The Critique of Power

The Critique of Power

Reflective Stages in a Critical Social Theory

Axel Honneth

translated by
Kenneth Baynes

The MIT Press
Cambridge, Massachusetts
London, England

First MIT Press edition, 1991.

Translation © 1991 Massachusetts Institute of Technology.

This work originally appeared in German under the title *Kritik der Macht. Reflexionsstufen einer kritischen Gesellschaftstheorie* (© 1985 Suhrkamp Verlag, Frankfurt am Main).

Set in Baskerville
by DEKR Corporation.
Printed and bound in the United States of America.

Library of Congress Cataloging-in-Publication Data

Honneth, Axel, 1949–
   [Kritik der Macht. English]
   The critique of power : reflective stages in a critical social
theory / Alex Honneth ; translated by Kenneth Baynes. — 1st MIT
Press ed.
      p. cm. — (Studies in contemporary German social thought)
   Translation of: Kritik der Macht.
   Includes bibliographical references and index.
   ISBN 0-262-08202-0
   1. Critical theory. 2. Horkheimer, Max, 1895–1973.
Philosophische Fragmente. 3. Habermas, Jürgen. 4. Foucault,
Michel. I. Title. II. Series.
   HM24.H582713 1991
301'.01—dc20   91-6950
                                                      CIP

Contents

Translator's Preface

When it was first published in Germany in 1985, *The Critique of Power* was immediately recognized as a significant and innovative contribution to debates concerning the normative foundations and emancipatory claims of a critical social theory. Honneth's study not only presents a systematic interpretation of the various attempts by the early Frankfurt School (notably Horkheimer and Adorno) to clarify the theoretical status and practical aims of their enterprise; it also brings to light the deeper continuities between this school and the later critical theories of Michel Foucault and Jürgen Habermas. Moreover, by situating the latter two theorists within the context of the earlier tradition of critical theory, Honneth provides a constructive framework for a comparison between them that (at least in the United States) has so far been conducted only at an initial, highly polemical level.

At the center of Honneth's reconstruction of the early Frankfurt School is the thesis that both Horkheimer and Adorno remained so tied to ideas derived from a comprehensive philosophy of history (e.g., social labor and the technical domination of nature) that they were unable to find a place within their theoretical analyses for a unique domain of the "social," that is, a domain in which individual and collective actors contest competing interpretations of their collective needs and normative orientations as well the distribution of scarce social resources. Insofar as a conception of social action becomes thematic for their theories, Foucault and Habermas are better able to attend to the domain of the social, albeit in quite different ways.

For Foucault, the social is construed as a domain of strategic interaction in which actors continuously confront one another in a "perpetual battle." According to Honneth, however, this analysis of the "microphysics of power" encounters difficulties in its attempt to account for the formation and maintenance of more complex structures of social domination. In the end, Foucault is compelled to abandon a model of strategic interaction in favor of a systems-theoretic analysis of power in which power is construed as a self-expanding property of social systems rather than as the product of struggle among strategic actors. Honneth thus presents a novel and systematic interpretation that is sure to find a place within current discussions of Foucault's work in the United States.

According to Honneth, Habermas' theory of communicative action offers a more promising point of departure for an analysis of the social, since it recognizes the role of consensual agreement as well as strategic conflict in both legitimate and illegitimate forms of power. However, two different and competing models of social change can be found in Habermas' writings: one that is indebted to his earlier critique of the "technocracy thesis" (a largely conservative thesis, hotly debated in the 1960s, that affirmed the spread of scientific reason and technocratic rule into more and more aspects of social life) and stresses the independence of "labor" and "interaction" and one that is more indebted to his reading of Marx and is better described as a moral "dialectic of class struggle" in which collective actors engage in conflict with one another about the interpretation of norms and the asymmetrical distribution of power. In *The Theory of Communicative Action,* with its two-tiered model of society as "system" and "lifeworld," Habermas displays a clear preference for the first model, with the result, according to Honneth, that the domain of the social is divided into a "norm-free" domain of strategic interaction and a "power-free" lifeworld. By way of an immanent reconstruction, Honneth thus offers a critique of Habermas' most recent formulation of critical social theory, which is still at the center of discussion (see *Communicative Action,* ed. A. Honneth and H. Joas [MIT Press, 1991]).

The result of Honneth's study is thus not merely a rich and at times provocative interpretation of the history of critical theory, but also a sketch of the contours of "the social" that should furnish that theory with its normative and practical orientation. Honneth pursues this latter task in greater detail in *Kampf um Anerkennung* (Suhrkamp, 1991).

In the following translation I have cited existing translations of both French and German texts whenever possible; any modifications are indicated in the notes. Axel Honneth was unduly patient in responding to my queries and offered many helpful suggestions during the long course of the translation. I would also like to thank Charles Wright for reading through the manuscript and for assuming primary responsibility for the translation of chapter 5. Shari Hartline assisted with the notes.

Author's Preface

In this study, I attempt to clarify the central problems of a critical social theory. At the *first level of a history of theory* I have been guided by the conviction that the two most influential new approaches to a critical social theory, that of Michel Foucault and that of Jürgen Habermas, are to be understood as competing developments of a set of questions opened by a critical theory: Both the theory of power, which Foucault has grounded in historical investigations, and the theory of society, which Habermas has developed on the basis of a theory of communicative action, can be viewed as attempts to interpret in a new way the process of a dialectic of enlightenment analyzed by Horkheimer and Adorno. If the history of critical social theory is reconstructed from this point of view, then Foucault's theory of power proves to be a systems-theoretic and Habermas' social theory a communication-theoretic solution to the aporias encountered by Adorno and Horkheimer in their philosophical-historical analysis of the process of civilization.

Insofar as the study traces historically the movement of thought that leads from Horkheimer's early essays through Adorno's philosophy of history and finally to the competing theories of Foucault and Habermas, there arises from an inquiry into the theoretical models a systematic viewpoint from which the construction and maintenance of social power can be apprehended. On the *second level of a clarification of the central problems of a critical social theory*, I examine the approaches de-

veloped by Adorno, Foucault, and Habermas in order to criticize the conception of contemporary societies as relations of
social domination. The purpose of such a comparison is to
work out in the represented positions the conceptions of action
that lie at the basis of social integration and thus, too, at the
basis of the exercise of power. From this background it is
shown, first, that Adorno must have failed in the task of an
analysis of society, since throughout his life he remained imprisoned to a totalized model of the domination of nature and
was thus uanble to comprehend the "social" in societies (chapter 3). Foucault and Habermas, by contrast, open up the domain of the social that was foreign to the tradition of critical
theory from two opposed extremes: in the action-theoretic
paradigms of "struggle" (chapter 5) and "mutual understanding" (chapter 7). The form that a "critique of power" should
assume today follows implicitly from a critical analysis of the
difficulties encountered, at different levels of reflection, within
both of these approaches. To that extent it provides, in the
movement of thought pursued from Adorno through Foucault
to Habermas, reflective stages in which the conceptual premises
of a critical social theory are gradually clarified.

The first six chapters of this work were submitted in 1983
as a dissertation to the Department of Philosophy and the
Social Sciences at the Free University of Berlin. I wish to thank
Birgit Mahnkopf and Hans Joas for constant discussions and
assistance and Urs Jaeggi for his display of impatience at just
the right moment.

Afterword to the Second German Edition (1988)

The Critique of Power is su... *Reflective Stages in a Critical Social Theory.* By this formula... on I wanted to indicate that the aim of the whole study was to present nothing more—but nothing less—than a history of theory with systematic intent. Since it was primarily the systematic intent of the book that has prompted doubts and questions in views, however, I have become acutely aware of the provisional character, and even the vagueness, of my own position.[1] Moreover, in the past few years there has been such an increase in the secondary literature on the authors included in this study that my own interpretations have acquired a greater burden of proof. The occasion of a new edition certainly does not present the appropriate context for a systematic response to all the questions that have been raised. But I also do not want to pass up the opportunity that is presented without at least arguing that the original goal of my investigation can still be theoretically upheld even in light of the new research.

I

The historically oriented study in this book indirectly develops a model of social conflict grounded in a theory of communication. The starting point for this proposal is, however, the reconsideration of a difficulty that has had a large impact on the history of critical theory in our century. When in the 1930s Horkheimer attempted to define the specific character of his theory by ascribing to it the capacity to have insight into its own origins and context of application, he thereby formulated not only a methodological requirement but a task for a social theory as well. Specifically, such a self-reflection called for a "sociological" analysis that would be in a position to explain social evolution in such a way that a moment of practical criticism also emerges as a constitutive condition of critical knowledge. The specific way in which Horkheimer, with reference to Marx, brought theory and practice together presupposes an analysis, from within the historical process, of those social impulses that call for a critique and an overcoming of established forms of domination. Only if the emancipatory interest, which also guides critical theory at a scientific level, can already be found within social life can it justly be conceived as a reflexive moment in social evolution. Within the tradition of thought founded by Horkheimer, the theoretical difficulty that results from this demanding task admittedly grew in significance to the extent that the emancipatory hope, nourished by prescientific considerations, became less convincing. The weaker the empirical indications for an already existing moment of practical critique became, the deeper did the analysis have to reach in order still to see it as an objective presupposition of the theory. The lapse of critical theory into the negativism of Adorno's social philosophy ultimately marks the historical moment in which the reflective task of a historical-social guarantee for critique succumbs. Thereafter, anyone who attempts once more to share Horkheimer's original aims first confronts the task of providing anew a theoretical access to that unknown domain in which the standards for critique are prescientifically anchored. A central problem for a critical social theory today is thus the question of how the conceptual framework of an analysis has to be laid out so that it is able to comprehend both the structures of social domination *and* the social resources for its practical overcoming.

The present study does not attempt to deal directly with the systematic problem provisionally outlined above, but to provide an answer indirectly via a history of theory. A necessary first step in formulating the question that serves as my starting point seemed to me to consist in a historical investigation that could provide a reconstruction of the history of critical theory in the form of a learning process. Thus, as a goal I had in mind a presentation that could argumentatively portray the historical succession of the individual theoretical stages in such a way that, gradually, at least the outline of a solution to the initial problem could be recognized. Such a procedure, which makes use of the Hegelian method for the history of philosophy, presupposes the anticipation of, if not a definitive conclusion, then at least the direction in which it seems to be attainable. The history of critical theory could be conceived as a learning process only if at least an indication of the standard was first specified by which insight or progress within that theoretical development was to be measured. The model of Habermas' theory has provided me with this sort of a direction, since his concept of interaction seemed to provide a theoretical way out of the philosophical-historical dead end into which critical theory was led with Adorno's negativism.[2] Thus, to a certain extent, I made use of the basic assumptions of action theory, which can already be found in Habermas' early work as an answer to Horkheimer's central problem, as a guiding motif. With it I was able to reconstruct the history of critical theory as a specific process of learning. The obvious circle in which I quite plainly moved by accepting such a conceptual presupposition I could only hope to overcome in the same way that every Hegelian history of theory attempts to succeed: by showing at the end of my critical reconstruction that I have argumentatively justified the theoretical premises I had presupposed from the outset.

Between early critical theory and Habermas' theory, I have introduced as a third model Michel Foucault's theory of power. I was motivated in this partly by the consideration that from the viewpoint of the history of theory Foucault's work presents an alternative to Habermas to the extent that it seems implicitly to realize a negative radicalization of the *Dialectic of Enlightenment* rather than its positive sublation in a theory of communication. Proceeding along these lines would create the framework for an illuminating interpretation of the relationship between poststructuralism and this major work in the philosophy of history, but such a hermeneutic perspective could not be a sufficient reason for such a decisive broadening of the conceptual horizon of the history of theory. What from the outset also motivated me to include Foucault in my study was the systematically guided hope that contrasting his theory of power to the communication-theoretic approach would allow a possibility to arise that would be significant for solving the basic problem. From the exchange with a social theory that follows the traces of Nietzsche, a conceptual impetus might perhaps arise that could push the movement of immanent reconstruction beyond the framework in which it was previously located in connection with Habermas' social theory.

Thus, from these different considerations taken as a whole the plan for the present study ultimately arose. The theoretical development of critical social theory from its starting point in Horkheimer's original approach, through Adorno's philosophy of history and Foucault's analysis of power, to Habermas' perspective is argumentatively reconstructed here in such a way that a view of a social practice gradually emerges in which a critique of social domination, in my opinion, is today more able to secure reflexively its own standards. I will have attained this tentative result of my investigation to the extent that in successive stages I have more specifically shown the following:

• Horkheimer is not in a position to solve the basic problem he himself sketched out, since his philosophy of history, which is tailored solely to the dimension of social labor, prohibited him from analyzing conceptually that social dimension of everyday cultural life and social conflict to which, in a few places, he attempted to relate his own theory.

• In reaction to the experiences of his time, Adorno undertook a conceptual reevaluation of that dimension of social labor which he had also privileged; the upshot was a negative philosophy of history in whose framework a practical zone of prescientific critique can no longer be discerned since it is forced to see in all social action only a mere extension of the human domination of nature.

• Foucault finds a productively new disclosure of that sphere of social interaction and conflict that Adorno systematically misunderstood by attempting, in his theory of power, to trace the origin of social domination back to a process of strategic exchange between subjects; this step was not able to provide the basis for a reflexive grounding of his critical claims, however, since it is conceived apart from all normative agreements and moral incentives and thus, in the end, is subjected to a purely systems-theoretic explanation.

• Habermas, with his concept of communicative action, first creates a theoretical approach that is able to recognize the beginnings of an answer to this basic problem since within its framework the structures of social domination can be explained as the result of processes of communicative agreement that underlie an internal claim to the fulfillment of intersubjective freedom that serves as the standard for a reflexive "critique of power."

• Habermas himself, however, finally developed his own approach in the direction of two different theories of society; of these, the only one which to me appears promising for a solution to the basic problem is the one in which social development is explained not with reference to a logic of rationalization, but with reference to a dynamic of social struggle that is structurally located within the moral space of social interactions.

With the last consideration I have attempted to bring my reconstruction of the history of critical social theory to the point where at least the initial contours of the idea of a model of social conflict grounded in a theory of communication begin to emerge. In contrast to the normativistic tradition of social theory, in such a model the process of social integration is conceived as a process that assumes the form of a struggle among social actors for the recognition of their identity until all groups and individuals possess the equal chance to participate in the organization of their common life. Thereby the philosophical-historical conception left to us as a heritage of the nineteenth century by Marxist theory, in the form of the doctrine of class struggle, is taken into account in a realistic manner.[3] However, in contrast to the tradition of social theory in which struggle is made into a universal feature of all social evolution, in the alternative model briefly identified social conflict should be conceived as a process that refers to the moral claims of individuals that can in principle be socially realized. In this way I take up, in an altered form, the basic idea that Habermas introduced in the project of a critical social theory when he grasped communicative practice as an intersubjective event whose idealizing presuppositions generate a moral development, so to speak, from themselves.

Now, sharp formulations of this sort cannot replace the theoretical arguments that would obviously be necessary for clarifying and developing such a conception. The essays that I have in the meantime published on the history of more recent social theory also represent at most only indirect approximations to the idea that has so far only been roughly outlined.[4] Only a study that succeeded in making Hegel's idea of a "struggle for recognition" systematically fruitful for a social theory could perhaps fill in some of the lacunae in the argument. But there are also basic considerations, opposed at once to my whole idea, that result from alternative interpretations of the theories I have critically investigated in my presentation. In the course of the argumentative steps that my reconstruction pursues, I have been confronted by the following questions: whether the critical potential of Adorno's social philosophy has not been underestimated if only his explicit contributions to the development of a social theory are investigated (section II below); whether the theoretical strength of Foucault's analysis of power is not misunderstood when it is reproached for its lack of a normatively demonstrable reference point within society (section III); and whether Habermas' objections to praxis philosophy are not taken too lightly when the underestimation of the comprehensive role of social struggle is held up against his own social theory (section IV).

II

It is not so much Horkheimer's programmatic writings when he was director of the Institute for Social Research as Adorno's contributions to a negativistic social philosophy that now stand at the center of the renewed interest in critical theory. Interest in the other members of the Frankfurt School has diminished in comparison with the attention Adorno's work is now receiving in a variety of contexts. At the center of this surprising return to Adorno is apparently the conviction that his critical conception of the nonidentical provides the best means for comprehending the conditions for a noninstrumental relation to inner and outer nature. For this reason, too, in the more recent literature precisely those portions of his writings from which philosophical formulations of an aesthetic concept of rationality can be derived acquire a privileged status. The impressive history of the Frankfurt School published by Rolf Wiggershaus in 1986 is written from a theoretical perspective that identifies with the aesthetic aims of Adorno's philosophy. That is, it is the image of a theory of mimetic experience that in the course of the historical presentation provides Wiggershaus with his answer to the question of what in the tradition is still enduring and holds future importance.[5] This indirect form of partisanship mellowed into the attempt at a more systematic justification in the monograph on Adorno that Wiggershaus brought out shortly after his larger study. A concept of rationality, which incorporates at a basic level an awareness of the instrumental uncontrollability of nature, is here put forward as the philosophical achievement that makes Adorno's work still relevant despite its many weaknesses.[6] The monograph published by Martin Jay in 1984 proceeds, in principle, in a similar fashion. Its argument is also primarily guided by the desire to clarify the relevance of Adorno's philosophical thought for a solution to those questions that have in recent times arisen from the problematic human relationship to nature.[7]

The same theoretical interests to which these two general studies are conceptually indebted also find expression in a series of more specific studies that deepen our knowledge about particular aspects of Adorno's philosophy much more than I was able to in my own interpretation. In an excellent study, Josef Früchtl has exposed the roots in the history of ideas from which, in Adorno's thought, the concept of mimetic experience could have been developed. For the first time all the elements from the psychoanalytic and anthropological tradition that could have influenced Adorno's critique of the domination of nature are made clear, even though these elements are nowhere explicitly mentioned in his texts.[8] Stefan Cochetti, in a comparable investigation, has examined the ethnological references inconspicuously introduced through the concept of myth in the *Dialectic of Enlightenment*. A scientifically deeper level of Adorno's philosophy that had not previously been disclosed in the interpretation of his work is thereby attained.[9] Finally, a few philosophical studies proceeding from these same theoretical interests have contributed to a wider clarification of Adorno's concept of rationality in that they are able to reconstruct his critique of identity logic by means of more recent philosophy of language. Above all, the penetrating interpretations of Albrecht Wellmer have in this way made clear that Adorno's ideal of a noncoercive knowledge of nature can itself still be defended if its grounding in the philosophy of language is supported with convincing arguments.[10]

As is easy to see, with these diverse research contributions the context of the discussion concerning Adorno's theoretical work has shifted considerably in the past ten years. In the center of the controversy today a question is advanced that could have arisen only after the communication-theoretic turn in critical theory has been accepted, at least in its central features. The studies mentioned above are almost unanimous in taking Habermas' program as an occasion for exploring, in various ways, new means for preserving Adorno's idea of mimesis. To that extent they commonly share the problem of how, under theoretically altered premises, a concept of the "uncoerced synthesis" has to be constituted so that it concerns "not the recognition of the nonidentical in the other, but the recognition of the nonidentical in the comprehension of reality and in the subject's relation to itself."[11] In my own presentation I did not take into consideration the theoretical possibilities that are again opened up by this turn in discussions of Adorno. In this respect, the criticism that I have attempted to raise against Adorno's social philosophy appears, on the whole, too one-sided. For this reason, too, the reservations that are offered by an orthodox repetition of Adorno's methodological reflections provide me with less to think about than the indirect objections that accompany the philosophical rehabilitation of his doctrine of mimesis.[12] Nevertheless, the new point of view that follows from it immediately gives rise to the difficult question of how the idea of an uncoerced relation to nature can appropriately be fitted not within the theory of knowledge or aesthetics but rather within the conceptual framework of a critical social theory.

At the conceptual level, a place for the reference to the human relationship to nature was not properly considered in the concept of the "social" which I briefly outlined in my book. Since my initial aim was primarily directed to clearly establishing the suppressed dimension of conflictual interaction within the tradition of critical theory, I let the aspect of the social relation to the natural world remain too far in the background. On the other hand, however, the research strategies that work with Adorno's concept of mimetic experience hardly present an appropriate basis for the further attempt to include this neglected aspect within the framework of a critical social theory. During his lifetime Adorno limited himself so exclusively to the possibilities of a noninstrumental relation to nature presented within the unique domain of the work of art that within the conceptual framework of his theory the different forms of the social experience of nature in their whole horizon can be taken up only with great difficulty.

A social theory whose central concern is to treat the practical relationship to inner and outer nature as a basic fact of forms of social life, however, must inquire about the access to precisely these everyday zones of social action. That is, the cultural models that are decisive within a society for organizing and regulating as a whole the exchange with the natural world are presented not within the sphere of aesthetic production, which has in the meantime become autonomous, but within the specific spheres of institutionalized everyday action. Practices concerning the preparation of food and the rearing of children, the cultivation of nature, and one's relationship to one's own body present domains of action of this sort in which the social relationship to nature is daily reproduced. The normative-practical rules that in turn guide these cultural activities can then be distinguished according to the question of whether they are more "mimetically" compliant or "instrumentally" controlling in their relation to the natural environment. In this way the line of thought that is currently being pursued in connection with Adorno's concept of "mimesis," above all within the context of aesthetic discussions, can be made sociologically fruitful within a critical social theory. Of course, the most useful considerations for this are to be found less within the Frankfurt School tradition than within French social anthropology, especially the work of Claude Lévi-Strauss. His writings, which are deeply shaped by the question of the social organization of the relationship to nature, thus present the starting point for a series of new attempts to introduce the dimension of the relationship to nature more deeply into the context of a social theory.[13] I am thinking especially of Johann P. Arnason's work, in which the cultural interpretation of nature is presented as a central dimension of social reproduction,[14] but also of Klaus Eder's recent study which, in the form of a comparative analysis of eating taboos, programmatically sketches the outline of a cultural sociology of the human relation to nature.[15] Only through an exchange with theoretical projects of this sort can the conceptual framework be attained within which Adorno's doctrine of mimesis could be reformulated today so that it would not remain tailored solely to the limited sphere of aesthetic production.

III

As has already been mentioned, the Foucault portion of my book is motivated by systematic aims as well as by considerations from the history of theory. In connection with its place within the history of theory, I have presented Foucault's writings as contributions to a project in which, by means of Nietzsche's philosophy, the *Dialectic of Enlightenment*'s tendencies toward a critique of reason are developed into a kind of systems theory. From the systematic perspective, by contrast, I wanted to show that the dimension of social conflict that Foucault makes central can only be invoked at the level of a social theory if it is grasped as the negative moment of a comprehensive process in the formation of social consensus. The secondary literature on Foucault since his death has progressed in so many directions that my own interpretation of his writings can no longer be judged so easily in the light of a single line of interpretation, as still seems possible to me in the case of Adorno's philosophy. In both complexity and vitality, the debate over Foucault's work is now comparable only to the discussion about Habermas' theory.[16] Nevertheless, two thematic points of difficulty so clearly rise above this unsurveyable field of research that an indication can be drawn from them of the theoretical problems that confront my interpretation today.

The two thematic complexes that especially dominate the Foucault discussion at the moment can best be characterized with the help of the brief formulation that Nancy Fraser introduced as a subtitle to her essay "Foucault on Modern Power": "Empirical Insights and Normative Confusions."[17] The various problems connected with the "normative confusions" of Foucault's theory of power are today primarily taken up in the theoretical debate in the United States. Here his writings have fallen upon the fertile soil of a theoretical field prepared by postempiricist philosophy of science and have quickly given rise to a productive controversy over the methodological status of a critical theory of power.[18] In the British and West German discussion, by contrast, which acknowledges Foucault's theory of power as a central feature, interest in the "empirical insights" has prevailed. Here it is primarily the various traditions of Weberian Marxism that have created a theoretical climate for the great interest in Foucault's historical analysis of modern techniques of power.[19] Corresponding to this rough distinction, it is, on the one side of the Atlantic, primarily questions about the method of the analysis of power that define the recent discussion of Foucault's work; on the other side, it is questions about empirical content.

In the United States the theoretical assumptions that have made possible the current controversy over Foucault's theory of power were set out in the excellent book by Hubert L. Dreyfus and Paul Rabinow.[20] In their comprehensive presentation of Foucault's theoretical work they were guided by the question of how the methodological procedure that emerges in his historical investigations is constituted. Along the path of a gradual delineation of adjacent theoretical traditions they were ultimately successful in determining that it is a method of "interpretive analysis" that gives Foucault's material studies their unmistakable character. By "interpretive analysis" Dreyfus and Rabinow meant a hermeneutic process that exposes the cultural practices of a form of social life without itself undertaking a transsituational evaluation. The theoretical advantage for cultural analysis promised by such a distancing hermeneutic is the advance in diagnostic precision that seems to accompany the renunciation of normative judgments. Of course they were both too conscious of the philosophical problems of contemporary theories not to see the difficulty Foucault must fall into with his neutral self-understanding. That is to say, if that normative standard of evaluation is supposed to be renounced, reasons why opposition should be directed against specific techniques of power at all can no longer be justified. As Dreyfus and Rabinow showed, with the complete surrender of a theoretical reference to norms, however they are to be justified, comes the danger of a relativism lacking any perspective. They thus conclude their book with a series of questions directed to Foucault that collectively refer to the difficulty of grounding a critique of the dominant forms of social control within his theory.[21]

In certain ways, the discussion in the United States took as its starting point the problems raised by such questions. It was also influenced from the outside by the arguments with which Habermas attempted to justify his critique of Foucault's theory of power.[22] The fronts that have so far formed in this controversy, which is being conducted at a high level, can be surveyed without great difficulty.[23] On the one side are those authors who consider Foucault's analysis of power a defensible undertaking precisely because it has sufficiently distanced itself from all claims to a noncontextual evaluation about forms of life. Against any attempt to provide a justification for universal norms, they raise the criticism that it must necessarily make use of metaphysical assertions, that it therefore draws upon unjustifiable convictions, and thus that it belongs to a traditional form of philosophical thinking. For them, by contrast, Foucault represents the type of skeptical philosophy that, in its objections to the prevailing order, only attributes to those objections the character of situation-bound statements or "negative maxims," so that it can apparently rightly renounce every further step toward a rational grounding. In his book, which represents the most radical interpretation of this kind, John Rajchman has given the name "historical nominalism" to this position of a "post modern" criticism no longer enchanted by theory.[24] In contrast, for Richard Rorty, who adheres only to a more moderate reading of this kind, Foucault is drawn into the vicinity of American pragmatism.[25]

If these interpretive proposals were completely unopposed, my own interpretation would be rendered problematic, since Foucault's analysis of power could no longer be construed as a methodological parallel to the approach of the Frankfurt School. For, viewed from the perspective that lies at the basis of the interpretations by Rajchman and Rorty, his historical studies can be understood only as elements of a diagnostic intervention that, in contrast to critical theory, has completely freed itself of any transsituational concept of human freedom or social emancipation. However, within the American discussion one can also find a group of authors who attempt, with good arguments, to counter such an interpretive proposal. In all the programmatic statements in which Foucault has announced his complete renunciation of normative justification they see a fundamental contradiction contained in his theory.

Even for this group of interpreters, to which such politically engaged theoreticians as Charles Taylor and Michael Walzer belong, Foucault's work is perceived as a significant challenge to contemporary philosophy. However, in this case, the fact that Foucault always wanted to avoid the task of explaining his normative perspective is taken as a sign of a systematic misunderstanding and is not regarded as an indication of a new interventionist form of theory construction. Thus, in an extremely circumspect criticism, Charles Taylor has shown that Foucault's concept of "power" can be made intelligible in general only if at least a vague "idea of liberation" is conceived as its complement.[26] Similarly, Walzer has made an interesting attempt to introduce into Foucault's social-theoretic exposition the moral distinctions by means of which his statements can initially acquire a politically unambiguous direction.[27] Through critical analyses of this sort, these authors wish to show that there is in Foucault's work a disquieting contradiction between theoretical claims and material investigations. Whereas the entire framework of Foucault's historical studies rests on moral convictions for which, to a certain extent, a universal validity must inevitably be claimed, one does not find even a hint of these once the theory is systematically explicated. Therefore, what the representative of the first interpretive direction takes to be a postmodern form of interventionist social theory is nothing more than the result of Foucault's deficient reflection on the normative conditions of his own writings. Thus, regardless of how the further justification of such fundamental norms is to be presented, Foucault should have systematically secured them at a theoretical level in order to avoid having his analysis of power fall into a basic contradiction.

However, from the perspective of the criticisms thus outlined, which are indirectly supported by my own ordering of the history of theory, a further problem arises that is connected with the premises of a critical social theory mentioned at the outset. If it is in fact moral convictions of a specific sort that guide Foucault in his critical diagnosis of the times, then an appropriate place for these must be found not only within his metatheoretical reflections but also within the conceptual framework of his social analysis. In my book, however, I defended the thesis that such a normative point of reference in Foucault's material investigations could not be assumed, since in them he allowed the entire dimension of sociality to be reduced to strategic interactions in which moral norms function only as a legitimating superstructure. In view of the enormous increase in the secondary literature, it thus remains to be determined in a further step whether, contrary to his own statements, Foucault's social-theoretical concepts still don't contain the conceptual presuppositions to supply his moral purposes.

With this question one enters the primary theoretical ground upon which the Foucault discussion moves today in England and the Federal Republic of Germany. In contrast to the controversy in the United States, sociological interests predominate here. Thus, it is the empirical content of Foucault's theory of power that now takes center stage. The significant discovery that this analysis of power was in contact with Max Weber's theory at surprisingly many points provided a decisive incentive for this orientation. Through this historical comparison, carried out in a series of studies published in England, there have emerged some implications of Foucault's work of which I myself had been insufficiently aware:[28] first, like Weber, Foucault made the disciplinary process the theoretical key to an analysis of changes in forms of the conduct of life [*Lebensführung*]; further the direction of various disciplinary processes is for him also defined with the help of the notion of a technical rationalization; finally, there is the methodologically interesting finding that, like Weber, Foucault traced the origin of modern disciplinary society back to a process of the historical convergence of techniques of rationalization that were suited to one another through an "elective affinity." The astonishing similarities indicated by these few remarks allow the emergence of a sociological level in Foucault's historical stuidies that in the future will make it easier to assess the value of his work for a theory of society.[29] Further, for the first time the possibility is opened up for explaining at a social-theoretic level Foucault's later studies in which he investigates in detail ancient forms of the conduct of individual lives.[30] Beyond that, theoretically significant suggestions result for investigating more empirically the value of types of self-thematization for the course of civilization.[31] Of course, the approach to Weber also unintentionally brings more clearly to light those weaknesses in Foucault's theory on which I attempted to base my own criticisms. Specifically, if his analysis of power is interpreted as a theory of increasing reification in the tradition of Weberian Marxism and then applied without any differentiation to empirical reality, then all the difficulties contained within Weber's sociological theory again become critical.

One can already find in Weber's sociology the problem that, within the framework he developed, the social or cultural resources that could oppose the modern process of the loss of freedom can no longer be identified. Nevertheless, from his concept of cultural rationalization one can still derive indications about the sort of personal, if not social, energies that are needed to free social life from the "iron cage" it has become.[32]

If this multilayered concept of "rationalization," which at least still includes intimations of possible forms of resistance, is, in connection with Foucault, interpreted simply in the sense of a growth in disciplining, then the problems that already exist for Weber take on even more importance. Specifically, within the reality described in this way there is no remnant of any kind to which theory could systematically refer as a cultural source of resistance in order to ground within society its own critique of the prevailing conditions. Thus, those commentators, such as Bryan Turner, who attempt to explain Foucault's analysis of power with aid of Weberian sociology finally arrive at the same objection with which I also concluded: "and nowhere does he [Foucault—A.H.] provide an analytically coherent approach to resistance."[33] The only chance that I can see for avoiding this fatal conclusion in the future lies in the alternative, which I developed in this book, of reconstructing Foucault's analysis of power not from the concept of discipline but from the basic concept of social struggle. Of course, to allow such an alternative to fulfill the tasks that would fall to it within the context of a critical social theory would require an extension of the concept of "social struggle" to just those moral norms that Foucault the theoretician constantly rejected.

IV

With the line of thought mentioned last, I have already indirectly appealed to the systematic idea that guided me in my interpretations of Habermas' work. On the other hand, in the portion of my investigation devoted to him I wanted to reconstruct the development of his theory in a way that would gradually eliminate the arbitrary character of the communication-theoretic premises of my own argumentation, thereby further grounding them. On the other hand, along the same path, I also wanted to show, at least in an initial outline, that the dynamic that arises in the historical development of social orders can be fully explained only by extending the sphere of communicative action to include the negative dimension of struggle. As the aim of such an internal connection between interaction and struggle I had in mind at the time the outline

of a social theory in which the process of practical rationalization is attributed to the development of a gradually widening
struggle for recognition. However, as already stated, not only
have the theoretical problems that I must deal with become
much clearer to me, but Habermas has also taken up some of
the points raised in my objections.[34] Accordingly, questions are
connected to my discussion of Habermas that today I am not
in a position to answer. Therefore, in conclusion, I will limit
myself to a brief review of my interpretive approach in view
of the more recent discussion.

Since Habermas' theory extends into considerably more disciplines, the secondary literature on him is even more difficult
to survey than that on Foucault.[35] Nevertheless, from the flood
of interpretations and responses a dominant trend can be
found in the questions that deal with the justification of rationality and with the corresponding challenges presented by the
recent critique of reason.[36] Since the publication of *The Philosophical Discourse of Modernity* this complex of themes has become even more significant and has produced a unique
discussion. By contrast, questions directed to problems in social
theory have receded more into the background. If I see things
correctly, the recent discussion has been provoked less by sociological questions than by an array of philosophical issues.
As far as the crucial premises of my own interpretation are
concerned, however, according to which the traces of two distinct models of society can be discovered, I have subsequently
found an important confirmation in the literature. In an essay
dealing with the normative problems in Habermas' theory,
Albrecht Wellmer has proposed distinguishing between two
competing alternatives that in certain ways converge with the
interpretation I have offered.[37]

With reference to the explanatory models by means of which
Habermas accounts for the process of practical rationalization,
Wellmer distinguishes between a model oriented to Freud and
one oriented to Piaget. According to the first model, the moral
learning process, which is supposed to lead to an emancipated
society, is represented as steps in a process of self-reflection
through which impediments to social interaction are made conscious. According to the second model, by contrast, it is success

in the formation of a new stage of moral consciousness that is supposed to propel the process of emancipation. Thus, in each model, the structure of the process of moral learning and that from which individuals are to be freed are defined in different ways. On the one hand, it is the conditions of distorted communication that are to be retrospectively dissolved through collective acts of self-reflection. By contrast, in the other case, it is a matter of stages of "limited reflexivity" that are overcome through progress in the development of cognitive competencies.

These oppositions coincide with the division I propose only insofar as an initial difference between the representations of the same basic historical conflict is seen as the crucial difference between the two models: In the case of the Freudian model the disturbances are represented within social interaction, whereas in the Piagetian model the deficit in a logically specifiable development of consciousness represents the primary reference point from which the different concept of practical rationality begins. Moreover, for Wellmer, as for me at the time as well, the differences just described also reflect differences in the tasks assigned to critical social theory in each model. According to the first model, theory is continuously related hermeneutically to the consciousness of the subjects involved, since it is supposed to be through the sketch of alternative interpretations of historical development that their insight into the conditions of distorted communication grows; according to the second model, it is the "objectively" given system problems as such for which theory seeks a solution along the path of a formal analysis of deficits in rationality.[38] In the development of his argument, however, Wellmer is primarily concerned with the question of the conclusions that follow from these differences for the problems that the concept of emancipation raises today. Thus, although methodologically important contributions for my own questions also result in general from the considerations he offers, they are initially of little significance for the original aim of my investigation.

The two competing models were at the time primarily important for me because I wanted to find within the development of Habermasian theory an alternative to the approach

that Habermas has since worked out with the distinction between "system" and "lifeworld." In the outline of a conception
of historical evolution that can be found in his book *Knowledge
and Human Interests* I saw the sketch for a model of society that,
on a theoretical level, was able to avoid that dualism by giving
more importance to moral conflict. That is, within this conceptual framework, which Wellmer has called the "Freudian
model," the forms of the institutional organization of production and political administration are also still conceived as the
result of a "moral" struggle between social groups and classes,
so that in principle the possibility of historically independent
systems of purely strategically rational action cannot arise. Of
course, along with the social-theoretic problems that arise for
me with Habermas' separation of "system" and "lifeworld," the
theme is also mentioned that has so far received the most
attention within the sociological discussion of his work. My own
objections, which even then could refer to some critical studies,[39] have been confirmed by a series of more recent essays,[40]
to which Habermas has already responded in a second round
of the controversy.[41] At this point I will not again address his
critical counterobjections by merely pointing to an alternative
action-theoretic model. Only if I were to succeed in developing
that frequently mentioned program at least to the point that a
renunciation of systems theory can be made plausible would
by arguments lose their provisional character and acquire a
critical force.

However, I do not want to conclude without at least having
indicated that at the moment the term "praxis philosophy,"
employed polemically by Habermas, has greatly contributed to
a confusion of the fronts in the debate. The theoretical position
so designated has two possible interpretations. On the one
hand, it is a tradition of thought in which the constitution and
reproduction of societies is represented by the model, still presented in the concept of labor, of a relationship of humanity
to itself. In this case, all the critical objections that Habermas
has convincingly made since his initial controversy with
Luhmann over the fiction of "higher-level subjectivities" apply
equally to this conceptual model.[42] But these objections do not
apply to the tradition of thought, to which in a few places he

gives the same name, in which the formation of the intersubjective consensus of a society maintained by cooperative efforts
represents the guiding model. On the other hand, "praxis
philosophy" refers to a tradition of social-theoretical thought
in which the constitution and reproduction of societies is in
the last analysis to be explained in action-theoretic terms and
thus gives the sustaining ground to a concept of "praxis," whatever the kind (labor, communication, etc.). But then this theoretical tradition of "praxis philosophy" cannot be refuted with
objections against forms of thought belonging to the philosophy of consciousness, but only with proof of the definitive limits
of action theory and thus the unavoidability of systems theory.
However, in his own concept of "praxis philosophy" Habermas
has brought the two alternative uses together within a single
tradition of thought, so that in his judgment, with his correct
objections to a concept of society indebted to the philosophy
of consciousness, he has already refuted any action-theoretic
criticism of his concept of system. If this peculiar conceptual
confusion is removed, however, it is then theoretically still a
completely open question whether a praxis philosophy might
not be able to do without the idealistic fiction of "the subject
on a large scale."

I

The Incapacity for Social Analysis: Aporias of Critical Theory

Critical theory, which originated more than fifty years ago under the intellectual authority of an individual person but as the work of a group of scientists, was conceived from the outset as a continuation of Marx's intentions under altered historical circumstances. It first took shape in Max Horkheimer's inaugural address at the Institute for Social Research; it was subsequently represented above all in the writings of Theodor Adorno. Since then it has been for many the paradigm of a theory in which the intention of a philosophically guided diagnosis of the time is combined with an empirically grounded social analysis. In this first part I will attempt to work out the basic theoretical assumptions of critical theory that from the outset stood in the way of that goal, which is still exemplary today. I shall retrace the developmental steps in the line of thought presented by Adorno and Horkheimer by investigating, first, Horkheimer's early programmatic writings (chapter 1), then the jointly authored *Dialectic of Enlightenment* (chapter 2), and, finally, Adorno's later writings on social theory (chapter 3).

1

Horkheimer's Original Idea: The Sociological Deficit of Critical Theory

In his essay "Traditional and Critical Theory," which appeared in the sixth year of publication of the *Zeitschrift für Sozial-forschung* (1937), Horkheimer attempted to sum up the theoretical claim and the political position of a critical theory of society.[1] His essay, written in exile in America, formulates the self-understanding of the Institute for Social Research during the 1930s. Horkheimer's aim is to expose the practical roots of the modern conception of science in order to be able to ground critical theory, as the self-conscious expression of processes of social and political emancipation, in the practical context that is made visible.

Horkheimer takes up the modern (or what he calls "traditional") model of science in connection with Descartes' reflection on method. According to this model, the task of scientific theories consists in the collection of deductively acquired statements that are hypothetically applied to empirically observable reality. The explanatory value of theory increases to the extent that the experimentally controlled observation of reality confirms individual statements within a logically consistent set of statements. The truth of a scientific theory is identical with the prognostic explanatory force of its body of statements. Horkheimer is not interested in the corrections to and modifications of this ideal of a unified science developed by post-Cartesian philosophy of science. The difference between deductive and inductive acquisition of general statements, in terms of which the classical schools of epistemology can be distinguished, or even the difference between experimental and phenomenological observations of reality, which distinguishes developments in the philosophy of science up to Horkheimer's own time, are secondary for him. He is interested much more in the basic model according to which the modern age envisions the relationship between scientific theory and reality. According to Horkheimer, the distinctive feature of traditional theory is defined by the following characterization of this relationship: "There is always, on the one hand, the conceptually formulated knowledge and, on the other, the facts to be subsumed under it. Such a subsumption or establishing of a relation between the simple perception or verification of a fact and the conceptual structure of our knowing is called its theoretical explanation."[2]

The merely external application of a set of statements (however they are acquired) to a natural process or to a historical event should make possible the explanation of the empirical state of affairs insofar as it becomes part of a series of propositions. In this way, as more and more segments of reality are caught in the net of hypothetical statements, natural and social processes as a whole can finally be theoretically predicted and controlled. Horkheimer sees in this function of traditionally conceived theories (that is, in their capacity to predict, control, and finally direct real processes) the constitutive context of modern science: "The manipulation of physical nature and specific economic and social mechanisms demand alike the amassing of a body of knowledge such as is applied in an ordered set of hypotheses."[3] The function of control that is presupposed by a scientific theory that seeks to explain and predict empirical states of affairs within a general set of statements betrays its origins: It is part of the practical process of reproduction in which the human species preserves its life through increasing control over its natural environment and its own social world. Horkheimer implicitly relies upon an assumption drawn from the philosophy of history for an explanation of how the achievements of social labor have made possible the emancipatory process that has freed the human world from the oppressive power of nature and produced a civilization that dominates nature and increasingly expands in relation to it. But—and this is the perspective in which Hork-heimer is interested—traditional theory does not recognize its own constitutive context. Although it is "a factor in the conservation and continuous renewal of the existing state of affairs,"[4] it has fictively cut itself off from all social processes of production: Reflecting a significant misunderstanding, traditional theory views itself as "pure" theory. As a result, Hork-heimer, in a manner reminiscent of the early Marx, can ascertain not only how its specific object but also how the type and manner of its contact with reality is shaped by the prevailing condition of the forces of social production, that is, by the accumulated effects of the control over natural and social processes:

The objects we perceive in our surroundings—cities, villages, fields, and woods—bear the mark of having been worked on by man. It is not only in clothing and appearance, in outward form and emotional make-up that men are the product of history. Even the way they see and hear is inseparable from the social life-process as it has evolved over the millennia. The facts which our senses present to us are socially preformed in two ways: through the historical character of the object perceived and through the historical character of the perceiving organ.[5]

The knowing subject and the object known are mutually determined from the beginning by the social process of the cultivation of nature, the product of which is the history of the species as a whole. However, the self-deception in which modern science considers itself free from all ties, even to this labor process, is clarified further by reference to a second assumption derived from the philosophy of history and more or less arbitrarily introduced into his essay: The production of social life has itself not yet been understood in the history of the species as the synthesizing, cooperative achievement of all laboring subjects. Of course, the process of production sketched out, oriented to the domination of nature, has so far brought about historical progress, but the acting subjects have not recognized their common constitutive accomplishments. This lack of awareness is simply continued in the self-understanding of traditional theory. Just as the human species is unaware of its historically constitutive productive activity, so modern science is unaware of the historically constitutive context to which it belongs as a result of all its cognitive achievements.

In order to illustrate this line of thought, Horkheimer draws an analogy between the still-unconscious synthesizing accomplishments of labor already achieved by the human species throughout history and the synthetic achievements of the transcendental ego in Kant's epistemology. This analogy admittedly also reveals for the first time the idealist fiction to which Horkheimer's construction of a unified species-subject leads[6]:

> The internal difficulties in the supreme concepts of Kantian philosophy, especially the ego of transcendental subjectivity, pure or original apperception, and consciousness-in-itself, show the depth and honesty of his thinking. The two-sidedness of these Kantian concepts, that is, their supreme unity and purposefulness, on the one hand, and their obscurity, unknownness, and impenetrability, on the other, reflects exactly the contradiction-filled form of human activity in the modern period. The collaboration of men in society is the mode of existence reason urges upon them, and so they do apply their powers and thus confirm their own rationality. But at the same time their work and its results are alienated from them, and the whole process, with all its waste of labor-power and human life, and with its wars and all its senseless wretchedness, seems to be an unchangeable force of nature, a fate behind man's control. In Kant's theoretical philosophy, in his analysis of knowledge, this contradiction is preserved.[7]

Horkheimer uses Kant's epistemological model to clarify the construction derived from the philosophy of history: Just as Kant traces the world of objects of possible experience back to the structurally given capacities of a transcendental subject, so the social world is regarded as the still-unconscious product of human cultivation of nature. The transcendental manner of speaking called for by this materialistic reading of Kant's epistemology requires a singular subject, employed by Horkheimer, in order to characterize the human accomplishments of labor lumped together as "the" activity of the species. Horkheimer must assign to it all the ordering accomplishments that Kant ascribed to the transcendental ego. Thus, as a singular subject of history, the human species always already produces the social world, and does so in a continuously better way. However, it remains unaware of its constitution up to the present time. This lack of awareness on the part of the species is the ultimate cause of the catastrophic blindness of the present course of history. Modern science is itself still an unconscious moment of this perpetually productive yet blind self-preservation. The materialistic interpretation first clarifies traditional theory in this situation by tracing it back to the labor process from which it grew and to which it remains methodologically tied. Along the path of this interpretation, traditional theory finally recovers its "positive social function,"[8] the rational domination of nature.

Horkheimer attempts to explain the self-misunderstanding of traditional theory in terms of this interpretive framework, derived from the philosophy of history, which unambiguously ascribes to the historical expansion of productive forces, to the rational means for dominating nature, an emancipatory potential, one virtually guaranteeing progress. His sketch, which seems to be derived directly from the "model of the estrangement of labor" that lies at the basis of Marx's early critique of capital,[9] treats the civilizing process of history as the process of a progressive perfection of the human domination of nature. The species is separated from the enjoyment of its power only as a result of its own lack of historical understanding. It is this interpretation of the contradiction between productive forces and productive relations that now governs Horkheimer's attempt to provide a foundation for a critical theory of society: The productive forces are seen as an emancipatory potential whose unplanned organization in capitalism is regarded only as the expression of human self-deception.

Horkheimer can initially derive the first feature of a critical theory without any difficulties *ex negativo*, that is, by avoiding the basic errors of traditional theory. Whereas traditional theory, insofar as it believes it can ground its methods through criteria immanent to knowledge alone, is separated from its own practical origin, critical theory is continuously conscious of its constitutive context. The self-knowledge with which the materialistic interpretation must first encounter traditional theory, so to speak, from without, is the first task and the deepest principle of critical theory: More of less repeating Karl Korsch's formula that historical materialism must always be applied to itself, in this essay Horkheimer states that "the influence of social development on the structure of the theory is part of the theory's doctrinal content."[10] But how can Horkheimer now define with greater conceptual precision the practical context to which critical theory is constitutively related if its starting point in the philosophy of history still reduces all social practice to the productive activity of the human species? The reply to this question reveals a first ambivalence, forced upon Horkheimer by his philosophy of history, in his solution to the claims made by a critical theory of society.

On the one hand, Horkheimer is simply being consistent when he traces critical theory back to the same mode of activity of the human species from which traditional theory is also supposed to proceed, though against its own self-understanding. Both types of theory would in the same way be dependent forms of expression of the civilizing process of the domination of nature. However, critical theory also introduces a knowledge that goes beyond given reality and is informed about the immanent evolutionary potential of the productive forces. Horkheimer is closest to this interpretation when he speaks of a tendency toward the "maintenance, increase and development of human life" inherent in the labor process.[11] Critical theory is thus itself the awareness of this immanent evolutionary direction:

Now, inasmuch as every individual in modern times has been required to make his own the purposes of society as a whole and to recognize these in society, there is the possibility that men would become aware of and concentrate their attention upon the path which the social work process has taken without any definite theory behind it, as a result of disparate forces interacting, and with the despair of the masses acting as a decisive factor at major turning points. Thought does not spin such a possibility out of itself but rather becomes aware of its own proper function.[12]

Within the conceptual framework of the philosophy of history proposed by Horkheimer this line of thought is, at first glance, conclusive: If the process of human history as a whole can be understood as a process of the gradual perfection of the domination of nature, then every society whose organizational form retards or does not fully exhaust the possibilities of freedom represents a condition of only partially realized reason. Corresponding to complete reason, which would be "identical with the domination of outer and inner nature" through free decision,[13] is a knowledge that is able to clarify the potential of the productive forces to explode the present because it is inherent in the progressive development of the human domination of nature. In this sense Horkheimer speaks of "the idea of a rational organization of society that meets the needs of all . . . and is inherent in labor."[14] However, the logic of this argument still leaves unclear how a critical theory so tailored (that is, as an intellectual extension of a second-order labor process) should be of a methodologically different structure, namely one that ought to be able to carry out a critique of the existing society. If Horkheimer is correct in tracing traditional theory back to the cognitive achievements introduced by the activity of labor, then the knowledge furnished by this type of theory is primarily suited only for the explanation and prediction of empirical processes. It does not contain the reflective moment that would be necessary to call into question the range that an existing social order grants to the development of productive forces. This methodological gap also cannot provide a higher-order knowledge, a knowledge about the direction of the domination of nature through science. A theory that consciously refers back to the process of social labor and has as its object the immanent developmental logic of the accomplishments of social labor rather than the actual processes of nature could, of course, fictively project this developmental course into the future, but it could not then use it as a criterion for a critique of social life. For the latter such a theory would still require knowledge derived from a philosophy of history, which must in fact lie at the basis of Horkheimer's own argument, in order to criticize a society in terms of its development-inhibiting organization of labor. Horkheimer himself obviously sees the contradiction to which this interpretation of the constitutive social conditions would lead: "An activity that, oriented to this emancipation, aims at an alteration of society as a whole might well be of service in theoretical work carried on within reality as presently ordered. But it lacks the pragmatic character that results from traditional thought as a socially useful professional activity."[15]

Traditional thought represents an intellectually objectified form of knowledge, collected in the historical process of the domination of nature. It possesses a practical character because it solves scientific problems, resulting from the reproduction of an existing organization of production, through the schema of a set of propositions which permit only the explanation and prediction of real natural processes. Just as theories of this sort arise from the practical conflict between humans and nature, so they again flow back into the process of the social domination of nature as knowledge of optimal control. Even a higher level of reflection upon the same practical origin, which makes conscious the immanent developmental dynamic of the process of social labor, cannot escape this framework of application. The consequence of Horkheimer's argument is that theory can only yield a technical knowledge that at best anticipates the future conditions of application of more developed productive forces, but does not permit a critique of its present mode of organization. The scientific perfection of the domination of nature does not itself lead to the "rational decision" that, in assigning the emancipatory potential of the productive forces to the conscious control of the producers, breaks through human self-deception.

At this point, alongside this first inadequate version, Horkheimer introduces another interpretation of the constitutive social conditions of critical theory. In this version, critical theory is not an immanent component of the developmental process of human labor but a theoretical expression of a prescientific "critical activity." This type of activity is not "pragmatic," like the activity of labor contained in the process of the self-preservation of society, but is critically related, in a distanced way, to the whole context of social life:

We must go on now to add that there is a human activity which has society itself for its object. The aim of this activity is not simply to eliminate one or another abuse, for it regards such abuses as necessarily connected with the way in which the social structure is organized. Although it itself emerges from the social structure, its purpose is not, either in its conscious intention or in its objective significance, the better functioning of any element in the structure. On the contrary, it is suspicious of the very categories of better, useful, appropriate, productive, and valuable, as these are understood in the present order, and refuses to take them as nonscientific presuppositions with which it has had nothing to do.[16]

This line of thought now leads Horkheimer not only to a different formulation of the constitutive social conditions of critical theory but also to an elaboration of its second theoretical feature. Initially this set of considerations presents a kind of human activity that has not nature but "society itself" as its object. It is concerned not with an extension of the domination of nature to social life as social control but with an activity that goes beyond the societally established functional system. Horkheimer quite obviously has in mind a kind of practical, socially transformative activity to which critical theory is itself connected. Of course, this argument, which makes direct reference to a dimension of social struggle, has no systematic place in the framework of the philosophy of history that Horkheimer has presupposed thus far: So long as this framework reduces the course of human history to the quasi-natural developmental process of the domination of nature, there is no conceptual possibility for a different form of social praxis which aims not at constantly expanding productive self-preservation but at a new mode of organizing societal self-preservation. With this Horkheimer repeats a conceptual dilemma of the early Marx. From the perspective of both epistemology and the philosophy of history, Marx's "Theses on Feuerbach," with its vague, genereal concept of "praxis," treats the history of the species as a nature-transforming, productive activity without thereby securing a place in the conceptual framework for the concept of "practical-critical activity" which in the same text clearly denotes a politically emancipatory, revolutionary activity.[17] But the line of thought that Horkheimer opens up with the concept of "critical activity" becomes clearer when it is developed to the point where the second methodological feature of a critical social theory is worked out.

Horkheimer pursues the methodological delineation of critical from traditional theory by attempting to define the different ways in which the two types of theory respectively relate the knowing subject to the object of investigation. In nature-transforming activity, of which traditional theory is the theoretically objectified form of expression, the acting subject relates to a natural event that represents a praxis-independent reality. To be sure, humans manipulatively intervene in this natural process, but only in a way that makes use of a lawfulness that transcends the subject. At the level of scientific theory, the experiment represents this nature-transforming activity. Like the acting subject, in the scientific experiment which produces artificial processes of natural reaction for the purpose of "visual instruction," the knowing subject relates to a reality that also remains unchanged by experimental intervention. Thus, in the case of traditional theory, scientific knowledge is external to the object of investigation. Of course, the relation between the knower and the known must change as soon as it is a matter of a critical theory of society. Horkheimer now shows that since critical theory has "society itself" as its object, "critical activity," whose intellectually objectified expression it is, is itself part of the reality investigated. Thus, in critical theory, subject and object are not externally opposed to one another in the same way as in traditional theories.[18]

Horkheimer firmly retains and develops this second interpretation, which understands critical social theory as the scientific objectification of a practical-critical activity. Theory is no longer only the intellectual product of an extra-theoretical transformative praxis; in addition, it continuously has a voice in its direction. From this Horkheimer now draws a conclusion: Only because critical theory constantly influences in an action-guiding manner the same social praxis through which it is known to have been produced is it a practically transformative moment in the social reality it investigates. The altered relation of subject and object denotes a second methodological feature of critical theory. Henceforth, it is no longer only knowledge of the practical conditions of its own origin; at the same time, it is the controlled application of an action-guiding knowledge to present political praxis. Since theory attempts both to make conscious its constitutive historical conditions and to anticipate its political context of application, it is potentially, as Horkheimer still describes it in 1937 using the language of the left-Hegelian Marxism of the 1920s, the "self-awareness of the subjects of a great historical transformation."[19] This formulation, which unambiguously grounds critical theory in a dimension of social struggle rather than in the societal domination of nature, dramatically reveals the disparity between its epistemological characterization and the philosophy of history that underlies it. In his analysis of the constitutive conditions of critical theory Horkheimer invokes a concept of social praxis that is more comprehensive than that permitted by his conception of the philosophy of history. At the level of the philosophy of history, the formation and the evolution of human societies are traced back to the process of the human domination of nature. The appropriation of nature represents that dimension in which human history moves along a line of increasing material abundance. The natural character of this progress is initially overcome in the historical moment in which the species first recognizes itself in its productive activity. However, in his second version, at the level of the methodological self-reflection of critical theory, Horkheimer is concerned with a dimension of practical-critical activity. The socio-cultural development moves within the orbit of both social production and social struggle. To be sure, this struggle is mediated by the economic development of productive forces, since the "protest" directing it, as Horkheimer unclearly puts it, arises from an "economic mechanism."[20] On the other hand, the structure of action which lies at the basis of social struggle is of a different kind than that of the nature-appropriating activity of labor.

Whereas in social labor the human species preserves and expands its social life in proportion to the practical conquest of natural processes, critical activity calls into question precisely the existing mode of organization of this process of societal self-preservation. An objective, pregiven power of nature corresponds to the activity of labor. Man is emancipated from it through a technical knowledge which assembles the practical results of this goal-directed manipulation of natural events. By contrast, the historicity of a socially established productive relation corresponds to practical-critical activity. This relation is connected with force and oppression so long as the "material and ideological power operates to maintain privileges."[21] A critical knowledge that has as its goal the "intensification of the struggle"[22] liberates man from this social power relation. If social labor derives its incentive from an objective pressure for survival, the incentives for practical-critical activity grow out of the subjective experience of a "prevailing injujstice"[23] which is structurally connected to a given distribution of social labor among social classes. For this reason, Horkheimer ascribes the nature-transforming labor that guarantees socio-cultural survival in general to the human species as a whole, as a transcendental subject that has become actual, whereas he ascribes the critical praxis of social struggle only to social groups that are excluded from the privilege of the appropriation of social wealth.

The restriction of the subject of critical activity to individual groups or classes indicates that social conflict—in contrast to the cultivation of nature objectively attained by the species—is embedded in a process of the experientially mediated interpretation of the historical situation. Only a framework of action in which the activity of the subject is prompted not by a single, common perspective united by the force of self-preservation but rather by varying perspectives shaped by experience can explain why Horkheimer allows only groups, as bearers of action, to correspond to practical-critical activity. In this dimension of social practice, namely social conflict, particular interpretations of reality, which are the forms of expression of conflicting constellations of interests, emerge in opposition to one another in order to struggle over the justness of an organization of social production. Therefore, Horkheimer understands Critical Theory's practical framework of application as the process of a dialogically mediated interpretation of social reality in the light of injustice experienced by the oppressed class:

If, however, the theoretician and his specific object are seen as forming a dynamic unity with the oppressed class, so that his presentation of societal contradictions is not merely an expression of the concrete historical situation but is also a force within it to stimulate change, then his real function emerges. The course of the conflict between the advanced sectors of the class and the individuals who speak out the truth concerning it, as well as of the conflict between the most advanced sectors with their theoreticians and the rest of the class, is

to be understood as a process of interaction in which awareness comes
to flower along with its liberating but also its aggressive forces which
incite while also requiring discipline.[24]

Horkheimer did not further clarify the specific structure of
the social practice characterized by the phrase "critical activity."
To be sure, the idea of a dialogically mediated application of
critical social theory opens up the insight into the interpretive
dependence upon social experiences. But Horkheimer does
not make use of this for a conceptually broadened demarcation
of the category of "critical activity" in contrast to the category
of "social labor." At the theoretical level the concept of practical-critical activity remains peculiarly undefined. To the contrary, at the level of his basic assumptions concerning the
philosophy of history, Horkheimer omitted completely the dimension of a critique of everyday life in which theory is known
to be located since that theory participates in the cooperative
process of an interpretation of the present in the interest of
overcoming suffered injustice. This conceptual reductionism
prevents Horkheimer from grasping the practical dimensions
of social conflict and struggle as such. Despite his epistemological definition of critical theory, he does not seriously treat the
dimensions of action present in social struggle as an autonomous sphere of social reproduction. But, for that reason,
Horkheimer gives up the possibility of considering sufficiently
the interpretive organization of social reality. The result is, as
will be shown, a sociological deficit in the interdisciplinary social
science that Horkheimer views as the solution offered by the
program of a critical social theory.

The lack of political orientation that seemed to confront the
Institute in the 1930s may have contributed to the conceptual
ambivalence of Horkheimer's arguments. In this case, concrete
uncertainty about the practical application of theory would
have hindered an adequate consideration of the dimension of
social struggle from the perspective of the philosophy of history. The realm of critical activity would have been completely
excluded from the conceptual framework of historical interpretation because the theory of society is unsure of its role at
the present historical moment. In fact, a political confusion,

which could well be the source of such a precipitous generalization, characterizes Horkheimer's political writings from this period: On the one hand, there is no doubt that under the conditions of capitalism a critical theory of society aimed at political praxis must look for its addressees only among the social class of the wage laborer, the proletariat. For reasons connected with the social structure, only this group is open to theoretical enlightenment and ready for political revolution. On the other hand, in these writings, as a result of the experiences of the National Socialists' seizure of power and of Stalinism, the doubt has increased about whether, under the conditions of postliberal capitalism, the proletariat still bears the potential for transformation resulting from its experience of oppression and crisis, as the Marxist concept of revolution assumes.[25] A major portion of the theoretical construction and social research of the Institute during the 1930s was an attempt to provide an empirical answer to the problem expressed in this tension. Its guiding motif is formed by the question "What psychic mechanisms have come about that enable the tension between the social classes to remain latent, even though it borders on conflict as a result of the economic situation?"[26] The program of an interdisciplinary social science, outlined by Horkheimer at the beginning of the 1930s, is tailored to the investigation of this phenomenon.

In his 1931 inaugural lecture, "The Present Situation of Social Philosophy and the Tasks of an Institute for Social Research," Horkheimer already makes it clear that a critical theory of society that accepts the difficult project of reflecting upon its social origins as well as upon the political possibilities for its realization can fulfill its task only within an interdisciplinary context. The model he presents for this task is that of a "continuous dialectical interpenetration and development of philosophical theory and particular scientific practice."[27] Horkheimer has in mind a critical theory that analyzes the structural conditions and consequences of capitalist crises through a constant interaction between philosophical diagnoses of the present and research projects within the particular sciences. "History and Psychology," an essay published the same year in the *Zeitschrift*, attempts to expand and concretize this roughly sketched theoretical program. The paradigm derived from the philosophy of history, which will later provide the framework for the methodological approach of critical theory, is found here in the form of a materialist reinterpretation of Hegel's philosophy of history. It provides an interpretive background for the task of integrating the individual scientific disciplines into a theoretical structure appropriate to the subject matter. According to Horkheimer, the materialist interpretation of history is indebted to Hegel's concept of history since it includes the idea of a context of action that goes beyond the intentions of individual agents. Nevertheless, it is also opposed to it since it traces the course of human history back to the development of the human domination of nature rather than to the unfolding of absolute Spirit. It is this idea, critically directed against Hegel, that now ushers in the idea of a process of social labor that shapes socio-cultural progress, an idea characteristic of the early Horkheimer: "The knowledge of actual relations dethrones Spirit as an autonomous power shaping history and puts in its place, as the motor of history, the dialectic between the different human forces that arise as a result of the conflict with nature and the antiquated forms of society. . . . According to it [the economic interpretation of history—A.H.], the maintenance and renewal of social life forces its own specific arrangement of social classes on humanity."[28] Horkheimer makes basic a process of the development of productive forces which, with each new level of the technical domination of nature, also produces a new level in the social organization of production. The dimension of social struggle which, as the constitutive ground of critical theory, will later assume such a divided role in the epistemological essay is nevertheless still completely absent from this concept of social evolution. The domination of nature, self-preservation solely through the processes of social labor, is the only dimension in which socio-cultural progress takes place. Horkheimer explicitly equates the "life process of a society" with the "conflict with nature."[29] This conceptually limited model of history, a decisive component of Horkheimer's early critical theory, forms the theoretical base upon which he erects the edifice of an interdisciplinary social science. Political economy is then the individual science that assumes the uncontested role of the fundamental discipline within the social sciences. Only economic concepts grasp the objective structure of the process of social life, since the history of civilization is disclosed as the process of a gradual development of productive forces freed from the fetters of outmoded productive relations: "If history is divided according to the different ways that the life process of human society is realized, then it is not psychological but economic categories that are historically fundamental."[30] As a result of this argument, Horkheimer can identify the central concepts of Marx's analysis of capital as the social-scientific concepts which express the capitalist form of the species-historical process of the domination of nature.

Of course, Horkheimer is aware that the economic theory of capitalism, which is supposed to form the backbone of interdisciplinary social science, must, so to speak, shift historically along with its object of investigation. Critical theory, if it wants to be an expression of an actual historical situation, must impartially comprehend the internal structural change that the capitalist system has undergone since its liberal era. Thus, for Horkheimer during the 1930s, the task of economics consisted in investigating the tendency of capitalism, as a result of the process of concentration, to move toward planned economic organization. Friedrich Pollock was at the Institute at this time to assist in this project.[31] The legal and political work of Franz Neumann and Otto Kirchheimer, which had as its object the judicial and political "mediatization" of the capitalist crisis dynamic, are also relevant here.[32] Horkheimer viewed the postliberal phase of capitalism as a mode of production in which the planning organ of an economic power elite replaced the steering medium of the market and the "monopolist" of the planned economy replaced the "manufacturer" of the liberal period.[33] However, it is largely thematized as an economic structure whose internal psychic dynamics were to be explained by the second discipline of interdisciplinary social science: psychology.

The argument in which Horkheimer presents psychology as a discipline complementing economic theory sounds familiar. It reflects the theoretical consensus that formed the common background of the "Freudian left" (Marcuse) in the 1920s and the 1930s in its efforts to integrate historical materialism and psychoanalytic theory.[34] Horkheimer turns against a sociological overburdening of the explanatory model presupposed in economic theory. A theory of society that reasons from motives of action hypothetically assumed by economic theory to the level of actual action implicitly relies upon a trivial psychology, indebted to utilitarian thought, that only recognizes "economic egoism" as a motive in social action. All the psychic motives that operate in a context of social action other than the purposive-rational pursuit of private interests are bypassed in an economic theory arbitrarily elevated to a psychology. In the place of such a trivial psychology, based on the rationalistic model of action in utilitarianism, a psychology that begins with the malleability and displaceability of human instincts should be developed. We can theoretically explain the modes of action of those social groups that participate in social repression against their own rational interest only if we consider that the needs motivating a subject not only exhibit extraordinary variation but also, under pressures of frustration, are forcibly deferred to compensatory goals. Therefore, a critical theory of society that investigates the causes of the latency of the class conflict it predicts must rely upon a psychology that has abandoned the theoretical presupposition of the purposive-rational motivation of all human action:

In any event, human action does not simply arise from the psychic strivings for self-preservation, nor simply from immediate sexual drives, but also, for example, from needs related to participation in aggressive forces, to recognition and confirmation of their own person, to concealment in a collectivity, and other movements affecting drives. Modern psychology (Freud) has shown how such claims are distinguished from hunger in that the latter demand a direct and continual satisfaction, while the former can be deferred, altered and made accessible to imaginary satisfaction.[35]

The psychological concept offered to analyze the social integration of the subject into a self-contradictory mode of production must be so constituted that it permits the instinctual life of humans to be viewed as an initially plastic, instinctual process that is shaped by societal demands upon action and constantly prepared for psychically constructed substitutes. It then becomes clear why the experience of social dependency and oppression is, so to speak, blocked and repressed by "an instinctual motor falsifying consciousness" even before it becomes "knowledge."[36] The cognitive disclosure of social reality which the ego would repair when it perceived injustice is thwarted by a dynamic process of denial and repression that substitutes perceived impotence with the imaginary experience of personal or collective power. Projection and identification are the psychological means that make this phantastical inversion possible.

It is this dualism of a knowledge adjusted to reality and an irrational instinctual process that marks the point at which Horkheimer introduces psychology into the interdisciplinary structure of critical social research. The capitalist domination of nature, in which there is a striking discrepancy between the developmental state and the mode of organization, is joined to a process of individual socialization that adjusts the instinctual potential of the subject to prevailing relations of oppression. This takes place in a process of instinctual dynamics that, by diverting socially undesirable needs to goals secured through domination, force the subject unconsciously to a constant misapprehension of reality that undermines the accomplishments of rational knowledge. Consequently, the economic reproduction of the capitalist system of domination rests upon the fluid basis of this constantly recurring instinctual process: It is, Horkheimer writes, "the historically developed psychic properties or set of drives that determines whether outmoded relations between productive elements are to be maintained and, with them, the social structure built upon them."[37] Therefore, within an interdisciplinary social science that empirically investigates the capitalist situation of crisis, economics requires a psychological theory that analyzes the socialization process of individual drives through which a social system that controls nature is integrated into the socially accepted unity of a life process. Psychoanalysis offers the theoretical paradigm that, according to Horkheimer, has the explanatory capacity to solve this problem. Its basic idea, the structuring of libidinal energies through the child's interaction with his parents, thus provides the second theoretical model that emerges as a complement to the basic mode of social labor derived from the philosophy of history.

Horkheimer assumes the version of psychoanalysis found in Erich Fromm's analytic social psychology. Within the intellectual circle of the Institute for Social Research, Fromm was entrusted with the task of working out a psychology that could be linked to economics without any fissure. His proposal thus conforms to the idea that led Horkheimer to include psychology within interdisciplinary social research: "Neither the external power apparatus nor rational interests would suffice to guarantee the functioning of the society, if the libidinal strivings of the people were not involved. They serve as the 'cement,' as it were, without which the society could not hold together, and which contributes to the production of important social ideologies in every cultural sphere."[38] Fromm links together two concepts arising from different sources in order to analyze the process of socialization that forces libidinal energies into the behavioral system required by society.[39] First, like other Marxist psychoanalysts of his time, he begins with the assumption that the institutional demands raised by the capitalist system of social labor are conveyed to the adolescent by the parents. The family is thus the social medium in which the socio-economic imperatives for behavior are preserved and passed on in a socially effective manner. Second, from an interpretation of Freud's psychoanalytic personality theory, mediated via the lectures of Karl Abrahams, he derives the idea that the personality structure of an individual consists in stabilized behavioral traits on the level of psychosexual development. Individual character is a bundle of firmly bound impulses taken from early childhood eroticism. Taken together, these concepts yield the basic categories of Fromm's social psychology: Parental rearing practices that reflect the external force of society within the family fix the psychosexual development of the child at the level appropriate to the socially required system of behavior. In contrast to this, the instinctual elements that strive to go beyond the forms of expression valued in the family are either repressed or sublimated—the libidinal strivings of the adolescent subject are incorporated into the societally desired frameworks of action.

When he speaks of psychology as a subdiscipline of a critical social theory, Horkheimer has in mind Fromm's social psychology. In his essays from the early 1930s Fromm developed his theory with reference to class-specific personality structures, a model he later replaced with a class-transcending notion of the sadomasochistic character in the Institute's study "Authority and the Family."[40] Insofar as Horkheimer does not make any conceptual revisions, he must inevitably adopt the weaknesses of Fromm's earlier model. Fromm lets the basic concepts of a psychoanalytic personality theory mesh directly with the basic concepts of an economic theory of society; the dimension of *social action*, the concrete reality of which gradually forms individual instinctual potential, is, so to speak, crushed between these two conceptual frameworks. The family, which represents the whole communicative context of society in Fromm's conceptual framework, appears as the mere function of an all-encompassing economic process: The functional imperatives of the capitalist economy are simply reflected as behavioral constraints within familial interaction. Within the structure of these systemic demands, shaped by the parent's rearing practices, the libidinal strivings of the adolescent apparently develop without friction. The closed functionalism into which this model falls is the hidden core of Fromm's social psychology. As Helmut Dahmer states, it moves in the direction of a "theory of total socialization,"[41] since, in opposition to the systemic forces of the economy, it does not grant a libidinal surplus to individual needs nor any autonomy to social action.

Horkheimer seems to be aware of this. As if to guard against the economic reductionism that would characterize a social theory short-circuited by a combination of Fromm's social psychology and Pollock's analysis of capitalism, Horkheimer inserts a third dimension of social reproduction between the realm of the socialization of individual instincts and the encroaching system of social labor—namely, culture. The concept of "culture" apparently represents the conceptual means with which he hopes to resist the danger of leading critical social theory astray into a latent functionalism through the theoretical merger of political economy and psychoanalysis alone. But the enigmatic significance and ambivalent place this concept admittedly acquires within the idea of interdisciplinary social science is the price of the conceptual reductionism of Horkheimer's own philosophy of history.

On the one hand, Horkheimer deals with a sphere of cultural action that extends beyond the socially differentiated subsystems of aesthetic or intellectual production and includes the realm of symbolic expressions and social interactions. In his inaugural address as director of the Institute he begins with the assumption that culture is a third dimension of social reproduction which, together with the system of social labor and the socialization of individual instincts, interdisciplinary social science must consider if it wants to analyze the integration of the functional imperatives of the economy into the always-fragile unity of social life. Critical social theory thus rests upon the three bases of economic, psychological, and cultural disciplines:

Not simply within social philosophy narrowly conceived, but rather within the circles of sociology as well as within those of philosophy in general, discussions about society have gradually crystallized around a question that is not simply of contemporary significance, but is at the same time the contemporary formulation of the oldest and most important philosophical problems, namely, the question of the relationship between the economic life of society, the psychic development of the individual and the changes within the cultural sphere in the narrower sense (to which belong not only the so-called intellectual content of science and religion, but also law, ethics, fashion, public opinion, sport, leisure, life-style, etc.). The intention of investigating the relationships between these three processes is nothing more than a formulation, appropriate to the state of our knowledge and methods, of the ancient question of the connection between particular existence and universal reason, reality and idea, life and Spirit, only now related to a new set of problems.[42]

The category of culture invoked here, which also recalls the use of the concept now adopted in Germany from British cultural history and working-class sociology,[43] denotes a field of social action in which social groups create common values, objectify them in the institutions of everyday life, and hand them down in the form of symbolic utterances. The dimension of social reproduction that Horkheimer thus seems to aim at with the help of such a concept of culture is one in which cognitive as well as normative self-interpretations are produced and secured within the medium of social action. These patterns of value orientation, produced within specific groups and communicatively reinforced, mediate between the system of social labor and the formation of individual motives since within them the economic constraints upon action are reinterpreted within the context of everyday practices and thereby accumulated in a socially effective manner. The natural potential of human drives and the socially independent forces of economic reproduction are refracted by the foundation of everyday interpretive accomplishments in which subjects reciprocally secure social meanings and values. Through the filter of these collective norms of action that are fixed in the group-specific interpretations of "law" and "morality" and that are symbolically represented in the habitualized forms of "fashion" and "lifestyle," the constraints upon action pre-given from above and the action motives repressed from within first become effective in subjects socialized in a life situation. The "cement" of a society, which in Horkheimer's words "artificially holds together the parts tending toward independence,"[44] consists in the culturally produced and continuously renewed action orientations in which social groups have intepretively disclosed their own individual needs as well as the tasks required of them under the conditions of the class-specific division of labor. However, Horkheimer does not draw this conclusion. Rather, even before he becomes aware of the action-theoretic logic of his own use of the concept, his use of the category of culture reverts back to a traditional line of thought that no longer refers to a specific domain of social action but rather refers to a realm of socially generalized agents of socialization. Within the conceptual framework that lies at the basis of Horkheimer's program of an interdisciplinary social science, this second concept of "culture" is instructive:

The process of production influences men not only in the immediate contemporary form in which they themselves experience it in their work, but also in the form in which it has been incorporated into relatively stable institutions which are slow to change, such as family, school, church, institutions of worship, etc. To understand why a society functions in a certain way, why it is unstable or dissolves, therefore demands a knowledge of the contemporary psychic make-up of men in various social groups. This in turn requires a knowledge of how their character has been formed in interaction with all the shaping cultural forces of the time.[45]

It is the system of reference and not only the conceptual range that has shifted in the context of this argument. Here Horkheimer deals with a series of cultural institutions that mediate between the behavioral requirements of social production and the subject through the stably institutionalized processes of education and acculturation. Parental rearing practices, school curricula, and religious rituals are media that affect all social classes and continuously reflect the behavioral constraints of the economic system back upon the individual psyche, albeit indirectly and in a fragmented manner. In one such use the concept of culture approximates the central Marxist notion of the "cultural superstructure," despite the fact that Horkheimer emphasizes the peculiar inner dynamics of cultural institutions more strongly than his predecessors.[46] Namely, the referential system decisive here restricts the concept of culture to permanently fixed institutions that are apparently removed from the everyday course of action. Not the cooperative production of normative patterns of orientation, i.e., cultural action, but rather the socializing function of formative institutions, the institutions of culture, provides the real paradigm toward which Horkheimer's second concept of culture is oriented.

Horkheimer has quietly transformed the action-theoretic concept of culture that he apparently has in view in his inaugural address into the institution-theoretic concept of the "cultural apparatus."[47] Culture now appears between the system of social labor and malleable human instincts in the obstinate form of organized learning processes that anchor the behavioral expectations required by the economy as libidinally charged goals of action in the individual psyche. In almost all the texts that Horkheimer published in the *Zeitschrift* during the 1930s this concept of the cultural institution has replaced the action-theoretic concept. In this way the conceptual reductionism of his philosophy of history is secured within Horkheimer's theory of social science. At the conceptual level he cannot pursue further the notion of cultural action, since the basic model of his philosophy of history leaves no room for another type of social action alongside the societal cultivation of nature.

Only an institution-theoretic concept of culture that attempts to get hold of the socially integrative function of education and religious institutions is compatible with a view of history that limits the development of civilization to the gradual expansion and refinement of human capacities for labor. In this process an institutionalized structure of cultural agencies undertakes the function of generating at the societal level the action motivations required by the social organization of labor and ideologically supporting the established distribution of privileges. The institutions of culture are thus stabilizing factors, reaching through individual instincts, in the species-historical process of the social domination of nature. However, within this model of history Horkheimer is no more able to entertain a concept of cultural action that designates the cooperative activity of producing and securing group-specific action orientations than he is the epistemological concept of critical activity, since both are conceptually ruled out by referring all human action to labor. With both concepts Horkheimer strives for more than he is able to achieve at the level of a philosophy of history. Between the Marxist model of social labor and the psychoanalytic model of the socialization of individual instincts there is no third theoretical model available in connection with which he could conceptually develop the structure of cultural action or social struggle. This is the reason why Horkheimer is finally compelled to leave unutilized the action-theoretic concept of culture just as he did the concept of critical activity, although he introduced both of them.

If we follow the implicit suggestions of Horkheimer's early writings, social struggle is the conflictual counterpart to cultural action. In their everyday action, members of a social group have harmonized their class-conditioned interests and their specific needs within relatively stable value orientations and interpretive patterns that enable them, without losing their psychic identity, to participate actively in the institutionalized structures of a social order. Within the horizon of such cultural systems of action, which have acquired a certain permanence in traditional forms of interaction and symbolic orders, class-specific burdens appear reduced to a biographically bearable degree and individual drives appear integrated into a calculable organization of needs. A group-specific horizon of orientation, which is supposed to fulfill both tasks, is, of course, extremely fragile since it must be renewed and confirmed constantly by group members. Unexpected events and information previously unknown interrupt the reproduction of established orientations and endanger the disrupted normative structure of a social group. Critical activity is then the directed process of a cooperative testing and problematizing of interpretations worked out within the group. This process encounters experiences, which have not yet been interpretively disclosed, that put in a new light the previously accepted proportion of social burdens and libidinal renunciations. The disruption of culturally secured everyday action forces the group member to correct and expand the traditional horizon of orientation in the face of unmasked reality. Critical activity is thus also the reflexive continuation of an everyday communication shaken in its self-understanding. On this basis, social struggle can be conceived as the cooperative organization of this everyday critique: It would be the attempt by social groups, forced by the conditions of the class-specific division of labor and excessive burdens, to realize within the normative structures of social life the norms of action acquired in the repeated experience of suffered injustice. However, since he does not know how to decipher the normal case of everyday action, Horkheimer must leave this paradigm of critical activity theoretically undefined. The force of his basic model of the philosophy of history is so strong that he cannot help but compress culturally guided everyday action and the critical-practical activity of social groups into a conceptual framework limited to social labor and the socialization of individual instincts. It is not the social actions of societal members but an institutionalized ring of cultural agencies that mediates between the economic imperative of societal self-preservation and the complimentary task of the socialization of individual needs.

As a result of this conceptual inconsistency, Horkheimer screens the whole spectrum of everyday social action out of the object domain of interdisciplinary social science. In contrast to the sociological task of investigating social reality with reference to group-specific background experiences and the cooperative process of creating social patterns of orientation, he seems to be locked within the programmatic structure of critical social research. Neither the familiar cultural communication within social groups nor the everyday clash between cultural action orientations of social groups is taken seriously as an object of specific scientific research. Within the interdisciplinary structure of Horkheimer's critical social theory, sociology thus assumes the marginal position of an auxiliary science. Since it does not occupy an independent theoretical model, it is simply pushed aside in favor of political economy or psychoanalysis when the cultural stabilization of the economic process or the social mediation of need formation are themes of investigation. However, Horkheimer is not concerned with providing a conceptual foundation for sociology. The action-theoretic programs in which Max Weber, on the one hand, and George Mead, on the other, attempt to give sociology the form of an autonomous science are foreign to him. Therefore, like Fromm—the functionalistic consequences of whose concept he hoped to correct through the construction of a theory of culture—he must finally be satisfied with a critical social theory that combines political economy and psychoanalysis. When he wants to analyze the process through which a system of dominating nature is integrated with the culturally accepted unity of social life, Horkheimer is thrown back to the dualism of a knowledge adapted to reality and irrational instincts. A tremendous gulf remains between rational insights into reality and libidinally induced misunderstandings of reality such that only empirical information concerning the mechanism of social integration can be obtained. This is the fundamental consideration behind the research project of the Institute, "Authority and the Family," directed by Horkheimer, on the latent readiness of the German people for fascism.

The entire edifice of interdisciplinary social science that Horkheimer attempted to sketch out during the 1930s rests upon the disciplines of economics and psychoanalysis alone. Within it a theory of culture is simply the failed attempt at a systematic consideration of social action. But the theory of culture actually applied in the work of the Institute is based not upon a theory of action nor upon a theory of institutions, but rather upon a third version of the concept of culture. At this point, in a (so to speak) second step of reduction, the traditionalistic concept of culture, limited to aesthetic products, once again prevails over the use Horkheimer had originally made of this concept. Leo Löwenthal and Theodor Adorno, who within the division of labor in the Institute were responsible for the sector of cultural theory, made use of this limited perspective in their research into cultural events. The goal of their research was the ideological-critical deciphering of the social content of the work of art. A materialist sociology of literature and music emerges in the place that, in Horkheimer's program of an interdisciplinary social science, should have been assumed by a theory of culture whose task was the analysis of the social mediation of processes of economic development and human instincts. Within the quiet transformation of the concept of culture from one based in a theory of action to one restricted to institutions, and finally to one articulated aesthetically, the change of perspective in the philosophy of history is already announced—namely, the change critical theory undergoes at the end of the 1930s in the work of Adorno.

2

The Turn to the Philosophy of History in the *Dialectic of Enlightenment*: A Critique of the Domination of Nature

Horkheimer concluded his essay "Traditional and Critical Theory" with reflections that did not fit well with the philosophical-historical framework of his argument. The theoretical confidence in the rational process of the social domination of nature, which gives a hopeful tone to the essay, finally yields to an unexpectedly pessimistic diagnosis of the times that depicts the postliberal phase of capitalism as an altered lifeworld. The formation of a capitalist planned economy, which took economic decisionmaking away from the small entrepreneur and handed it over to the administration of the large manufacturer, brought with it far-reaching changes in the conditions of individual socialization. Besides losing his decisionmaking capacity, the clarity and efficacy of which sustained his authority in liberal capitalism, the factory owner also loses the cognitive and moral bases of his identity. Through the erosion of his personality, in light of whose exemplary appearance the growing child could form a stable, morally guided identity, the features of individuality for the entire society gradually changed. Horkheimer sees in the weakening of the small independent entrepreneur the historical trend toward the end of personality:

Once the legal owners are cut off from the real productive process and lose their influence, their horizon narrows; they become increasingly unfit for important social positions, and finally the share which they still have in industry due to ownership and which they have done nothing to augment comes to seem socially useless and morally dubious. . . . Under the conditions of monopolistic capitalism, however, even such a relative individual independence is a thing of the past. The individual no longer has any ideas of his own. The content of mass belief, in which no one really believes, is an immediate product of the ruling economic and political bureaucracies, and its disciples secretly follow their own atomistic and therefore untrue interests; they act as mere functions of the economic machine.[1]

Apart from all class-specific differences,[2] Horkheimer infers from the growing centralization of economic decisionmaking the loss of personality in socialized individuals. To the extent that the process of the monopolization of capital absorbs the efficacy of cultural institutions along with the economic freedom of subjects, the control of behavior by the authority of individual conscience passes directly over to the authoritative planning of social administration. Subjects are directed less and less by a socially developed superego and are thus more directly susceptible to influence through external guides. Of course, the empirical background for this social-psychological hypothesis is derived not solely from the process of economic concentration but also from the worldwide creation of totalitarian state systems. Horkheimer derives the image of a mass managed by external domination, which appears in the last pages of his programmatic essay, from the experience of a public that applauds the fascist or Stalinist seizure of power. This consciousness of a global system of domination, consented to by the suppressed subjects, is combined with the experience of the American culture industry and, from now on, determines the self-understanding and the concept of critical theory.

The last volume of the *Zeitschrift für Sozialforschung*, which appeared in 1941, contains two studies by Horkheimer that clearly express the modified interpretation of his theory. The essay "Art and Mass Culture" marks a turning point in Horkheimer's theory of culture.[3] "Culture" is no longer a general concept for the institutionalized structure of autonomous media of socialization. Since the process of capitalist industrialization has in the meantime penetrated the inner regions of cultural institutions and opened them up to direct influence by powers of social administration, the cultural superstructure has lost its "relative power of resistance." This new stage of cultural reproduction is retained from now on in Horkheimer's concept of "mass culture." It refers to the institutional complex of mass art that arose with the new reproductive techniques as well as to the monopolistically organized leisure industry, through which individual needs can be arbitrarily manipulated and norms of action can be artificially produced. But the power of resistance that Horkheimer believes to be absent from the new cultural institutions has, in his view, been gathered in the works of modern art. This small sector of aesthetic production assumes in the present the emancipatory function that formerly belonged to the free domain that protected individual identities within the cultural superstructure as a whole. The concept of "new art" thus represents the second pole of Horkheimer's reformulated theory of culture. It refers to "authentic works of art . . . monuments of a solitary and despairing life that find no bridge to any other or even to its own consciousness."[4] The manipulative culture industry and the incommunicable work of art are opposing sides of the contemporary culture that abandon the socialized subjects without protection to the imperatives of the apparatus of domination because they no longer can supply them with the resources for personality formation.

The second essay Horkheimer published in the final volume of the *Zeitschrift*, "The End of Reason," contains the rough outline of a philosophy of history that attempts to provide this modified theory of culture with an appropriate interpretive framework.[5] The category of labor contained in the concept of self-preservation also forms the basis for this revised philosophy of history. However, with its aid, Horkheimer now outlines not the emancipatory process of the human domination of nature but the process of a self-destruction of reason. His argument is based on the conviction that from the very beginning human reason stands in the service of the self-preservation of the subject. This thought is the key to a theory of the self-dissolution of human reason: With the monopolization of all competencies of economic decisionmaking in a planned economy and the centralization of all competencies of political decisionmaking in the authoritarian state, the region of individual identity-formation is restricted to the point that it is no longer able to form guided interests and normative orientations. As a result the acting subject is deprived of the purposive-rational thinking that serves both the technical domination of external nature and the prudential disciplining of his inner nature. Instrumental reason, originally the means for the rational domination of nature and the self, has, through the same process in which personality ceases to be its bearer, been transformed into the means of "monopoly rule."[6] As victims to their own reason, human beings are helplessly subjugated by this subjectless system of strategic and technical thought. Thus, from the fate of the present the insufficiency residing in the human domination of nature itself is disclosed: "The new order of fascism is reason revealing itself as unreason."[7]

In the context of this argument, in which the idea of a critique of instrumental reason is accompanied by a culture-theoretic diagnosis of the present, all the elements are already included that would henceforth determine the modified form of critical theory. In the last essays of the *Zeitschrift* Horkheimer enters upon a new phase of his thinking.[8] The idea of a self-destruction of human reason, the social-psychological concept of the loss of personality, the concept of mass culture, and the ideal of the authentic work of art are the building blocks of a theory of society that has its inner content the central experience of the commonality of fascist and Stalinist domination. Its most prominent author is, of course, not Max Horkheimer but Theodor Adorno. His thought is shaped profoundly by a historical experience that shows the present to be a socio-cultural destiny. The central nerve of his theory is not (as it was for Horkheimer in the 1930s) the disappointment of revolutionary hopes, but the horror of the catastrophic culmination of the process of civilization. Adorno sees the social situation of his own time as an instance of totalized domination. He discovers the unity of a single process of domination within the arena of political power systems ranging from the Stalinist Soviet Union, through fascist Germany, to the state capitalism of the United States. The defeat of the Russian revolution with the rise of Stalin's dictatorial state bureaucracy, the terroristic founding of the fascist power apparatus in Europe, and the apparently interminable growth of American capitalism are for him barely distinguishable developmental forms of one historical process, which culminates in a system of total domination.⁹ Unlike any other, Adorno's social theory is motivated by the philosophical-historical question of the possibility of this world-historical convergence.

From the beginning Adorno moved within different philosophical regions than Horkheimer. In the 1930s he was already interested in the theoretical problems that Horkheimer ran up against when he was forced to drop the program of an interdisciplinary social theory in its original form. Adorno was indifferent, if not completely skeptical, toward the original program of Horkheimer's Institute—namely, the multidisciplinary and practically oriented investigation of the crisis of contemporary capitalism.¹⁰ Rather, the essays in the sociology of music that Adorno published in the *Zeitschrift* move in the direction of a theory of mass culture.¹¹ In those essays his task was to derive the socially integrative function of mass culture from the commodity form of standardized and mass-produced works of art. This attempt at a critique of the regressive mode of reception wherein aesthetic enjoyment is fused with the mere consumption of commodities was directly influenced by the analysis of fetishism found in Marx's critique of political economy. On the other hand, Adorno's early philosophical essays, which were primarily products of the academic requirements of his university studies, already moved in the direction of a critique of instrumental reason.¹² In them he attempts to sketch out the methodology of a philosophy aimed at deciphering the socially determining configurations of action in an alienated world. The concepts of historical image and configurative language, which are supposed to be the means for an interpretive technique removed from the instrumentalizing spirit, indirectly disclose a sympathy with the hermeneutic method of Walter Benjamin.¹³

Both motifs—the theory of mass culture developed in conjunction with the fetishistic character of music and the idea of a hermeneutic that unlocks an unconscious process of human natural history—thus gain the upper hand in the critical theory of the 1940s. Although as a result of these themes Adorno maintains throughout his career an ambivalent attitude toward the project of an empirically controlled and interdisciplinary theory of society, they henceforth form the central elements of the theoretical model that guides the Institute for Social Research. The core of this new conception of critical theory is a philosophy of history with which Adorno hoped to clarify the historical genesis of total domination. To a certain degree it represents the inverse of the principal themes of the philosophy of history that initially underlies Horkheimer's program for a critical theory of society.

Adorno took the similarity between the different systems of totalitarian domination so seriously as the historical starting point of his theory that it became the thematic horizon for an entire model of history. In the same way that Marx conceives the demystified productive relations of capitalist society as the conceptual key to a reconstruction of human history, Adorno views the relations of domination that have become visible in his own time as a structural paradigm from the development of which the hidden logic of the whole process of civilization is to be read. Critical theory is henceforth "the theory of the fascist present in which the hidden side of things comes to light."[14] From this despairing perspective (which, as will be seen, Adorno retained even after the historical situation of German fascism had been overcome), the progress of civilization is exposed as the concealed process of human regression. Socio-cultural evolution, which on the testimony of a cumulative growth in productive forces gives the impression of continuous progress, turns out to be the extended act of regression in the history of the species. The title that Adorno gives to this process is "retrogressive anthropogenesis." It forms the internal organizing principle of his philosophy of history.[15]

The *Dialectic of Enlightenment*, jointly authored by Adorno and Horkheimer at the beginning of the 1940s, represents the attempt to present this historical experience of the regressive history of the species in the unsystematic form of a collection of essays. Its primary material consists in an interpretation of literary and philosophical works—Homer's *Odyssey*, the novels of de Sade, and essays by Kant and Nietzsche. Adorno and Horkheimer reconstruct the course of European civilization not from sources in social history but from these indirect witnesses from intellectual history. The basic concept that implicitly guides the literary interpretations of this investigation is that of instrumental rationality. It functions to clarify the origin and the dynamic of the process of civilizing regression. From now on the concept of 'rationality' restricted to objectivating thought provides the key for a critical theory of society. With Horkheimer, Adorno accomplishes this by generalizing Marx's critique of capitalism, making it possible to view from the theoretical perspective of an increasing reification not only the history of liberal-capitalist society but the whole course of civilization. In the tradition of the Marxist analysis of capital from Georg Lukács to Alfred Sohn-Rethel the forms of consciousness of bourgeois society are thought to have developed from the forces of abstraction of commodity exchange, in which subjects acting with reciprocal disregard for their needs and experiences are transformed into "objects."[16] By contrast, in the totalizing view of the *Dialectic of Enlightenment* commodity exchange is merely the historically developed form of instrumental rationality. To be sure, in a few passages in his writings Adorno follows the fundamental idea of Sohn-Rethel's formal-genetic epistemology in which the abstractive accomplishments of modern thought are explained by the cognitive requirements of capitalist commodity exchange.[17] A few passages in the *Dialectic of Enlightenment* also attempt to describe (albeit metaphorically) the first steps in the human intervention into natural processes through a description of sacrifice as the original act of a fraudulent exchange between humans and the gods.[18] Admittedly, such interpretations, which direct attention to a pattern of organization in intersubjective relations rather than to the relation of humans to external nature, remain secondary to the central argument that Adorno and Horkheimer develop from the perspective of the philosophy of history. In the latter, commodity exchange assumes the role of a social medium that extends to society the mode of rationality formed in the original process of human self-preservation in opposition to external nature.

It is on this prehistorical act of human self-preservation that the philosophical-historical analysis of the *Dialectic of Enlightenment* initially concentrates. Adorno and Horkheimer describe the process by which the human species, released from the security of instinctual bonds, liberates itself from the threat of an inscrutible nature, as the process of a gradual substitution of mimetic forms of behavior. Humans raise themselves above animal conditions of existence to the extent that they initially learn to master the reflexive sort of conditions that prehuman forms of life physically imitate in situations of fear before threatening natural objects and, finally, to replace them completely through the prophylactic control of nature. By being able to transform modes of behavior aimed at imitating nature into the process of working upon nature, the human species steps beyond the boundary of animal life: "Civilization has replaced the organic adaptation to others and mimetic behavior proper, by organized control of mimesis, in the magical phase; and, finally, by rational practice, by work, in the historical phase."[19]

Magic is a form of collectively orchestrated mimesis. The artificial assimilation of the group to the natural environment here fulfills the function of either fictively mitigating the threatening effects of practically uncontrollable natural processes or imaginatively influencing them in their course. But only the manipulative intervention into natural processes themselves replaces the merely passive defense against natural dangers with active control. Humans employ the constantly accumulating experiences of the natural environment in order to make the regularities of natural processes into a means for the acquisition of their own livelihood. In the same process in which they learn to control and master nature, they begin to abstract from the threatening majesty of nature and henceforth to make it into an objectified reality in accordance with repeatable experiences suited to the goals of manipulative intervention. In conjunction with the requirements for instrumental action, humans take from the chaotic manifold of their natural environment only those conceptual components that possess functions for their practical intervention. It is in the act of labor that humans learn to overcome the ever-present threat of nature by forcing its sensory manifold into a conceptual schema that provides them with a surveyable and controllable world: "In thought, men distance themselves from nature in order thus imaginatively to present it to themselves—but only in order to determine how it is to be dominated. Like the thing, the material tool, which is held on to in different situations as the same thing, and hence divides the world as the chaotic, manysided, and disparate from the known, one, and identical, the concept is the ideal tool, fit to do service for everything, wherever it can be applied."[20]

The anthropological argument that Adorno and Horkheimer develop in these remarks scattered throughout the text is related to the analyses that Arnold Gehlen undertook in his philosophical anthropology. However, in comparison with this work the passages in the *Dialectic of Enlightenment* are less articulate and materially impoverished. They undertake solely the task of indicating the prehistorical background from which the process of regression in the history of civilization occurs. As they can be read in these few passages, the anthropological considerations of Adorno and Horkheimer do not, however, simply represent the thin remnants of the biologically better-informed anthropology of Gehlen. Rather, they initially form the framework for an alternative philosophical-historical account. Whereas Gehlen regards the activity of conceptual orientation, by which humans in the practical realization of the appropriation of nature harness its overflowing plenitude, as a "productive accomplishment of unburdening" that compensates for the deficit of human instinct,[21] Adorno and Horkheimer conceive the same process of the conceptual structuring of reality as the initial phase of reification. From this point of view, the process through which humans, under the imperative of self-preservation, place the natural environment at their conceptual disposal, emerges as the compulsive counterpart to a nature congealed into pure objectivity:

'Recognition in the concept,' the absorption of the different by the same, takes the place of physical adaptation to nature. But the situation in which equality is established, the direct equality of mimesis and the mediated equality of synthesis, the adaptation to the condition of the object in the blind course of life, and the comparison of the objectified thing in scientific concept formation, is still the state of terror. Society continues threatening nature as the lasting organized compulsion which is reproduced in individuals as rational self-preservation and rebounds on nature as social dominance over it.

Science is repetition, refined into observed regularity, and preserved in stereotypes. The mathematical formula is regression handled consciously, just as the magic ritual used to be; it is the most sublimated manifestation of mimicry. Technology no longer completes the approximation to death for the sake of survival by physical imitation of external nature, as was the case with magic, but by automation of the mental processes, by converting them into blind cycles. With its triumph human statements become both controllable and inevitable. All that remains of the adaptation to nature is the obduracy against nature.[22]

In the act of orientation that accompanies the process of working upon nature, humans have so consistently purified objectified nature of all uncontrollable surplus that, on this developed level, modern technology and science can now be interpreted as the perfected institutions of a society in league with death. In these systems of an organized mimesis at a second level, which no longer reflect living nature but which rather reflect conceptually reified nature, the force of nature that social labor was originally supposed to overcome continues: Just as the methodological form of science merely repeats the regularities that reveal themselves from the viewpoint of obtaining practical disposal over nature, technology reproduces the elementary components of human administrative practice on an automated level. As the comparison with Gehlen's anthropology also suggests, the presupposition of this argument, which is already contained in the basic idea of the *Dialectic of Enlightenment*, is an instrumentalist epistemology negativistically construed. It is the result of a radical reevaluation of the process that, in connection with the early Marx, Horkheimer in the 1930s still conceived as the emancipatory process of a gradual completion of the domination of nature.

The *Dialectic of Enlightenment* also initially interprets the development of productive forces that were perfected with the modern achievements of natural science and technology as the systematically driven growth of knowledge acquired in the original act of a control-oriented intervention into natural processes. Under the guiding perspective of social self-preservation, the natural environment is objectified, and with the goal of augmenting social power, it is gradually developed. Thus, the primary interest of the analysis is no longer the increase of social wealth that accompanied this process, and which occupied the argumentative center of Horkheimer's early philosophy of history, but rather those effects of reification that are primordially embedded in this process. The cultivation of nature, which is secured by the cognitive subsumption of natural processes under the perspective of control, is paid for by the neutralization of its sensible manifold and variety, that is, at the cost of the exclusion of living nature. In the end, from within the human practice of control the only aspect of reality that is perceived is that revealed by the requirements of operative manipulation and reproducibility. Thus the development of productive forces dilutes nature to the mere projection of social control: "Men pay for the increase in their power with alienation from that over which they exercise their power. Enlightenment behaves toward things as a dictator toward men. He knows them in so far as he can manipulate them. The man of science knows things in so far as he can make them. In this way their potentiality is turned to his own ends. In the metamorphosis the nature of things, as a substratum of domination, is revealed as always the same."[23]

Thoughts of this kind reveal the fundamental element upon which the philosophical-historical construction of the *Dialectic of Enlightenment* rests. Its theoretical basis is formed by a theory of domination[24] that makes its starting point the instrumental control of nature. Such a theory sees in the identity logic of instrumental reason—the subsumption of the particular under the universal—the original model of domination, of which every other form of domination is merely derivative. In this conclusion (which, as we shall see, is not drawn in all of Adorno's writings with the same consistency), the *Dialectic of Enlightenment* approximates that traditional form of cultural criticism in which the objectification of nature through technology and science is itself taken to be a sign of a process of the decay of civilization. As it is expressed in the *Dialectic of Enlightenment*— in startling agreement with the cultural criticism of Ludwig Klages or Alfred Seidel (which was itself influenced by "life philosophy")[25]—the "division of life into spirit and its object" is then as such the original cause of the self-alienation of humanity. Today, a decade and a half after Adorno's death, one catches from this one-sided perspective a surprising glimpse into the clandestine similarity that his thought has with that of his opponent Heidegger.[26]

Within the *Dialectic of Enlightenment* a critique of the mastery of nature forms, however, only the starting point for deciphering, with the aid of a philosophy of history, the complementary civilizing phenomenon of the instrumental working up of nature. As the motif of "retrogressive anthropogenesis" reveals, these are its essential themes. Its analysis is founded in the evidence of a forceful entwinement of social self-preservation and human self-renunciation. The attempt to comprehend the inner-psychic parallel to the process of the control of nature is initially represented by a sketchy theory of the ego that takes up again the thread of anthropological reflection. Adorno and Horkheimer interpret the development of the individual ego as a process that is played out solely between the individual conscious subject and his or her natural environment. Just as the formation of the socio-cultural mode of life was interpreted only against the twofold backdrop of the practical conflict between a single group and the threats of nature, that is, between subject and object, so the formation of the human capacity for identity is conceived as the primarily individual process of formation of a subject in relation to natural reality. The human ego, according to these few indications, emerges as the intra-psychic product of a process in which the perceiving subject learns to distinguish between outer sense impressions and inner experiential states. Under prehuman living conditions the experiential frame of the more developed life forms is initially the result of a projection upon external nature of various survival impulses that remain unconscious. Now, to the degree that humans are able to transcend animalistic conditions of existence, they are compelled by the pressure for social differentiation that sets in to distinguish between their individual projections and that which belongs to sense impressions coming from without. Along this path the ego emerges through the individual's projecting himself or herself as the antithesis to a gradually fixed nature. Reflected by a constant external world, which is the product of the individual's growing consciousness of the cumulative projections, humans experience themselves as the unified organ of all their experiential states. Thus, in a certain way, the ego is the result of a concluding (that is, internally directed) projective accomplishment of the subject: "The subject creates the world outside himself from the traces which it leaves in his senses: the unity of the thing in its manifold characteristics and states; and he therefore constitutes the 'I' retrospectively by learning to grant a synthetic unity not only to the external impressions, but to the internal impressions which gradually separate off from them. The real ego is the most recent constant product of projection."

This unconvincing anthropological observation, which attempts to explain the development of individual identity as a formative process of the subject in relation only to the natural world, introduces one of the few places in the *Dialectic of Enlightenment* where the boundaries of a purely negative argument are crossed and the basic features of a positive conception of ego autonomy can be perceived. They constitute the normative background whose contour is retained in the philosophical-historical claim concerning a process of human self-renunciation that reaches back to the beginning of the domination of nature. Adorno and Horkheimer sketch the outlines of an autonomous ego identity within the context of the same theory of perception in which they also explain the origin of ego identity. They want to show that the formation of identity leads to an ego free of compulsion and identical with itself to the extent that the subject allows outer sense impressions and its inner experiential states to communicate equally and freely with one another: "The inner depth of the subject consists in nothing other than the delicacy and wealth of the external world of perceptions. . . . Only in that mediation by which the meaningless sensation brings a thought to the full productivity of which it is capable, while on the other hand the thought abandons itself without reservation to the predominant impression, is that pathological loneliness which characterizes the whole of nature overcome."

Within the argumentative totality of their philosophical-historical conception, this thought of Adorno and Horkheimer appears unusually utopian. It provides, on the basis of the characteristics of a nondominating relation between the human spirit and the natural environment, the outlines of an ego identity free from coercion. The autonomous ego is thus only the correlate of a nature recognized in its own individuality. It achieves a degree of freedom commensurate with the extent to which it noncoercively takes over in its inner cognizing capacity the sensible manifold of the impressions given by nature. This aesthetic concept of ego identity, which makes the formation of individual identity independent of social recognition by other subjects, defines the argumentation in which Adorno and Horkheimer now attempt to explain human self-renunciation as a civilizing effect of the human domination of nature. Its thesis merely expresses the conclusion that results when the instrumental objectification of nature by humanity is observed from the viewpoint of an aesthetic model of ego identity. The cognitive leap, in which the acting subject learns to perceive his natural environmment from the fixed perspective of control, must then be interpreted as the beginning of an interruption of that free association between outer sense impressions and inner sensory experience in which the autonomous ego grows. The objectification of nature is thus the complementary process to a rigidification of individual identity: "if the links [between the outer world of perception and subjective experience—A.H.] are broken, the ego calcifies. If it proceeds positivisitically, merely recording given facts without giving anything in return, it shrinks to a point. . . ."[29] The subject that comes about with the instrumental intervention into nature is no longer allowed to respond openly and flexibly to the sense impressions that it receives from it. Rather than resonating with the sensible abundance of nature, its sensory possibilities are concentrated in the cognitive schematism of control. The ego of the instrumentally acting subject is forcefully directed to the maintenance of this posture. Therefore, it can stabilize its identity only through the continual exclusion of all sense experiences that threaten to impair the direct pursuit of the principle of control.

In another passage referring to the practical function of the principles of logic, Adorno repeated the same line of thought, that is, the assertion of an unavoidable civilizing link between social domination of nature and rigidification of ego identity. The passage, found in *Against Epistemology*, stresses once again the fundamental role assumed in this argumentative context by the negative version of an instrumentalist epistemology: "Genetically logic presents itself as an attempt at integration and the solid ordering of the originally equivocal—as a decisive step in dymythologization. . . . By virtue of logic, the subject saves itself from falling into the amorphous, the inconstant, and the ambiguous. For it stamps itself on experience, it is the identity of the survivor as form. And the only assertions about nature it lets be valid are those which are captured by the identity of those forms."[30]

However, the instrumentally acting person who gradually reduces the threatening abundance of nature is not only a knowing subject but also an instinctual subject. The rigidification of the individual's senses must therefore be reflected in a repression of his organic drives. Beyond making sense perception rigidly one-sided, social labor also demands the permanent channeling of amorphous natural impulses. In this Adorno and Horkheimer see the side of the civilizing process of human self-renunciation that affects instinctual dynamics. In the *Dialectic of Enlightenment* the largest part of the philosophical-historical interpretation is dedicated to this process. The basic thesis with which they interpret the destiny of the ego's instincts is essentially clear and compelling, but it remains in an undeveloped theoretical framework: The motivational basis for the domination of nature arises with the repression and rejection of all instinctual impulses that impede labor. Since labor requires single-minded vigilance and directed energy, the subject is allowed to take up in his ego only those instinctual impulses that can be channeled into his instrumental performances. All diverting, distracting, or superfluous instincts, by contrast, must be either sublimated or suppressed. In contrast to the passages that serve to explain the sensible one-sidedness of humans on the basis of the continuous pressure of social labor, Adorno and Horkheimer here leave almost completely out of consideration the intra-psychic processes that underlie the original suppression of instincts. Although psychoanalysis is part of its theoretical inventory, an explanatory framework that could make intelligible the mechanisms of the formation of individual needs and that would be comparable to the explanatory model implicit in the theory of perception is not found in the *Dialectic of Enlightenment*. Thereby, however, both the socializing process in which the subject's motive energies are shaped in the service of labor and the intra-psychic process whereby it deflects from itself energies that impede labor must drop from view. Neither social norms, in whose form the ego in communication with other subjects learns the motivational demands of society, nor the authority of individual conscience, which represents within the psyche the repressive demands of society, form reference points for the analysis. Accordingly, it seems as if the same attitude of control through which the instrumentally acting subject learns to work upon nature also makes him capable of independently modeling his own instinctual potential. The impression is strengthened by a central metaphor of the book—Odysseus strapped to the mast of the ship for the purposive-rational reason of averting desire: The process of the domination of nature repeats itself in the control of instincts, as the individual conquest of inner nature.

This image, suggested by the *Dialectic of Enlightenment*, is theoretically misleading since it permits the repression of human instinctual potential to appear as the work of an isolated subject.[31] It nevertheless furnishes the second component that within the context of the philosophy of history enters into the conception of the self-denial of humanity. It sets aside the thesis of the sensory one-sidedness of the subject sketched out in the theory of perception in order to complete the picture of the socializing effects of the societal domination of nature. It is primarily in the interlacing of sensory impoverishment and rigorous suppression of instinct in the process of human self-disciplining that the character traits in terms of which Adorno and Horkheimer see the instrumentally acting subject as being shaped become intelligible: "Men had to do fearful things to themselves before the self, the identical, purposive, and virile nature of man, was formed, and something of that recurs in every childhood. The strain of holding the I together adheres to the I in all stages; and the temptation to lose it has always been there with the blind determination to maintain it."[32]

With this summarizing remark Adorno and Horkheimer reach a point in their argument from which the basic traits of their philosophical-historical thesis can be seen for the first time. Adorno and Horkheimer assume that the human species has freed itself from the superior strength of a threatening environment once it has learned to overcome the limits of a merely passive resistance to natural dangers and to transform mimetic modes of reaction into instrumental acts of control. In the activity of social labor carried out from the perspective of control, the natural environment is now objectified and gradually cognitively deprived of its sensory richness, which frustrated intervention. Adorno and Horkheimer are, further, convinced that this original act of subsuming natural processes under the action schema of technical control, that is, of the domination of nature, provides the impetus for a process of human self-denial. The instrumentally guided objectification of nature is accompanied by the process of the self-objectification of humanity. With this thesis Adorno and Horkheimer presuppose that, for the sake of labor, individuals must forcibly constrict their capacity for sensory experience as well as their organic instinctual potential in order to realize the discipline of instrumental functions. From the perspective of a philosophy of history, the conclusion to the *Dialectic of Enlightenment* is drawn from this line of argument: namely, that to the extent that human subjects systematically increase their instrumental control over external nature, they at the same time gradually forfeit their inner nature, since they must treat it in the same way as external nature. Thus the progressive process of the social domination of nature is only one side of a simultaneous process of decline of a humanity alienated ever more profoundly from its own nature:

With the denial of nature in man not merely the *telos* of the outward control of nature but the *telos* of man's own life is distorted and befogged. As soon as man discards his awareness that he himself is nature, all the aims for which he keeps himself alive—social progress, the intensification of all his material and spiritual powers, even consciousness itself—are nullified, and the enthronement of the means as an end, which under late capitalism is tantamount to open insanity, is already perceptible in the prehistory of subjectivity. Man's domination over himself, which grounds his selfhood, is almost always the destruction of the subject in whose service it is undertaken; for the substance which is dominated, suppressed, and dissolved by virtue of self-preservation is none other than that very life as functions of which the achievements of self-preservation find their sole definition and determination: it is, in fact, what is to be preserved.[33]

This argument, which gives the impression of a compressed synopsis of the *Dialectic of Enlightenment*, is content with the assertion of a forceful entwinement of social self-assertion and human self-denial. But Adorno and Horkheimer's philosophical-historical construction, referring solely to the history of philosophy and literature, is not exhausted in driving this civilizing cycle out from cover. Even the reference to 'capitalism' in the cited passage suggests that the *Dialectic of Enlightenment* must also include elements of a theory of the forms of social domination that can supplement the anthropologically backed conceptions of the social domination of nature and individual self-domination. The basic framework for such a third concept, oriented to the relations of domination within a society, is found in the rudimentary conception of a theory of the social division of labor. This explains social inequalities of labor not by reference to the functional requirements that arise with the intensification of the society's work upon nature, nor by reference to problems of distribution that are posed with the production of surplus products, but by reference to a contingent act of the collective seizure of privileges at the beginning of the process of civilization.

As Joseph Schmucker has shown,[34] for Adorno the category of "privilege" represents generally the key to a conception of social domination. It is supposed to portray the unjustified coercive act that lies within all social labor. It also provides the motif with whose help the fragments of a theory of the social division of labor can be put together in the *Dialectic of Enlightenment*. The resulting interpretation of the process of the formation of social domination is extremely vague[35]: In an "archaic act of despotism,"[36] after the close of the nomadic era, social groups forcibly appropriate the privilege of being allowed to be permanently replaced by other members of society in the performance of socially allocated tasks. On "the basis of fixed property,"[37] which with a varying degree of control socially safeguards the violently secured privilege, "the ability to allow oneself to be replaced" is from then on "the measure of domination," and "he is most powerful who is able to be discharged from the most tasks."[38] To the extent that the collective monopolization of this social privilege is able to separate the resulting reproductive tasks of the species into instrumental activities and activities of control, into physical and mental labor, the collective behavioral traits of domination and bondage must also be distinguished from one another. "The enjoyment of art" and "manual labor,"[39] "self-preservation and physical strength,"[40] are the respective products of socialization according to the two modes of activity into which members of society are separated by the original act of a violent division of labor. In the few passages in their investigation in which they pursue at all the interest in a theory of social domination, Adorno and Horkheimer primarily inquire into these side-effects of socialization within a coerced separation of mental and physical labor:

But even though, despite all submission, the savage nomad still participated in the magic which determined the lines of that submission, and clothed himself as his quarry in order to stalk it, in later times intercourse with spirits and submission were assigned to different classes: power is on the one side, and obedience on the other. For the vanquished (whether by alien tribes or by their own cliques), the recurrent, eternally similar natural processes become the rhythm of labor according to the beat of cudgel and whip which resounds in every barbaric drum and every monotonous ritual.[41]

The formation of a socially privileged class that can be exempted from all manual labor is necessarily accompanied by the development of a socially oppressed class that, under the threat of force, can be encumbered with all manual labor. Since it must alone bear the entire monotony and discipline of the purposively regulated work upon nature, this class of physical laborers must directly reproduce within itself the rigid character or reified nature. Such a line of thought, which has major significance for Adorno's perception of the behavior typical of oppressed groups, is on the one hand designed to correct a misunderstanding to which the *Dialectic of Enlightenment* itself gives rise: the misleading idea according to which the process of civilization is driven by the successful productive activity of a unified species-subject. Once the archaic inequality in the distribution of social labor is theoretically taken into account, this idea must give way to a more complex conception which has as its point of reference a fundamentally conflict-ridden society divided into social classes. With the division of society into classes, the social subject loses its unity. As a result, Adorno and Horkheimer complete with a third term, namely the dimension of social conflict, the bipolar model of their philosophy of history in whose context the developmental dynamic of the history of civilization is explained solely by the confrontation between human spirit and natural reality. This implicit correction is admittedly somewhat incomplete, since it seems as if the hypostatization of a collective subject capable of engaging in intentional action like an individual subject is simply carried over from the level of whole societies to the level of social classes. On the other hand, the line of thought contained in the cited passage lets one perceive how the crude assumptions of a theory of social domination come to be inserted into the philosophical-historical leitmotif of the *Dialectic of Enlightenment*. Adorno and Horkheimer begin with the view that, in order to be able to adhere to the coercively imposed compulsion of the continuous tasks of labor, the socially suppressed class must habitually continue in itself the blind regularities disclosed by nature to humanity from the perspective of control. This allows them to speculate that the social domination of the privileged class over the working class is a kind of intrasocial extension of the human domination of external nature. The technical control of nature by the species thus extends to the social control exercised by the dominating class over the members of society forced to labor, just as, conversely, the complementary despiritualization of nature continues in the cultural impoverishment of physical laborers. As a result of this line of thought, Adorno and Horkheimer do not hesitate to describe the historically suppressed class as the "social descendant of physical nature."[42] This pointed formulation blatantly reveals the implicit presupposition that creates in the *Dialectic of Enlightenment* an argumentative bridge between the philosophical-historical construction and a theory of social domination. The knitting together of these component concepts represents an attempt to form the concept of social domination in correspondence with the concept of the domination of nature. Only with the silent presupposition of this analogy is it meaningful to conceive of the techniques of social domination as products of an intra-social utilization of the means of domination acquired by working upon nature. The "restriction of thought to organization and administration," which serves the "manipulation of the small" in ways that secure domination, is only the civilizing consequence of the original bias of human thought in favor of instrumental reason that serves social self-preservation against nature.[43] It is the same with the complementary half of the train of thought in which Adorno and Horkheimer attempt to interpret the social groups forced into physical labor as the intra-societal representatives of repressed nature. This too is a plausible argument only with the silent presupposition of a corresponding relation between social domination and the domination of nature. For only if the suppressed class is comprehended as an unresisting object of the mechanisms of technical control in the same way as nature is it meaningful to speak of the cultural impoverishment of physical laborers generally as a direct product of social domination as well as of the despiritualization of nature as a necessary correlate to the social domination of nature. Then, of course, it is incumbent on Adorno and Horkheimer to assert that "submission," "experiential poverty," and "impotence of the worker" are the "logical consequence of industrial society."[44]

As now becomes clear, the theory of the domination of nature that supports the philosophical-historical construction of the *Dialectic of Enlightenment* also forms the argumentative backdrop for a very vague concept of social domination. Adorno and Horkheimer are so strongly fixated on the model of the instrumental control of nature, which is the real interest of their philosophy of history, that they also want to conceive the manner of functioning of intra-social domination according to this model. Therefore they are conceptually compelled to comprehend the process of the creation and exercise of social domination in such a way that they can rediscover in it all the properties of the social domination of nature. That process of social domination is then, to a certain extent, the structural analogue to the process of instrumental control within the boundaries of society. In both processes a collectivity represented as a subject—that of the human species in the first, that of the privileged class in the second—dissociates itself from its own natural or social environment by making it into an object of control-oriented action. Just as the instrumentally acting subject subsumes natural processes under the abstract perspective of control in order to be able to make it subject to his goal-oriented manipulations, so too the socially privileged subject arranges all other members of society according to the perspective of control in order to let them become organs for the execution of socially allocated work assignments. In both processes language only serves the function of transforming the chaos of natural or social phenomena into a referential system specifying events relevant for control.[45] Both types of controlling action are in time consolidated in apparatuses of domination: Social organizations in which the successful procedures of control and manipulation of the oppressed members of society are embedded correspond, on the side of social domination, to the technical instruments in which rules are gradually embodied in repeatable operations upon nature. Finally, an immanent developmental potential is common to both processes: The instrumental control of objectified nature and the social control over the oppressed classes increase to the extent that technical apparatuses as well as the social organizations are for their own part able to produce the controlled processes artificially. One cannot find in the *Dialectic of Enlightenment* such a statement about these key analogies. Nevertheless, the philosophical-historical argumentation in which Adorno and Horkheimer attempt to comprehend forms of social domination as the intra-social continuation of the domination of nature permits one to draw such conclusions. The social-theoretic implications of the *Dialectic of Enlightenment* first genuinely appear in light of these conclusions. Because they also base the analysis of intra-societal relations on a concept of the domination of nature, Adorno and Horkheimer must comprehend the process of the acquisition and exercise of social domination as a process in which an individual or collective subject influences other subjects in order to realize his or her plans and intentions. This subject acquires power through an act utilizing physical force and compelling other members of society to endure the dictates of an unequal distribution of social labor. It conceals the violently seized privilege in institutional forms in order to make its own position of power socially permanent. In order to guarantee the obedience of the oppressed groups with respect to the institutions that secure domination, the subject now makes use of the means of physical and psychic force: In the first case, it employs the means of power it controls as a property owner in order to directly compel the obedience of the oppressed subjects through the actual use of force or the open threat of force. In the second case, it makes use of the means of persuasion or manipulation to indirectly compel the obedience of the oppressed subjects for its own benefit.

These cases of direct and indirect force are the only forms of social domination that are conceptually suited to the social theory implicit in the *Dialectic of Enlightenment*. Any form of social domination that is not traced back to the active oppression of the member of society under the general aim of control (namely, the goal-oriented influence of individual obedience) but is conceived rather as the result of an agreement between members of society, however it comes about, is, by contrast, effectively excluded from this theoretical framework. In this further case, it is not the directly or indirectly produced obedience but the horizon of normative orientations of the oppressed groups itself that forms the basis that supports the social domination by privileged groups. It concerns a double-sided relation of social domination: The cultural self-understandings and action-guiding value orientations through whose filter all social groups apprehend for themselves an established institutional framework fuse into a fragmented but nevertheless effective consensus that is able to secure a high degree of normative recognition for an institutionalized inequality in the distribution of social goods. Of course, such a case of consensually secured domination poses for social theory the difficult task of identifying those institutional and cultural mechanisms that channel and block the process of the production of normative action orientations among the members of a group so that, despite socially perceivable inequalities, they are able to join in the building of social consensus. Only if this difficulty is solved in a theoretically promising way can one explain the social situation in which the imbalance in a society of institutionalized privileges is based nonetheless upon consensual recognition.

However, in the *Dialectic of Enlightenment* Adorno and Horkheimer must not even pose such a problem, which under the concept of "structural violence" is a theme in the social sciences,[46] since as a result of the construction based on the philosophy of history they must already deny the conceptual possibility of any kind of consensually secured domination. The analogy between domination of nature and social domination does not allow them to take into account any other kind of social domination than that anchored in the techniques of direct or indirect force. They are prevented in principle from acknowledging the cultural activities and the interpretive accomplishments of the oppressed groups in a social system. The influence of the basic themes of the philosophy of history on the social-theoretic argument of the *Dialectic of Enlightenment* is so strong that Adorno and Horkheimer cannot but comprehend the socially oppressed subject as a passive and intentionless victim of the same techniques of domination that are aimed at nature. It seems as if the procedures of control shape individuals without running into attempts at social resistance and cultural opposition.

Since with their philosophy of history they interpret the history of civilization as the heightening process of the domination of nature, social class domination, and the domination of individual instincts, Adorno and Horkheimer are driven to a conclusion that, from the perspective of social theory, must ignore the existence of an intermediary sphere of social action. The collective force of self-preservation is transferred so unproblematically into the class-specific coercion that secures domination and into the individual coercion of self-discipline that a social space for the creative achievements of interacting groups no longer remains. It is easy to see that the social-theoretic reductionism evident in this conclusion furnishes the antithesis, in the form of a pessimistic philosophy of history, to the conceptual path that led the early Horkheimer to the optimistic variant of a materialistic philosophy of history. In both versions of critical theory the action-theoretic categorial framework is exhausted in the concept of labor. In both versions, the history of human societies is consequently conceived only in connection with the dynamic of the human domination of nature. In the two versions, however, the same process of the domination of nature receives two very distinct interpretations: Whereas in the 1930s Horkheimer entrusted to the technologically guided cultivation of nature the uninterrupted potential for civilizing liberation, the *Dialectic of Enlightenment,* less than a decade later, attributes the original impetus for the decay of civilization to the same process of a technologically progressing domination of nature.[47]

3

Adorno's Theory of Society:
The Definitive Repression of
the Social

Although they initially discover the process of a historical regression of the species within the historical reality of fascist Germany and, to a certain extent, project it back to the beginning of civilization, the authors of the *Dialectic of Enlightenment* do not view this process as coming to an end with the defeat of fascism. A metaphor from the "Notes and Drafts" appended to their joint investigation enables one to see that, from the perspective of a philosophical-historical theory of the domination of nature, fascism is only one historical stage in the ineluctable process of the decay of civilization:

In Germany, fascism won the day with a crassly xenophobic, collectivist ideology which was hostile to culture. Now that it is laying the world waste, the nations must fight against it; there is no other way out. But when all is over there is nothing to prove that a spirit of freedom will spread across Europe; its nations may become just as xenophobic, pseudo-collectivistic, and hostile to culture as fascism once was when they had to fight against it. The downfall of fascism will not necessarily lead to a movement of the avalanche.[1]

The gloomy presentiment expressed in the last sentence delineates the argumentative horizon in which Adorno's critical theory remains even after fascism's defeat. Although he was not free from all ambiguity, Adorno held firmly to the basic convictions of a critique of the domination of nature even under the altered conditions of postwar capitalism. He has made the philosophical-historical construction of the *Dialectic of Enlightenment,* which initially was supposed to serve as a genealogical interpretation of National Socialist totalitarianism, into the organizing framework of a theory that has the task of critically diagnosing the welfare-state democracies of late capitalism. The social-theoretic tools that earlier were implicit in the philosophy of history are, to a certain extent, henceforth relieved of historically informed control. Although the empirical focus of the theory shifts from the state's organization of direct force to the institutional strategies of indirect force, the framework guiding the investigation nevertheless remains that of the *Dialectic of Enlightenment*. From the perspective of a philosophical-historical interpretation of fascism, the critical theory of Adorno's postwar writings surveys the Germany restored by capitalism. The theory is in a paradoxical situation; it is equipped with the conceptual tools for an analysis of totalitarian domination, although these are not obviously useful for an investigation of the normal form of capitalist domination. Nevertheless, wherever the theory attempts to evade the evident incompatibility between concept and reality by abandoning the framework prescribed in the *Dialectic of Enlightenment*, it falls to a certain extent behind the ongoing claims to radicality of its own philosophy of history. As will be shown, this paradox belongs to the peculiarities of the social theory that Adorno brought to Germany from exile in the United States and which he erects on the basis of an unhistorically retained philosophy of history. It is, of course, only an expression in social theory of a deeply situated aporia that critical theory fell into with the *Dialectic of Enlightenment*. The interdisciplinary analysis of society, which in the 1930s Horkheimer placed alongside philosophy as an equal partner, is now merely the subordinate auxiliary to an aporetic critical theory vacillating between a negativistic philosophy and philosophical aesthetics. It will be useful to make evident this reordering within the theory (a) before examining the content of Adorno's later social theory (b).

(a) The structural transformation of critical theory that comes to light with this altered emphasis on the disciplines is indebted to a far-reaching implication of the *Dialectic of Enlightenment*. With the critique of the domination of nature, Adorno and

Horkheimer have not only imported a heretofore foreign element into the tradition of critical social theory; they have, at the same time, significantly altered its theoretical status and its scientific conception. The model of the philosophy of history that Adorno and Horkheimer construct on the basis of a concept of the domination of nature leads to a methodological revision in critical theory that is rather cursorily announced in the introduction to the *Dialectic of Enlightenment:*

> Even though we had known for many years that the great discoveries of applied science are paid for with an increasing diminution of theoretical awareness, we still thought that in regard to scientific activity our contribution could be restricted to the criticism or extension of specialist axioms. Thematically, at any rate, we were to keep to the traditional disciplines: to sociology, psychology, and epistemology. . . . However, the fragments united in this volume show that we were forced to abandon this conviction. . . . [I]n the present collapse of bourgeois civilization not only the pursuit but the meaning of science has become problematical in that regard.[2]

The difference that emerges between the original project of a social research guided by philosophy, on the one hand, and a philosophy of history exempted from scientific confirmation, on the other, is systematically grounded. This change becomes inevitable if the scientific disciplines are no longer viewed from the perspective of a cumulative self-enlightenment of the human species, as was still the case for the early Horkheimer, but rather from the viewpoint of an increasing self-alienation of humanity. That is the perspective from which the *Dialectic of Enlightenment* must view science as a whole when it gives a negative interpretation to the enterprise of an instrumentalist epistemology. Of course, the scientific disciplines thus represent systematic developments of a practically acquired and life-preserving knowledge. They belong, as one passage puts it in excessively anthropological terms, to the evolutionarily adaptive accomplishments of humanity "as teeth belong to a bear."[3] Nevertheless, at the same time they also increase the distance that, in the first instances of control-oriented action, humans open up between themselves and nature. So viewed, the sciences continue in methodically systematized ways the process in which society learns to maintain itself through the instrumental control of its external nature and then through the social control of its inner nature. They participate in the civilizing course of the human domination of nature and of social reification precisely because they rationalize the socially stored knowledge of control that relieves society of its situational contingency. No type of scientific objectification can escape the narrow framework which is thereby posited, since science itself, and not simply one of its interpretive forms, is structurally bound to the conditions of control-oriented action. All differences that might exist between the natural sciences and the social and humanistic sciences become insignificant in comparison with this highest functional determination. The *Dialectic of Enlightenment* directly forces its authors to such a crude definition of the sciences:

> It is not difficult to see where science fits into the social division of labor. Its task is to accumulate facts and their functional relationships in the greatest possible quantities. The storage system used must be clearly designed, so that any industry can instantly pick out the particular assortment of intellectual goods it is seeking. . . . Historical works, too, furnish material. Ways of applying it are to be sought not directly in industry but indirectly in the administrative sphere.[4]

Adorno and Horkheimer develop a compelling interpretation of the sciences, but they remain content with illustrations of this sort. They subsume all types of scientific knowledge, irrespective of their methodological peculiarities, under the highest concept of knowledge aimed at control. The plausibility of their thesis is demonstrated, however, only with the obvious examples of technical and administrative knowledge. The *Dialectic of Enlightenment* is correct in this restricted demonstration if its theoretical premises are accepted—that is, if every accomplished form of conceptual orientation is initially tied to an act of instrumental control and every form of scientific knowledge is itself subsequently understood as a generalized form of conceptual orientation, it is only logical to regard the whole of science as an instrument of technical or social control. Since Adorno and Horkheimer explicitly draw this definitive conclusion, they are compelled to take a further step: They must distinguish their own considerations from every form of scientific knowledge in order not to be drawn into the framework of control-oriented knowledge. Taken on their own terms, the philosophical-historical premises of the *Dialectic of Enlightenment* separate critical theory from the very theoretical impulse of the particular sciences in relation to which it was so far necessarily oriented as, to be sure, a philosophically guided but nevertheless empirically controlled program of social research. Adorno and Horkheimer must free critical theory from the grip of the empirical social sciences and relinquish the sole responsibility for it to philosophy. From now on, within the general framework of Adorno's theory, social-scientific research is given the status of an auxiliary discipline that remains bound to a generalized ideological reservation whenever it is invoked again.

This displacement within the theory represents, however, only the methodological side of the revisions required by the philosophical-historical model of the *Dialectic of Enlightenment*. The other side concerns the task and the reflective mode of the discipline that now assumes almost the entire burden of proof for critical theory: philosophy. Since philosophy cannot remain completely unaffected by the critique of instrumental reason, Adorno and Horkheimer are inclined to revise its epistemological claims as well. In Horkheimer's original program of a critical social theory, philosophy still appeared in the guise of a self-assured form of a materialistically applied philosophy of history. Since it can refer to a real rational potential inhabiting the process of social production, it secures its own legitimacy. But now that the model of progress found in the philosophy of history has been abandoned, this must change as well. The critique of the domination of nature, in which aspects of the philosophy of history and of epistemology inseparably flow into one another, provides a definition of instrumental reason that is so general that it also seems to include philosophical thought. In that case, however, its own status is contradictory: To the extent that it already makes the pure act of conceptual operation into an elementary form of instrumental reason, it cannot justify any form of discursive thought, even its own. Philosophy is the reflective form of a critical theory that discovers in each step of conceptual reflection a piece of the continued history of domination. Therefore, strictly speaking, it prohibits itself. The *Dialectic of Enlightenment* does not pursue this difficulty any further. But a note entitled "Philosophy and the Division of Labor" indicates the task that still remains for philosophy within the context of critical theory once it has certified its own questionable status from the standpoint of the philosophy of history: ". . . unlike those who administer it, philosophy is concerned with thought, in so far as this does not succumb to the prevailing division of labor or allow it to dictate its tasks. . . . Philosophy is not synthesis; and it is not the fundamental or master science. It is the attempt to resist this suggestion, the determination to hang on to intellectual and real freedom."[5]

Adorno and Horkheimer anticipate critical theory's path of a "negativistic return" to philosophy.[6] Admittedly, they assign the theoretical task of social criticism solely to philosophy, but at the same time they no longer allow it to have any confidence in the achievements of a synthesizing thought that is able to survey the present with the aid of a historically maturing reason. Rather, since they know that philosophy itself is lodged within the civilizing structures of instrumental thought, they must deny it any claim to positive knowledge. Accordingly, in the end they can only entrust to it the negative function of a self-criticism of conceptual thought. Philosophy can then be understood as the reflection that inquires into the logic of conceptual formation in which it is shown that within this logic the particular qualities of a state of affairs encountered by the subject are categorially effaced. At the same time, the reflection is turned against its own linguistic medium in order to call into question for itself the dominating character of discursive thought. Only along the path of a negativistic return of philosophical reflection upon itself can the *Dialectic of Enlightenment* uphold a philosophical claim to knowledge without coming fully into conflict with its own premises. In their joint work, however, Adorno and Horkheimer aim at this solution only vaguely. Adorno made this task of a self-criticism of conceptual thought, in all its radicality, his own for the first time in the subsequent development of his philosophical theory. In *Negative Dialectics,* published in 1966, he attempts "to transcend the concept by means of the concept"[7]—that is, to demonstrate immanently by means of a philosophical analysis philosophy's own questionable status.

The difficulty presented by the central philosophical-historical thesis of the *Dialectic of Enlightenment* is not, of course, thereby solved. It is merely postponed. Philosophical reflection transformed into self-criticism does not escape the horizon of conceptual thought, since only conceptually comprehended language is able to give it determinacy and communicability. It cannot simply divest itself of the defect which the critique of instrumental reason discovered in philosophy; it must instead consciously attempt to assimilate it into itself. The problem thus remains: How is critical theory still possible under the premises of a philosophical-historical construction that always immediately discovers in each act of conceptual knowledge the sign of a powerful human domination of nature, one by means of which humanity is also alienated? How, on these premises, is it able to make justifiable assertions about reality if it is initially able to disclose reality only with the aid of conceptual knowledge? So long as it remains tied to the medium of objectivating thought, which is alone permitted to attain theoretical insight, critical theory will remain imprisoned in the very reason that, according to its own conviction, brings about the process of civilizing decay. How, then, can it overcome the conceptual force of instrumental rationality without relinquishing the claim to genuine knowledge? The *Dialectic of Enlightenment* also suggests an answer to this last, decisive question— an answer that, in fact, already anticipates the development upon which critical theory first clearly embarks in Adorno's later writings. In a brief note devoted to the outline of a "theory of crime," Adorno and Horkheimer outline the form of a noninstrumental approach to reality:

The ability to stand apart from the environment as an individual, and at the same time to enter into contact with that environment— and gain a foothold in it—through the approved forms of communication, was eroded in the criminal. He represented a trend which is deep-rooted in living beings, and whose elimination is a sign of all development: the trend to lose oneself in the environment instead of playing an active role in it; the tendency to let oneself go and sink back into nature. Freud called it the death instinct, Caillois "*le mime-tisme*." This urge underlies everything that runs counter to bold prog-ress, from the crime which is a shortcut avoiding the normal forms of activity, to the sublime work of art. A yielding attitude to things, without which art cannot exist, is not so very remote from the violence of the criminal.[8]

The briefly summarized characteristics of the form of action in which humanity learns to maintain itself over against nature here provides only the outline for the attempt to describe the properties of a second, nondominating approach to reality. In the form of the classical criminal Adorno and Horkheimer discover the traits of an attitude toward things that is shaped not by the viewpoint of instrumental control but rather by the capacity for flexible surrender. From this surprising perspec-tive it is now possible for them to correlate the criminal and art under a common characteristic: They represent different cases of a reactive behavior in which the force of self-preser-vation yields to an impulse of self-surrender. Each represents a mimetic relation to reality in which the subject selflessly gives itself over to things. The comparison that Adorno and Hork-heimer present sounds forced, since it is tied to an excessively romanticized picture of the criminal. But it permits one to see the answer that the *Dialectic of Enlightenment* gives to question of how, under the premises of its philosophy of history, gen-uine insight that does not immediately fall under the verdict of a critique of conceptual thought can still be gained. For the "sublime work of art" represents a cognitive medium in which nonconceptual knowledge about reality can be acquired if it mimetically draws near to things, just as the classical criminal does.

In his early contributions to aesthetic theory, published in the *Zeitschrift für Sozialforschung,* Adorno had already identified aesthetic experience as a privileged medium for the appropri-ation of reality. In the essay "Art and Mass Culture" Hork-heimer, obviously under the theoretical influence of Adorno, saw in an avant-garde art that shunned the flow of social com-munication the last power of resistance against a culture that gradually fell under the imperative of capitalistic industry. Leo Löwenthal, for many years the principal editor of the *Zeitschrift,* was motivated in his critical studies of literature by the conviction that the capacity for seismographic perception of situations of social conflict belonged in unique ways to artistic production. Finally, the studies in culture theory by Walter Benjamin and Herbert Marcuse—the former an occasional and the latter a more constant collaborator in the Institute for Social Research—apart from all differences, convey the common image that aesthetic experience assumes a historically leading role in the process of social transformation.[9]

In the argumentation of all five of the aforementioned authors, the work of art, as a sort of aesthetic compensation for the lost confidence in the revolutionary potential of the oppressed class, becomes a central theme of critical social theory. But it is in the *Dialectic of Enlightenment* that aesthetic experience first receives a philosophical-historical interpretation that ascribes to it a systematically privileged position above all other forms of knowledge. Art owes this favored status to a line of thought that belongs to the deep normative stratum of the *Dialectic of Enlightenment* from which the aesthetic model of successful identity formation already emerged. Since the conceptual objectification of natural processes sets in motion a process of man's domination not only over external nature but also over his inner nature and his social world, the idea of a nonconceptual approach to nature attains the status of a normative explication of the conditions of freedom and social emancipation: A society is free in an emphatic sense only if its members are able noncoercively to encounter themselves and others in such a way that they relate to nature no longer from the viewpoint of technical control but rather with a readiness for communicative surrender. A mimetic relation to nature, in which things are valued not as objects for manipulative intervention but as counterparts to sensory experiences, is the presupposition of a society freed from the repression of individual instincts and social power. The work of art now represents the artificial form of such a mimetic approach to the world of things.[10] This feature gives it a special position in the civilizing process in a twofold sense: First, it represents the historically unique type of experience in which the individual is able to acquire his substantiality without being forced under the conceptual scheme of instrumental control. Artistic activity thereby bears witness to the possibility of a nondominating approach to reality in which nature, because it is no longer simply the material for human self-maintenance, becomes an equal partner in a communicative act. In a line of thought that deals with the convergence of natural and artistic beauty, Adorno allows the special position of aesthetic experience to become clear:

> Just how inextricably natural and artistic beauty are interlocked can be seen by looking more closely at the essence of what appreciation of natural beauty is. First of all, it focuses exclusively on nature as appearance, never on nature as the stuff of work and material reproduction of life, let alone as a substratum of science. Like the aesthetic appreciation of art, that of nature centers on images. Nature is perceived as appearance of the beautiful and not as an object to be acted upon. This abnegation of the purpose of self-preservation, then, is just as crucial to the aesthetic perception of nature as it is to that of art.[11]

If the work of art is today able to represent the only model of an experience in which, as in aesthetic perception, sensible impressions are no longer filtered through instrumental conceptual schemas, and if the emancipation of society is tied to the presupposition of a nondominating appropriation of the natural environment, then only the work of art is still able to represent in undiminished form the normative claim of social freedom. That is, so long as the compulsion toward the domination of nature is extended into the dominating order of social life, only artistic activity, since it represents an alternative to the prevailing practice of self-preservation, promises in the "idea of the redemption of historically repressed nature"[12] the possible future of an emancipation from civilizing domination. With the help of the famous formulation "artist as representative," Adorno, in an essay on Paul Valéry's aesthetic theory, has expressed this thought, which indicates the second normative position of art within the philosophy of history introduced in the *Dialectic of Enlightenment*. In one passage, after an introductory sentence that assembles the decisive features of his analysis of contemporary society, Adorno outlines the representative function that from now on is normatively given to art in his version of critical theory:

He [Valéry—A.H.] presents the alternative to the anthropological transformations under late capitalism brought about by totalitarian regimes or mass culture directed by giant corporations in which the human is reduced to a mere apparatus of reception, a reference point of conditioned reflexes, and is thus prepared for the condition of blind domination and new barbarism. The work of art, which he opposes to humanity as it is, remains faithful to the possible portrayals of humanity. . . . The densely organized, flawlessly structured work of art, sensuously materialized through its conscious power and in which the artist immerses himself, barely lets it be realized, but it embodies resistance to the immense pressure that mere existence exercises over humanity. . . . The artist who bears the work of art is not simply the individual who produces it, but rather through his work, through passive activity, he becomes the representative of the subject of all society. Insofar as he yields to the necessity of the work of art he removes himself from everything that could be attributed simply to the contingency of his individuation. However, in such a representation of the subject of society as a whole, that of the entire, undivided humanity, to which Valéry's idea of the beautiful appeals, a condition is also conceived which abolishes the fate of blind individualization in which the whole subject is finally realized.[13]

It is easy to see that in this passage Adorno assigns to the artist all the normative tasks that another significant interpretation of historical materialism, Lukács' *History and Class Consciousness,* still entrusted to the proletariat. Precisely with reference to this formulation, which Lukács chose in order to describe the reflective process of the representative proletarian who unites in himself all cognitive competencies, Adorno now attributes to the artist the function of vicariously articulating in his aesthetic work the unreleased potential of the human species—that is, the combined capacity for sensory receptivity and for goal-directed material mastery.[14] The work of art, in connection with this representative function, is two things at once: It is the representative of a reason that divests itself of the constrictions of instrumental rationality in that it learns to take up the mimetic capacity of aesthetic experience, and it is the cognitive medium in which alone substantive insights are still to be gained that provide information about the social situation without at the same time succumbing to the critique of instrumental reason. These achievements, taken together,[15] induce Adorno, in the theoretical development of the *Dialectic of Enlightenment,* to give aesthetics the leading role in the general construction of critical theory. For, at the moment in which the normative and cognitive potential of a reason that transcends the limits of instrumental rationality is gathered together in the immanence of the work of art, a theory designed for the purpose of social criticism must be able to be so thoroughly revised according to the epistemological model of artistic activity that it can, to a certain extent, view society from this perspective. Just as critical theory in the early writings of Horkheimer still claimed to capture the self-consciousness of the revolutionary social movement, so now, after the turn in its basic philosophical-historical assumptions introduced in the *Dialectic of Enlightenment,* critical theory is allowed to understand itself only as the reflective form of the redemptive claim inhabiting the work of art. *Aesthetic Theory,* which Adorno worked on in the last years of his life, serves the task of raising critical theory to this new epistemological level. It seeks to fulfill the function of decoding for art its own logic in order to let a critical theory of society be joined to it.

If in his postwar writings he gradually gives the competencies of critical knowledge to art, Adorno is merely drawing the conclusions that follow from the model of the philosophy of history that, from the perspective of a universal history, he had first sketched out with Horkheimer in his interpretation of fascism. If philosophical reflection and (especially) scientific research are not able to escape the suspicion of complicity in the civilizing process of reification, then the monopoly of critical knowledge must finally fall to aesthetic experience. The radicality of Adorno's writings lies in the self-critical application of this conclusion to the methodological structure of critical theory. In order to make the form of presentation of his theory also conform to the cognitive requirements negatively contained in the *Dialectic of Enlightenment,* his mode of argumentation tries to approximate the mimetic achievements of the work of art so that in specific texts he lets the traditional norms of methodological rigor and systematic proof fall behind the requirements of a noncoercive approach to the subject matter under consideration.[16] In order to oppose the subsumption of particularity asserted in his philosophy of history even within the confines of theoretical discourse, he wanted to confer the status of argumentative statements on the content of individual experiences.[17] And finally, to a certain extent as the last consequence, he obliged critical theory to admit that the cognitive capacity of the work of art is higher than that of theoretical reflection. Admittedly, this final conclusion only shifts to another level the aporia into which the project of a conceptually apprehended critique of conceptual thought must in principle fall. Since even a philosophical aesthetic can in each case only refer to other experiential modes of artistic production, it cannot itself create this experience. The critical theory that emerges in Adorno's postwar writings thus vacillates helplessly between philosophical reflection and aesthetic experience, not wanting to be the one and not able to be the other.[18]

(b) This inner construction of Adorno's critical theory leaves only a little room for the project of an empirically oriented analysis of society. Wedged between a philosophy oriented to conceptual criticism and a philosophical aesthetics, to which the task of genuine knowledge must be conceded so long as the implications of the underlying philosophy of history are followed consistently enough, social-scientific research assumes the place of an auxiliary discipline whose methodology is not quite acknowledged. From the perspective of the critique of science contained in the *Dialectic of Enlightenment,* sociology represents the paradigmatic example of a science of bureaucratic control that serves the maintenance of intra-societal domination. With this in mind, Adorno speaks of the "administrative structure" of social-scientific research.[19]

The first of two tasks that Adorno assigns to social science within the context of his critical theory arises out of the need for an ideological critique of such established social research. Thus, here too, just as in the corresponding case of philosophy, he regards the indirect path of self-criticism of previously established science as the appropriate method for elaborating a critical theory of society. The imagination of his sociological studies is thus fueled by an assessment of the intentions, the conceptual presuppositions, the methodological tools, and the substantive results of the empirical as well as the theoretical social sciences in terms of their historical truth-content. The methodological key that he employs in order to realize this task of ideology-critique is derived from Hegel's logic of essence.[20] Adorno uses the conceptual distinction between essence and appearance as a way of showing that although the social sciences gathered together by him under the vague title "positivism" might be able to comprehend the empirical world of appearance of contemporary societies, the true essential core, the law of capitalist exchange, remains unexplored in principle.

Adorno's ideological critique of "positivistic" social science is, however, only incidentally concerned with the modest thesis that the tradition of sociological theory dissociated its object from the economic conditions of capitalism and thus isolated the object from its determining relations. Adorno is too good a student of Marxism not to know that ideologically suspect theories always also contain elements that, from a normative perspective, can be understood as materially appropriate conceptions of a "false" object. This historical relation to truth is what is of primary interest to Adorno in established social research. The argumentation of his ideological studies serves primarily to establish that the methodological techniques and the basic conceptual convictions of the conventional social sciences—that is, therefore, the methods of empirical social research and the systems-concept of sociological functionalism— can be understood as adequate research methods of a contemporary sociology because the mode of socialization assumed within them has in fact also approximated the reality of capitalist society. Thus, according to its own basic intention, Adorno's critique of sociology is designed for the exposition of a historical convergence of the "positivistic" concept of society and actual social development. It deals with the conviction that the conceptual framework of positivism only reflects a movement that, as a reification within the nexus of social life, is itself being completed in the processes of a coercive integration of all domains of action and a destruction of the capacity for individual identity. To that extent, the quantitative increase in techniques testifies to the actual standardization of the model of individual behavior in the same way that the positivistic model of society mirrors the actual coercive condition of society: "A social science which is both atomistic, and ascends through classification from the atoms to generalities, is the Medusan mirror to a society which is both atomized and organized according to abstract classificatory concepts, namely those of administration."[21]

The critical point of all Adorno's sociological essays is found in sharp conclusions of this sort. It discloses the immanent connection that exists between the project of an ideological critique of social science and the philosophical-historical construction of a process of civilizing decay. Adorno seems to depict for the present the picture that the *Dialectic of Enlightenment* draws of totalitarian societies of its own time in order to rediscover all the social phenomena that had been condensed in the form of theoretical premises in the established social sciences. Nevertheless, such a model already presupposes for its own part the critical outline of a concept of contemporary society, however vaguely it is defined. Critical social research can hardly be content with an ideological critique of established social research. If, in order to be able to present the historical kernel of truth in contemporary social science, Adorno simply extends to the present situation the lines of social-scientific analysis that are rudimentarily sketched out in the joint study with Horkheimer, an independent anticipation of present society is required that is able to justify this provisional extension. Therefore Adorno cannot avoid, in a sort of tentative social theory, setting out from the beginning those properties of contemporary capitalism that can only be indirectly confirmed in the self-critique of sociology. This is the second task that Adorno assigns to social science in the framework of his critical theory. It takes over the function of developing and continuously modifying the picture of late-capitalist society that is presupposed in the philosophical essays and the ideological-critical studies.

In Adorno's postwar writings the social theory entrusted with these tasks assumes the form of a social-scientific analysis of the integrative accomplishments of late capitalism. In accordance with its conceptual system, it is tailored from the outset to an attitude that makes it possible to perceive the coercive mechanisms of social integration but not the latent boundaries of social conflict. The analysis singles out three complexes: political-economic reproduction, administrative manipulation, and psychic integration. On all three levels Adorno works with a concept of domination into which, I maintain, the implications of the theory of domination developed in the *Dialectic of Enlightenment* indiscreetly flow. The result, however paradoxical it may sound, is the definitive repression of the social from the social analysis of critical theory.

The central element of Adorno's analysis of society, the determination of the socio-economic structure of contemporary society, already reflects conceptual ambiguities and substantive uncertainties that can only be attributed to the peculiar irrelevance of empirical sociological questions for his late work. Even here Adorno still allows himself to be guided by the concept of "state capitalism" initially imported into the research context of the Institute by Friedrich Pollock.[22] At first, it was supposed to serve the scientific analysis of the National Socialist economic order alone.[23] However, it was subsequently elevated, in Horkheimer's famous essay "The Authoritarian State" and in the *Dialectic of Enlightenment,* to the means for defining the postliberal phase of capitalism generally.[24] Already in its original, professional interpretation, in which it had grasped the tendencies of a transition within capitalism to a bureaucratic "command economy," the concept of state capitalism encountered considerable criticism and was weakened empirically by the studies of Neumann and Kirchheimer, who demonstrated the continuation of a capitalism that was admittedly monopolistic but was nevertheless still steered by the market. In the global interpretation with which Adorno and Horkheimer now take up this concept, the category of "state capitalism" asserts a mode of organization of capitalism in which the steering of the entire economic process by the mediating sphere of the competition of individual capitalists is transferred over to the centralized administrative activity of an apparatus of domination. The calculated interests of the major corporations and the planning capacity of the state organs come together in a technical rationality to which all domains of social action are uniformly subordinated.

Adorno makes use of such a vague conception as early as

1942 in "Reflections on Class Theory." In that essay the point of his interpretation of "state capitalism" is still formulated in terms of the philosophical-historical claim that to a certain extent the cycle of civilization comes to a close with the end of liberal capitalism since, with the formation, after the interlude of economically induced class conflict, of an administrative elite who exercise control, a piece of human prehistory returns— the arbitrary and violent appropriation of power by social groups. The sharply formulated opposition between a noninterventionist market economy and a state-capitalist central administration, which in view of fascism Adorno subsequently used as the basis for regarding the liberal phase of capitalism as simply an episode in the history of noneconomic acts of domination,[25] remains the theoretical element that also provides an argumentative framework for his postwar sociological writings. Admittedly, the influential essay "Late Capitalism or Industrial Society?," which Adorno delivered in 1968 as the opening address to the sixteenth Congress of German Sociologists, is free of the philosophical-historical tone that allows "Reflections on Class Theory" to look like a further excursus to the *Dialectic of Enlightenment*. The concept of state capitalism returns unchanged in a vague form, however, even if it is no longer under the same title.

The concept initially developed with a view to the political-economic analysis of fascism is now supposed to help answer the question of whether, with the transition to the highly industrialized societies of the capitalist West and the Soviet Union, a new mode of social organization has come about that renders superfluous the classical distinction between capitalist and postcapitalist productive relations. In a silent correction to the philosophical-historical theory of domination contained in the *Dialectic of Enlightenment*, Adorno initially answers by emphasizing the dependency of technological development upon conditions within the socio-economic framework—"its interconnectedness with the social relations in which it is embedded."[26] In his presentation of the productive relations responsible for the developmental level of the Western industrial societies, however, he repeats with only slight modifications the insights of the analysis of fascism—the thesis, that is, concerning state capitalism. The "regressive tendency within liberal capitalism" toward a centrally administered, thoroughly organized society is the process that Adorno still regards as the definitive event in the formation of highly developed societies.[27] As was already the case in the analysis of the 1940s, the simplicity of the thesis of a totally administered society leaves a host of unanswered questions in the background—questions such as the following: Is purposive-rational domination concentrated solely in a state-organized administration, or is it additionally institutionalized in nonstate administrative bodies? Does the administrative activity of the centralized organs of domination simply fulfill the clearly circumscribed imperatives of the capitalist economy, whether it helps to correct or to create compromises for the conflicting demands of the economy, or does it autonomously realize its own logic of political power? Finally, do the administrative means of domination represent the present embodiment of a rationality of control formed at the beginning of the civilizing process, or did the subsequent development of a purposive rationality first form with capitalist industrialization?

None of these questions is conclusively answered in Adorno's essay. Rather, dispersed throughout the text one finds support for each of the conflicting sets of interpretations.[28] They appear to be of only secondary importance for Adorno, since the traumatic picture of a totally administered society seems to occupy the complete attention of his sociological analysis. Where theoretical differentiations should be substantively supported, one finds formulations that only describe in other words the process of the administrative penetration of society. The most impressive phrase that Adorno seems to find for the result of this process that so dominates this analysis is "the end of mediation." It arises out of the context of the *Dialectic of Enlightenment,* and it dominates the sociological writings of the 1960s as a guiding motif. It reveals the large extent to which Adorno's analysis of late capitalism relies upon the contrasting model of a liberal-capitalist market economy.

Adorno's picture of liberal capitalism is shaped by the idealizing conception that, so long as it remains free of state intervention, the market is the sole social sphere for the type of action in which identities are secured. Since, with the mutual calculation of interests, the market creates space for experiences of social identity, the purposive rational conflicts of action of individual subjects can still be mediated within it by the requirement for economic reproduction. For Adorno the market is the prototypical form of social mediation in capitalism. As a result, the places of social communication that lie outside it—the institutions of the bourgeois public sphere, the proletarian cooperative enterprise, or the plebian subculture, all of which delay the path of capitalist industrialization—as well as the interest organizations directed toward it, in which social groups attempt to realize their economic interests, are bypassed in Adorno's description of the social infrastructure of liberal capitalism. The subject closed within the private sphere of the nuclear family comes into contact with the social environment solely via the market process. Thus, it is only logical for Adorno to infer globally from the political-administrative paralyzing of the market a deformation of the social connections between economic reproduction and particular acting subjects.

Against the background of a concept of liberal capitalism emptied of the basic dimensions of the public sphere, it must seem as if the administrative centralization of processes of economic decisionmaking threaten to undermine the internal social infrastructure of capitalism in general, for the very process that through the bureaucratic steering of the economy has deformed the space opened by the market for interest-oriented action destroys thereby at the same time the only social institution mediating individual action. In the centralized administration of the process of capital utilization, which he contrasts to the strongly overemphasized phase of a market economy free from intervention,[29] Adorno thus perceives for the present a global "end of mediation." The imperatives of a productive system that has become independent through bureaucratic planning, so it must seem to him, now directly encounter individualized members of society without being filtered through any spheres of social action.

This concluding line of thought is decisive for the interpretation of capitalism that Adorno worked out in his postwar writings. The central argument arises not from an empirically oriented analysis of late capitalism but from a prior logical consideration: With the transition to centrally organized capitalism society must have lost its inner sociality, since a medium of social action that was institutionalized only within the market sphere has now been destroyed. Adorno is driven to the disquieting conclusion of a totally administered society, since his analysis of the structural changes in capitalism is guided from the outset by an extremely reductionistic conception of the internal social relations of capitalism. Neither the cultural institutions of collective self-understanding (that is, class-specific forms of the public sphere) nor the organizations for securing collective interests (that is, professional and task-specific types of social corporations) receive appropriate conceptual consideration. This view of capitalist society, hardened into a one-dimensional picture, lets fade out of view the deeper dimensions of those pre-state domains of action in which normative convictions and cultural self-interpretations, as well as the purposive-rational deliberations of individuals, become socially effective. Nevertheless, as will now be shown, this conception forms the theoretical backbone of the further investigations in which Adorno completes his structural analysis of late capitalism with an analysis of the processes of social integration.

Initially Adorno can let a theory that investigates the institutional mechanisms which compel individuals to strict adherence to the goals of action set by the economic and political bureaucracies be tied unproblematically to the model of centrally organized capitalism derived from the original diagnosis of state capitalism. Just as the socio-economic analysis serves to define the structural properties of highly developed capitalism, so the theory of the culture industry, which must fulfill this second task, now has as its object the administrative side of the process of social integration. Its basic idea refers to the assumption that with centrally controlled mass media the instrument of an effective manipulation of consciousness accrues to the administrative power. In the essay just mentioned, which is intended to address the question "late capitalism or industrial society?," Adorno offers a brief reflection on the social consequences of an industrial-administrative control of consciousness:

If society is so organized that it automatically or deliberately blocks, by means of the culture and consciousness industry and by monopolies of public opinion, even the simplest knowledge and awareness of ominous political events or of important critical ideas and theories; if, to compound it all, the organization of society paralyzes even the very ability to imagine the world differently from the way it in fact overwhelmingly appears to its inhabitants, then this rigid and manipulated mental condition becomes every bit as much a material force—a force of repression—as its counterpart, i.e., free and independent thought, once sought its elimination.[30]

The second component of Adorno's sociological diagnosis of the present, the theory of the culture industry touched upon in these sentences, is also derived from investigations in which the experience of German fascism and the American exile originally were reflected. Adorno's early essays on the commodity character of works of art produced on a standardized scale and Horkheimer's studies on the bifurcation of contemporary culture were joined together in a chapter in the *Dialectic of Enlightenment* entitled "The Culture Industry: Enlightenment as Mass Deception."[31] This chapter examines the administrative use of electronic media as a "means for the enchainment of consciousness"[32] and sets forth a model that Adorno simply carries over into his later studies on the cultural scene in the postwar era. According to this model, on the basis of a monopolistic economic system, the modern reproductive techniques of film, radio, and television are fused with the rapidly spreading entertainment industry into a cultural-industrial complex whose manipulative products make it possible to control individual consciousness at the level of motivations. Adorno is also convinced that, in aesthetic presentation as well as in informational content, the products of the culture industry affect the members of society in such a way that they willingly undertake administratively sanctioned tasks.

Two of the tendencies in the transformation of cultural modes of perception that were released by the immanent formative power of the electronic media appear to have been the major reasons why Adorno remained convinced, to the end of his life, of the empirical cogency of the theory of the culture industry worked out in the 1930s and the 1940s. On the one hand, he assumes that with the capitalistically driven expansion of mass media all elements of the world of sense perception are drawn into an artificially produced reality.[33] This tendency, which Adorno sees as culminating in the technical innovation of television, allows the appearance of the media world to assume characteristics that are increasingly accommodated to reality and thus ever more effective. On the other hand, he is guided by Walter Benjamin's observation that the distance between cultural products and the public which enjoys them is drastically diminished by the electronic techniques of reproduction.[34] In direct contrast to Benjamin's cultural-revolutionary hopes, however, Adorno detects in the destruction of the aesthetic aura the tendency toward an ever stronger imposition upon the observer of the perceptual pattern of a passive, nonreflective consumer.[35] Deprived of all distance through the spatial and temporal incursion of the media world into private life and blinded to reality by the abundance of the media, each person now stands powerless before the flow of information working through the channels of the mass media. In both tendencies—the continuously perfected synthesizing of the world of sense perception and the advance of media consumption into everyday life—Adorno sees a transformation of the usual modes of reception that leaves the individual a helpless victim of an all-pervasive media reality. It is the conviction, gained through the perception of this radical cultural change, concerning the suggestive power emanating from the products of the cultural industry, concerning its power over the representational world of the public, that seduces Adorno into the supposition of the capacity for an intentional manipulation of consciousness by the administrative measures of the mass media, which are apparently fused with the organs of the state. As Adorno attempts to show in his analysis of their content, the conformity-creating messages produced and distributed by the culture industry are so easily able to influence individuals only because they penetrate into the deepest of consciousness along the paths prepared by the suggestive power of the mass media.[36]

Adorno does not shy away from the consequences of his theoretical argument concerning late capitalism. He is of the opinion that it is in principle possible that an expansion of ideological stereotypes which is administratively controlled and which makes use of the channels of the mass media is sufficient for securing the required measure of social consensus formation in late-capitalist societies. According to Adorno, under the influence of the pseudo-worlds of the media, subjects become willing recipients of conformity-inducing messages. Only in light of such a basic conviction can he regard the theory of the culture industry as an adequate basis for a sociological analysis that investigates the institutional mechanisms of social integration. He can be content to answer the questions raised by an explanation of social conformity in terms of an investigation of the content of the products of the cultural industry because he is firmly convinced of its direct effect on its addressees. The limited perspective present in this conviction can already be judged by the fact that Adorno is able to overlook completely the subcultural horizons of reception (that is, group-specific interpretive accomplishments and models of deciphering) as well as the national peculiarities of the organizational form of mass media. Of course, this limited perspective is surprising only when one does not relate the theory of the culture industry to its own background in a global structural analysis of late capitalism. The roots of such a crude version of a theory of manipulation, in which his theory of the culture industry finally concludes, are found here in Adorno's socio-economic diagnosis of the times.

The claim that with the destruction of the market introduced by the transition to a postliberal era of capitalism society forfeits that medium which at the societal level helped to bridge the gap between the demands of the economic structure and individual acting subjects is central to Adorno's socio-economic structural analysis. Since the market was the historically unique place for an institutionalized coordination of individual actions, to the extent that the bureaucratic centralization of processes of economic decisionmaking undermine the market, the inner life of the society must itself cease to exist. If the track of this conclusion by Adorno, about whose radicality he was not in doubt, is pursued in the theory of the culture industry, then its rough-hewn hypotheses, large omissions, and oversimplifications no longer sound so surprising: At the level of his struc tural analysis of late capitalism, Adorno was so convinced of the disintegration of socially mediated modes of action that on the level of his analysis of mass media he did not notice the obstacles to cultural-industrial manipulation: subcultural interpretive styles and forms of perception—that is, cooperative interpretive accomplishments. He could not perceive the patterns of group-specific value orientations and everyday interpretations that, as horizons of meaning, guide the individual in working through the flood of media information, since he was so certain about the destruction of the capitalist infrastructure built on the basis of just such achievements of social action. Therefore, he could not believe that the suggestive influence of the culture industry could find its limits in the fact that the process of the cooperative production of group-specific horizons of orientation was itself not subject to manipulation. Adorno did not make room in his social theory for an autonomous sphere of cultural action in which members of a social group bring their everyday experiences and interests into agreement in one common world view. Only in one particular passage, which seems unusually strange within the context of his sociological writings, did he concede, in view of the results of an empirical research project, the possibility that the messages could simply reverberate against the walls of an everyday world skeptical toward the pseudo-reality of the media:

. . . many—this may be due to the representation—suddenly behave quite realistically and critically evaluate the political and social importance of those same well-publicized events, the uniqueness of which they had breathelessly viewed with astonishment on television. Thus, what the culture industry sets before people in their leisure is, if my conclusion is not too hasty, admittedly consumed and accepted, but only provisionally, like the naive experience of the theatre or film, not simply as reality.[37]

Adorno did not pursue the remarks contained in this passage. They would have directed his sociological theory along the path of an inquiry into the subcultural orientation-horizons that are the result of an interpretive praxis based on the ongoing common experiences of social groups. An analysis of the rules of understanding embedded in them would have enabled him to ask about the interpretation that the members of society give themselves about the messages of the mass media that affect them. Instead, in his writings on the culture industry, Adorno lapses into a theory of manipulation that reasons directly from the informational content of the products of the culture industry to its individual effects and thus assumes an especially crude form. According to its conception, the ideological messages unfold their media force by reaching right through the subcultural horizons of association of subjects so that they can produce conformist attitudes without any resistance.

However, a criticism that rejects the manipulation-theoretic curtailment found in this conclusion but does not pursue its causes within Adorno's overarching theory of society is admittedly too brief.[38] It omits the fact that in his analysis of the organizational form of late capitalism Adorno is so preoccupied by the idea of an "end of mediation" that he cannot consider the intermediary sphere of the everyday communicative praxis of social groups. The one-dimensionality of Adorno's analysis of the culture industry is simply the theoretical result of a conceptual reductionsim in his theory of society. With the scant means of an analysis of capitalism that can only perceive a medium for the social mediation of individual action in the sphere of the market, he diagnoses an irreversible destruction of the market in the highly industrialized society of postliberal capitalism. He can subsequently infer from this the dissolution of internal social relations generally, the desocialization of society. This enables him to conclude finally in the pointed formulation that the "Sisyphusian labor of individual instinctual economy" today seems to be "taken over by the institutions of the culture industry."[39]

However, this sentence also reveals that for the task of an investigation of the process of social integration Adorno cannot allow himself to be satisfied with a theory of the culture industry. For the ideological apparatus of the culture industry can assume the task of regulating the instincts, which formerly was carried out independently by individual subjects, only to the extent that it is not only capable of controlling the reflective activities of individuals but also able to exercise control over their instinctual life as over objectified natural processes. Since

Adorno attributes to the mass media in late capitalism not only the effects of a meticulous control of consciousness but also the effect of a control over instincts that penetrates into organic life, he must be able to show why members of society no longer possesses the strength for the mastery of individual instincts. The task of explaining this is taken up in Adorno's sociological diagnosis of the times by a psychoanalytically informed theory of ego weakness, which appears alongside the theory of the culture industry in the analysis of processes of social integration. Although the institutional basis of the administratively directed consensus formation in late capitalism does appear in the latter, its inner-psychic presuppositions are now supposed to be revealed in this socio-psychological diagnosis of "the end of personality."

It is not difficult to find the internal connection that links Adorno's social-psychological essays from the outset with his general theory of late capitalism. As in the case of the culture industry, here too it is brought about by the uniquely idealized concept of the market. For this Adorno can initially draw upon the social-psychological work in which, since the time of Horkheimer's pessimistic prognosis in the conclusion to "Traditional and Critical Theory," the Institute for Social Research had investigated the historical structural changes in the development of personality. In the earlier essay Horkheimer only hinted at an explanatory approach that saw the disappearance, along with the central function of the small private entrepreneur, of the prospect for the individualization process kindled by paternal authority. But after the war, Horkheimer worked this explanation out in an essay that tried to resume the social-psychological research activity of the Institute.[40] His guiding idea, which derived the loss of paternal authority and hence the renunciation of individual ego formation from the socio-economic transition to state-organized capitalism, later informed the simultaneously published works of Marcuse and Mitscherlich on the "fatherless society"—which, despite their differences, agree in discovering a new social type shaped by the destructuring of the superego.[41]

Adorno can see his own essays included in the ranks of this social-psychological work since he lets them take their point of departure from the conviction that the prospect for the formation of individual autonomy first comes about historically at the moment in which liberal capitalism and the market institutionalized a space for individual economic responsibility and freedom of discretion. Since the newly created sphere of action in socially transparent ways requires on the part of members of society the capacities to calculate interests, to make decisions, and for labor discipline, it represents for Adorno the sociostructural presupposition for a process of socialization in whose course the maturing subjects learn to perceive in their fathers the professional virtues required by the market, to respect their authoritative influence, and thus to internalize them as demands of conscience. Once these conditions of socialization for the formation of individual conscience disappear, he can infer that if the centralized steering of the economic process renders the personality traits of the father superfluous, then with the postliberal structural change in capitalism the zenith of bourgeois autonomy is passed. Such a model of the history of human individuality, synchronized with the development of the market, forms the general background to Adorno's social-psychological reflections:

As the free market economy displaces the feudal system and demands entrepreneurs as well as free wage laborers, it forms these types anthropologically as well as professionally. Concepts such as self-responsibility, precaution, self-satisfying individuality, fulfillment of duty, but also stark force of conscience and internalized obligation to authority, emerge. The individual itself, as the term is used until today, barely attained its specific content before Montaigne or Hamlet, in any case not before the early Italian renaissance. Today competition and the free market economy are increasingly losing importance in the face of concentrated large industry and its corresponding collectivities. The concept of the individual, which arose historically, attains its historical limit.[42]

Inasmuch as Adorno's postwar sociological publications now undertake the task of investigating this "historical limit" (that is, the tendency toward an erosion of individuality which accompanies the structural change of capitalism), they concentrate basically on the question of the historically appropriate relation between psychological and sociological theory formation. Only two studies concerning Freud's theory of mass psychology deal, within the immediate context of an argument concerning psycho-social reality, with the general social conditions of the weakening of the ego—although even here it is primarily with an eye to the analysis of the psychic preparation of the German people for fascism. Their primary interest is the enormous effect that the manipulative techniques of the fascist leader could have attained through the utilization of the narcissitic energies of individuals.[43] The majority of Adorno's psychoanalytic essays deal, by contrast, with the individual mechanisms of the loss of the ego only in the indirect context of a metatheoretic argument that raises ideological objections against the sociological reception of psychoanalysis through North American Neo-Freudianism. Here Adorno's urgent concern is to demonstrate that any premature appropriation of sociology by psychoanalysis, be it via an expansion of its foundations in a theory of the instincts or via a reception of extrafamilial influences in theories of socialization, underplays the real split between atomized individuals and the independent subsystems of domination.[44]

The picture that arises from these contributions by Adorno concerning the psychic process of the destruction of the ego is not free of contradictions. To be sure, the inner-familial cause and the socializing result of the process, which are their topic, are defined identically in these specific essays so that they correspond to the image suggested from the outset by a social psychology of late capitalism that accompanies the theory of the culture industry. The loss of paternal authority, which is the inner-familial result of that political restriction of economic independence and human control of dispositions, allows for a direct socialization of the child through administrative power. That is, so long as the growing child could form a moral conscience through the internalization of the norms and sanctions authoritatively represented by the father, he was capable of controlling his instincts—in ways conforming to society, to be sure, but nevertheless independently—and was thus secured against behavioral requirements stipulated from outside. Now, however, since along with the father's social authority his attitude of strict expectations within the family has been shaken, to a certain extent the child lacks the personal counterpart required for internalizing the norms of prohibition that form the conscience. Thus the apparatus of the culture industry is able to assume as a surrogate the task of regulating the instincts. Adorno now connects to this argument, which so far corresponds to the thesis of the "outwardly directed character," a further line of thought that in specific ways posits a narcissistic regression of the ego as a complementary process alongside the destructuring of the superego.

Adorno begins with the assumption that the ego, permanently overburdened with the dual tasks of tireless mastery of the instincts and rational self-preservation, regresses to a condition of the libidinal cathexis of the self in order to be able to avoid the experience of real powerlessness.[45] The ego-libido thereby set free is directed toward the mass idol, which functions as a replacement for the father and which is so removed from impoverished everyday life that the powerless individual can projectively secure an "infinite celebrity" in it. The parallel psychic processes of a destructuring of the superego and a weakening of the cognitive achievements of the ego, both of which are far-reaching consequences of the dissolution of the market sphere for the process of socialization, allow the individual subject to become a victim to an apparatus of domination that exploits the potential of the organic instincts for its own ends:

The social power-structure hardly needs the mediating agencies of ego and individuality any longer. . . . The truly contemporary types are those whose actions are motivated neither by an ego nor, strictly speaking, unconsciously, but mirror objective trends like an automaton. Together they enact a senseless ritual to the beat of a compulsively repetitive rhythm and become emotionally impoverished: with the destruction of the ego, narcissism, or its collectivistic derivatives, is heightened. A brutal, total, standardizing society arrests all differentiation, and to this end it exploits the primitive core of the unconscious. Both conspire to annihilate the mediating ego; the triumphant archaic impulses, the victory of id over ego, harmonize with the triumph of society over the individual.[46]

The socially compelled regression of the individual to the early-childhood stage of narcissism is supposed to make intel-

ligible the unbroken power that the media of the culture industry are able to exercise upon the organic instinctual life.
Since the capacities of the ego for intellectual and moral control
are breaking down (the process announced by the formula,
employed here, of the "renunciation of the moment of mediation"), the human instinctual potential can become directly tied
by the administrative power to the tasks of social reproduction
through the utilization of narcissistic energies. Attached to the
collectivized ego ideal manipulatively proffered by the culture
industry, the individual instincts from below feed supportively
into the system of domination centrally administered from
above as long as no conflicting dynamics arise—something that
Adorno seems more convinced about than Marcuse. But already this last argumentative step, in which the human instinctual dynamic appears as the "cement" of late-capitalist
societies,[47] is surprising within the context of Adorno's social
psychology: On the one hand, since Adorno—in strict opposition to the psychoanalytic "revisionism" of Erich Fromm or
Karen Horney[48]—is convinced that there is an instinctual nature that in its core remains resistant to social influences, the
capacity for (complete) socialization of the natural instincts is
excluded. But on the other hand, since he perceives in the
human instincts precisely the organic foundation for an apparatus of domination independent of the individual, he challenges attributing a surplus potential to inner human nature.
It follows that Adorno must think that the organic substrate of
human instincts is so designed that it fits without any remainder
into the model of the offers for satisfaction borne by the
system.[49]

But the presupposition of such a conception of instincts (in
which, to be sure, the possibility of a social molding of the
individual instinctual life is contested, but in which an unhindered manipulation of the formation of human needs is nonetheless allowed) is not the most surprising thing about Adorno's
social psychology. The argument in which the whole underlying assumption of a decomposition of the superego is joined
to the thesis of a narcissistic regression of the ego is also not
very convincing from a purely immanent point of view. The
first assumption, as was shown, is directly connected to social-

psychological considerations, which lead back from the empirically unsubstantiated phenomenon of the loss of paternal authority to an epochal disturbance in the process of the formation of the child's conscience. The second assumption (that is, the thesis of a structurally induced regression of the individual to the early-childhood stage of narcissism) relies on psychoanalytic considerations that are informed by a historically significant increase in narcissistic personality disturbances. But the explanation that Adorno offers for this second phenomenon is not fully compatible with the concept that served in the explanation of the first phenomenon. For Adorno clarifies the process of the narcissistic regression of the ego in connection with "the continuous failure [of individuals] to satisfy their own ego demands"[50]; but how is the individual supposed to learn how to form its own exacting ego-ideal, on whose biographical realization it could founder, if the intrapsychic process of the formation of conscience is itself permanently destroyed?

It seems that in his social-psychological hypotheses on the social causes of ego loss Adorno has combined two explanatory approaches which, as he has proposed them, cannot be brought together. On the level at which he pursues the investigations, influenced by Horkheimer's observations, on the psychic effects of the loss of paternal authority, he insists upon an externalization of the superego which is taken over by the artificial "group-ego."[51] But, if he derives the narcissistic regression of the individual from a repression due to the failure experienced in the realization of authentic ego-claims, then he is not allowed to postulate precisely this externalization. Thus, Adorno makes use of two irreconcilable explanatory models in order to account for the decline of the individual's capacities for psychic control. In the first case he presupposes the actual destructuring of the imperatives of the superego; in the second case he attempts to understand psychic regression in terms of their unsuccessful realization. In a penetrating study, Jessica Benjamin traces this theoretical unclarity in Adorno's social psychology back to conceptual confusions that prohibited him, under the category "internalization," from sufficiently distinguishing between the acquisition of capacities for cognitive-instrumental action and the appropriation of norms of moral action: "He tends to use the concept of internalization confusingly to signify two different but related phenomena, the development of the ego and the super-ego. The identification with parental authority as super-ego is collapsed into the identification with parental competence or the reality of childhood autonomy as ego formation."[52] An undifferentiated concept of "internalization" that does not distinguish precisely enough between the development of the ego and the formation of the superego would explain why Adorno so quickly combines the destructuring of the superego (analyzed in social psychology) with the loss of the cognitive capacities of the self, despite the fact that the two explanatory models that he employs in the sociological interpretation of the two respective processes are incompatible with one another. In his basic categories, Adorno implicitly assimilates the interactive process of identification with other subjects, which enables the child to learn norms and commands represented within the family, to the process of the rational appropriation of external reality, which makes possible to an increasing extent the cognitive mastery of the environment by the child. He conceives the moral development of the child in terms of the same model according to which he understands the adolescent's acquisition of capacities for instrumental action, that is, as a process in which the growing individual, by assuming paternal behavioral models, learns to control his own instinctual life as well as external nature. Since Adorno understands moral and cognitive socialization of the child as two sides of an acquisition of paternal competencies of action, he cannot see that "the loss of internalized conscience is not the same as the lack of conscious rational control over the environment which an autonomous ego could exert."[53]

However, the unclarity of the concept of internalization, which seems to force Adorno into the contradictions of his social-psychological hypothesis, also reveals a deeper deficiency in his appropriation of psychoanalysis. Jessica Benjamin is concerned above all with this particular deficiency, since she attempts to establish the superior explanatory potential of the revisionist psychoanalysis which Adorno criticized throughout his life, namely, the theory of object relations and ego psychology. She uncovers therewith the basic monistic assumptions in Adorno's theory of personality development, which we have already encountered in connection with the interpretation of the *Dialectic of Enlightenment.*

When Adorno joins together in the concept of "internalization" the processes of the formation of conscience and the development of intelligence, the difficulties that emerge can be understood as the consequence of a conception of the genesis of the self in which the attainment of individual identity appears as a sort of inner-psychic extension of the societal conquest of nature. Organic instinctual potential is thus, to a certain extent, simply the inner-psychic complement to external nature, which the subject must learn to control effectively. This conception, which dominates the sections of the *Dialectic of Enlightenment* dealing with the theory of personality, suggests that the process of the formation of conscience be interpreted as an internalization of the capacities for controlling the environment, that is, as an internally directed act of the domination of nature. So conceived, the growing individual is confronted with an objective world of natural objects which he or she learns to control in the course of socialization. Similarly, the father is also not just one partner interacting with the child, but rather the exemplary representative of an externally and internally directed domination of nature. From this it is easy to see that in his social psychology Adorno must attribute such a philosophical-historical significance to paternal authority only because in his appropriation of psychoanalysis he collapsed the child's environment into a world consisting solely of natural events:

The crucial problem in both conception of the ego and of nature is therefore the lack of a concept of intersubjectivity—of subject to subject relations or societal interaction. Consciousness appears to be a property of the individual monad. The world is not conceived of as an intersubjective realm in which the objects encountered are really themselves subjects who have the capacity to act and be affected by another's actions. In their [Adorno's and Horkheimer's—A.H.] use of the abstract category "outside world," in their analysis of reason itself in terms of ego and outside, subject and object, they are unable to overcome the subject-object dualism from which, in their view, domination ultimately springs. The source of their objectification of the outside world, as well as their inability to transcend the reason which objectifies, is the development of the categories of reflection and self-reflection solely out of the relation between subject and object.[54]

From this basic objection, a perspective can easily be attained that enables one to see retrospectively a few theoretical short-circuits in Adorno's social psychology. Specifically, only when we take into consideration that in his interpretation of psycho-analysis the social world of communicative action and the pressing nature of inner needs are assimilated to an undifferentiated world of objective states of affairs which the subject learns to control solely through the internalization of paternal competences does it become evident within his social-psychological writings to what a limited range of social encounters the communicative framework of socializing events has been allowed to dwindle. At the level of theory, Adorno has systematically considered as a communicative dimension in the environment of the child only the figure of the father, whom he conceives as the intra-familial representation of the societal domination of nature. He leaves out of consideration all other communicative partners for the formative history of the individual. This prevents him generally from giving the appropriate weight to the socializing capacity of the dimension of social interaction. He does not take up the wide-ranging medium of social communication that forms the framework for processes of individual socialization. It is as if the schematic manner in which Adorno narrows the perspective on the adolescent's environment to the representative role of the father lets him disregard the communicative infrastructure of his object at every concrete level of his social psychology. Consequently, it is not easy to see that

• such a close relation should exist between the behavioral patterns required in the economic sphere of the market and actual personality structures—whereas it may be that the personality patterns which in certain ways were called for by the pressure of economic activity are formed precisely in the pre-economic arena of public realms of society and thus can be influenced by group-specific learning processes;

• such a direct connection should exist between the social reduction of the central function of private entrepreneurs and a
structural change in the forms of familial relations—whereas
it may be that the class-specific patterns of family communication should be considered so that the different effects of the
structural changes in capitalism would be judged according to
the respective family types[55];

• such a direct relation should exist solely between paternal
authority and the formation of the child's conscience—whereas
the nexus of the child's communicative interaction might be
conceived such that the psychic role of all the child's communicative partners become visible: "The peer group is considered invariably conformist. . . . It [the social-psychological
concept of Horkheimer and Adorno—A.H.] ignores the role
of maternal authority and pre-Oedipal development as well as
the difference in female child development. . . ."[56]

If Adorno had given greater recognition to the internal relations of social action at every argumentative level of his social
psychology, then it would have become clear that the behavioral
traits required by the market are not simply reflected in the
personality patterns of the individual, but rather become socially effective only through the medium of communicative
experiences within groups; that the structural change of capitalism can only be directly expressed in the loss of paternal
authority if the father's familial hegemony was also actually
grounded in the experience of economic sovereignty; and that
the societal weakening of paternal authority (whatever its
cause) does not automatically lead to a disturbance in the process of individualization, but, conversely, might provide room
for an increase in the psychic significance of the child's other
communicative partners. However, Adorno did not consider
these alternative viewpoints which result from a heightened
attentiveness to the significance of social action for the process
of socialization. The conceptual framework designed for the
process of the domination of nature, within which he took up
the theoretic impetus toward psychoanalysis, did not permit
considering the conditions for the communicative framework
of the process of individual formation other than in a one-

sided concentration on the role of paternal authority which corresponds to the rational principle of the domination of nature. Only this permitted him, in abstraction from all mediating social links, to infer directly from the economic tendencies toward a destruction of the market sphere, through the restructuring of the family, to the conclusion of a destruction of the individual capacity for identity.

In arriving at this gloomy conclusion, Adorno's social psychology completes the picture that had already been sketched out in his socio-economic and critical postwar writings on the form of domination in late capitalism. The dispersed and scarcely elaborated socio-economic analyses, which took their starting point from the model of state capitalism, were supposed to dissect the tendencies toward a concentration of the performance of all societal regulation in the planning of large bureaucracies: The regulation of social life had been detached from the mediating organ of the market and passed over to an administrative management. To the centralized administration of political-economic events corresponds an administratively directed social integration. The studies on the culture industry, which make up the largest portion of the postwar sociological writings, are likewise supposed to make transparent the institutional mechanism that helps to secure the requisite measure of social conformity in late-capitalist societies. The right of disposal over the electronic mass media has been transferred to cultural-industrial management and, because of the suggestive power of media broadcasts, can be utilized as instruments for the manipulation of consciousness. The mass media can develop as an effective means for controlling instincts, of course, only if individuals themselves have lost the capacity for autonomous regulation of their drives. For that reason, finally, the social-psychological essays should analyze those processes of socialization that gradually open the space for an unmediated socialization of the individual's instinctual potential by the culture industry. The transformation in the family that comes about with the passage to organized capitalism has disrupted the inner-familial conditions for the formation of a successful identity inasmuch as paternal authority as well as the authoritative model for the formation of the child's conscience have been destroyed. Adorno has now supplemented this definitive prognosis with the claim concerning a narcissistic regression of the individual, generalized it into the speculative thesis of the "end of the individual," and, as a complementary social-psychological argument, placed it alongside the equally handy thesis of the "totally administered society." Taken together, these two elements allow the theory of late capitalism to lead into a diagnosis of the times that confirms word for word the picture of a coercively unified society that was assumed from the beginning in Adorno's philosophical argument.

This social-scientific conclusion represents the principle of integration, which secures the unity of social life in late capitalism, as a one-sided relation of social domination. In the regulation of political and economic events, the apparatus of administrative control is independent of normative expectations and of the consent of the members of society. The unity of late-capitalist societies results exclusively from the interplay of the bureaucratic planning of the economy and the manipulative production of mass loyalty. On the level of economic reproduction, a highly monopolized economic system provides the prerequisite that the ruling bureaucracies are able to regulate undisturbed the entire process of social production through the means of technical rationality. On the level of social integration, the destruction of the capacities for psychic control additionally create the condition that the centrally linked mass media are able to harness the libidinal energies of individuals for societal tasks. Thus, the necessary presuppositions for the integration of society as a whole can be created "from above"—that is, through the planning and manipulative activities of a ruling administration.

It is no longer difficult to see how the conceptual model presented in the *Dialectic of Enlightenment* still figures so prominently in the concept of late-capitalist domination. Up through his last writings Adorno is convinced that in late capitalism it is solely the administrative means of direct and indirect force that bring individual actions together into the order of a social system. Apart from any measure of prevailing political liberties and the corresponding degree of social democratization, he

attributes the characteristics of a totalitarian system of domination to late-capitalist societies generally. From the oversim-
plified perspective offered by Adorno's analysis of society in
the 1950s and the 1960s, the differences between the various
forms of late-capitalist rule fade within the nebulous picture
of a coercively unified society. This alone already gives rise to
the suspicion that in Adorno's theory of late capitalism the
model of society built on the paradigm of the "domination of
nature" found in the *Dialectic of Enlightenment* reappears unchanged and that it is forced within the rigid confines of a
theory of totalitarianism. This suspicion first seems justified,
however, when the guiding concepts with which Adorno attempts to comprehend the operative modes of late-capitalist
domination also come into view: It is, above all, the categories
of "pressure," "force," "training," and "manipulation" from
which the conceptual apparatus of his model is built[57]—concepts which, as a whole, describe the effects of an instrumentally acting subject upon things or living beings. The basic
presuppositions and conceptual apparatus of his theory of late
capitalism show that, even in his later writings, Adorno cannot
give up the model of the domination of nature, of purposive
rational control over unresisting natural processes. This allows
him now, as already in the *Dialectic of Enlightenment,* to conceive
the exercise of social domination as a process in which the
macro-subject of the centralized administrative apparatus influences the members of society through the means of direct
and indirect force in order to make them tractable for the
purposes of its global plan.

The conceptual model of the domination of nature, which
remained unchanged, allows Adorno to ignore without the
slightest reservation those problems that, in classical Marxism,
were posed under the rubric of ideology and, in the contemporary Marxism influenced by Gramsci, were brought into the
open in the concept of social consensus. Since Adorno, under
the conceptual sway which the *Dialectic of Enlightenment* held
over him until the end, conceives of the modes of integration
in late-capitalist societies fundamentally as a one-sided relation
of social domination, he can generally overlook the question
concerning the latent mechanisms that allow individuals to

assent to an established structure of privileges. Although the altered political reality in postwar Germany should have convinced him of the urgency of investigating the institutional conditions for the formation of social consensus, he directed the gaze of his theory solely to the manipulative techniques and psychic presuppositions of a pressure toward conformity exercised from above. With regard to the dominated individuals, this one-sided concept of domination admittedly leads to a further conclusion: Just as he implicitly views the dominant side of social control according to the model of the subject exercising control over natural processes, so must Adorno consequently interpret the subordinate side according to the model of a nonintentional, merely reactive life process. As in the *Dialectic of Enlightenment,* he is also forced by the underlying model of domination to treat the oppressed individual as a passive victim of the techniques of domination. Along with the possibility of a social consensus that normatively supports an established system of social inequalities, Adorno had to take issue with its counterpart: the possibility of social struggle, as the early Horkheimer put it. He was thereby able to keep his social analysis free of the problems that are forced upon Marxist-oriented social research by the necessity of analyzing the potential for social resistance.

Adorno remained so captured by the concept of the domination of nature throughout his life that, in his analysis of the modes of integration in late-capitalist societies, he falls into a social-theoretic reductionsism that simply passes over the level of the cultural accomplishments of social groups, the sphere of social action in general, and thus is confined to the two poles of "individual and organization."[58] The wrong track of his social theory announced therein culminates in the paradoxical attempt in his later sociological writings to gradually deny within the medium of social-scientific analysis the possibility of a distinct social science. Since, with the political-administrative undermining of the market sphere, the medium of social mediation between the economic system of reproduction and individual acting subjects seems to be destroyed at every level, an independent object domain for a critical social science no longer emerges. As has been shown, this conclusion arises from the conceptual impossibility of a social theory fixated on the civilizing process of the domination of nature being able to comprehend systematically another dimension of social action alongside the sphere of the market. However, Adorno made this necessity into the virtue of a critical theory that no longer permitted a third dimension between a systems analysis suited to the techniques of administrative domination and a psycho-analysis fitted to the fate of individual instincts. It may be that, as in a distorted image, the error of Marxist social analysis in general during this century is reflected in such a displacement of sociology. For this analysis has selected and designed con-cepts in such a way that the fundamental category of social action, the dimension of the social, can no longer be discerned between a hypostatized system of economic reproduction and a complementary sphere of individual socialization.

II

The Rediscovery of the Social:
Foucault and Habermas

The history of critical theory from its beginnings with Hork-heimer to the later philosophy of Adorno is characterized by a conspicuous omission: Neither Horkheimer's original project for the Institute nor Adorno's fragmentary social theory proved capable of comprehending the mode of the *social* organization of societies. The early Horkheimer overlooked the entire spectrum of everyday cultural action since a reductionistic philosophy of history prohibited him at a conceptual level from developing any other dimension of action than social labor. Since he was compelled to leave the constructive role of social action out of view, he could only place the model of economic reproduction directly alongside the psychoanalytic model of the socialization of individual drives and integrate the two in an ultimately functionalistic model of society. The framework of an interdisciplinary research program, as it was still formulated for the Institute by Horkheimer in the 1930s on the basis of this reductionistic model of society, was of course completely abandoned with the definitive turn to the philosophy of history that critical theory took in the *Dialectic of Enlightenment* under the weight of fascism. From there on, the philosophy of history within critical theory remains one-sidedly concentrated on social labor. Through a kind of normative inversion, it is interpreted as an act of the original domination of nature and is, to a certain extent, regarded as the basis for a process of the decay of civilization that culminates in the totalitarian rule of fascism. The *Dialectic of Enlightenment* reveals the inner-psychic and social consequences that result from the species-wide advance to an instrumental control over natural processes. Forms of social domination now appear as the social spinoff of the activity of the control of nature, in which, in a metaphorical analogy to an instrumentalized nature, oppressed subjects are viewed as passive victims.

This basic model of the philosophy of history also does not permit a proper conceptualization of the organizational mode of societies, since it conceives of processes within society as a whole as facsimiles of processes of the control of nature. It also completely abandons the project of an interdisciplinary social analysis, which had held such a prominent position in Hork-heimer's original program. Horkheimer and Adorno now present the philosophical-historical critique of the domination of nature so generally that it implicates every form of scientific knowledge (even social-scientific research) as a cognitive aspect of the reifying dynamic of civilization. They are thus compelled to free critical social theory from its ties with the empirical sciences and make it once more the sole responsibility of philosophy. This resignative turn is reflected in the methodological structure that critical theory assumes in Adorno writings after the war. Empirically oriented social science acquires the function of merely confirming the picture of a totally integrated society that is tacitly presupposed in the specific domains of the critique of domination, namely, the projects of a philosophical critique of the concept and a philosophical aesthetics. Adorno pursues this task in a series of sociological essays that investigate, under the title "the end of mediation," the administrative mechanisms that forcefully integrate social life in late capitalism by exploiting the subject's loss of identity. In the end, however, critical theory seems to have renounced the theoretical possibility of determining whether, and to what degree, social groups actively participate in the integration of society.

A conception of critical theory that is connected to the disciplines of political economy and psychoanalysis in a merely external manner loses sight of the everyday cultural action of social groups in the same way that a psychoanalytically supported concept of the totally administered society loses sight of the consensual basis of administrative domination. Both ignore the the cognitive and moral synthetic accomplishments of which social groups are capable through the cooperative interpretive efforts of their members. The conceptual model, guided by a philosophy of history, of the social domination of nature is in both cases extended by a psychoanalytic theory of socialization, but not burst asunder. It only shifts the perspective to the inner relations of society. Processes of the production of horizons of orientation within groups are as unrecognizable as the everday conflicts that result from the opposing moral convictions of different groups. Insofar as behavioral patterns required by the economy and the state are, under the guidance of socialization processes, anchored directly in the needs of individuals, what thus emerges is only the simple view that late-capitalist societies are in general reproduced independent of the communicatively acquired norms of action of their members.

In Horkheimer's programmatic sketch of critical social research this takes the form of a latent functionalism, to which Horkheimer's own model of society is finally reduced as a result of the abridgement of his concept of culture to a theory of institutions. In Adorno's later social theory it is expressed in the concept of total domination (which remained unchanged from his analysis of fascism) that completely ignores the entire dimension of social action and is committed to the idea of an administrative manipulation of psychically weakened members of society. Horkheimer's original project and Adorno's late social theory define the beginning and the end of the classical period of critical theory, which could never find a productive access to the social sciences since under the preconception of a one-sided philosophy of history it could not provide any room for the analysis of social action. In the place of the sociological question concerning the modes of social integration and social conflict there appeared the question concerning the reciprocal influence of individual psychic drives and economic reproduction—that is, the possible rapprochement of psychoanalysis and the analysis of the economic system.

This incapacity for posing the problem in a sociologically fruitful way became the unmistakable sign of the tradition of critical theory that appeared first in Horkheimer's inaugural address and ended in the resignative philosophy of Adorno's later period. Of course, important trends for the solution of aesthetic and philosophical problems have now emerged from this tradition.[1] But in the field of critical social science these authors were not able to produce a similar effect. To be sure, Horkheimer's writings and Adorno's entire corpus have been the objects of distinguished interpretive efforts,[2] but for use as a theoretical tool in the analysis of late-capitalist societies one finds their theories unmodified only among close-minded epigones. In the West German discussion, however, the Frankfurt School has so steadfastly monopolized the self-interpretation of a critical social theory that it has impeded a productive appropriation of alternative traditions for a long time. This is especially evident in its wide-ranging critique of positivism, which went beyond an objectivistic theory of science and beyond American pragmatism to include systems theory and Durkheim's sociology and which thus significantly hindered an unbiased exchange with the American and French sociological traditions.[3] It is also evident in its one-sided concept of culture, tailored initially to institutions directly involved in socialization and ultimately only to those connected with aesthetic production, which thus blocked the reception of those traditions in the sociology of culture (such as English cultural history and research on the working class) that employ categories open to the cultural phenomena visibly preserved in the social life of specific groups.[4]

The obstacles encountered by the attempt at a nondogmatic continuation of critical social theory could be overcome only after basic theoretical concepts that were able to replace the philosophical-historical concept of the domination of nature that characterized the tradition represented by Horkheimer and Adorno were found. The unprofitable dualism of psychology and economics, to which the Frankfurt School remained tied in all phases of its development, could no longer be effectively conquered from within in basic agreement with its guiding conceptual model, but only by a new theoretical framework that promised to take the *uniqueness of the social* seriously in a different way.

In the 1960s and the 1970s, attempts at such a change of orientation within the context of a critical social theory obviously develop primarily out of two positions that alone seem to have renounced the philosophical-historical model of the domination of nature while still attempting to answer the central question, for Marxism as well as for critical theory, concerning the mode of domination and the form of integration in late-capitalist societies. The social theory of Michel Foucault and that of Jürgen Habermas are today viewed as competing schools of thought, each of which continues Adorno's critical theory.[5] They share the goal of replacing the picture that portrays society as the result, in whatever way, of the cognitive achievements of a species-subject that acts instrumentally with a theoretical model that begins with a definition of social action. Of course, the joint dismissal of a philosophical concept of labor that for so long limited access to the domain of the social for critical theory is also the only common denominator of the social theories of Foucault and Habermas, since they gain access to the field of social action from completely opposite sides.

Foucault's social theory initially develops out of the context of a structuralist critique of traditions in the human sciences indebted to the philosophy of the subject.[6] The goal of decoding forms of social knowledge as textual edifices without a subject defines the first phase of his theoretical project (chapter 4). Only when Foucault is first able to overcome the paradoxes of such a program is the domain of the social opened up to him as a network of strategic actions. A model of strategic action, as I would like to show, is the theoretical core of the theory of power taken up by Foucault in the second phase of his work (chapter 5). Nevertheless, the attempt to construct a social theory solely on the foundation of a concept of "social struggle" leads to easily demonstrable difficulties that force Foucault, in the historical investigations guided by his theory of power, to yield to a systems-theoretic model. From this perspective Foucault's social theory can finally be represented as a "systems-theoretic" solution to the *Dialectic of Enlightenment* (chapter 6). By contrast, as I subsequently would like to show, Habermas' social theory can be broadly conceived as a "communication-theoretic transformation" of the *Dialectic of Enlightenment*.

Foucault's Historical Analysis of Discourse: The Paradoxes of a Semiological Approach to the History of Knowledge

Foucault stands within the tradition of the Durkheimian school, at least to the extent that he accords ethnology a privileged position among the human sciences. To be sure, it does not occupy this special role because, as a discipline complementing sociology, it investigates the modes of integration of primitive societies and thus provides an empirical basis for a knowledge that can be contrasted to the study of industrially developed societies.[1] Foucault grants ethnology a methodologically privileged status for different reasons than Durkheim. This status is justified for him by the fact that ethnology does not simply explore the historically evolved regions of human knowledge, but seeks to comprehend all the unconscious decisions and formations of norms which first make culturally possible the cognitive self-understanding of humans. Ethnology is distinguished from the older human sciences [*Geisteswissenschaften*] as well from the newer social sciences through the insight that the common object of social-scientific knowledge—that is, the human subject—is not something self-evidently given, but is something that is first produced through the cognitive and normative codifications of a culture. Ethnology understands more deeply, so to speak, than other disciplines, since it makes conscious the general cultural presuppositions of scientific knowledge. This allows it to stand out from the canon of the remaining human sciences as a theory of the "cultural unconscious" and to fulfill a role comparable only to that of psychoanalysis. Foucault concludes *The Order of Things* with this pointed characterization of the methodological similarities between ethnology and psychoanalysis. At the conclusion to an investigation which has historically reconstructed, in the form of an "archaeology," the cultural epistemic conditions for the origin of the modern human sciences, the scientific knowledge contained in these two disciplines is supposed to signal the end of the epoch of the human sciences, since they have called into question the self-assuredness of humanity from two sides:

Ethnology, like psychoanalysis, questions not man himself, as he appears in the human sciences, but the region that makes possible knowledge about man in general; like psychoanalysis, it spans the whole field of that knowledge in a movement that tends to reach its boundaries. . . . Ethnology is situated within the particular relation that the Western *ratio* establishes with all other cultures; and from that starting-point it avoids the representations that men in any civilization may give themselves of themselves, of their life, of their needs, of the significations laid down in their language; and it sees emerging behind those representations the norms by which men perform the functions of life, although they reject their immediate pressure, the rules through which they experience and maintain their needs, the systems against the background of which all signification is given to them. The privilege of ethnology and psychoanalysis, the reason for their profound kinship and symmetry, must not be sought, therefore, in some common concern to pierce the profound enigma, the most secret part of human nature; in fact, what illuminates the space of their discourse is much more the historical *a priori* of all the sciences of man—those great caesuras, furrows, and dividing-lines which traced man's outline in the Western *episteme* and made him a possible area of knowledge.[2]

Foucault obviously has in mind the structural anthropology of Claude Lévi-Strauss when he introduces ethnology as a "counterscience" that is directed toward a system of rules that unconsciously determines human action and thus indirectly problematizes the naive trust in the objects of the human sciences. It was Lévi-Strauss who imputed to the investigation of archaic societies a scientific procedure that initially comprehended the ethnologically interesting phenomena of marital behavior or the narration of myths linguistically as a self-contained sign system, then, in a second step, reduced this to its respectively smallest elements of information, and finally, in the reconstruction of their specific rules of combination, exposed a piece of the unconscious logic of a culture.[3] Here, however, it is not so much the methodological characterization of ethnology as a science of the "cultural unconscious" that is of interest—though even this is not obvious and is today, at least in the form given to it by Lévi-Strauss, contested.[4] What is surprising is that, without perceiving any difficulties, Foucault extracts ethnology from its substantive connection with primitive civilizations and presents it as a universal science of the "system of a given culture." Ethnology is no longer a theory of cultures with writing, however it might be presented; it is a theory of the unconscious presuppositions of thought and normative systems of any possible culture in such a general sense that even Foucault's own project of an archaelogy of the modern human sciences seems to fall under it. This encourages the suspicion that in the methodological sketch of ethnology Foucault outlines the self-understanding of his own research activity. If this is correct, *The Order of Things* concludes with a chapter that presents the procedure of that discipline on whose methodological basis it operates from the beginning as the history of science.

Insofar as the final chapter of *The Order of Things* is not misleading, Foucault's social theory initially appears with the understanding that it is a science like ethnology. At first glance this is paradoxical. For in his three large investigations from the 1960s—*Madness and Civilization, The Birth of the Clinic,* and *The Order of Things*—Foucault works out the basic features of a theory of European modernity in the form of a historical reconstruction of the systems of knowledge culturally determining it. How is this "history of science" period of his work, which marks the end of a phase including literary criticism and the history of psychology[5] and which only later (in the metatheoretical investigations in *The Archaeology of Knowledge* and "The Order of Discourse") receives a methodological basis, supposed to be brought under the unifying title of an "ethnology" if its analyses apply primarily to those cultural forms of orientation that have integrated societies of enlightened Europe since the end of the eighteenth century? The task Foucault assigns to his theory of society is apparently in conflict with the understanding he has of his own science. Within it ethnology not only assumes the central role of a counterscience that itself shakes the so-far-uncontested confidence of the human sciences, but ethnology is at the same time the theoretical discipline that he seems to associate with his own investigations. Foucault thus claims for the scientific-historical analysis of the very culture to which he himself belongs a discipline whose theoretical trait is marked by the fact that it was developed in the analysis of foreign cultures. In order to expose the aim of a theory of the European forms of knowledge, he makes use of the title of a science that originally arose in connection with the analysis of non-European civilizations.

This initial paradox in Foucault's writings disappears as soon as we understand the basic social-philosophical idea that, so to speak, provides the underlying motivation of his earlier work. The literary experiences of the postsurrealist novel as well as the theoretical motifs of social-scientific structuralism are expressed in it. It is the goal of an artificial distantiation from its own culture that, in an interview with Paolo Caruso, allows Foucault to confer the title "ethnology" on his scientific-historical investigations:

One could define it [Foucault's research project—A.H.] as an analysis of the facts of civilization that characterize our culture, and thus it would be a matter of something like an ethnology of the culture to which we belong. I actually attempt to place myself outside the culture to which we belong in order to analyze its formal conditions for the purpose of, so to speak, achieving its critique; not, however, in order to devalue its accomplishments, but rather to see how they actually arose. By analyzing the conditions of our rationality, I also call into question our language, my language, whose origins I am analyzing.[6]

If Foucault regards the unique feature of his historical research as the analysis of the elementary components of his own Western European culture "from outside," then the disciplinary title he selects for his investigations becomes plausible. Ethnology is that discipline within the social sciences to which, according to its theoretical origins, falls the task of investigating, apart from the coordinated horizon of understanding characterizing its own scientific culture, the culture of an archaic civilization which is foreign to it. The methodological difficulties which are connected to a scientific work of this sort,

since it must be able to bridge the differences between culturally specific conceptions of reality in order to be able to analyze
the unfamiliar life context at all, are present in the history of
ethnology from the outset. Foucault now uses the perspective
of the unique constellation in which ethnology is presented as
science to explicate the specific claim that emerges with his own
theory of society: that it observes the "facts of civilization" of
European culture from the same "external" position that ethnology also necessarily adopts when investigating the culture
of a civilization previously unknown to it. Foucault, who in
terms of his theoretical development is a historian of science,
understands by "facts of civilization" primarily the systems of
knowledge that determine the culture of a society. He comprehends historically, as products of the changes of the nineteenth
century, those systems of cultural knowledge that shape the
face of European modernity. The attempt to analyze the cultural systems of knowledge solely from the perspective of an
external observer constitutes the unique contribution and the
particular attraction of Foucault's original social theory.

The theoretical advantage that Foucault promises from this
sort of attempt is easy to discern: The elementary components
of a cultural life-context are supposed to be able to appear to
an equal extent unbiased and raw, because they are observed
from the perspective of a science foreign to it. The peculiarity
of a culture is first revealed to us just to the extent to which
we step outside its initially intelligible horizon of experience
and thus learn to take up the viewpoint, so to speak, of an
estranged observer. Of course, Foucault places on himself a
substantial burden of proof with the claim that his own social
theory takes up this perspective external to its own culture.
That is, he must be able to show how sociological research in
connection with an investigation of its own cultural context is
supposed to be capable of such a perceptual estrangement,
since in its own understanding of reality, in its conceptual
framework and its logical convictions, it is initially so closely
bound up with the cultural context to be examined. The question can be avoided only if it is assumed that within a society
sociology must in principle recapitulate the scientific results
that ethnology should supply when it is confronted by a society

unknown to it. Those sociological theories that begin with such premises are convinced that, within one and the same society, social groups have formed such different interpretations of reality and everyday experiences that they stand opposed to one another as if to foreign or strange cultures. Under this theoretical assumption, which Foucault certainly does not share, the research strategy recently proposed in English sociology of culture with the project of an ethnography of working-class culture makes sense. Here the problem of sociology is presented in an exact analogy to the problem of ethnology, since it is assumed that from the familiar horizon of its elaborated scientific culture sociological research encounters the "second" culture within its own society in as foreign a manner as ethnological research encounters the culture of archaic civilization.[7]

For Foucault, however, for whom the sociological hypothesis of the existence of different cultural worlds within one society is left completely out of consideration, sociological research does not from the outset necessarily adopt an external perspective with respect to the other environments within the context of social life. As will be shown, the linguistic concept of culture, which he implicitly makes use of in his scientific-historical investigations, is, when he speaks of *"episteme"* or "discourses," presented in such a way that it designates the pattern of thought that determines a society as a whole for a specific period. For this reason Foucault is faced with the task of first showing how it is that his own social theory is methodologically at all able to adopt a foreign or alien perspective toward its own culture, since, like all the other sciences, it is initially bound to the form of thought prevailing in its own time.

This is a problem that is theoretically difficult to solve. For in order to be able to distance itself from its own culture such that it appears just as any other culture, methodological operations are required that purge the specific theoretical language so thoroughly of any traces of the culturally coordinated form of thought that it acquires, so to speak, a neutral character. Foucault thus ought rightly to claim for his social theory the perspective of an observer who has become alienated from his own culture only if he is able to show how it is gradually able to free itself from the traditional context of its scientific culture and thus actually adopt a neutral position with respect to it. This undertaking allows the guiding methodological theme and the social-philosophical point of Foucault's original approach to emerge. Through an act of conceptual self-purification, social theory must free itself from all modes of thought belonging to the culture which is to be investigated in order to be able to achieve with respect to it the distanced perspective of an ethnology. From this position the specific function that a critique of the tradition of the philosophy of reflection assumes for Foucault can be seen, and the particular value that the adoption of structuralist basic assumptions occupies for him can also be surmised.

Foucault may have originally received the impetus for the idea of an ethnology of one's own culture from literary texts. In a well-known essay dealing with the central motifs of Maurice Blanchot's novels, he summarized the experience that converged in French literary avant-gardism in the phrase "thinking from outside": "This thinking keeps itself outside every subjectivity in order to let its limits stand out from the outside, to announce its end, to let it be dispersed about, and to confirm its final absence."[8] Foucault has in mind such authors as Antoine Artaud, Pierre Klossowski, or even Maurice Blanchot when he speaks of the "disappearance of the subject" in the French literature of his day. To its aesthetically estranged depiction of a world in which the human subject is subjugated to the sexual automatism of his body, the silent laws of his language, or the anonymous sequence of events of the day, there corresponds in the artificial positivism of the "new novel" the picture of a society in which the human is encountered as a being devoid of feeling. Foucault also devotes an essay to this current within French postwar literature in order to show in it the comparable attempt of a literary externalization of reality in a process of events detached from subjective experiences of meaning.[9] Foucault thus attempted to understand both literary tendencies as testimony to an aesthetic estrangement in which actions are displaced from the horizon of meaning of the subject into the objectivity of a sequence of events devoid of meaning. Each segment of a context of social action is presented as a state of affairs that cannot be further interpreted—and thus also from the perspective of an observer who does not rely upon an unreflectively accepted horizon of meaning.

Now, the postsurrealist avant-garde could naturally provide Foucault with little more than the first impetus for the idea of a methodically self-conscious distantiation from one's own culture. But it had obviously also already pointed him in the direction in which he carried forward the attempt at a neutralization of his scientific concepts in order to let his social theory adopt an external perspective removed from its own culture. For Foucault perceives the "opening to a language from which the subject is excluded" as the underlying point of convergence in those literary experiments undertaken in the novels by Blanchot, Klossowski, or Robbe-Grillet.[10] Thereby, in that here the linguistic structure becomes, so to speak, the bearer of action-events, the human individual forfeits the favored position of the action-determining subject attributed to him thus far and becomes the object of an encompassing linguistic event. The human is no longer the experiential center of a course of action which he encounters and oversees, but the arbitrary effect of a network of events out of which he can no longer make sense and which is produced by the rules of language. This is the consequent, though not terribly clear, line of thought to which Foucault's literary-theoretic interpretation leads.[11] He attempts in the domain of social philosophy to make this more precise and to render it fruitful for the purpose of an ethnologically oriented social theory. With the insight that individual subjects are themselves subordinated to encompassing linguistic rules, he is apparently given the key that allows for the detached observation of European culture.

Foucault indirectly gathers from the novels with which he deals an indication of the model of thought that shapes the self-understanding of European modernity and thus becomes the main feature of that culture from which his own social theory methodically attempts to distance itself. If the experiments of the literary avant-garde commonly point to an aesthetic disclosure of the entanglement of the subject within an event that transcends its individual horizon of meaning, then the opposite of that experience—that is, the supposition of a subject with the power of action—is at the center of the model of thought in the prevailing culture. A theoretical distance is to be gained from this culture in order to be able to place social analysis in an "external" position comparable to that of avant-garde literature. This line of argument already basically reveals the starting point and the solution of the methical operation by means of which Foucault attempts to extract his social theory from the conceptual horizon of its own culture and put it in the position of an estranged observer. The starting point of the methical operation lies in the depiction and critique of the concept of the subject that dominates the tradition of European thought. According to this concept the human individual attains its individuality by virtue of the fact that it knows itself to be objectified in action and, at the same time, returns to itself by reflecting upon its objectifications. In an important chapter in *The Order of Things* Foucault pursues this model of theory in the tradition of the philosophy of reflection from its historical origins in the transition from the eighteenth to the nineteenth century, and in the equally central introduction to *The Archaeology of Knowledge* he investigates its implications for the theory of history.[12] Here the first step in the project of a methical neutralization of social theory assumes the form of a critique of traditional philosophy of history. Consequently, in its place a social-scientific model emerges that has rid itself of all the conceptual impurities of the theoretical tradition of the philosophy of reflection. Foucault undertakes the task of sketching out the conceptual framework of such a neutralized social theory in the complex line of argument in *The Archaeology of Knowledge*. The second step in the project of a methical neutralization of social theory is found here in the construction of a new theoretical language. Foucault thus allows himself to be led by the structuralist currents of French historical and social sciences while developing a system of basic concepts that operates without any reference to the activities of a conscious subject and thus is able to encounter the European tradition of thought as something alien or foreign.

Foucault initially clarifies the theoretical character of the concept of the subject in the philosophy of reflection only at the level of the history of science. In *The Order of Things* he locates the origin of European modernity, which he considers to have produced the form of thought represented in the philosophy of the subject, at the end of the eighteenth century.[13] His hypothesis is that on the threshold of the nineteenth century the classical world of representation, which was convinced that reality was symbolically constituted, began to break down, because the sciences of organic nature and the social world encountered a phenomenal domain of a peculiar sort—a reality not reducible to its sign function—and the human subject moved directly into the center of the domain of cultural perception. From thence forth in European modernity the human subject took over the central cognitive function that had belonged to language in classical thought because it represented the only mediation between the all-encompassing system of signs and the self-subsisting reality. The human individual can now appear in the place of language since, owing to a transformation of the whole system of knowledge, it suddenly becomes constitutive not only for the subjective side but also for the objective side of knowledge—that is, it becomes the transcendental condition of the possibility of a knowledge directing itself again to empirical man and his world.

Foucault does not distinguish among the various versions of the modern philosophy of the subject any more than do other structuralists. What is alone decisive for him is that under the ontological presuppositions of the newly emerged worldview the human is conceived simultaneously as an active subject in the order of knowledge and as a material element in the order of nature. To that extent he is the point of intersection of both orders and thus the self-knowing middle point of the world. By contrast, the classical worldview (or, as Foucault says, *episteme*) viewed the human individual as a symbolically endowed being but not as a part of the internally stable order of nature, so that under its ontological presuppositions such an privileged position of man, as "subjugated sovereign" or "observed observer," was not conceptually possible:

The modern themes of an individual who lives, speaks, and works in accordance with the laws of an economics, a philology, and a biology, but who also, by a sort of internal torsion and overlapping, has acquired the right, through the interplay of those very laws, to know them and to subject them to total clarification—all these themes so familiar to us today and linked to the existence of the 'human sciences' are excluded by Classical thought: it was not possible at that time that there should arise, on the boundary of the world, the strange stature of a being whose nature (that which determines it, contains it, and has traversed it from the beginning of time) is to know nature, and itself, in consequence, as a natural being.[14]

In the system of knowledge of European modernity the human subject inhabits the double role of a subject and an object of knowledge since he can know himself as a part of that natural reality to which, in knowing, he devotes himself. Thus, from now on, those domains of reality (such as economic wealth or cultural linguistic forms) that previously could have been taken seriously only in their function as signs appear as historical modes of being [*Daseinswesen*] of humans. The world now becomes divisible into just as many dimensions as there are functions for human self-realization to fulfill. This is the basic idea of the human sciences. Their epistemological justification relates to the idea that they represent those instruments of historical-empirical research activity through which humans discover the regularities of their own mode of existence. In the argumentative framework of *The Order of Things,* an analysis of the internal scientific consequences of the epistemological break between the classical and the modern *episteme* now stands in the forefront. Foucault is primarily interested in the dispersion of the basic ideas of the philosophy of the subject among the various branches of the sciences that arose at the same time as the new system of thought. His historical reconstruction of the knowledge systems of European modernity is therefore primarily a descriptive analysis of the internal construction of those scientific disciplines that, with the cognitive impetus of the new concept of the subject, were able to emerge since the beginning of the nineteenth century.

Of course, in the exposition of his (not uncontested)[15] table of the human sciences Foucault also takes into consideration immanent problems. He uncovers the major difficulties that result for the new disciplines of research from the fact that in the advancing self-reflection of the subject they encounter not only the preconditions of human existence, which are independent of consciousness, but also the zones for carrying out individual action, which lie beyond consciousness. However, just as Foucault does not attempt to explain the historical dissolution of an established worldview according to the problems immanent in the development of science, he does not directly inquire into the immanent validity of the theoretical model in the philosophy of reflection. With the type of history of science that lies at the basis of his investigation in *The Order of Things*, Foucault initially raises only the claim of a descriptive analysis. What should be described are those discontinuous phases in which an epoch-determining model of thought is dissolved through a new revolutionary model of thought that cannot itself be explained according to the immanent constellation of problems within the development of science. In this way, the disparate sciences of an epoch emerge as dependent elements of a unique mode of thought that is itself dependent on a limited number of preliminary conceptual decisions about the condition of reality. This basic idea lets Foucault's early scientific-historical work converge with the self-reflection of analytic theory of science stimulated by Thomas Kuhn's notion of "paradigms" and join with those currents of thought that answer skeptically the old question concerning the possibility of scientific progress by referring to the historical evidence for different styles of rationality. Consequently, Jean Piaget was able earlier to work out the similarity between Foucault's and Kuhn's point of departure, and the significance of Foucault's descriptive history of science for the historical development of analytic theory of science has in the meantime been noticed by its representatives.[16]

Now, each relativist or historicist in the field of the history of science must address the question as to which type of scientific rationality he himself uses to analyze and classify the disparate types of scientific rationality. Foucault is compelled to leave behind the descriptive framework of his theory in order to be able to give an answer to this question. This occurs in *The Archaeology of Knowledge* (published in 1969, three years after *The Order of Things*). The argument is directly concerned with the methodological justification of the procedures implicity utilized in the historical investigations into the history of European science. Indirectly, this difficult work attempts, at the level of social philosophy, to purge the concepts employed therein from all elements of a philosophy of the subject and, to that extent, to create the methodological framework for an ethnological analysis of its own culture.

Foucault can no longer avoid debate with competing theoretical positions, and thus, generally, the argumentative evaluation of the culturally predominant patterns of thought, since the method of his own conception could otherwise barely be theoretically justified. He thus opens his methodological discussion with a brief critique of the concept of the subject in the philosophy of reflection which in many respects resembles the argument that Louis Althusser developed first in the collection of essays in *For Marx* and then later, with Etienne Balibar, in *Reading Capital*.[17] For Foucault, as for Althusser, the principal error of the philosophy of reflection is exemplified by its consequences for the concept of history, and this connection is primarily demonstrated in Hegel's philosophy of history. That is, what results from the conceptual strategy of the philosophy of reflection is the necessity of comprehending the whole of history as a product in the same way as the world of objects which human spirit reflexively views as the result of its own objectifications is a product. To the totality of historical events is thus assigned the same producing subject as the world of human experience. The singular subject, which is required for the constitutive activity of producing objects of possible experiences as well as for bringing about historical events, guarantees the unity and thus the continuity of history. The human spirit can retrospectively grasp all events in the course of history as the steps that it must necessarily take in the process of its self-realization.

Hegel's thought serves as the model in connection with which Foucault now also accounts for the post-Hegelian versions of the philosophy of history. He sees them as being bound together by this common reference to a subject, identified with the human spirit, or to a social class, to which all historical

events are imputed as conscious or unconscious externaliza-
tions. In order to be able to defend such a globalizing thesis,
Foucault must of course have removed all the substantive differences that exist between the ontological claim, the methodological supposition, and the purely normative projection of a
unifying subject of history. Only through the resulting abstraction from all post-Hegelian distinctions within the concept of
history[18] is it possible to reduce German historicism and the
Hegelian-Marxist tradition to the same "discourse of the
continuous"[19] and then, as Foucault does, to conceive this as
simply a derivation of Hegel's philosophical-historical thought.
Foucault once again shares with Althusser's critique of historicism the simplifying perspective that permits this reduction.
Here too the idea of historical continuity as the theoretical
correlate to the assumption of a unifying subject of history was
criticized.[20] However, Althusser accounts for the model of history in the philosophy of reflection by referring to the interest
in self-justification of the revolutionary bourgeoisie that, via
the theoretical presupposition of a historically empowered actor, secures for itself its role as a rationally acting subject.[21]
Foucault does not adhere to an ideological-critical account of
this sort. What is particular to his argument is that it derives
the problematic application of basic concepts of the philosophy
of reflection to social processes from the "fear" of "conceiving
of the *Other* in the time of our own thought"[22]:

If the history of thought could remain the locus of uninterrupted
continuities, if it could endlessly forge connexions that no analysis
could undo without abstraction, if it could weave, around everything
that men say and do, obscure syntheses that anticipate for him,
prepare him, lead him endlessly towards his future, it would provide
a privileged shelter for the sovereignty of consciousness. Continuous
history is the indispensable correlative of the founding function of
the subject: the guarantee that everything that has eluded him may
be restored to him; the certainty that time will disperse nothing
without restoring it in a reconstituted unity; the promise that one
day the subject—in the form of historical consciousness—will once
again be able to appropriate, to bring back under his sway, all those
things that are kept at a distance by difference, and find in them
what might be called his abode.[23]

The assumption that leaves the different versions of the history of philosophy convinced of a continuity of history is apparently due to a kind of theoretical projection. The philosophical theories of history transfer to the historical process without any reservation the outcome of the epistemological self-reflection of the ego, the insight into its own constitutive achievement. As a result, they are able to treat it as the product of an identity-maintaining subject. The alien or foreign event of the historical past is conceived as the expressive form of human experience, as the objectification of a self-externalizing spirit, or as the unrecognized product of labor of a social class— in each case, as the production of a human agent. The historically other thereby becomes a familiar part of its own subjectivity and loses it fear-instilling alterity. Even if one does not share its cultural-psychological assumptions, this argument is of interest because it points to the danger of an uncontrolled application of the philosophy of reflection. Its domain of competence is carelessly overstepped as soon as the model of thought of the meaning-constituting ego is projected into social and historical events. That is, the social world then appears as the production of a single conscious subject [*Geistsubjekt*], and the historical process appears as the trace of its permanent self-objectifications. This, in turn, has as its consequence philosophies of history that already presuppose, at an ontological level, a continuous meaning to history, while nevertheless failing to give due weight to the manifold and disparate historical events. Thus the traditional idea of historical continuity, even as it is found in the *Dialectic of Enlightenment* in the negative version of a "logic of disintegration," is in the meantime problematized within an epistemological context and criticized in connection with analytical philosophy of history.[24] Foucault recognizes the theoretical error a philosophy of history makes when it transfers the idea of a "constitutive function of the subject" to social processes. In order to avoid the snares of the philosophical conception, he must keep the basic concepts of his new conception free from taints of the traditional philosophy of reflection. But instead of questioning the singularity of the historical subject, to which the constitutive achievements are assigned, and substituting the more convincing model of a plurality of historical actors, Foucault adopts the opposing approach of an elimination of the concept of the subject in general. He does not question the monological character of the philosophy of reflection, but rather rejects its underlying model of thought generally. This radical conclusion, which becomes very significant for Foucault's goal of an ethnological analysis of society, first emerges, however, when the next step of his critique of the philosophy of history is made clear.

Within Foucault's argument the two concepts of "the document" and "the monument" serve as illustrations for the existence of two competing ways of viewing history. In the concept of "the document" the meaning of written testimony from a time past is examined because of the meaning that is symbolically represented within it. The document preserves the experiential content of a previously existing epoch in written form. It first acquires significance to the extent that it is understood as the objectification of projections of meaning: "The document was always treated as the language of a voice since reduced to silence, its fragile, but possibly decipherable trace."[25] If the document is regarded as a significant system congealed into a text, however, then that also means conceiving it as a form expressing human intentions, however this claim might be further qualified. Foucault abruptly concludes from this that a view of history supported by the interpretation of documents cannot avoid comprehending historical events as the meaningful product of a singular subject. This conclusion is plausible, however, only on the condition that every symbolic expression is regarded as obviously the product of a monological pattern of meaning. Only then can the text retained in a document appear as the objectification of the intention of a unique and collective subject, and the process of history as a kind of diachronic succession of its intentional significant acts. It would be represented otherwise if a meaning, as it is expressed in a historical document, were understood as the result of interaction between at least two subjects. That would lead to the result that a view of history which dealt with the hermeneutic interpretation of documents would not automatically be ensnared in the misunderstandings of a concept of history based in the philosophy of reflection, since it would have reckoned with a plurality of historically active subjects from the outset. Although it would be relevant to the demands of his theory, Foucault does not attend to this distinction. He is thus able to judge the hermeneutic conception of the "document" as an element of a view of history that remains conceptually bound to the metaphysical error of traditional philosophy of history. In opposition to this, he introduces the concept of the "monument" as a means of historical research:

To be brief, then, let us say that history, in its traditional form, undertook to 'memorize' the *monuments* of the past, transform them into *documents*, and lend speech to those traces which, in themselves, are often not verbs, or which say in silence something other than what they actually say; in our time, history is that which transforms *documents* into *monuments*. In that area where, in the past, history deciphered the traces left by men, it now deploys a mass of elements that have to be grouped, made relevant, placed in relation to one another to form totalities.[26]

Foucault has, of course, chosen the concept of the "monument" deliberately. It originates from the field of architectural history, not intellectual history. In contrast to the concept of the "document," it indicates a material and only indirectly symbolic witness to the past, such as a building. Its original form is initially reconstructed through archaeological activity, that is, through the exacting technical labor of uncovering and assembling scattered parts of a building. The success of such an archaeological procedure is tested primarily by the criterion of the functional harmony of the reconstructed edifice and only secondarily with reference to the historical appropriateness of the simultaneously reconstructed structure of meaning.[27] All these associations of meaning occasioned by the concept of the "monument" point to the same conclusion: They are supposed to describe an approach in which the historical tradition is characterized not through the hermeneutic interpretation of contexts of meaning but through the quasi-objectivistic analysis of textual edifices. To the extent that a written document becomes a monument in the eyes of the observer, it loses its symbolically mediated form of expression and becomes the fact, emptied of meaning, of an *oeuvre* composed of textual elements. The theoretician encounters the tradition not as a context of meaningful symbols but as a structure of merely empirically given signs. Foucault must mean this when he construes the task of a renewed history as follows:

> ... not the interpretation of the document, nor the attempt to decide whether it is telling the truth or what is its expressive value, but to work on it from within and to develop it: history now organizes the document, divides it up, distributes it, orders it, arranges it in levels, establishes series, distinguishes between what is relevant and what is not, discovers elements, defines unities, describes relations. The document, then, is no longer for history an inert material through which it tries to reconstitute what men have done or said, the events of which only the trace remains; history is now trying to define within the documentary material itself unities, totalities, series, relations.[28]

As monuments, the documentary traditions of the past do not possess an intentional content. They no longer symbolically constitute an historically buried experience; they are empirically encountered formations of textual elements. As such they do not force the theoretician necessarily to interpret them retrospectively as intentions encoded in a piece of writing; rather, they confront him with the task of ordering and classifying the scattered textual units from a functionalist perspective. Of course, Foucault's methodological proposal, as clear as it thus appears, does not provide a lot to go on. It first acquires contours when it is seen in the context of those arguments with which semiological structuralism responded to the philosophy of consciousness within the phenomenological traditions dominant in France in the 1950s.

The category of the "sign," which goes back to Saussure's linguistics, is the means employed by semiological structuralism to oppose the movement in phenomenological philosophy of consciousness represented primarily by Sartre and also, initially, by Merleau-Ponty.[29] Saussure's insight into language as an endless order of discrete linguistic elements constitutes the point of departure. Language forms a primordial inventory of units marked by internal differences out of which the speaker in the act of speech constructs meaningful sentences. The individual speech act is thus itself dependent upon the semiotic structure of the language employed, that is, the specific ordering of elementary significant units among themselves. This is in principle already the core of the argument that shaped semiological structuralism in its critique of the tradition of the philosophy of consciousness.[30] The target of the critique is the thesis concerning the self-certainty of the ego. If the semantics of meaning depends upon a system of signs that itself constitutes an autonomous entity, then each act of individual meaning is, so to speak, determined by something foreign. Thus, if in the act of self-reflection the ego attempts to turn inward upon its own accomplishments, it is always already subjected to the foreign and largely external order of signs defined merely by difference. The subject is consequently only the fictive author of its meaningful acts; behind its back operates "the strict external algebra"[31] of the sign, which has already provisionally determined the possibility and the means of the pattern of meaning.

From out of this basic idea there arose, during the 1960s in France, the impetus for a number of theoretical attempts to establish at a universal level and in a variety of scientific domains the priority of the system of signs over the meaningful acts of the subject. Alongside the studies in literary criticism,[32] the most prominent examples are Jacques Lacan's psychoanalytic presentation of the basic difference between individual need and the symbolic order[33] and Jacques Derrida's philosophical-historical critique of the category of "self-consciousness."[34] In both cases the guiding theoretical point of view is the idea of a system of linguistic signs to which the meaning-bestowing acts of the subject are subordinated. Foucault also seems to be influenced by the same motifs of semiological structuralism when he programmatically begins *The Archaeology of Knowledge* with the concept of the "monument," for the assumption contained in this concerning the expressive power of historical documents beneath the level characterized by meaningful referents is plausible only if one accepts that the entity of the order of signs—the organizational system of the textual elements as such—generally has a decisive influence upon the self-understanding of historically acting subjects.

The basic motif of *The Archaeology of Knowledge* is thus of semiological origin, as the category of the "monument" already seems to indicate. The dimension of symbolically represented meaning, which a hermeneutically guided interpretation of the historical tradition encounters, is for it not something ultimate but rather something determined by the independent linguistic order of textual elements. Foucault contests the scientific value of interpretations that attempt to derive from written testimony of the past a reference to the experiential content of a historical epoch or the pattern of meaning of a social group. The subjective intentions, which can still be viewed as the source of the objectifications which are to be hermeneutically deciphered, cannot be taken as something primary, since they themselves are subordinate to an order of signs outside them. Humans experience themselves and their environment meaningfully only within the semantic framework of a conceptually ordered world. This linguistic order is not, however, the product of the meaning-bestowing acts of subjects; rather, it is the product of an arbitrary arrangement of linguistic elements. The state of the system in which signs determined solely by mutual differences are located at any one time governs what meaning humans are capable of realizing in their understanding and experience. A hermeneutically oriented view of history that pursues a symbolically represented meaning in the discovered document thus remains in the apparent world of a subject empowered by its own intentions. Only a view of history that perceives the document as a monument to be investigated in terms of the modes of organization of textual elements has consistently enough destroyed the self-deceptions of the subject about itself. Without any illusions, it takes into account that human intentions are, so to speak, composed in the language— foreign to them—of an anonymous system of signs.

The methodical plan Foucault sketches when he critically opposes the concept of the "monument" to the concept of the "document" can be detected in this network of arguments. What becomes clear is that he is not concerned simply with overcoming a concept of history idealized in the philosophy of reflection; he actually attempts to go beyond the horizon of a model of thought in which the cognitive achievement of producing their own experiential world is attributed to human individuals. Foucault does away with the project of testing and correcting the weaknesses in traditional versions of the philosophy of reflection; in a conclusion that is characteristic for semiological structuralism as a whole, he completely replaces them with an opposing model of thought in which the quasi-transcendental function of world-constitution is attributed not to the monological actions of an ego or to the intersubjective interpretive accomplishments of subjects but rather to nonintentional systems of signs. The structure of a neutral order of signs determines the subjectively necessary form of possible experience.[35] If this is the basic assumption of a social theory schooled in semiological structuralism, then its immediate result is another concept of intellectual history. If the cognitive order of the social world is conceived as the product of a subjectless system of signs in Foucault's sense, then human intellectual history can no longer be regarded as a historical process that follows a continuous course of learning or that is generally propelled by the cognitive initiatives of subjects. Since the elementary cognitive operations of human individuals are themselves always caught up in the ontological schematism of an order of rules that precedes them, those rules—which bring the materially arbitrary signs into a specific order—represent the true bearer of intellectual history. The orders of signs synthesized through the anonymous power of rules change not in response to the systematic stimulus of problems in learning but in response to the contingent impetus of historical events. The historical process, once it is viewed without anthropocentric illusions, can also be understood as the discontinuous succession of internally ungrounded orders of signs which force humans into the semantic framework of a particular worldview.

In this rough sense Foucault can place a revised concept of intellectual history at the head of his reflections on the theory of science. The title "archaeology," which corresponds to the concept of the "monument," is meant to signal this characteristic. Terminological hints of Gaston Bachelard's epistemology[36] and of the concept of history associated with the "Annales" school[37] also enter into the formulations that Foucault selects to characterize his new mode of writing history. Once again the view of history found in the philosophy of reflection constitutes the negative contrast for his characterization, this time from the diachronic perspective of a "global history":

> The project of a total history is one that seeks to reconstitute the overall form of a civilization, the principle—material or spiritual—of a society, the significance common to all the phenomena of a period, the law that accounts for their cohesion—what is called metaphorically the 'face' of a period. Such a project is linked to two or three hypotheses; it is supposed that between all the events of a well-defined spatio-temporal area, between all the phenomena of which traces have been found, it must be possible to establish a system of homogeneous relations. . . . it is also supposed that one and the same form of historicity operates upon economic structures, social institutions and customs, the inertia of mental attitudes, technological practice, political behavior, and subjects them all to the same type of transformation; lastly, it is supposed that history itself may be articulated into great units. . . . These are the postulates that are challenged by the new history when it speaks of series, divisions, limits, differences of level, shifts, chronological specificities, particular forms of rehandlings, possible types of relation. This is not because it is trying to obtain a plurality of histories juxtaposed and independent of one another: that of the economy beside that of institutions, and beside these two those of science, religion, or literature; not is it because it is merely trying to discover between these different histories coincidences of dates, or analogies of form and meaning. The problem that now presents itself . . . is to determine what form of relation may be legitimately described between these different series; what vertical system they are capable of forming; what interplay of correlation and dominance exists between them.[38]

Now that this programatic view of the concept of the "monument" and the corresponding concept of history has been clarified in its broad features, one should not, of course, forget that Foucault's methodological project as a whole is indebted to the goal of an ethnological investigation of European civilization. In this sense *The Archaeology of Knowledge* constitutes an ethnology within the field of the history of ideas. For, since the archaeological view of history sees the documented bodies of knowledge of the European tradition as monumental textual structures consisting of pre-intentional linguistic elements, it has apparently taken on the role of the external observer who happens upon the unintelligible bits of writing of a deceased cultural world. This is quite obviously the background meaning that Foucault associates with the title "archaeology."[39] It originates in the fact that a social theory starting out with the basic assumptions of semiological structuralism obviously seems to adopt an external perspective removed from its own society, since in principle it forbids itself hermeneutic access to the symbolic reality of a culture. In Foucault's understanding, the leitmotif of the semiological approach uniquely collapses into the request for an ethnology aimed at its own culture. Its reflection on linguistic theory is at the same time the strategic means employed to place the theory in the position of the external observer.

Only if the epistemological background of *The Archaeology of Knowledge* is kept in mind—if, that is, its argument is also supposed to serve the methodical exercise of a culturally neutral observer's perspective—are the aim and the organizing principle of its reasoning easily discerned. The category of the "monument" and the structuralist concept of history are there only to provide a preliminary sketch of the goal of Foucault's investigation; its proper task first begins when it takes up the "cathartic" work on the concept. Its function is to replace those categories in a historical theory of cultural knowledge whose lineage can be traced to hermeneutics or the philosophy of the subject with terminology that makes do without reference to the meaningful activity of subjects. Foucault makes this goal of his argument unmistakably evident:

In so far as my aim is to define a method of historical analysis freed from the anthropological theme, it is clear that the theory that I am about to outline has a dual relation with the previous studies [*Madness and Civilization, The Birth of the Clinic*, and *The Order of Things*—A.H.]. It is an attempt to formulate, in general terms . . . , the tools that these studies have used or forged for themselves in the course of their work. But, on the other hand, it uses the results already obtained to define a method of analysis purged of all anthropologism.[40]

As soon as the task of *The Archaeology of Knowledge* is defined in this way, the methodological schema it follows in its conceptual labor can also be easily seen. Foucault apparently arranges his procedure according to the methodical model of a two-stage operation that Roland Barthes described as the "structuralist activity."[41] It states that a given material for research should initially be broken down into its smallest elements, and that these are then investigated in terms of their rules of formation. Finally, the newly discovered ordered groups hold out the possibility of reconstructing the unconsciously effective structure of the analyzed object domain. Each part of this two-stage operation of "analysis" and "new arrangement," as Roland Barthes puts it, now shapes Foucault's argument, to the extent that both must be completed before the new conceptual framework and field of tasks for an archaeology of knowledge is fully constituted.

If one disregards for the moment the methodological vagueness in Barthes' procedural proposal, what initially follows from it for Foucault is the task of filtering out from the whole field of the production of cultural knowledge the units that cannot be further analyzed. It is easy to see that this beginning step essentially entails two separate tasks: Before the research material is broken down into the smallest elements defining it, it must be possible to observe it in an unbiased manner, that is, independent of scientifically well-defined typologies. Foucault fulfills the first of these two tasks by means of a process of conceptual bracketing that excludes all those ideas, traditionally tied to the phenomenal domain and to its symbolic expression, that entail conceptual references to the meaningful accomplishments of a subject.[42] This is thus the step in Foucault's argument that, from the viewpoint of the aim of achieving an ethnological observer's perspective, fulfills the task of purifying the concepts to be used of all traces of meaning linked to hermeneutics or to the philosophy of reflection.

The list of the categories from intellectual history which Foucault shows to be dependent upon the incriminated tradition of hermeneutics, and which he thus excludes from his own theoretical language, is extensive, but it is meant only to be indicative. It stretches from the concepts of "tradition" and "evolution" employed in the history of philosophy, which are also suspect within analytic philosophy, of history,[43] to the elementary classificatory concepts of the "*oeuvre*" or the "book," which are difficult to do without even in everyday language. The radical character of Foucault's procedure can be measured by the fact that he also attempts to exclude such ordinary terms from his conceptual framework. If one accepts that even such familiar references to acts of meaning are to be avoided, then it makes sense that these constitute the ideal reference point under which a portion of the totality of all literary expressions are chosen and brought together as an example under the unifying title of the "*oeuvre*":

> But it is at once apparent that such a unity, far from being given immediately, is the result of an operation; that this operation is interpretative (since it deciphers, in the text, the transcription of something that it both conceals and manifests); and that the operation that determines the *opus*, in its unity, and consequently the *oeuvre* itself, will not be the same in the case of the author of *Le Theatre et son Double* (Artaud) and the author of the *Tractatus* (Wittgenstein), and therefore when one speaks of an *oeuvre* in each case one is using the word in a different sense. The *oeuvre* can be regarded neither as an immediate unity, nor as a certain unity, nor as a homogeneous unity.[44]

The association of meaningful acts ascribable to individuals, which Foucault has taken to be just as constitutive for the guiding concepts of the philosophy of history to be overcome as for the central terminology of everyday speech, recurs within to the traditional methods of the human sciences. The method of empathetic understanding and the idea of a meaning-begetting hermeneutic are likewise accompanied by the idea that it is the meaningful performances of a subject that have been objectified in the text which is to be interpreted. Thus, methods of this sort, like the concepts whose preconscious connotative meanings have already been exposed, must also be excluded from the inventory of the theoretical means of an "archaeology" of cultural knowledge.[45]

The hastily drawn up and partially completed bracketing procedure to which Foucault submits the concepts and methods of the discipline of intellectual history is held together by the theoretical hope that, after retreating from all the obstructing means of knowledge, the object domain in view will be revealed, so to speak, in an unadulterated form. According to Foucault, the task of systematic bracketing is so constituted that it delegitimates the traditional reference system of intellectual history in order then to be able to lift this like a veil from the reality of symbolic states of affairs existing in themselves. As a result, the research material that is to be investigated in cultural history then appears neutral from the observer's perspective:

Once these immediate forms of continuity [that is, the theoretical suppositions of a hermeneutic philosophy of history—A.H.] are suspended, an entire field is set free. A vast field, but one that can be defined nonetheless: this field is made up of the totality of all effective statements (whether spoken or written), in their dispersion as events and in the occurrence that is proper to them. Before approaching, with any degree of certainty, a science, or novels, or political speeches, or the *oeuvre* of an author, or even a single book, the material with which one is dealing is, in its raw, neutral state, a population of events in the space of discourse in general. One is led therefore to the project of a *pure description of discursive events* as the horizon for the search for the unities that form within it.[46]

Seen epistemologically, this precritical line of thought already contains not only Foucault's answer to the second problem that is presented with the task of analyzing the research material into elementary units but also a decisive indication of his solution to the difficulty that is connected with the subsequent methodological step toward a new classification of the units removed from their former contexts. For by "effective statements" are obviously meant those smallest components of which the entire field of cultural knowledge as such is supposed to consist, and by the concept of "discourse" those formations are briefly mentioned into which, from the archaeological perspective, the initially isolated elements are supposed to be brought together again.

Considered once more against the background of Roland Barthes's methodological plan, after the conclusion of the procedure of conceptual bracketing, Foucault is confronted with the task of analyzing into its smallest elements the research material that has now been freed from misleading representational associations. Since, however, he seems to be convinced in a strangely naive manner that after a complete separation from all hermeneutic barriers to knowledge the object is revealed in an unveiled form (that is, as it is in itself apart from knowledge), he can simply set aside this methodological step. The analytic activity that Roland Barthes has in mind is, for

Foucault, immediately connected with the procedure of bracketing, since in it the domain of phenomena to be investigated is not only freed from all false representations but is also disclosed in its raw and unadulterated existence. Foucault represents the reality that remains after the removal of the ordering concepts of the human sciences as a chaotic heap of linguistic statements, a huge quantity of "discursive events." These form the raw material of which the entire field of cultural knowledge is then shown to consist once it is observed from the archaeological viewpoint.

However, the definition of what he wants included under the term "statement" (*enoncé*) gives rise to a difficulty for Foucault. In order to perceive the difficulty that he necessarily runs up against, it is necessary to recall once again the central theoretical role that this concept holds in *The Archaeology of Knowledge*. The investigation sets for itself the exacting goal of developing the conceptual framework for a theory of cultural knowledge that views its object as a hermeneutically indecipherable and objectively given text. In order to make good on this claim, which stems from the basic intention of an ethnology of his own culture, Foucault makes use of conceptual initiatives of semiological structuralism. The basic thought thus outlined, which is finally supposed to allow for an objective analysis of texts, is admittedly of only limited use for Foucault. He claims to be able to explain not isolated acts of meaning whose elementary units are the words of a linguistic system, but such complex symbolic structures as systems of knowledge whose elementary units are groups of words (that is, assertions about states of affairs). Thus, whereas semiological structuralism orients its argument initially to the linguistic level of words alone, Foucault is compelled to extend the same argument to the level of sentences, since only on this level can the elementary components of complexes of ideas and modes of thought be found. He is consequently oriented toward a conceptual equivalent to the semiological concept of the sign, which like the sign is uniquely defined by its position in a pre-significant system of rules but which, in contrast to the sign, also lies above the level of words at the level of propositional expressions—the "statement" is supposed to represent such a specific linguistic unit.

The contradictory-sounding formulations needed to describe the task assigned to the concept of the "statement" already make clear the entire difficulty in which Foucault finds himself: On the one hand, Foucault is unable to avoid understanding the statement, in a first approximation, as an in-principle-meaningful combination of words. The statement is a component in the use of language or speech, no longer a component of language. In the statement the significant elements of a linguistic system are arranged from the viewpoint of establishing a validity claim. A constitutive role is thus imputed to the subject insofar as it alone is able to bring the word units together meaningfully for the purpose of an assertion: "Generally speaking, it would seem, at first sight at least, that the subject of the statement is precisely he who has produced the various elements, with the intention of conveying meaning."[47] Moreover, at the moment in which it appears in speech with the aim of raising a validity claim with an intentional reference, the meaning of the sign is no longer determined solely by its position in the semiological system of relations; it is also determined by its referential relation to an asserted state of affairs. At any rate, Foucault seems to concede just this: "A series of signs will become a statement on the condition that it possesses a specific relation to 'something else'. . . ."[48] As can easily be seen, both claims violate the theoretical presuppositions with which semiological structuralism argues, for a statement can then no longer be regarded as a mere element of an autonomous entity consisting of relations of internal dependency if it is conceived as a subjectively intended and referentially related combination of words. As soon as we understand the statement as a linguistic unit that is filled by an intended meaning, we can no longer analyze it is connection with its position in a pre-significant relational structure; we can analyze it only in connection with the intended state of affairs. Foucault seems to be aware of the danger that threatens his argument as a result of this reference to the individual meaning-intention and the state of affairs asserted by a statement. As if to avoid the risk of sounding like the philosophy of the subject, he now sets out to work against all that he has just offered in his definition of the "statement," and thus also again to deny the characteristics of a meaningful combination of words.

It is not easy, however, to follow the proposals for a definition that Foucault sets out with the aim of providing the statement with a status comparable to the semiological concept of the sign. Toward this end he first separates it from the grammatical unit of the sentence, the logical unit of the proposition, and the pragmatic unit of the speech act. The criteria that are here respectively introduced for limiting the elementary units of speech do not apply to the statement because it as a whole permits a greater possible number of legitimate connections between signs. According to Foucault, "a graph, a growth curve, an age pyramid, a distribution cloud are all statements."[49] Although it should not be difficult to recognize propositions formally gathered in statistical tables or graphic representations, he cites such cases to demonstrate the unsuitability of the proposed definitions of "statements" found within linguistic analysis. In their place he finally offers a conceptual characterization that sees the only element common to all conceivable cases of statements as lying in the common function of bestowing "existence" upon a combination of signs. His concluding definition is thus correspondingly vague: "The statement is not therefore a structure (that is, a group of relations between variable elements, thus authorizing a possibly infinite number of concrete models); it is a function of existence that properly belongs to signs and on the basis of which one may then decide, through analysis or intuition, whether or not they 'make sense,' according to what rule they follow one another or are juxtaposed, of what they are the sign, and what sort of act is carried out by their formulation (oral or written)."[50]

If it is only subsequently that one is supposed to be able to decide if a statement "makes sense," then neither the individual meaning-intention nor the referential relation to a state of affairs belongs to its defining characteristics. Rather, every symbolic utterance that represents a combination of at least two words or signs can claim to be a "statement." A few pages earlier, however, Foucault had himself rejected such an unserviceable definition: "Let us look at the example again: the keyboard of a typewriter is not a statement; but the same series of letters, A, Z, E, R, T, listed in a typewriting manual, is the statement of the alphabetical order adopted by French typewriters."[51]

This line of thought provides a good illustration of why we take a series of signs or words for a statement the moment we can infer that an intended reference or assertion is connected to it. In an instruction manual this intended meaning is surely noted specifically by virtue of an illocutionary element; thus the series of letters in such a case is the propositional element of a grammatically constructed or symbolically abbreviated sentence. However, Foucault does not take seriously the implications of his own example. It would have required explicitly taking into account the fact that we can comprehend a symbolic utterance as a statement when an intended meaning can be imputed to it. The identification of a textual element or a symbol as a statement is connected to a hermeneutic presupposition. From the outset we must have already attributed to it the feature of a meaningful and intentional utterance before we can examine the content of the statement. The attempt at a quasi-semiological definition of the "statement" must fail.[52] Either the statement is free from any intended meaning, in which case it is no longer to be distinguished from an arbitrary combination of signs, or it is characterized as a symbolic relation precisely by virtue of an intended meaning, in which case it can only be understood with a view to the intended state of affairs and is no longer presignificant.

To the extent that he wants to avoid any reference to the intentions of speaking subjects, Foucault does not allow himself to take up properly a definition of the "statement." He nevertheless undertakes the attempt and thus ends up in the plain contradiction of wanting to introduce the statement throughout as the basic element of meaning in language use, but needing to avoid completely the concept of meaning itself. This leads him astray into the rather useless conclusion of representing the statement as an "existence function of the sign." According to this conceptual arrangement, the statement is the linguistic medium in which the sign is able to emerge from the domain of mere possibility in a linguistic system and enter into the real domain of language use. The different types of linguistic utterances, including as well the "sentence" or "proposition" analyzed in traditional linguistics, thus fulfill only the one common function of letting the sign appear socially in the form of speech. The statement is, so to speak, the sign as it appears socially in action. As such it partakes of the anonymity of an unintentional linguistic structure. Foucault can now conclude from this that, rather than being produced by a speaker, the statement itself first determines the role that a speaker must assume as soon as he makes use of it:

. . . the subject of the statement should not be regarded as identical with the author of the formation—either in substance, or in function. He is not in fact the cause, origin, or starting-point of the phenomenon of the written or spoken articulation of a sentence; nor is it that meaningful intention which, silently anticipating words, orders them like the visible body of its intuitions. . . . It is a particular, vacant place that may in fact be filled by different individuals; but, instead of being defined once and for all, and maintaining itself as such throughout a text, a book, or an *oeuvre,* this place varies. . . . If a proposition, a sentence, a group of signs can be called 'statement', it is not therefore because, one day, someone happened to speak them or put them into some concrete form of writing; it is because the position of the subject can be assigned. To describe a formulation *qua* statement does not consist in analyzing the relations between the author and what he says . . . but in determining what position can and must be occupied by any individual if he is to be the subject of it.[53]

Foucault thus repeats at the level of *parole* or language use the basic semiological idea that individual acts of meaning are subordinate to the independent order of signs. The thesis that this move must justify states that every factually existing statement, to a certain extent, determines as its executive organ the subject corresponding to it. This remains within the spirit of semiological structuralism, but it makes sense only on the basis of that defining artifact of a nonintentional statement which is initially without meaning. Only if the linguistic utterance is regarded, in a way that can barely be reconstructed, as an event which precedes an individual intention to speak does it make sense to place the role of the speaking subject in a unilateral dependency upon the prevailing type of a statement.

As a brief glance at the procedural model proposed by Roland Barthes reminds us, the definition of the "statement," and thus the characterization of the elements at the basis of the entire field of cultural knowledge, constitutes only the first move in the two-stage activity of the structuralist. A second step must expose the anonymous operations of rules of formation by means of which the analytically isolated elements are brought together in empirically observable groups. Consequently Foucault is now faced with the task of analyzing the laws of construction on the basis of which the groups that are effective as systems of cultural knowledge are formed out of the chaotic mass of all existing statements. The symbolic orders which thus newly emerge for view assume the place that in the hermeneutic conception of the history of ideas would have been designated by the traditional classificatory concepts of the "epoch," the "*oeuvre*," or the "book." Foucault calls "discourses" the linguistic units that are revealed in the domain of symbolically represented knowledge, if that domain is viewed at the level of the rules of formation of statements. They are the true theme of his archaeologically estranged history of ideas.

The concept of "discourse" marked a theoretical achievement in Foucault's social analysis from the beginning. It is not only introduced as the appropriate means for a renewed critical theory[54]; it also provides the impetus for working out an independent conception of theory.[55] The attraction of this category, central to Foucault's original approach, is, of course, on the level at which it is theoretically introduced in *The Archaeology of Knowledge,* still barely to be comprehended. Here the concept owes its meaning first of all to the simple conceptual decision to call "discourses" all linguistic systems in which several statements are connected to one another in a rule-governed manner. In any case, this is how the summary passage in which Foucault presents his own use of the concept of discourse is to be understood:

We can now understand the reason for the equivocal meaning of the term *discourse,* which I have used and abused in many different senses: in the most general, and vaguest way, it denoted a group of verbal performances; and by discourse, then, I meant that which was produced (perhaps all that was produced) by the groups of signs. But I also meant a group of acts of formulation, a series of sentences or propositions. Lastly—and it is this meaning that was finally used (together with the first, which served in a provisional capacity)— discourse is constituted by a group of sequences of signs, in so far as they are statements, that is, in so far as they can be assigned particular modalities of existence.[56]

On the assumption that the concept of the "statement" actually possesses the clarity which it would claim, this definition could easily be accepted. If the statement is the elementary unit of knowledge that characterizes the culture of a society, then the systems of empirical statements that arise through the rule-governed combination of several statements are called "discourses." Discourses are systematic connections of statements in time. From this it follows that the order of the discourse can thus first be studied when the rules by which individual statements actually relate to one another become clear. Foucault immediately continues with his definition:

... if I succeed in showing ... that the law of such a series is precisely what I have so far called a *discursive formation,* if I succeed in showing that this discursive formation really is the principle of dispersion and redistribution, not of formulations, not of sentences, not of propositions, but of statements ... , the term discourse can be defined as the group of statements that belong to a single system of formation; thus I shall be able to speak of clinical discourse, economic discourse, the discourse of natural history, psychiatric discourse.[57]

The heavy burden of proof which the concept of discourse assumes must now therefore provide a reconstruction of those rules of formation through which the individual statements are joined into a system. We encountered such anonymously operative rules, upon the correct analysis of which the success of Foucault's project now consequently seems to depend, when in connection with the concept of the "monument" we first attempted to make clear the idea of an archaeological view of history. There we saw that Foucault, in attempting to view the European history of ideas from the standpoint of an external observer, attempted to conceive systems of cultural knowledge as subjectless orders of signs which are formed through the synthesizing effect of anonymous rules. Meanwhile, the relevant framework in which this concept of rule is placed has been further clarified; but now a difficulty appears that is due to the peculiar definition of the "statement." Since in its pure "exteriority" the statement is regarded as a presignificative fact,[58] the rules according to which individual statements are combined into the unity of a discourse can have their origin neither in a speaking subject nor in an impinging reality. The problem that arises from this for the concept of discourse is obvious: Statements are first supposed to exist as pure linguistic events apart from any referential relation and from any human act of meaning. Thus those statements that are joined in a discourse cannot have their common element in the fact that they presuppose the same individual or collective subject or that they have the same state of affairs as their object. Then what kind of principle of formation is it by virtue of which individual statements are connected in a discourse?

The Archaeology of Knowledge steadfastly struggles with this problem, without definitively resolving it. It raises the nagging questions that finally compel Foucault to abandon completely the framework of a social theory oriented primarily to the linguistic order of cultural knowledge. Foucault is fully conscious of the peculiarity of the problem presented to him in the reconstruction of the formative rules of discourses. He considers false those solutions to his problem that assume that the unifying principle of a discourse lies in a common object to which the statements therein gathered refer, or that assume a reality given independent of discourse. What such an account leaves out of consideration is the fact that a discourse to a certain extent first produces by means of its own terminology the domain of phenomena. That is his central topic. He illustrates this with the example of mental illness:

It would certainly be a mistake to try to discover what could have been said of madness at a particular time by interrogating the being of madness itself, its secret content, its silent, self-enclosed truth; mental illness was constituted by all that was said in all the statements that named it, divided it up, described it, explained it, traced its developments, indicated its various correlations, judged it, and possibly gave it speech by articulating, in its name, discourses that were to be taken as its own.[59]

Foucault rejects the existence of something like a prediscursive and thus objective problem with regard to which a specific group of mutually linked statements could be understood as an attempt at a theoretical solution. Beyond the discourse which, as Foucault says, "constitutes" it, there is no state of affairs corresponding to the thematic object that can be regarded as real.[60] In the example cited, this assertion also helps to forge the argument Foucault employs a few pages later in criticizing his own historical investigation of the social treatment of madness. *Madness and Civilization* now appears inadmissible, at least to the extent that the sequence of different theoretical discourses and treatment practices were described with reference to one identical domain of phenomena: the "prediscursive" experiential content of the schizophrenic. If the scientifically treated states of affairs have been exposed as realities dependent in principle upon discourses, the thoretical presupposition of such an external object which is common to all psychopathological discourses is not tenable.[61]

Together with the proposal of explaining the unity of a discourse by reference to its own object domain, Foucault discusses three other proposals. He treats them under the headings of "style," "concept," and "theme," and they each have the disadvantage of too quickly reducing the structural richness of a discourse to one dimension.[62] Foucault does not consider the completely different possibility of making explicit the fact of the immanent organization of statements within a system—that is, the proposal of explaining the unity of a discourse by reference to the cognitive achievements which subjects intersubjectively bring about is so incompatible with the basic assumptions of his theory that he need not even discuss it. Thus Foucault is aware of the problem posed by his analysis of discourse. He is obliged, without referring to its empirically describable domain of phenomena or to an epistemologically analyzable subject, to identify the principle of formation that brings the disparate statements into the order of a discourse. However, the part of his argument where he introduces this difficulty and attempts at the same time to give a first answer is not very illuminating:

> Concerning those large groups of statements with which we are so familiar—and which we call *medicine, economics,* or *grammar*—I have asked myself on what their unity could be based. On a full, tightly packed, continuous, geographically well-defined field or objects? What appeared to me were rather series full of gaps, intertwined with one another, interplays of differences, distances, substitutions, transformations. . . . On the permanence of a thematic? What one finds are rather various strategic possibilities that permit the activation of incompatible themes, or, again, the establishment of the same theme in different groups of statement. Hence the idea of describing these dispersions themselves; of discovering whether, between these elements, which are certainly not organized as a progressively deductive structure, nor as an enormous book that is being gradually and continuously written, nor as the *oeuvre* of a collective subject, one cannot discern a regularity. . . . Whenever one can describe, between a number of statements, such a system of dispersion, whenever, between objects, types of statement, concepts, or thematic choices, one can define a regularity . . . we will say, for the sake of convenience, that we are dealing with a *discursive formation.* . . . The rules of formation are conditions of existence . . . in a given discursive division.[63]

However, what is now up for debate is precisely what sort of conditions these are that integrate "a specific number of statements" in a "similar system of dispersion"—that is, that place the "objects," "styles of utterance," "concepts," and "themes" of individual statements into a rule-governed relation such that they form a discourse. Thus the line of thought that Foucault repeats here contributes little toward answering the genuinely interesting question. To be sure, he provides criteria for distinguishing between different levels of discourses, but he has not yet solved the recurring problem. The stubbornness with which it apparently pursues Foucault arises from the fact that a discourse-creating principle generally is demonstrated only if a discourse is seen as more than an entity consisting of mere linguistic events, of thoroughly context-free symbolic structures. For so long as statements are regarded not only as nonintentional but also as generally unmotivated functions of signs, what a rule grouping them into the order of a discourse consists of remains unintelligible. Foucault therefore cannot avoid attaching an increase of meaning or function to discourse, as he has thus far done in his provisional definitions; he cannot treat discourse so trivially as an unmotivated combination of statements which are themselves unmotivated if he would like to identify a principle that produces the order of a discourse. Only in an incidental remark does Foucault concede this, although he thereby unambiguously abandons the argumentative framework thus far presented: "Of course, discourses are composed of signs; but what they do is more than use these signs to designate things. It is this *more* that renders them irreducible to the language (*langue*) and to speech. It is this 'more' that we must reveal and describe."[64] A few lines prior to this text Foucault has already given the description for the function that the discourse assumes beyond its function as a sign, which he surprisingly again acknowledges here. There it states that the rules of discourse "define . . . the control of objects."[65] The unmediated claim to a "function of control" for discourse provides the means which Foucault uses to resolve the thus-far-unclarified difficulty in his argument. At the same time, however, it is the theoretical element that finally drives him beyond the original framework of a semiologically conceived analysis of knowledge.

Foucault does not find the characteristic of discourse in its representative function, nor in its communicative function, but in its function as a means for control. Whereas with respect to the first two functions he assumes that they make sense only when intentionally acting subjects are introduced, he believes a function of control can be claimed for discourse without such an assumption. Foucault's concept of discourse results not from the immanent rules of language use, but from an objective social context in which language use fulfills only one function: comprehending and controlling natural and social processes. Regarded in this way, individual statements are arranged into a group of statements according to the measure of their common achievement in bringing about the "control" of some object. The order of discourse is established through social rules which are located within a functional circuit of trans-individual techniques of domination. Undoubtedly the attractiveness of this concept in general is initially due to this preliminary characterization.[66] Now, however, in an explanatory section of his investigation, one more associative than others and based on examples, Foucault gives it two different interpretations which are barely compatible with one another.

On the one hand, Foucault attempts to locate the rules of discourse, explained with the help of the newly introduced functional characterization, immanently within a discursive formation itself. This idea first serves to shift the focus to the concept of discourse, which is now supposed to designate not a stable and latent order of knowledge but rather a fluctuating system of statements, a "discursive praxis."[67] By this Foucault naturally cannot mean the activity of speaking subjects. His concept of praxis arises, like Althusser's corresponding category, from a translation of Sartre's concept of praxis back into a structuralist framework of thought; thus it designates nothing more than the purposive-rational operations of a system that maintains itself in accordance with functional imperatives.[68] A discursive praxis so understood itself actively establishes, for the purpose of controlling a given material, the rules according to which it then operates: "We sought the unity of discourse in the objects themselves, in their distribution, in the interplay of their differences, in their proximity or distance—in short, in what is given to the speaking subject; and, in the end, we are sent back to a setting-up of relations that characterizes discursive practice itself; and what we discover is neither a configuration, nor a form, but a group of *rules* that are immanent in a practice, and define it in its specificity."[69]

Foucault no longer includes only linguistic statements under the elements among which the discursive praxis establishes a rule-governed relation. Since by "style of utterance," which is specific to a given discourse, he also attempts to comprehend the social space in which the discursive statements are obtained, institutional orders and socio-structural positions also belong among the elements which are fused into an order of knowledge by a discursive praxis. Foucault makes this clear through instructive examples from *The Birth of the Clinic*. In that work he accounts for the origin of clinical medicine through the historically unique combination of the physician's improved situation of observation, his increased professional status in society, and the altered system of medical institutions. Thus clinical medicine can be viewed as

the establishment of a relation, in medical discourse, between a number of distinct elements, some of which concerned the status of doctors, others the institutional and technical site from which they spoke, others their position as subjects perceiving, observing, describing, teaching, etc. It can be said that this relation between different elements (some of which are new, while others were already in existence) is effected by clinical discourse: it is this, as a practice, that establishes between them all a system of relations that is not 'really' given or constituted *a priori;* and if there is a unity, if the modalities of enunciation that it uses, or to which it gives place, are not simply juxtaposed by a series of historical contingencies, it is because it makes constant use of this group of relations.[70]

According to this reflection, the discourse forms a rule-governed combination of institutional techniques and cognitive procedures. It appears as the unintended result of an anonymous synthetic achievement that joins institutionally fixed strategic action and cognitively accessible potential for knowledge into a practically effective order of knowledge whose function is to control the natural or social processes of the environment. As can quickly be seen, however, with such a conception Foucault contradicts his original definition in which he had to describe discourse solely as a systematic combination of statements, of linguistic events. Moreover, it is difficult to see how the act that combines institutional techniques and cognitive procedures without relying upon the cognitive initiative of subjects, and which thus produces the discourse, is supposed to be portrayed. The idea of discourse associated with the concept of "discursive praxis" is thus barely plausible once this unclarity is considered. However, there is also another interpretation with whose help Foucault attempts to explain the functional definition of discourse which was directly introduced.

On the other hand, in the same context of argumentation, Foucault would also like to conceive discourse according to an economic model. Like money, it is regarded as a scarce resource for whose possession social actors compete.[71] The discourse has general social value because it provides space for the exercise of cognitive control as well as for the *mise-en-scène* of expressive needs. It constitutes, so to speak, a social medium that is flexible enough so that interests in domination and instinctual impulses are equally capable of being expressed. From this perspective Foucault can attempt to derive discourse from the position it acquires in relation to the two "nondiscursive practices" of "power" and "desire":

This practice also involves *the rules and processes of appropriation* of discourse: for in our societies . . . the property of discourse—in the sense of the right to speak, ability to understand, licit and immediate access to the corpus of already formulated statements, and the capacity to invest this discourse in decisions, institutions, or practices—is in fact confined . . . to a particular group of individuals; in bourgeois societies that we have known since the sixteenth century, economic discourse has never been a common discourse. . . . Lastly, this practice is characterized by the *possible positions of desire in relation to discourse:* discourse may in fact be the place for a phantasmatic representation, an element of symbolization, a form of the forbidden, an instrument of derived satisfaction. . . .[72]

Foucault here anticipates lines of thought (which he worked out later in his 1970 inaugural lecture at the College de France) the task of which is to provide a schematic overview of the institutional strategies through the exercise of which a social system "at once controls, selects, organizes, and redistributes the production of discourse."[73] Foucault discovers techniques of domination of this sort in processes of cultural control over the possible themes of discourse, in the scientific elaboration of the contents of discourse, and in the social regulation of access to discourse. Together, these institutional strategies work an effect consisting in the production of an order *within* discourse, not *of* discourse. For Foucault now conceives of discourse as an omnipresent stream of linguistic events, in contrast to the characterization of the concept in *The Archaeology of Knowledge;* this leads him to a linguistically renewed *Lebensphilosophie* that finds in human speech, rather than in the organic life process, an "incessant and disorderly buzzing," something "discontinuous" and "violent."[74] But if discourse constitutes a linguistic event that is itself unstable, contingent, and mediated, then every rule concerning it appears like a violent act that disrupts its free-moving flow. The institutional techniques that socially organize discourse thus only second-arily form a means for social domination. They function pri-marily as cultural strategies used by civilization as a whole to curb the danger of disorderly speech.[75]

The argument of *The Archaeology of Knowledge* is not yet encumbered by motifs of this sort from life-philosophy (*Lebens-philosophie*), which had a detectable influence upon French post-structuralism.[76] One even finds in it remarks that sound like a warning against a linguistic application of life-philosophy. Thus it is all the more surprising when, in the passage just cited, Foucault makes use of the concept of discourse that he first introduces later under the influence of life-philosophy. For to conceive of discourse as a social medium which social actors competitively seek to appropriate means that it must be pre-supposed as something that is already given, as a linguistic reality. Discourse must already be a finished symbolic reality before interests in domination or even instinctual demands are able to possess it. However, so far *The Archaeology of Knowledge* had presented things in just the reverse order. Discourse is the rare case of a system of statements that in general first comes about when statements are systematically connected to one another under the common function of controlling reality. The system of statements is first constituted by the impulse of an interest in domination. In the first interpretation, discourse is a previously given linguistic event which can then serve as a means for interests in domination; in the second interpretation, by contrast, discourse is the product of an activity directed by interests in domination.

Foucault defends both interpretations equally, but he does not take their incompatibility into consideration. Taking the two interpretations together, discourse is a stream reaching beyond space and time as well as a highly selective organiza-tional form of linguistic events. On the other hand, each inter-pretation taken by itself admittedly does not solve the difficulty it was originally intended to answer—that is, to explain the principle of formation by virtue of which contingent and dis-united statements are connected in the order of a discourse. The first interpretation simply evades the difficulty by suddenly introducing another definition of discourse. The second interpretation deals with a systemically achieved operation that is capable of joining institutional techniques with cognitive procedures—not, however, statements with statements—into an order of knowledge. Both characterizations are incompatible with the definition of "discourse" provided by Foucault at various points in his argument. These paradoxes, in which *The Archaeology of Knowledge* is increasingly entangled, do not reveal an inconsistency primarily in the answers, but already in the questions that Foucault presents in his methodological work. It can be seen as soon as we recall the theoretical starting point of his investigation in order to survey once more, against this background, the path of his argument. Foucault's archaeological view of history can then be seen as the ontologized formulation of an originally methodological concern.

The problem with which *The Archaeology of Knowledge* systematically begins arises for Foucault primarily in connection with the methodological issues raised by the project of an ethnology of one's own culture. In order to be able to transpose social theory into the position of an external observer so that it is able to appear as an ethnology in relation to its own culture, one must make methodical efforts which artificially distance it from the models of thought and conceptions of reality familiar to it. Initially influenced by the experiences of the post-surrealist avant-garde and supported by specific investigations in the history of science, Foucault defends the view that the model of thought determining cultural modernity is rooted in the philosophical supposition of a constitutive ego, a subject which creates meaning. Therefore, the methodical distancing of social theory from the understanding of reality that reigns in its own culture must assume the form of a systematic exclusion of all forms of thought shaped by the philosophy of the subject. At the level of the conduct of research, this means that the ideas and concepts employed in social theory must be freed from the implications of the philosophy of the subject and thus from references to the meaningful activities of a monological subject. This is the theoretical point at which, in *The Archaeology of Knowledge*, the argument concerning the theory of science begins.

However, alongside this project there immediately appears an objective that is more radical than these methodological considerations. The introductory chapter, which briefly lays out the leading ideas, makes clear in the concept of the "monument" that it is not simply a question of the conceptual bracketing of ideas connected with the philosophy of the subject, but their substitution with a conception of reality completely purged of the notion of meaning. The difference between the initial methodological considerations and what *The Archaeology of Knowledge* actually produces results form an important misunderstanding on Foucault's part. From semiological structuralism he borrows the model that determines the conceptual critique. From a theory that claims the general priority of a subjectless, rule-governed system of signs over the meaningful activity of subjects he derives the means by which he is supposed to place social theory in an external position over against the European intellectual tradition. This basic idea leads Foucault unintentionally beyond the methodical starting point that was the reason he first became concerned with semiological structuralism. For it requires stepping out of the horizon of the model of thought in which the cognitive act of producing its own symbolic and social world is attributed to the human individual. The semiological themes cohere only with a theory that has replaced a conceptual framework designed with reference to contexts of human meaning with a conceptual framework suited to a nonintentional rule-governed order of signs. Such an altered theory naturally not only prohibits reference to the meaningful activity of a monological subject; it forbids as a whole an interpretive access to social reality. Thus Foucault not only transforms his social theory into the unique situation of an ethnology in which the contexts of meaning of a preestablished social world are initially distant; beyond that, he seems to be convinced that the alien social world is not an intentionally constructed life-context at all. In the place of the attempt to distance artificially its own familiar culture, in which the basic convictions and conceptions of reality within it are methodically bracketed, the attempt to comprehend the specific culture as an actually nonintentional, anonymous rule-governed social event appears. Ontological statements about the constitution of linguistic reality thus finally account for the object domain which was originally only supposed to be observed *as if* it could appear independent of its own meaningful references. The project of an ethnology of a specific culture has silently acquired the form of a semiological ontology that accounts for the formation of cultural knowledge out of the elementary units of "statements." Foucault entangles himself in the web of this fundamental misunderstanding when he, in the end, is no longer able to provide a consistent meaning for the central concept of "discourse." This finally compels him to abandon completely the program of a semiologically structured analysis of knowledge and thus more consistently to pursue the path he has already opened up with the functional characterization of discourse as a means of domination.

From the Analysis of Discourse to the Theory of Power: Struggle as the Paradigm of the Social

The theme that brings Foucault's writings within the vicinity of Adorno's critical theory becomes visible only after his abandonment of the framework of a historical analysis of discourse marked out in *The Archaeology of Knowledge*. Of course, the material investigations Foucault had undertaken in the 1960s with the intention of constructing an archaeology of the human sciences already converged on the question of the historical conditions under which the concept of humans as individuated subjects could emerge. To that extent, even in this period, Foucault also engaged a position that profoundly shaped Adorno's philosophy of history.[1] But the different answers that Foucault's analysis of the history of knowledge offers for the formulation of the problem he shares with Adorno do not yet form a unified hypothesis. The aporias of a semiotically oriented analysis of knowledge prohibit Foucault from reaching a sufficiently clear and internally consistent answer to the recurring question concerning the 'origin of the individual'. The ontologizing starting point of elementary statements, which are not to be characterized by intentional meaning or by reference to objects, at a methodological level allows for no explanation of the constitution of knowledge contents, or even of the concept of discourse itself, other than a more or less accidental relation to the functional requirements of institutions.

Foucault's explication of the analysis of discourse, which ontologically misconstrues the methodological intent of artificially distancing oneself from one's own culture, gets caught up, as has been shown, in self-contradictory hypotheses concerning how the historical development of knowledge systems is to be explained. The inconsistencies in the analysis of discourse are reflected in the historical investigations bound to its methodology. Despite their descriptive wealth, they offer only vague explanations and obscure conjectures when they are supposed to provide the historical presuppositions for the origin and transformation of particular systems of thought. It remains undecided whether the discovery of new contents of knowledge, and thus also whether the discovery of the individuated subject as an object of knowledge, is to be traced back to the historically accidental concurrence of institutional and cognitive conditions or to a historically unique constellation of social problems.[2] Because the theoretical foundation of Foucault's historical investigations itself remains unclear, those investigations cannot provide a consistent answer that allows them to be placed in relation to Adorno's philosophical-historical hypotheses.

This changes the moment Foucault finally gives up the theoretical project of a semiologically oriented analysis of knowledge and enters upon the ground of social analysis. Until this point his work represented only a kind of indirect social theory. As culturally valid knowledge systems, discourses form the media of social integration. Their cognitive systems, however, are initially supposed to be elucidated immanently—that is to say, solely through the analysis of the rules of composition of their linguistic elements. The context of social structures thus remains only a vague background to the analysis of discourse even when Foucault is finally compelled by his own arguments to explain the constitution of discourses by reference to the functional requirements of society. At this point systems of knowledge should be examined according to the manner in which they assume functions for the extra-discursive social order. But Foucault takes up this functional determination itself without a corresponding conception of system, without a developed notion of a social structural framework. This allows for a certain degree of arbitrariness in the notion of power, with which Foucault attempts to understand the specific functional accomplishments of discourses in *The Archaeology of*

Knowledge. He is himself undecided about the fundamental distinction between social power over subjects and instrumental power over objects. Thus, his early work remains, to a certain extent, below the threshold of real social analysis.

Foucault introduced the first revisions of this original model of the analysis of discourse inconspicuously in his inaugural lecture, entitled "The Discourse on Language."[3] From now on the institutional conditions of the production of knowledge, and thus the context of social structures as such, come to the fore of the theory. This change in perspective arises in the first place as Foucault, with one eye on the philosophy of Nietzsche, seeks to identify basic social dispositions [*soziale Grundaffekte*] that underlie the institutional processes of the maintenance of social systems. A common object of these constitutive instinctual energies, which constantly enter into the reproduction of society, is discourse, which Foucault, to be sure, attempts to comprehend within the interpretive framework, already illustrated above, of a life philosophy refurbished by linguistic theory. Society can thus be interpreted as a social system nourished through the twin dispositions of 'power' and 'desire' in which discourse, portrayed precisely as an omnipresent stream of linguistic events, is an object of strategic conflict.[4] The institutional organization of society is in turn to be explained as a social constellation of those strategies and techniques through which groups seek to embody the conflicting dispositions of power and desire in the medium of discourse.

This dualistic conception now offers the theoretical possibility of comprehending institutional procedures for the control of knowledge as technologies of social control, and so also of redressing the social-theoretic deficit of the original analysis of discourse. But it remains extremely vague and obscure in its social-philosophical foundations, in the abruptly introduced notion of disposition, and thus in the conception of society it permits. Moreover, this construction suffers from the ambiguous synthesis of elements of life philosophy and a theory of power. Foucault thus very quickly replaced this dualistic conception with a monistic conception of power[5] which is more consistent in its theoretical presuppositions and more distinct in its leading concepts. This monistic conception hereafter forms the socio-philosophical basis of his social theory.

Whereas it is the aporia of a semiotically oriented analysis of knowledge that provides the immanent theoretical impetus for a gradual transformation of Foucault's theory in the direction of an analysis of the relations of social power, at the political and biographical level the events of the French student movement lead in the same direction. Foucault himself time and again attributed the thematic shift that had taken place in his work by the end of the 1960s to the experiences that the Western European left had undergone during the suppression of the May rebellion. The fundamental motive for the theory of social power on which Foucault subsequently worked would therefore have been the rudely awakening experience of the strategically perfected reaction of an established system of power to social uprisings. Of the theoretical conclusions that Foucault drew, however directly, from these events, it is first of all of decisive importance for the still-incomplete conception of discourse that from this time onward he conceived of social systems in general as networks of social power in which knowledge formations assume the special function of augmenting power. Discourses are thus systems of social knowledge that owe their genesis to the strategic requirements of an established order of power even as they may in turn effectively act upon a given order of power. With this train of thought, which on first impression has systems-theoretic resonances, Foucault not only discards the vitalistically tinted conception of discourse that he had in the interim allowed to enter into his writings; more important, he is now in the position to abandon definitively the framework of a semiotically oriented analysis of knowledge. In the place of an analysis that seeks to investigate the cultural systems of knowledge on the basis of the internal relations among significant linguistic components, a social-theoretic analysis can now emerge that investigates the external (i.e., functional or causal) relations between the empirical constituents of a social system, between knowledge formations and power relations. In hindsight Foucault himself sought to characterize the shortcomings of his earlier writings in terms of their inability to do justice to the functional aspects of social systems of knowledge that were disclosed through the conception of power: ". . . what was lacking here was this problem of the 'discursive regime', of the effects of power peculiar to the play of statements. I confused this too much with systematicity, theoretical form, or something like a paradigm. This same central problem of power, which at that time I had not yet properly isolated, emerges in two very different aspects at the point of junction of *Madness and Civilization* and *The Order of Things*."[6]

The restrained self-criticism presented here, however, does not sufficiently allow us to recognize that a change in the object of knowledge corresponds to the shift in methodological orientation mentioned above. The order of knowledge is transformed into an order of social power. With the introduction of a monistic conception of power, Foucault not only leaves the methodological framework of semiological structuralism definitively behind; he also gives his theory in general a new object domain. In the place of culturally determining forms of knowledge, whose history during the period of European modernity should be investigated, institutional and cognitive strategies of social integration now emerge, whose stabilizing effect for the societies of modern Europe are to be analyzed. The theory of knowledge becomes the theory of power. It is precisely here that Foucault's work first moves into the territory also inhabited by the tradition of the Frankfurt School.

In order to be able to see the position that Foucault's social theory takes up here, it is of course necessary first to become familiar with the peculiar conception of power he utilizes. In connection with the just-cited self-critical remarks, Foucault continues with a claim that allows us to measure the unacknowledged extent of the conceptual reorientation of this theory and that also affords a first insight into the basic assumptions of his conception of power:

From this follows a refusal of analysis couched in terms of the symbolic field or the domain of signifying structures, and a recourse to analysis in terms of the genealogy of relations of force, strategic developments and tactics. Here I believe one's point of reference should not be to the great model of language (*langue*) and signs, but to that of war and battle. The history which bears and determines us has the form of a war rather than that of a language: relations of power, not relations of meaning. History has no 'meaning', though this is not to say that it is absurd or incoherent. On the contrary, it is intelligible and should be susceptible of analysis down to the smallest detail—but this in accordance with the intelligibility of struggles, of strategies and tactics.[7]

Foucault develops the essential features of a theory of social power, as is indicated in these sentences, in the form of an exchange with two competing theoretical traditions. It is his conviction that both classical political science and Marxist social theory fail in the project of adequately understanding the predominant mechanisms of social integration in developed societies because both are to an equal extent bound to the theoretical prejudices of a conception of power suited to premodern forms of power. According to this conception, power is represented as a contractually regulated or forcibly acquired possession that justifies or authorizes the political sovereign in the exercise of repressive power. In both cases it is supposed that an actor who is in possession of power utilizes apparently suitable means to carry out those prohibitions and instructions that allow the objectives of rule to be realized. Following the model of the legal contract, classical political science thinks of the possession of power as a transference of rights. The Marxist theory of power, following a statist model of thinking, understands the possession of power as an acquisition of the state apparatus.[8] In opposition to both theoretical traditions, Foucault proposes a strategic model of power whose uniqueness results from the attempt to translate the naturalistically informed ideas of Nietzsche's theory of power[9] into the framework of a theory of society.

Foucault objects to both of the central components of the traditional conception of power, i.e., to the ideas concerning the subject and the means of social power. Regarding the assumption of a social actor to whom power is ascribed as a contractually arranged or forcibly acquired possession, Foucault proposes the hypothesis that becomes for the time being the decisive assumption of his own conception of power: that power should be thought of not as a fixable property, as the enduring characteristic of an individual subject of a social group, but rather as the in principle fragile and open-ended product of strategic conflicts between subjects. The acquisition and maintenance of social power thus takes place not in the form of a one-sided appropriation and exercise of rights of decree or instruments of compulsion but rather in the shape of a continuous struggle of social actors among themselves. Foucault clothes this central objection in the formula (borrowed from Nietzsche) of the "diversity of power relations," which seems to start out from a multiplicity of competing subjects rather than from one subject holding power, and thereby would unexpectedly have already gone beyond the structuralist starting point:

It seems to me that power must be understood in the first instance as the multiplicity of force relations immanent in the sphere in which they operate and which constitute their own organization; as the process which through ceaseless struggles and confrontations, transforms, strengthens, or reverses them; as the support which the force relations find in one another, thus forming a chain or a system, or on the contrary, the disjunctions and contradictions which isolate them from one another. . . .[10]

Even though Foucault uses the physicalistic language of mechanics here, the course of thought presented above suggests that we may assume an action-theoretic model of relations as the basis of his theory of power. Strategic action among social actors is interpreted as the ongoing process in which the formation and exercise of social power is embedded. Power is rooted in a "perpetual battle"[11] insofar as every unilateral achievement of strategic objectives appears to be bound to situations of direct confrontation between subjects. Above all, those formulations in which he traces the genesis of social power to the inconspicuous conflicts of everyday social life speak in support of this action-theoretic interpretation of Foucault's theory of power:

Power comes from below: that is, there is no binary and all-encompassing opposition between rulers and ruled at the root of power relations, and serving as a general matrix—no such duality extending from the top down and reacting on more and more limited groups to the very depths of the social body. One must suppose rather that the manifold relationships of force that take shape and come into play in the machinery of production, in families, limited groups, and institutions, are the basis for wide-ranging effects of cleavage that run through the social body as a whole.[12]

At one place in his theses concerning "The Power and the Norm," in which he had summarized his theory of power, Foucault even makes a similar claim that power is "always a particular form of momentary and constantly repeating clashes within a definite number of individuals."[13] The basic action-theoretic thought, which is otherwise wrapped in more mechanistic terminology, here steps unconcealed into the light of day: the emergence of social power can be studied on an elementary level in the action-situations in which subjects with competing objectives meet and contend for the achievement of their aims. Social power is then admittedly not, as the cited statement misleadingly suggests, these strategic confrontations themselves, but rather results from the outcome in which one of the competing subjects is able to settle the dispute in his favor. "Constant repetition" of such direct conflicts means that the situationally secured power is not to be conclusively stabilized in the regulation of social interaction (that is, in established institutions) but rather remains permanently dependent upon confirmation in elementary situations of social struggle. Each society is, insofar as it is understood solely as a nexus of strategic relations between individual or collective actors, in a constant and in principle unending state of war: "Between every point of a social body, between a man and a woman, between the members of a family, between a master and his pupil, between every one who knows and every one who does not, there exist relations of power which are not purely and simply a projection of the sovereign's great power over the individual; they are rather the concrete, changing soil in which the sovereign's power is grounded, the conditions which make it possible for it to function."[14]

This explanation, drawn from a conversation, unmistakably reveals that with the turn toward a theory of power Foucault attempts to understand the social first of all as an uninterrupted process of conflicting strategic action. From the outset this differentiates his theory of society from that of Adorno, which to a certain extent skipped over the phenomena of social action by seeking to understand social structures in general as coagulated forms of an activity of control directed at both outer and inner nature. Foucault starts from a specific dimension of social action. His basic model is the strategic intersubjectivity of struggle. The concept of action that forms the basis of this model is, however, not very definite, even crude. On a fundamental conceptual level it remains unclear whether he would like social conflict to be interpreted as taking place among individuals alone or also among collective actors. Substantial evidence for both interpretations can be found in Foucault's explanatory remarks. The basic theoretical model of the social tells us just as little whether the antecedent cause of the elementary situation of struggle is the in principle incompatible self-interest of individual or collective actors, or whether the mutual incompatibility of their interests is due only to certain historical conditions. However, Foucault's comments certainly speak here for the first of these two versions—that is, for the assertion, reminiscent of Hobbes, of an original state of war of all against all.[15]

Foucault is of course not interested now in the elementary situations of social struggle as such, but rather in the more complex power structures that proceed out of them. His problem thus consists in having to explain how a system of mutually interconnected positions of power, i.e. an order of domination, can emerge out of the perpetual process of strategic conflict among actors. On a fundamental conceptual level he tackles this difficulty only indirectly in the form of a critique of the Marxist theory of the state. According to that theory's presuppositions (which Foucault, to be sure, sketches too simplistically[16]), it appears that an order of power based in the economic authority of a social class is maintained by the instrumental interventions and manipulative procedures of a state apparatus. Social power relations are guaranteed through the centrally controlled employment of administrative means of compulsion or thought control. In opposition to this Foucault presents the thesis that an order of social domination, regardless of its character, cannot be steered from one point through the centralized activity of a political apparatus of power. Since it emerged out of a sequence of successful strategic acts, it can have its existence only in successfully regulating situations of conflicting action. In order to understand this objection, it is necessary to interpret it as a first, and admittedly still implicit, consequence of struggle as the basic model of action.

Foucault also seeks to understand the formation and reproduction of complex power structures solely on the basis of the strategic model of action. He starts out with the general idea that the emergence of social power relations is to be understood as a process in which situationally secured positions of power in different places are connected like a net into a centerless system. An order of control develops horizontally—that is, when examined from the fictive perspective of a synchronic slice through the continual stream of conflicts, in that moment in which the results secured on different social fronts combine with one another into a sum, into a common objective. In the first place, a system of power is to a certain extent nothing but a momentary linking up of similar outcomes of action in different locations of a social life-context. To the extent that it is able to make such interconnected outcomes repeatable in the same situations of conflict and thus to give them a certain continuity, a system of power obtains permanence from the longitudinal perspective of history. Considered in general, it is then an order of situationally secured and maintained positions of power temporally stabilized into a system.[17]

If this basic model is provisionally accepted, disregarding for the moment the persisting lack of clarity, then already a theory of society that fixates upon technologies of state control is shown to be inappropriate in its basic assumptions. This is because a social power structure cannot be instituted and maintained through the centralized activity of a state apparatus, but only through the 'decentered' activities of the most varied actors in diverse situations of struggle. In reductive statist conceptions of power, however, it is assumed that an existing order of power is able to reproduce itself through the utilization of the centrally directed measures of compulsion or the manipulation of consciousness (i.e., through the operations of the state apparatus), although it does then obtain stability only when at the same time it succeeds in maintaining in different places of the society the positions of power that are necessary for its continued existence. Systems of power thus must already have formed and established themselves on a substate level in social conflicts of action through a graduated sequence of strategic outcomes before an apparatus of state control can obtain scope for its own operations. And because the state's means of stabilizing power have a very limited radius of influence, they can offer only the roughest contribution to the process of struggle in which an existing system of power must steadfastly maintain itself in the daily staging of social conflict. Foucault writes:

I don't want to say that the State isn't important; what I want to say is that relations of power, and hence the analysis that must be made of them, necessarily extend beyond the limits of the State. In two senses: first of all because the State, for all the omnipotence of its apparatuses, is far from being able to occupy the whole field of actual power relations, and further because the State can only operate on the basis of other, already existing power relations. The State is superstructural in relation to a whole series of power networks that invest the body, sexuality, the family, kinship, knowledge, technology and so forth . . . but this meta-power [the state apparatus—A.H.] with its prohibitions can only take hold and secure its footing where it is rooted in a whole series of multiple and indefinite power relations that supply the necessary basis for the great negative forms of power.[18]

Foucault apparently wanted the critical argument, which can in this manner be extrapolated out of the model of strategic action, to be understood above all as a contribution to the discussion of Marxism within France, namely as an objection in principle against Althusser's theory of the "ideological state apparatus."[19] But, disregarding for now the ambiguities of the initial model, sufficient cause arises on the basis of his reflections to call the conception of power in Adorno's later theory of society into question, since it, as shown, indeed likewise posits social power unilaterally as the goal-directed activity of a centralized administrative apparatus, thus virtually ignoring the practical foundation of the exercise of power, the substate situations of social struggle.[20] Against the reductive statist conception of power, Foucault sets out as an opposing theoretical sketch the project of a "microphysics of power." This is oriented so that the formation of power, in correspondence to the action-theoretical premises, should be traced back to the strategic exchanges in everyday conflicts of action. The object domain of the still-to-be-worked-out analysis of power is formed, then, by relations of action that

> are not univocal; they define innumerable points of confrontation, focuses of instability, each of which has its own risks of conflict, of struggles, and of an at least temporary inversion of the power relations. The overthrow of these "micro-powers" does not, then, obey the law of all or nothing; it is not acquired once and for all by a new control of the apparatuses nor by a new functioning or a destruction of the institutions; on the other hand, none of its localized episodes may be inscribed in history except by the effects that it induces on the entire network in which it is caught up.[21]

Foucault is consistent enough to describe social systems of power first of all as structures that are fragile, to a certain extent continuous, and at all times subject to testing. The model of strategic action that forms the basis of his concept of power requires that the order of power that emerged out of the consolidation of situationally secured positions of power be understood only as a momentary systematic state that in all of its elements remains exposed to a continually renewed process of testing through social conflicts. Thus, in another place Foucault speaks also of "global, but never fully stable effects of power." These cautious formulations, though, which seem to do justice to the presupposed model of the "perpetual battle," themselves contain a problem that remains to this point unresolved: If a society is thought of exclusively as a nexus of types of strategic action, how shall the situationally and occasionally achieved outcomes of action actually be temporally stabilized and then also be socially connected to a system of outcomes of action achieved and stabilized in other places? When in fact each position of power obtained in a situation of social conflict is exposed to incessant testing, how can those aggregate states form themselves out of the flow of strategic action to which, as Foucault says, "power relations link themselves"? The solution to the problem, as is not difficult to see, is contained in the concept of "stabilization" or, as Foucault calls it, with the same meaning, "institutionalization." But just the interpretation of this concept causes Foucault considerable difficulties, which will be revealed when we turn our attention to a second consequence of the definition of the social as a perpetual condition of struggle.

Out of the action-theoretic premise that social life can be regarded as a process of strategic conflicts among actors and that social power can accordingly be interpreted on an elementary level simply as success in a situation of struggle, a critique of that tradition of social scientific theory centered on the standard case of the normative recognition of social power implicitly follows for Foucault. On the simplest level of a strategic conflict between two actors, social power is, as said, the momentary result of the success with which one of the two actors is able to bring about his objectives. Each situation in which the two actors clash anew represents in turn a test for the successful actor's position of power that resulted from the first confrontation, because now the underdog will try again to bring his suppressed interests about—that is, the underdog declares or behaves as if accepting the opponent's position of power. Foucault must mean this, and only this, when he imagines the possibility of a stabilization of strategically acquired positions of power. In any case, he may not now assume that this stabilization takes place in the form of an agreement between the two actors concerning the priority of competing objectives on the basis of commonly acknowledged norms and values. In a social world consisting merely of situations of strategic action, something like normatively motivated consent could in no way be formed, since after all the subjects encounter one another only as opponents interested in the success of their respective aims. For this reason a situationally secured position of power, understood as success in the unilateral realization of objectives, cannot be stabilized—at least not in the manner in which it takes on the shape of a claim to power that for a certain duration has normative recognition. As long as we find no explanation for the possibility of the institutionalization of positions of power obtained in a situation of conflict other than that of normatively motivated consent, those positions remain constantly exposed to the risk of unrestrained social conflict. Then, of course, something like an aggregate state of strategic social action might not be able to form.

From this train of thought, pointedly sketched here, there arises for Foucault the necessity of dismissing the legal norms and moral orientations that regulate the interaction of members of society with one another as mere illusions, as cultural deceptions. In the perpetual staging of social struggle, in which a social order of power to a certain extent has its being, legal norms and moral attitudes assume the sole function of hiding strategic objectives and veiling the everyday situation of conflict. Over against the substance of struggle, which remains the same, they represent, as it were, only historically variable superstructures. In his critique of a contract theory of society Foucault has only roughly referred to this consequence, which, on the conceptual level of his theory of power, follows from his model of action because it does not allow for a dimension of normative agreement. It is, of course, the unacknowledged source of the political decisionism that his writings on the theory of power reveal as soon as they are examined from a normative perspective.[22] In our context, however, it is of particular interest that the resolute theoretical exclusion of a practically effective dimension of normative agreement confronts Foucault that much more strongly with an unresolved problem: How can the (however momentary) aggregate condition of a structure of power, whose prerequisite should be precisely the interruption of the process of conflict, be derived from the social condition of an uninterrupted struggle, when the possibility of a normatively guided consensus among the subjects involved is excluded in principle? The indirect answer that Foucault seeks to give to this question may be inferred from a second complex of reflections by which he supplements the proposed conception of power with further determinations, and which to a certain extent lead us into the center of his social theory.

So far I have presented Foucault's model of strategic action in abstraction from those means which the actors are able to employ on the occasion of social conflict in order optimally to bring about, in opposition to the opponent, their own objectives. The elucidation of this instrumental component of strategic conflict—the analysis, that is, of technologies of power acquisition—is served by the second complex of arguments in Foucault's theory of power. Carried out at first in the form of a critique of competing formulations, this analysis is the theory's actual theme—and indeed its most insistent theme. However, Foucault now sees to the preparation of this concept— which for him is central—no longer on a general level but rather on a historical level.

The most general objection that Foucault raises from this perspective against competing theories of power addresses itself to the conventional tendency of looking at the means used to influence an opponent in strategic conflicts solely in terms of the alternative between "violence" and "ideology."[23] It remains unclear whether Foucault is alluding with this expression to the conceptual pair of "force" and "fraud" that comes out of classical social philosophy, but in practice he means the same thing. The opponent in social conflict is forced in the first place through the threat or use of physical force, and in the second place through "calculated" and "subtle" deception[24] concerning the particular objectives of action or the empirical conditions of action, to abandon his own purposes and to submit to the opponent's will. Foucault considers both ideas to be inadequate for explaining the mode of functioning in modern orders of power. With regard to the concept of ideology, though, which is still to be shown, Foucault makes objections not only on historical but also on theoretic-systematic grounds.[25] But the foundation of his argument is formed by the historically informed thesis that the uses of physical force and of ideological influence as means of power do not allow the degree of integration of highly developed societies to be understood. He therewith poses to himself as a historical question the same problem that Parsons, in his celebrated chapter on Hobbes in *The Structure of Social Action,* had clothed as the general question concerning the possibility of social order. How can we explain to ourselves the stability of an order of social life once we have recognized that for this purpose the strategic means of "force and fraud," of "violence" and "deception," alone are insufficient?[26]

This problem arises for Foucault, of course, in a context in which he inquires historically after typical means of exercising power within modern societies. That is why the answer he gives must, to a certain extent, contain the thesis opposite to that which Parsons chose as a solution to the "Hobbesian problem." Parsons answered the question concerning the possibility of social order, as is known, with the thesis, borrowed from Durkheim, that the actions of a society's members can be sufficiently connected with one another solely on the basis of commonly recognized values. Foucault supposes in contrast that social orders of power must always remain unstable, since the conflicts carried on in all regions of social action around positions of power cannot be brought to a halt through generally binding values. An order of power, which is to be imagined as an alliance of constantly threatened positions of power, can, however, reduce its own instability by employing technically more effective means for the preservation of power. Consequently the question that Parsons raised presents itself for Foucault as a historical problem that is, as it were, inverted. What means for the exercise of power do modern orders of power employ when they do in fact show a lesser degree of instability than would be achieved through the instruments of violence and ideology alone? Physical violence and ideological influence, Foucault believes, show a common characteristic as means of procuring power: They work by way of directly or indirectly forcing opponents to abandon their own objectives. The interests of the strategic opponent are repressed, whether now under the threat of physical violence or with the help of skillfully employed deception. Precisely therein lie the limits to the effectiveness of the traditional methods of power, of "force" and "fraud":

. . . this power is poor in resources, sparing of its methods, monotonous in the tactics it utilizes, incapable of invention, and seemingly doomed always to repeat itself. Further, it is a power that only has the force of the negative on its side, a power to say no; in no condition to produce, capable only of posting limits, it is basically anti-energy. This is the paradox of its effectiveness: it is incapable of doing anything, except to render what it dominates incapable of doing anything either, except for what this power allows it to do.[27]

Now, under no circumstances is it self-evident to understand procedures of ideological influence simply as methods of indirect suppression of needs, as repressive technologies of power. Indeed, ideologies work rather underground so that they induce a subject to intra-psychically adopt objectives which originally were external to the ego, whose practical realization they then honor. Foucault, however, does not consider this essential phenomenon of the mode of operation of ideologies. Without further ado, he lumps such acculturation through ideology together with such "repressive" methods of power as the use of violence and sets them together in opposition to a historically new type of method of power. The uniqueness of this new type is determined on the most general level through the concept of "productivity"; the methods of power that above all come into use in modern societies are, as Foucault says, defined by "productive effectiveness" and by "strategic resourcefulness."[28]

For Foucault the idea that the use of particular methods of power is able to bring forward productive effects is, to a certain extent, the key to a historically adequate theory of power. The philosophical impetus for this idea, for its part, comes from Nietzsche's conception of power, which sought to interpret creative achievements of every kind either as direct or as indirect forms of the expression of a will to power. Foucault picks up this basic thought, but reserves it for the analysis of the special achievement of modern methods of power. Now for the first time technologies of social power possess the productivity attributed by Nietzsche to all expressions of power, namely, the capacity on its side to produce social energy: "Since the classical age the West has undergone a very profound transformation of these mechanisms of power. 'Deduction' has tended to be no longer the major form of power but merely one element among others, working to incite, reinforce, control, monitor, optimize, and organize the forces under it: a power bent on generating forces, making them grow, and ordering them, rather than one dedicated to impeding them, making them submit, or destroying them."[29]

What it can mean for social theory that certain technologies of social power now display productive instead of repressive effects—that is, that they create rather than repress the energy of social action—is explained inadequately by Foucault. The meaning of the argument is illuminated, though, by the connection, initially difficult to grasp, with which the concepts of "norm," "body," and "knowledge" are found together within his conception of power.

The concept of "norm" represents the most general expression that Foucault chooses for the goal of that method of power that assumes not repressive functions but rather productive ones. Techniques of power of this kind, as said, do not aim at suppressing, directly or indirectly, the objectives of the strategic opponent's action. Their purpose is to routinize the modes of behavior of the social opponent through constant disciplining and, through that, to allow them to solidify. Foucault calls every kind of such conduct fixed by compulsion a "normalized" conduct. Norms of conduct are, when we so understand them, rigidly reproduced patterns of action (or, as they are in some places more simply and less ambiguously called, socially imposed habits).[30] But Foucault is not alluding to a dimension of morally obligatory action when in a first approximation he seeks to determine the achievements of modern methods of power through just this capacity to create "norms of conduct": "Since the nineteenth century a series of apparatuses have developed . . . whose purpose it was to produce discipline, to impose obligations, to develop habits. What took place in the course of this development [before the nineteenth century— A.H.] represents thus also the prehistory of the apparatus of power, which served as the base for the acquisition of habits as social norms."[31]

The category of "norm," though, taken for itself alone, remains in Foucault's expositions somewhat vague and hastily formulated. In the theoretical self-interpretation of his historical investigations into the techniques of the exercise of social power, not only is he often a victim of the unwarranted temptation to bring together the concept of "norm" that is geared toward compulsorily fixed patterns of conduct and the concept of the norm of moral action; above and beyond that, he associates the former with yet another concept: that of social normality.[32] These obscurities first disappear when the second category central to Foucault's argumentation steps into view and is referred back to the category of "norm." Foucault has brought together, under the concept of the "body," that region of the expression of life toward which the modern techniques of power direct themselves with the goal of the production of norms of conduct.

The category of the "body" assumes an essential function in Foucault's theory only in the moment in which, along with the starting point of a historical analysis of discourse, he drops the idea that the order of a society is produced primarily by way of an unconscious regulation of linguistic expressions or by way of forms of social knowledge. With the turn to the theory of power Foucault is at the same time won over by the apparently naturalistic conviction that it is less the cultural modes of thought than it is the body-bound expressions of life over which societies must be able to control in order to reduce their own instability. Moreover, the new thought that societies live solely from the bodily activities of the subjects contributes to such an idea.[33] In this context Foucault speaks of body and life processes. Under these he subsumes all expressions of life that are tied directly to the basic functions of the human body—on the one hand, purely motor and gestural movements; on the other hand, the elementary organic processes of procreation and illness. If a society's capacity for integration has to show itself according to whether it is sufficiently capable of controlling and coordinating such modes of bodily behavior with one another, then the strategic effectiveness of its methods of control is measured precisely by the extent to which they are able to regulate those regions of bodily processes. This is the fundamental thought that induces Foucault to allocate a fundamental role in his theory of power to the conduct of human bodies rather than to cognitive and moral attitudes.

From this last perspective the modern techniques of power are now distinguished for Foucault in that they are able not merely to suppress or simply control the conduct of human bodies but also systematically to produce it. The production and creation of the conduct of human bodies, however, means for him, on the one hand, to give an originally unsettled and fluid motor activity of bodies[34] [*Körpermotorik*] the fixed shape of a uniform pattern of conduct by means of perpetual disciplining, i.e., to normalize the sequence of motions of the human body. The concept of "bodily discipline," which is central to the historical investigation *Discipline and Punish,* is extracted from the idea that the techniques of social power can have their goal in the compulsory standardization of motor and gestural motions. Under this concept the most varied practices are assembled, by the power of which the motor and gestural movements of individuals are forced into the blind automatism of routinized acts and trained for productive work. Foucault is interested not in a historical psychology but rather in a historical "physics" of the disciplining of bodies. The human body is not understood as a unity of physical and psychical processes, but rather, following an intentionally physicalistic program, is imagined as a mechanically functioning system of energy. In a way different from the theory of civilization of Norbert Elias[35] and also different from the *Dialectic of Enlightenment* of Horkheimer and Adorno, Foucault therefore grasps the process of disciplining bodies—which he sees, with those authors, as a concise indication of the modernization of Europe—not as the psycho-physical process of a growing control of passions and bodies but rather as the exclusively physical process of an ever-more-perfect directing of sequences of bodily motions. Foucault disregards individual psycho-dynamics [*Trieb dynamik*], onto which, as always, such disciplining procedures radiate back. In this purposeful reductionism the structuralist *leitmotif* of the analysis of discourse returns in his theory of power in the form of an energetic hostility to psychology that will prove, in the end, to be incompatible with the model of action that theoretically underlies his concept of power.

But there is a second aspect to what Foucault understands as the productive domination of the behavior of human bodies. Since, when he applies his theory of power to the conduct of human bodies, he has in view not only the motor and gestural motions of individuals but also the fundamental organic processes of birth, procreation, and death, he takes into consideration a further complex of modern techniques of power. The goal of these is the control of the "biological" behavior of the population and not the disciplining of individual motor activity.

Foucault assembles the administrative strategies that contribute to the regulation of the organic life processes of humans under the provocative title of "biopolitics." In alliance with the techniques of disciplining bodies, they represent the institutional basis of the system of power formed during the modern age in Europe:

> In concrete terms, starting in the seventeenth century, this power over life evolved in two basic forms; these forms were not antithetical, however; they constituted rather two poles of development linked together by a whole intermediary cluster of relations. One of these poles—the first to be formed, it seems—centered on the body as a machine: its disciplining, the optimization of its capabilities, the extortion of its forces, the parallel increase of its usefulness and its docility, its integration into systems of efficient and economic controls, all this was ensured by the procedures of power that characterized the *disciplines: an anatomo-politics of the human body.* The second, formed somewhat later, focused on the species body, the body imbued with the mechanics of life and serving as the basis of the biological processes: propagation, birth and mortality, the level of health, life expectancy and longevity, with all the conditions that can cause these to vary. Their supervision was effected through an entire series of interventions and *regulatory controls: a biopolitics of the population.*[36]

It is at this point of decisive importance that Foucault sees these techniques for the exercise of social power upon bodies as, in each case, subordinate to rules that are the result of the scientific development of the corresponding body and life processes. The disciplining of the movements of individual bodies and the administration of the organic life processes is possible solely in proportion to information and knowledge about "humans" that was produced in accordance with the guiding perspective of strategic disposal. That leads to the third category, the concept of "knowledge," that Foucault brings to the analysis of the productivity of modern techniques of power.

In *The Archaeology of Knowledge,* as we saw, Foucault had already played with the idea of interpreting discourse merely as an instrument of a linguistic "seizing hold" of reality. To this thought, though, which there remains unmediated, fell only the task of helping to resolve the virtually insoluble paradoxes of a semiologically oriented analysis of knowledge. The turn toward the theory of power arose in the first place out of the radicalization of a particular argument, one that was for the original project of a historical analysis of discourse quite insignificant. If the contents of social knowledge, which under the application of semiological methods were not to be analyzed without contradiction, ought to be understood in general as means of power relations, then it is necessary to analyze the concealed structure of the social power relations before the role of scientific knowledge therein could be more exactly determined. Foucault seeks now, on the categorial level of his theory of power, to grasp societies as the momentary state of a perpetual process of strategic interaction among social actors. Endeavors to gain scientific knowledge assume, then, consistent with this, no role other than that assumed by all other activities of individuals and groups:

> Perhaps, too, we should abandon a whole tradition that allows us to imagine that knowledge can exist only where the power relations are suspended and that knowledge can develop only outside its injunctions, its demands and its interests. . . . We should admit rather that power produces knowledge (and not simply by encouraging it because it serves power or by applying it because it is useful); that power and knowledge directly imply one another; that there is no power relation without the correlative constitution of a field of knowledge, nor any knowledge that does not presuppose and constitute at the same time power relations.[37]

Within the framework of his theory of power, Foucault understands science in general as an activity in which reality is empirically opened up, conceptually subdivided, and theoretically explained from the perspective of the production of social power. The requirements of possible objectivity for scientific knowledge are therefore determined by the aim of the social subjugation of individuals. Apart from this strategic relation, methodologically produced knowledge fulfills no specifiable purpose. In correspondence with this it is also false to speak, as has been done until now, of science as an "instrument" or "means" of social control. Foucault goes beyond the conventional interpretation according to which social groups are able to monopolize theoretical knowledge and scientific information for the purpose of assuring power by means of institutional and cultural strategies of exclusion.[38] Scientific activity does not exist for him apart from a field of strategic conflict, so that it could serve the actors engaged there as a tool; rather, it is itself merely the reflective form of strategic action.

Foucault's "theory of knowledge," which is only indirectly laid out in the investigations of his theory of power, consists of the attempt to trace the conceptual framework and methodological procedures of the human sciences—and indeed of the natural sciences[39]—to a system of cognitive relations that is anchored in elementary situations of the exercise of social power, namely in inquisitions, investigations, and tests. In such prescientific procedures of inquiry, which aid in the constant control of the social opponent, reality is in general framed in advance as the strategic field of operation, as which it then appears in the sciences in a methodologically objectified manner. In opposition to Adorno (with whom, however, he shares the theme of the control-oriented character of the sciences), Foucault derives the conditions of scientific knowledge not from a framework of reference oriented toward instrumental access to nature but rather from a framework of reference placed within the strategic requirements of the social struggle. He is interested not in the concealed connection between scientific experience and the domination of nature but rather in that between scientific experience and strategic action. As a sociological disciple of Nietzsche, he insists upon developing out of this basic epistemological idea a critique of the human sciences, whose emancipatory self-understanding this critique triumphantly confronts with its practical origins: "These sciences, which have so delighted our 'humanity' for over a century, have their technical matrix in the petty, malicious minutiae of the disciplines and their investigations. These investigations are perhaps to psychology, psychiatry, pedagogy, criminology, and so many other strange sciences, what the terrible power of investigation was to the calm knowledge of the animals, the plants or the earth. Another power, another knowledge."[40]

Foucault's polemically pointed critique of science, which seeks to expose the connection in principle between efforts to gain theoretical knowledge and purposes of strategic action, is admittedly slightly articulated and almost superficial. Until now it has not been used to examine the character of particular sciences in a manner subject to critical scrutiny; nor has it addressed the problem of how knowledge derived solely according to the perspective of obtaining social power can be of practical value in contexts of action that are obviously differently oriented (for instance, the contexts of technical access to nature or the therapeutic treatment of disturbances in socialization). In the place where this critique of science is, once more, precisely directed toward a particular discipline, as in the case of psychoanalysis, it does not enter directly into its methodological structure, but instead is content yet again with the rather crude demonstration of its social function.[41] Finally, the kind of theory of knowledge that Foucault posits as the basis of his critique of the sciences would entangle him in the contradiction of no longer being able to justify epistemologically his own academic research activity, while it would itself be subject to the verdict of its own proposed claims (that is, it would have to expose itself as merely a reflexive form of strategic action).[42] As a result, Foucault's critique of science, taken as a whole, is too vague in its fundamental principles and too precipitate in its conclusions to be convincing as an outline of a theory of knowledge. In any case, it also has, at this point in Foucault's argumentation, just the task of providing a rough background for the theme that actually interests him: the mode of functioning of modern techniques of power which are centered upon the relationship of body, norm, and knowledge.

Now that all three concepts have been broadly elucidated, we can see clearly that they form a kind of regulated feedback system in which, as I understand Foucault, systematic knowledge about the modes of action and bodily processes of humans (sociology, medicine, pedagogy, psychology, etc.) is produced by means of suitable procedures of extracting information (inquisition, confession, interrogation, etc.). This knowledge is then translated into practices of the direct disciplining of bodies (disciplinary power) and of the administrative control of behavior (biopolitics). Of course, the regulated feedback system in which the symbolic processes of the production of knowledge are combined with the practical operations of the control of behavior is interpreted not statically but rather in the sense of a cumulative learning process. Every practically applied technique for the manipulation and control of human life processes at the same time expands the base of information for scientific knowledge, just as every insight gained into these events through the process of scientific research increases the scope of manipulation for procedures of disciplining and control. Foucault speaks now in a double sense of the "productivity" of these techniques of power that function as a kind of regulated feedback system, but without sufficiently clearly differentiating between the two manners of using the concept. Modern strategies for the use of social power are productive in that they are constantly able to optimize themselves in a reflexive manner as well as in that they know how to increase the bodily performance of the subject.

In this way Foucault develops ideas about the character of modern techniques of power, to which are imputed not only those nearly unlimited possibilities for the control of behavior but also the capacity for constant self-optimization. Accordingly, he no longer regards individual actors or social groups as the subjects of this developed form of the exercise of power, but instead social institutions such as the school, the prison, or the factory—institutions that he himself must comprehend as highly complex structures of solidified positions of social power. The frame of reference for the concept of power has, therefore, secretly been shifted from a theory of action to an analysis of institutions. But then the theoretical diagnosis of the techniques of power does not actually settle the problem on the agenda, but rather simply conjures it away. While the concept of power is supposed to have been developed out of the practical intersubjectivity of social struggle, without having been able to explain sufficiently the process of the social stabilization of positions of power, the analysis of the techniques of power unexpectedly uses the idea of power-wielding institutions without having to refer to the process of their social establishment. In between, the phenomenon of actual theoretical interest—the stabilization of practically secured positions of power in the form of their social institutionalization—disappears. Between the situationally unique securing of a position of power (which the basic action-theoretic model of conflict can only assert again and again) and the highly complex activity of social control by institutions (which is assumed in the conceptual explanation of the modern techniques of power), the emergence of social power relations remains, on a theoretical level, curiously unexplained.

This discrepancy is not accidental, but rather possesses a systematic character. It does not result from the fact that Foucault develops his model of strategic action only on the basis of simple examples of a direct confrontation among actors and then expands it into a theory of society, whereas he carries out his analysis of techniques of power with reference to historically concrete processes. To utilize the concept of struggle as the exclusive basis of a social theory is by no means free of contradiction: Each social stabilization of a position of power—that is, each establishing of however limited a relation of power—presupposes the interruption of the struggle in the form of a normatively motivated agreement, or of a pragmatically aimed compromise, or of a permanently emplaced use of force. Whereas the first two ways for the solution of a strategic conflict represent cases of a two-sided stabilization of social power, the third solution represents the improbable case of a merely one-sided stabilization of a position of social power. Because he initially supposes an uninterrupted string of strategic conflicts, Foucault excludes at the conceptual level any possibility of a mutual overcoming of the struggle in the provisional state of stabilized power. Thus, there inevitably remains for him only the possibility of interpreting the institutionalization of positions of power as a process of the constant use of force. Consequently, when he seeks theoretically to describe the modern techniques of power, he uses consistently, though unexpectedly, that third avenue of thought: At this point, he understands relations of social power as the aggregate states of strategic action obtained through permanent and technically highly perfected uses of force. Social institutions appear to him, as he explains in an unwarranted reference to Durkheim,[43] merely as means of a one-sided rule by force.

Because Foucault does not render an account of the aporias involved in the attempt to derive a concept of relations of social power solely from the idea of the omnipresence of strategic conflicts, he must on the level of social theory feel himself obliged once again to derive the order of societies from the effect of the use of force coagulated in institutional apparatuses. Contrary to his own claims, the social-theoretic determination of the character of modern techniques of power contains nothing more than the conceptually differentiated but nonetheless fundamentally reductionistic idea of a one-sided rule of force. Thereby, however, there emerges in Foucault's theory of power, as is easy to infer, a striking discrepancy between the model of action posited as the basis and the social theory carried out, between the assertion of an unlimited process of social struggle and the claim of an unlimited effectiveness of the modern power of discipline. In other words, in one and the same context of argumentation the theoretic confirmation of a "perpetual battle" faces a detailed picture of the manner of functioning of administrative institutions of compulsion, the social prerequisite for the development of which is precisely the interruption of the "perpetual battle." The idea of a plurality of socially competing actors fits only with the first hypothesis; the idea of bodily behavior that is unresistingly manipulated is compatible only with the second hypothesis.

This internal rift in Foucault's theory of power, due to the reduction of social to strategic conflict and thus the exclusion of other forms of social action, is first resolved when he changes over from the level of conceptual reflection to the field of historical writing. In the material investigations concerning the emergence of modern techniques of social integration, the model of strategic action no longer seems to play a theoretically determining role—indeed, the historical phenomena of social conflict in general, as will be shown, have disappeared behind the systematic process of the continuous perfecting of techniques of power. As soon as it takes on the form of historical investigation, Foucault's analysis of power finally, in an odd, systems-theoretic manner, approaches Adorno's social theory, from which, because of the initial action-theoretic model of social struggle, it at first so conspicuously stood apart.

6

Foucault's Theory of Society: A Systems-Theoretic Dissolution of the *Dialectic of Enlightenment*

The social theory implicit in Foucault's analysis of power is not well represented in the conceptual formulations and sociological considerations of the writings referred to thus far. As is to be expected, its real substance is indirectly raised in the historical investigations he conducted in the 1970s. There, in keeping with the complete turn to the theory of power, Foucault gives his historical writing the new form of "genealogy." This concept, which is once again oriented to Nietzsche, emerges as the successor to the original project of an archaeological approach to history.[1] The specific contours of the new discipline do not arise from methodological considerations, as was the case in the "archaeology," but follow necessarily from the shift in the object domain. So long as Foucault construes the task of his theory as the investigation of the culturally determining forms of knowledge of European modernity, his form of historical writing contrasts with the prevailing forms of the history of science by virtue of the methodological aim of an artificial distantiation of the object domain. Now, however, since it is the characteristic forms of the exercise of social power that first of all comprise the objects of the theory, his historical writing differs from traditional kinds of social history not by virtue of its unusual methodology, but in terms of the unsuspected dimensions of reality that can be discerned by an optics designed for the phenomena of power. In a text that aims at an interpretation of Nietzsche's understanding of a critical history, Foucault indirectly refers to these premises of his ge-nealogy of history: "Humanity does not gradually progress from combat to combat until it arrives at universal reciprocity, where the rule of law finally replaces warfare; humanity installs each of its violences in a system of rules and thus proceeds from domination to domination."[2]

However, it is not only the aim of consistently regarding all historical processes as the products of a general movement in the succession of systems of domination, thereby achieving a new meaning for historical events, that constitutes the special character of Foucault's genealogical writing of history. In ad-dition, within the framework of his theory of power, he takes up once more his initial question concerning the cognitive presuppositions under which humans could first be experi-enced generally as individualized subjects and gives it a more specific formulation. He is no longer interested in the abstract genesis of the concept of subjectivity in the modern sciences; now he is interested in the practical genesis of the modern representations of the subject and morality within the context of strategies of social power. Foucault is able to carry out this reformulation of his initial question by virtue of the basic idea of his theory of power, outlined above. According to this the-ory, the cognitive production of knowledge accompanies in principle the exercise of social domination over other subjects. Only on the basis of such a premise does it make sense to look for the origin of culturally influential concepts—and thus also for the genesis of the representations of the subject and mo-rality, which are central to the self-understanding of modern-ity—within the history of the techniques of social domination. A passage on the indissoluble connection between power and knowledge can thus be seen as programmatic:

A certain policy of the body, a certain way of rendering the group of men docile and useful. This policy required the involvement of definite relations of knowledge in relations of power; it called for a technique of overlapping subjection and objectification; it brought with it new procedures of individualization. . . . Knowable man (soul, individuality, consciousness, conduct, whatever it is called) is the ob-ject-effect of this analytical investment, of this domination-observation.[3]

Since his theory of power regards the production of knowledge and the exercise of domination simply as different sides of the same process, Foucault can easily combine the goal of a history of institutions with the goal of conceptual history [*Begriffsgeschichte*]. To the extent that research succeeds in exposing the historical development of modern techniques of social integration, it also reveals the conceptual roots of the modern representation of the subject. Following Nietzsche, Foucault now calls "genealogy" a kind of historical writing that integrates into a single investigation the tasks of the history of institutions and conceptual history.

However, Foucault has offered only one historical study that fully satisfies this self-imposed claim to a history guided by a theory of power. This is found in the history of the French system of criminal justice presented in 1975 under the title *Discipline and Punish*. By contrast, in 1976, the first volume of *The History of Sexuality*—subtitled *The Will To Knowledge*—presents only a kind of introduction to the initially planned six volumes. The two investigations stand in a complementary relationship to one another, fixed by the basic theoretical ideas of the theory of power. With the institutional foundation of the penal system, the first study pursues in an exemplary manner the prehistory of those administrative strategies of corporal discipline that were eventually connected to the firmly emplaced system of disciplinary power in advanced societies, whereas the historical prerequisites for the genesis of the "biopolitical" techniques (as Foucault calls the manipulative procedures aimed at the biological conduct of the population) are investigated in the large-scale history of sexuality. According to Foucault, what emerges from the results of the two investigations taken together is not only a social-historical overview of the institutional development of modern forms of social integration, but also a conceptual-historical glimpse into the history of the modern understanding of subjectivity.

Discipline and Punish initially appears to be the paradigm of a perfectly assembled, theoretically generalized history. According to it, the epochal process of change that underlies the modernization of the European penal system from medieval corporal punishment to contemporary forms of incarceration is, from another point of view, simply a social-historical process of evolution, one in which the historical development of contemporary systems of domination can be partially traced. According to Foucault, the form of social integration charac- teristic of modern societies is constituted through an institu- tional linking of disciplinary apparatuses that originated independent of one another. Of these, the prison is indeed a typical, though historically late, example. Foucault's choice of the prison as the object of his historical study already betrays, however, a bit of the prejudice at work in his analysis of the socially integrative achievements of contemporary social sys- tems. As will be shown, he represents the life of developed societies, in a paradoxical inversion of the action-theoretical assumptions of his theory of power, according to the model of total institutions.

The beginning and the end of the process of historical evo- lution, which Foucault treats as a mere segment of the com- prehensive process of the development of the modern system of power, are marked by two images that make up the intro- duction and the conclusion to his book[4]: the detailed descrip- tion of a cruel quartering in 1757 in Paris and the description of a plan in 1836 for a penal city designed as a system of total supervision. According to Foucault, the "birth of the prison," which is central to his investigation, lies between these vividly illustrated techniques of social control. The task of the inves- tigation is clearly defined by the context of the theory of power in which it is embedded: In order to demonstrate that the development of punishment can be seen as an institutional contribution to the construction of the modern system of power, Foucault must be able to show that the introduction of prison sentences, which initially had the effect of drastically reducing physical suffering, was not a process guided by con- siderations of humanity but an optimization of the process of social control. Concealed in the gradual reform of imprison- ment was, consequently, a continuous actualization of tech- niques of social power.

Describing a publicly celebrated execution, Foucault dra- matically illustrates the historical starting point of his argu- ment. It concerns a punishment, in which elements of medieval methods of torture are applied, aimed at restoring through a public forum royal sovereignty that had been injured by an offense. Foucault examines the classical system of punishment of the seventeenth and eighteenth centuries in a way that allows the mechanisms directed at the body of the delinquent to emerge. In this way he pursues the basic idea of his theory of power, according to which the characteristics of the techniques of social domination are measured primarily in terms of their effect on the bodily conduct of individuals. So construed, two ritualized treatments of the body dovetail with one another in the classical system of punishment. Initially, it is torture, i.e., the use of physical force in extracting a statement, that, together with the oath that the defendant is forced to swear before the trial, is supposed to bring about the confession in the criminal proceeding. Foucault describes torture as "a torture of the truth":

Torture was a strict judicial game. And, as such, it was linked to the old tests or trials—ordeals, judicial duels, judgments of God—that were practiced in accusatory procedures long before the techniques of the Inquisition. Something of the joust survived, between the judge who ordered the judicial torture and the suspect who was tortured; the 'patient'—this is the term used to designate the victim—was subjected to a series of trials, graduated in severity, in which he succeeded if he 'held out,' or failed if he confessed.[5]

Judicial torture, according to Foucault, is the essential element in a system of punishment in which the body functions as a locus for ascertaining the truth. After the summation of the evidence and the announcement of the sentence, this form of "corporal technology" is continued in carrying out the penalty, since in the ceremony of public chastisement or execution it is the body of the condemned that stands at the center of any measures. Foucault claims that judicial torture, staged as a spectacle before the public, joins together three juridico-political aspects: First, punishment continues the act of interrogatory torture in which the condemned publicly repeats his confession. Furthermore, torture is immanently connected to the confessed crime, since a kind of symbolic relationship is produced through the chosen means of corporal punishment. Finally, the long duration of the punishment or execution, as a conclusion to the judicial ritual, constitutes a kind of final examination. Of course, the carefully calculated "festival of torture" is itself introduced within the political context of a ritual of domination which contributes to the public manifestation of the sovereign's power. Punishment or execution acquires its central societal function initially in connection with these symbolic strategies of political rule in the "ceremonial by which a momentarily injured sovereignty is reconstituted."[6] It can be seen that the process of the publicly staged torture does not represent a juridico-political relic in the epoch of an enlightened monarchy, and concerns the restitution not of justice but of the power attacked through crime:

> We must regard the public execution, as it was still ritualized in the eighteenth century, as a political operation. It was logically inscribed in a system of punishment, in which the sovereign, directly or indirectly, demanded, decided and carried out punishments, in so far as it was he who, through the law, had been injured by the crime. In every offense there was a *crimen majestatis* and in the least criminal a potential regicide. And the regicide, in turn, was neither more nor less than the total, absolute criminal since, instead of attacking, like any offender, a particular decision or wish of the sovereign power, he attacked the very principle and physical person of the prince.[7]

After the description of the phase of penal justice determined by the practices of torture and punishment, the reforms in penal law which Foucault now takes up in his historical reconstruction are of great importance to his line of argument. As it was the "classical" system of thought in his lecture "The Discourse on Language," so now it is also the "classical" system of penal law that for Foucault above all represents the historical contrast with reference to which the specific features of modernization beginning with the transition to the nineteenth century should be sharply distinguished, be it in forms of knowledge or in penal practices. The reform of penal law, which has its philosophical roots in bourgeois social-contract theories and which becomes effective in the second half of the eighteenth century, makes "man" the limit of the legitimacy of punitive authority. In the critique of contemporary techniques of torture, with its argument that penalties should instruct and not take revenge, this reform calls for a humanization of the means employed in the punishment of offenders. At the same time, Foucault relates the many reform proposals that were developed on the basis of this moral argumentation to a calculus of the technique of power whose goal is the restriction of the monarch's judicial arbitrariness and the refinement of the instruments of social control. Thus the penal reform borne by the spirit of the Enlightenment turns out to be a transitional phase in penal techniques which, with the critique of the king's arbitrary will regarding punishments and its lack of principles, only prepares the ground for a thoroughly rationalized social control which precisely encompassed all illegalities:

In short, penal reform was born at the point of junction between the struggle against the super-power of the sovereign and that against the infra-power of acquired and tolerated illegalities. And if penal reform was anything more than the temporary result of a purely circumstantial encounter, it was because, between this super-power and this infra-power, a whole network of relations was being formed. By placing on the side of the sovereign the additional burden of a spectacular, unlimited, personal, irregular and discontinuous power, the form of monarchical sovereignty left the subjects free to practice a constant illegality; this illegality was like the correlative of this type of power. So much so that in attacking the various prerogatives of the sovereign one was also attacking the functioning of the illegalities. The two objectives were in continuity. And, according to particular circumstances or tactics, the reformers laid more stress on one or the other.[8]

Foucault argues in terms of a historically guided functionalism that steadfastly regards cultural traditions, and thus historically shaped ideas and values, only from the perspective of the objective function they perform in a systemic process characterized by the increase of power. The reform proposals born in the intellectual climate of the Enlightenment thus appear, apart from their subjectively intended content, simply as the means that help to replace a superfluous model of social control with procedures of control that correspond to historical conditions. According to Foucault's interpretation, insofar as the execution of a sentence, in keeping with the employed measures of reform, is no longer conceived as the ritualistic display of sovereign power, but rather is conceived as an act aimed at prevention and the imposition of sanctions, the entire field of delinquency is radically demarcated. Possible punishments are from now on sufficiently differentiated to be able to join, more or less symbolically and for the purpose of instruction and deterrence, a specific penalty to each particular type of delinquency. A perfection of means at the level of criminal prosecution corresponds to this functional transformation in punishment, which instead of referring only to the committed offense now refers to all possible offenses in the future. For the critique of the judicial will of the monarch, although it was influenced ethically by early bourgeois theories of democracy, brings about a decentralization of penal power, and as a result the fight against crime is able to invade recesses of society that were previously uncontrolled.

At this point, however, an obvious ambiguity is connected to the functionalistic reference system that Foucault has from the outset incorporated into his historical investigation. It is contained in the formulation asserting that the instruments of social control that are connected with the reformed methods of punishment are technologically "more effective." It is unclear whether the effectiveness of the means of social control is to be measured by criteria fixed by the institutional framework of a given social order or by the criteria set by a process of increasing social control that is independent of a specific social order. In the first case the standard that defines the exercise of social control changes with the transformation of the forms of social domination, and the measure of the effectiveness of social control would depend upon the particular conditions by which a specific form of social organization is shaped. In the second case the reference that defines the exercise of social control is historically invariant; it is determined by an objectively describable optimum of control which makes it possible to measure the effectiveness of individual forms of social control apart from the institutional framework in which they are administratively located.

Differences significant for Foucault's method are connected with the distinction between these two possibilities of a functionalist analysis. In the first case, it would be necessary to clarify the institutional conditions in terms of whose maintenance the worths of specific instruments for the exercise of social domination are measured. At the center of this analysis stands the economic and political order in relation to which the means of control appropriate to it are examined.[9] Corresponding to this within Foucault's study is a reference to a new range of criminal offenses that emerge with the capitalist transformation of the economy and to which the now-dominant bourgeoisie, by employing effective means of social control, must respond.[10] It is, of course, unwarranted to claim that the newly developed procedures of control are more effective than the instruments of social control found in prebourgeois forms of domination, since they serve the maintenance and stability of a different social order, a new institutional framework. However, Foucault seems to claim precisely this; comparing the two types of social control, he speaks of an augmentation of social power.[11] From this we can infer that he is secretly inclined toward the second model of a functionalist analysis. What stands in the center of this model is not a given social order but a process of increasing social power, from which it is assumed that this process fulfils functions in connection with invariant problems of reference. If Foucault follows such a methodological procedure, he must attempt to observe all social processes from the functionalist perspective, not of the maintenance, but rather of the augmentation of power; in other words, from the viewpoint of the objective aim of a maximum control of all processes of social life.

That Foucault in fact pursues the second version of a functionalist analysis, that he thus goes beyond the criteria of a given social order and makes the world-historical process of the augmentation of power of social systems as a whole the background of his investigation, can be clearly seen in the next step of his argument, which is connected to the concise presentation of the era of reform and which turns to the question that is now decisive. Foucault assumes that the penal reforms inspired by the moral spirit of the Enlightenment were of short duration and of little effect. Although the prison as a means of punishment had a subordinate importance in the differentiated system of publicly instructive punishment intended by the reformers, it actually assumed the dominant role in penal law within a short period of time.[12] With its institutionalization, a historically new principle of punishment is opposed to the model of punishment presented so far. What imprisonment designates is not the publicly staged correction of the absolutist epoch or the socially demonstrated penal practice of the reform phase, but the uninterrupted force achieved through a disciplining of the body concealed from the public. In view of these differences in the social logic of punishment, it is of course the rapid and all-encompassing process that, according to Foucault's interpretation, allowed imprisonment to become the central means of punishment within only a few decades that is the historical event which a history of penal law urgently needs to explain: "How then could detention," so reads the question decisive for the entire study, "become in so short a time one of the most general forms of legal punishment?"[13]

In the attempt to find an answer to this question, Foucault proceeds methodically in two stages. In one stage he attempts to identify the social problematic that at the end of the eighteenth century could force such a transformation of social techniques of punishment into the instruments of imprisonment. In the other stage he attempts, in a wide-ranging sketch, to bring out the contours of a prehistory of corporal discipline, reaching back to the Middle Ages, that created the technical and cognitive presuppositions that made possible the relatively quick application of the methods of punishment employed in the prison system. The most extensive and undoubtedly the most impressive part of Foucault's study is devoted to this second task. It takes the form of a systematic overview of the historical process by which the techniques of the methodically trained disciplining of the body were formed in European modernity. For this Foucault takes as a basis an administrative learning process in which different institutions of socialization, extending from the monasteries to the military schools, each within its own setting, gradually developed knowledges and procedures that, though not coordinated, brought about the goal of a detailed normalization of human bodily conduct. Within the historical panorama that arises on the presupposition of this basic idea, it is not difficult to perceive the institutional prehistory of those techniques of power that have already been presented on the theoretical level in connection with the three concepts of norm, body, and knowledge:

> The 'invention' of this new political anatomy [bodily discipline—A.H.] must not be seen as a sudden discovery. It is rather a multiplicity of often minor processes, of different origin and scattered location, which overlap, repeat, or imitate one another, support one another, distinguish themselves from one another according to their domain of application, converge and gradually produce the blueprint of a general method. They were at work in secondary education at a very early date, later in primary schools; they slowly invested the space of the hospital; and, in a few decades, they restructured the military organization. . . . On almost every occasion, they were adopted in response to particular needs: an industrial innovation, a renewed outbreak of certain epidemic diseases, the invention of the rifle or the victories of Prussia. This did not prevent them being totally inscribed in general and essential transformations, which we must now try to delineate.[14]

Foucault deploys all his scientific skill in the description of the methods, techniques, and knowledges that were formed out of the different disciplinary moments since the sixteenth century for standardizing and training the conduct of human bodies. Toward this end, he distinguishes between procedures of direct bodily training and strategies that accompany the control of conduct. Within the first class of disciplinary methods Foucault includes those techniques whose task it is to force the motor and gestural movements of the body into a routinized mode of conduct. Foucault uncovers four such training procedures[15]: First, there are the techniques of a spatial distribution of human bodies—in the monastery, in the school, or in the workhouse individuals are arranged according to function or rank in isolated locations and spaces. Second, there are the procedures of a temporal rationalization of all bodily conduct—bodily movements were dissected into individual acts that were specialized in terms of the handling of objects such as tools or weapons. Third, there is the attempt at a temporal formation of the methods of training themselves—the steps of discipline were located in an "analytic-evolutive" time so that they themselves could be organized and planned. Finally, there is the stage of a combination of the trained body and an ordered functional context—within the army or the workshop, the bodily activity of an individual is systematically synchronized with the activities of other individuals.

This list of disciplinary techniques enables Foucault to view the historical process of the discipline of the body not only within the usual context of the places of early capitalistic production but also as imbedded in a comprehensive complex of institutions effective for socialization.[16] In addition to this, Foucault presents a series of procedures in which the forceful routinization of modes of conduct is continuously regulated and theoretically evaluated. Here Foucault identifies three different procedures of control[17]: First, there is a constant and detailed surveillance of routinized activity that finally takes the form of an architectural design for places of education and work. Second, there is the practice of the "normalizing" judgment, in which unlawful violations of the regulations regarding time and the rules pertaining to the body are corrected by firm admonitions and punishment. And finally, as a third procedure, there is the method of "examination," which again brings together all the techniques of control: "The examination combines the techniques of an observing hierarchy and those of a normalizing judgment. It is a normalizing gaze, a surveillance that makes it possible to qualify, to classify and to punish."[18]

Foucault's historical survey culminates in the image of the "examination" not only because he sees the regulated combination of all other methods of control at work in it, but, primarily, because he perceives in it the institutional source of the modern mode of thinking that views humans as individuated subjects. This is, accordingly, the place in *Discipline and Punish* where the goals of a history of institutions are combined with those of a conceptual history [*Begriffsgeschichte*], as this was programmatically announced under the name "genealogy." Foucault thus begins with a basic idea that is instructive. He assumes that the institutional possibilities for an experience of personal individuality increased in Western modernity in connection with the power of a social class. Under the conditions of the absolutist monarchies, Foucault argues, only the members of the feudal manor who were free to assert themselves in ritual, in written accounts, or in visual reproductions were capable of becoming individuals. This social gradient marking

the individual was reversed, however, with the gradual establishment of the examination as the central mechanism of
control, since only with it could members of the subordinate
classes now be individually documented: "In a disciplinary
regime, . . . individualization is 'descending': as power becomes
more anonymous and more functional, those on whom it is
exercised tend to be more strongly individualized; it is exercised by surveillance rather than ceremonies, by observation
rather than commemorative accounts, by comparative measures that have the 'norm' as reference rather than genealogies
giving ancestors as points of reference; by 'gaps' rather than
by the acts of superiors."[19]

What would today be investigated in sociologically oriented
biographical research as the administrative constitution of individual courses of life is perceived in this line of argumentation as a process historically rooted in the examination
procedures of the early poorhouses, workhouses, and hospitals.[20] Thereby, the capacity to report one's own biography in
standardized form also becomes understandable as the peda-
gogical result of a process that serves to control social conflicts.
But Foucault seeks more for his study from this fruitful line
of thought. Beyond this social-historical line of argumentation,
he also attempts to derive an insight relating to the sociology
of knowledge. This occurs when he abruptly derives from the
thesis that in disciplinary centers individual courses of life were
produced for administrative ends the conclusion that the
psychic inner life of humans is first capable of developing
under the force of a gradually intensifying bodily discipline.
Thus, not only the capacity for biographical self-presentation
but even the capacity for individual experiences of the self is
a practical consequence of the discipline imposed on bodily
conduct. Furthermore, Foucault then infers that the concept
of the "soul," in which the psychic processes were comprehended, must also be derived solely from the contexts of the
institutional practices of bodily domination. In this way he is
finally able, apparently without any difficulty, to derive a "genealogy of the human soul" from the history of the methods
of administrative control:

Rather than seeing this soul as the reactivated remnants of an ideology, one would see it as the present correlative of a certain technology of power over the body. It would be wrong to say that the
soul is an illusion, or an ideological effect. On the contrary, it exists,
it has a reality, it is produced permanently around, on, within the
body by the functioning of a power that is exercised on those pun-
ished—and, in a more general way, on those one supervises, trains
and corrects, over madmen, children at home and at school, the
colonized, over those who are stuck at a machine and supervised for
the rest of their lives. This is the historical reality of this soul, which,
unlike the soul represented by Christian theology, is not born in sin
and subject to punishment, but is born rather out of methods of
punishment, supervision and constraint. This real, non-corporal soul
is not a substance; it is the element in which are articulated the effects
of a certain type of power and the reference of a certain type of
knowledge, the machinery by which the power relations give rise to
a possible corpus of knowledge, and knowledge extends and rein-
forces the effects of this power.[21]

Of course, to the extent that Foucault's coarsely woven epistemology is unconvincing, the attempt, from within a theory
of power, to derive the concept of the "soul" from the historical
process of bodily discipline will also sound implausible. Foucault's argument not only leaves peculiarly unclear whether it
is the origin of psychic life itself or the origin of the conceptual
representation of psychic life that he wants to uncover; it also
contradicts in a striking way the results of investigations, such
as Durkheim's sociology of religion, that are more empirically
founded and that attempt to deduce sociologically the genesis
of the concept of the "soul."[22] But the specific deficit of Foucault's argument undoubtedly consists in the fact that it de-
duces first from social influences (which are themselves
presented as merely external coercive procedures that produce
subjects) the formation of a sort of psychic life of humans, and
it then connects the representation of the "human soul" directly
to this. If Foucault really supposes he has in this way worked
out the origin of human subjectivity, then he must have been
led astray by a very crude version of behaviorism that represents psychic processes as the result of constant conditioning:
Under the pressure exercised on them in the confession and
the obligation to speak the truth, humans would have discovered motives and experiences in a place where nothing "in

itself" exists. Such an odd picture, in which psychic life is interpreted as the artificial product of a socially induced confession and in which the concept of the "soul" is conceived as its image within the world of human ideas, subsequently explains why Foucault so stubbornly refuses to regard the discipline of the human body as a historical process in which physical and psychical processes are inseparably affected.

However, the disquieting consequences to which Foucault's "genealogy of the soul" leads now have a twofold significance for the question that interests us. For what urgently needs clarification is the question of what kind of functionalist method of analysis Foucault employs in the explanation of the historical development of the techniques of punishment and especially of the rapid expansion of incarceration at the beginning of the nineteenth century. So far it is only clear how he can make intelligible the technical and cognitive conditions that within this time period made possible a rapid reorientation of the punitive procedures around the means of corporal discipline. Toward this end Foucault begins with what can be called a strategic learning process of pedagogic, military, and industrial institutions in which, since the Middle Ages, methodical knowledge and technical ability were gathered which at the end of the eighteenth and beginning of the nineteenth centuries only needed to be applied to enable the extensive formation and administration of the prison. Nevertheless, as has been said above, only the technical and cognitive presuppositions have thereby been clarified—but not the historical causes that in a relatively short time were able to bring about the introduction of imprisonment as the central technique of punishment. Foucault is thus logically driven to a second step in his argument in which the social-historical conditions that actually brought about the transformation in penal politics in the presumed time period have to be identified. The way that Foucault now attempts to answer the second question raised by his explanatory account reveals for the first time the basic systems-theoretic idea that finally connects his social theory to the historical investigations.

Foucault does not approach the question directly, but by way of a theoretical detour. He is convinced that the establishment of the prison system is realized in connection with a universal transformation of techniques of social power. Hence he must first analyze the process and the cause of this comprehensive process of transformation before he can consider, as an accompanying phenomenon, the "birth of the prison." From Foucault's point of view, the new techniques of power result from the fact that during the course of the eighteenth century the disciplinary institutions that had existed alongside one another in society in an unconnected manner grew together into a kind of self-regulating system. What was historically new was thus not found in the peculiarity of the employed methods of corporal discipline; rather,

what was new, in the eighteenth century, was that, by being combined and generalized, they attained a level at which the formation of knowledge and the increase of power regularly reinforce one another in a circular process. At this point, the disciplines crossed the 'technological' threshold. First the hospital, then the school, then, later, the workshop were not simply 'reordered' by the disciplines: they became, thanks to them, apparatuses such that any mechanism of objectification could be used in them as an instrument of subjection, and any growth of power could give rise in them to possible branches of knowledge; it was this link, proper to the technological systems, that made possible within the disciplinary element the formation of clinical medicine, psychiatry, child psychology, educational psychology, the rationalization of labor. It is a double process, then: an epistemological 'thaw' through a refinement of power relations; a multiplication of the effects of power through the formation and accumulation of new forms of knowledge.[23]

This line of thought is valid only to the extent that additional information, beyond what we already know from our basic conceptual reconstruction of Foucault's theory of power, can clarify how the historical formation of those modern techniques of domination, which are presented as a process of circulation between the increase in knowledge and the expansion of power, could have taken place. Foucault assumes that this occurred as the social product of a historical process in which the disciplinary centers that initially operated independent of one another were connected to a network of mutually coordinated and reciprocally linked institutions. That is, only to the extent that the thus-far-autonomous organizations were first brought together in a way that permitted the regulated exchange of information could the constant circulation of knowledge that is henceforth supposed to represent the presupposition of an optimal exercise of power be institutionally secured. However, Foucault does not identify the social groups through whose practical initiatives the initially isolated disciplinary centers were institutionally linked, nor does he characterize the societal institution generally responsible for bringing about such an intermeshing of systems of action. Rather, he is content with a pointed sketch of a historical problem under the weight of which he assumes the process of institutional fusion took place. He thus distinguishes two aspects of a social conjuncture that, according to his view, occurred in those societies of the eighteenth century that underwent capitalist development:

One aspect of this conjuncture was the large demographic thrust of the eighteenth century; an increase in the floating population . . . ; a change of quantitative scale in the groups to be supervised or manipulated (from the beginning of the seventeenth century to the eve of the French Revolution, the school population had been increasing rapidly, as had no doubt the hospital population; by the end of the eighteenth century, the peacetime army exceeded 200,000 men). The other aspect of the conjuncture was the growth in the apparatus of production, which was becoming more and more extended and complex; it was also becoming more costly and its profitability had to be increased.[24]

Foucault apparently takes the increase in population and the development of productive forces to be the problems to which societies respond through the formation of power strategies. Since now, in the process of capitalist modernization, these two problems assume such drastic proportion—largely because the peasants were driven from their original places of production and because the economic process was accelerated through the beginning of capital formation—society must respond, Foucault concludes, to the historically acute situation with an increase in its capacity to control; that is, with an optimization of the strategies of power socially established thus far. This occurs precisely on the way to an institutional linking of the initially isolated disciplinary centers:

The development of the disciplinary methods corresponded to these two processes, or rather, no doubt, to the new need to adjust their correlation. Neither the residual forms of feudal power, nor the structures of the administrative monarchy, nor the local mechanisms of supervision, nor the unstable, tangled mass they all formed together could carry out this role: they were hindered from doing so by the irregular and inadequate extension of their network, by their often conflicting functioning, but above all by the 'costly' nature of the power that was exercised in them.[25]

In view of the specific problems determined by the increased mobility of the population and by accelerated economic growth, the disciplinary moments represent an appropriate means for securing social power. First, they are able to do without the prestigious expenditure of feudal forms of power, and thus they are cheaper; second, they represent a system of surveillance that reaches across every sphere of social life, and thus they are more effective in terms of control; finally, through the continuous discipline of bodily conduct they increase the capacity for individual achievement, and thus they are more productive in economic output. Foucault thus speaks of the "threefold aim" of the "disciplinary regime":

. . . the peculiarity of the disciplines is that they try to define in relation to the multiplicities a tactics of power that fulfils three criteria: firstly, to obtain the exercise of power at the lowest possible cost (economically, by the low expenditure it involves; politically, by its discretion, its low exteriorization, its relative invisibility, the little resistance it arouses); secondly, to bring the effects of this social power to their maximum intensity and to extend them as far as possible, without either failure or interval; thirdly, to link this 'economic' growth of power with the output of the apparatuses (educational, military, industrial or medical) within which it is exercised; in short, to increase both the docility and the utility of all the elements of the system.[26]

From this perspective, in which the functional qualities of the newly established techniques of power are once again presented as a whole, the methodological process that *Discipline and Punish* implicitly seems to follow can be fully seen for the first time. Foucault evidently conducts his historical research within the framework of a systems theory that conceives the form of social organization as a temporary complex of power strategies by which the invariant problems of demographic growth and economic reproduction are overcome. The institutions and mechanisms of social domination are grasped as temporary solutions for tasks posed within society by the fact that the conduct of a steadily growing portion of the population must be coordinated with the requirements of a correspondingly expanding process of production.[27] The institutional solutions are temporary because each new stage in the development of the population and in the expansion of productive forces requires an increase in societal steering capacities, that is, an optimizing of strategies of social power. Societal institutions can do this because, by way of a trans-subjective learning process, they cumulatively improve the means of exercising power. Under the conditions of early capitalism, both cardinal problems in the maintenance of social power become especially acute because the need for controlling the growth of the population increases along with the need for maintaining the productive process. The system of social power responds to this historically acute situation of conflict through an institutional linking of the disciplinary institutions into one circulating system. The prospect is thereby opened up, historically for the first time, for a social condition in which the organized complex of power is itself now able to control the initially independent problems to the extent that, with the help of applied techniques, it learns to manipulate directly biological behavior as well as the productive achievements of individuals, that is, the growth of the population and the capacity for labor.

If such a pointed sketch of the systems-theoretic model of thought that underlies Foucault's historical research has been appropriately rendered, some aspects of his argument that have hardly been noticed so far are easily accommodated within a common frame of thought.

First, it becomes clear why Foucault consistently gives such scant attention to the form of economic organization of the societies he studies. From the perspective of a systems theory, as is apparently to be found in *Discipline and Punish*, the economic process is presented as a mere backdrop to the system of social power; thus, it merits increased interest only when, owing to changes, it confronts the exercise of social power with new problems of adaptation.

Second, if the proposed systems theory is assumed as a framework for argument, it is also understandable why in his social-historical studies Foucault gives only scant attention to the strategic considerations with which social groups seek to secure and widen their positions of social power. In fact, there is now a theoretical reason why, in his historical examination, Foucault disregards the dimension of social struggle, even though he had initially grounded his theory of power conceptually in a model of strategic action: As soon as societal evolution is conceived only as a process of the augmentation of social power carried out according to the logic of periodic adaptations to the environment, as is obviously the case in Foucault's historical examination, it follows that the classes that dominate at any given time are viewed as the mere bearers of systemic processes, that is, as a quantity that can in principle be ignored. Rather than forming the practical ground for the institutionalization of forms of domination, social conflicts are the everyday plain over which the systemic process paves the way.

From the other side, finally, those elements of Foucault's argument that bear the traits of a crude behaviorism also acquire a fundamentally mechanistic conception. From the perspective of a systems theory that views societal processes as systemic processes of the augmentation of power, modes of human conduct themselves, especially their bodily life expressions, are only material to be shaped by the power strategies operative at a given time. By contrast, had Foucault consistently followed the trace of his original model of action, in which existing forms of social domination were judged to be products of social conflict and not merely results of a systemic process of adaptation, he would not have been prevented from conceptually endowing social actors with those motives that first make it possible in general to produce political revolution and thus social conflict.

Thus, a systems theory one-sidedly restricted to steering processes is exposed as the juncture at which Foucault's theoretical convictions come together like threads. But even if the scattered elements of the argument gradually come together in a united whole we are still not finished with our reconstruction of Foucault's historical exposition. His explanation of the social processes that led to the transformation in penal practices at the beginning of the nineteenth century and that thus permitted the prison to become the basic means of punishment still remains. The interpretation Foucault offers for this process at the conclusion of his study is extremely terse. It follows as a simple conclusion to the functionalistic argument with which he has already explained the historic transformation of the techniques of social power in general. If it is viewed in this comprehensive context, the generalization in criminal law of carceral punishment turns out to be merely the consequence of an accommodation of punishment to the new mechanisms of the exercise of power, that is, an institutional assimilation of the methods of punishment to the disciplinary institutions that have, in the meantime, blended together into a complex whole: "One can understand the self-evident character that prison punishment very soon assumed. In the first years of the nineteenth century, people were still aware of its novelty; and yet it appeared so bound up and at such a deep level with the very functioning of society that it banished into oblivion all the other punishments that the eighteenth-century reformers had imagined. It seemed to have no alternative, as if carried along by the very movement of history."[28]

Internally, the prison operates according to the same methods that were already typical in other disciplinary institutions. It subjects the legally condemned to the force of a constant surveillance and a continuous disciplining of the body. Since it employs these procedures so exclusively that its organizational existence, so to speak, consists in them, in a final turn in his study Foucault now attempts to present the prison as institutionally paradigmatic for all other organizations in highly developed societies: "Is it surprising that the cellular prison, with its regular chronologies, forced labor, its authorities of surveillance and registration, its experts in normality, who continue and multiply the functions of the judge, should have become the modern instrument of penalty? Is it surprising that prisons resemble factories, schools, barracks, hospitals, which all resemble prisons?"[29]

Foucault does not distinguish between social organizations in which membership is regulated on the basis of juridically free contracts and total institutions in which membership is coerced on the basis of legal orders. He can pass over these decisive differences without notice because he has already defined law and morality as mere means for the cultural concealment of strategic goals.[30] Admittedly, legal norms and moral ideas no longer represent the historically variable superstructure to the invariant core of social struggle, as they initially did in his theory of power; rather, they function as the cultural superstructure of a systemic process of the augmentation of power, insofar as he has silently replaced the action-theoretic model with the systems-theoretic concept. In a sort of diagnostic conclusion to his historical argumentation in which he projects the results of the structural change of power into the present, Foucault can define the type of social integration that underlies modern societies according to the model of total institutions without substantially having to take into consideration the universal achievements of bourgeois law. Just as in the prison, in which the confined are subjected to a complex system of constant observation and continuous disciplining, so today the population as a whole is controlled through a network of disciplinary institutions spanning all spheres of social life. The title that Foucault gives to this compulsory form of social order is "panopticism." It is supposed to make clear that social conformity is secured only by way of a permanent and detailed regulation of conduct wherein the leading organs are those institutions of control that are linked together in a closed and regulated system. Thus, Foucault's study ends with a new vision of a "one-dimensional society" in which subjects are forced to adapt not through the manipulation of their psychic drives but through the disciplining of their bodily behavior:

Historically, the process by which the bourgeoisie became in the course of the eighteenth century the politically dominant class was masked by the establishment of an explicit, coded and formally egalitarian juridical framework, made possible by the organization of a parliamentary, representative regime. But the development and generalization of disciplinary mechanisms constituted the other, dark side of these processes. The general juridical form that guaranteed a system of rights that were egalitarian in principle was supported by these tiny, everyday, physical mechanisms, by all those systems of micro-power that are essentially non-egalitarian and asymmetrical that we call the disciplines. . . . The real, corporal disciplines constituted the foundation of the formal, juridical liberties. The contract may have been regarded as the ideal foundation of law and political power; panopticism constituted the technique, universally widespread, of coercion. It continued to work in depth on the juridical structures of society, in order to make the effective mechanisms of power function in opposition to the formal framework that it had acquired. The 'Enlightenment', which discovered the liberties, also invented the disciplines.[31]

As if to underscore the intellectual kinship once more, the last sentence cited above reiterates the quintessence of Foucault's study in words that could have been taken directly from the *Dialectic of Enlightenment*. In fact, viewed from this conclusion to the study of the prison, the agreement between Adorno's philosophy of history and Foucault's social theory, evident in these common formulations, is at first so striking that it threatens to conceal specific differences. Apparently like Adorno, in his historical investigation Foucault equates the course of European history with the force of a rationalization process in which the means of domination are gradually perfected under the veil of moral emancipation. What Foucault calls the "dark side" of the modern civilizing process Adorno and Horkheimer in the *Dialectic of Enlightenment* conceive as the "subterranean history" of Europe.[32] Apparently like Adorno, Foucault also assumes that the process of technical rationalization that determines the course of European history from below ground and is vaguely circumscribed by the period of the "Enlightenment" accelerates and intensifies to the extent that the practical realization of domination was methodologically controlled and reflexively optimized by the development of the natural and human sciences. As a result, both theoreticians are compelled to view the outcome of scientific activity as a whole, notwithstanding methodological characteristics and real relations, as a knowledge of domination. Finally, like Adorno, Foucault seems to see the process of technical rationalization as culminating in the "totalitarian" organizations of domination of highly developed societies. Both theoreticians conceive its stability solely as the effect of the one-sided activity of administratively highly perfected organizations. According to the common view of Adorno and Foucault, neither social groups nor the normative convictions and cultural orientations of socialized subjects have a role in the social integration of late-capitalist societies. It is solely the work of the steering accomplishments of an independent systemic organization. Adorno sees these steering accomplishments as produced by the planning and manipulative activities of a centralized administration. Foucault, by contrast, believes that the necessary accomplishments secured by the controlling and disciplinary procedures are produced by organizations institutionally linked together, such as the school, the prison, and the factory.

However, the minor variations already contained in this last point indicate a difference between Adorno and Foucault that proves to be significant if we consider the list of similarities once more. To be sure, both authors obviously ignore the fact that in normal cases social groups support or endure the process of maintaining relations of social power through their normative convictions and cultural orientations—thus, to put it sharply, they participate in the exercise of domination. Adorno and Foucault, therefore, both place a coercive model of societal order at the basis of their social theory. But Foucault, when he attempts to analyze the means of social coercion that correspond to this basic idea, is satisfied with a conception of technique that works solely on the human body, since he regards the psychic properties of subjects, and thus their personality structures, entirely as products of specific types of corporal disciplining. Because of his structuralist beginnings, Foucault, as soon as he gives his theory of power the form of historical investigations, portrays subjects behavioristically, as formless, conditionable creatures. Adorno represents this process differently. He attributes such contemporary importance to manipulative strategies because he regards it as one of the characteristics of the postliberal era of capitalism that subjects have lost the psychic strength for practical autonomy. The techniques of manipulation are able to have disposal over individuals as well as over objectified natural processes only because subjects are beginning to lose those ego capacities that were acquired in the course of the history of civilization at the expense of aesthetic capacities. What Foucault in his theory of power appears ontologically to presuppose—the conditionability of subjects—Adorno grasps as the historical product of a process of civilization that goes back to the early stages of human history.

The critical spirit of a philosophy of history that interprets the triumphal march of instrumental reason as a process of human self-denial is distinguished in this regard from the objectivistic spirit of a systems theory that views the history of society solely as a process of the augmentation of social power. Of course, Adorno and Foucault may agree in the diagnosis of a process of technical rationalization of the means of social domination, but the theories that respectively permit them to reach this common result are basically different. Adorno's philosophy of history attempts to trace the intrapsychic and societal consequences that result from the historical step of an instrumental disposition toward natural processes. It is in the position to make this claim because it takes as its basis an—admittedly unconvincing—concept of the domination of nature in which the intrapsychic processes of personality formation are regarded as complementary to the practical activity of labor. However, as a result, for Adorno the growth of capacities for administrative control is only one of three dimensions in which the process of civilization initiated by the original act of the domination of nature moves. Societal production, social domination, and the formation of individual personality are simultaneously included in this—the inexorable triumphal march of instrumental reason is reflected in the changes in the organization of social power and in the psychic properties of the subject. By contrast, the theory on the basis of which Foucault views the process of civilization in his historical investigations is directed solely to the second of these three dimensions. He portrays the history of societies solely as a systemic process of the increase of the capacity for administrative steering.

In addition, Foucault and Adorno arrive at the theoretical assumptions of their historical analyses in completely different ways. The basic model with which Foucault analyzes the process of the technical perfecting of the means of social domination is not that of the mastery of nature but rather that of strategic rationality. He assumes that societies are compelled toward the formation and development of strategic means of social control because the requirements of steering are steadily raised as a result of population growth and the corresponding development of productive forces. In his historical writings, Foucault's approach is reduced to this systems-theoretic version of a theory of social power because he is not able to grasp the social solely as a field of strategic conflicts. The manner in which the formation of complex structures of power, relations of social domination, might come about could not be explained on the exclusive basis of a concept of social struggle. Foucault does not abandon an account of the difficulties thereby raised for his argument; rather, he simply dissolves them when in his analysis of the peculiarity of modern techniques of power he suddenly puts the image of social force in the position held by strategic action. This coercive model of social order, in which the original concept of the social as a field of social struggle is transformed into the concept of a network of disciplinary social institutions, takes on a systems-theoretic form in Foucault's historical studies. In this form a single dimension is cut out of that process of civilization, already described in a one-sided manner by Adorno's philosophy of history, and is conceived functionalistically as the augmentation of social power. Thus, given the presuppositions with which Foucault operates, it is no longer a question of the complementary process of a gradual human self-alienation as found in Adorno's philosophy of history. To that extent, in the form of historical investigations, his theory of power represents a systems-theoretic solution to the *Dialectic of Enlightenment*. In its positivistic indifference, the historical process, which for Adorno took the form of a critique enveloped in resignation, becomes the objective event of the augmentation of social power.

Admittedly, neither Adorno's critical theory nor its systems-theoretic continuation in Foucault's theory of power yields the appropriate tools for analyzing the forms of integration in late-capitalist societies. What is required for that is a consistent working out of those dimensions of social action so far only indirectly and vaguely encountered in Horkheimer's early work, namely that of "culture" and that of "social struggle." By contrast, Jürgen Habermas' social theory offers the best chance for a substantive development of these concepts. In his attempt at a communication-theoretic transformation of critical theory, he has made the dimension of social interaction the center of his approach. Habermas initially developed his theory by way of a critique of positivism based on an anthropology of knowledge. The first phase of his theoretical work is determined by the goal of tracing the different types of scientific knowledge back to prescientific interests of the species so that critical social theory might be justified as an element of the societal life-process (chapter 7).

Habermas extends the communication-theoretic insights of his critique of positivism into the basic assumptions of a social theory in which he attempts to establish a primacy for processes of social interaction in the formation of the species and thus for social evolution. In this second phase of his work Habermas presents mutual understanding [*Verständigung*] as the paradigm of the social. Yet he locates the basic ideas of social theory that result from this within two competing versions of the history of the species. As I will try to show in chapter 8, two different versions of social theory from within the perspective of a theory of communication follow from this. Habermas develops further only the first conception, one oriented to systems theory. In the 1970s his social theory was worked out, in several stages, from the approach initially developed in his critique of the technocracy thesis. This developmental process, in which the traces of an alternative model of society gradually disappear, is finally formulated in *The Theory of Communicative Action* (see chapter 9 below).

Habermas' Anthropology of Knowledge: The Theory of Knowledge-Constitutive Interests

In his inaugural address at Frankfurt, "Knowledge and Human Interests" (1965), Jürgen Habermas, like Max Horkheimer thirty years earlier, outlined the program of a critical social theory.[1] Like Horkheimer, Habermas pursues in his contribution the goal of clarifying the theoretical claim and the methodological peculiarity of a critical social theory which he attempts to distance, step by step, from a traditionally conceived form of theory. Again like the Horkheimer of the 1930s, Habermas states the opinion that in the traditional understanding of theory science can be viewed as a "pure" undertaking, freed from practical interests, only because its own mooring in social practice remains epistemologically unclarified. Therefore, both Horkheimer and Habermas see the primary task and vocation of a critical social theory to be that it—in contrast to traditional theory—must first make conscious at a general epistemological level its own origins as well as the origins of traditional theory. But in the working out of this thesis, that is, in the reconstruction of the specific practical relation of the different forms of theory, Habermas departs from Horkheimer at decisive points. Different conceptions of human knowledge lie at the basis of the common approach to a critique of traditional theory from which Horkheimer in the 1930s and Habermas in the 1970s attempt to develop a critical social theory. These differences reveal that, from the beginning, Habermas attempts to locate his social theory within the framework of a theory of action that is more complex than Horkheimer's critical theory or Foucault's theory of power.

Just as Horkheimer, in "Traditional and Critical Theory," originally used Descartes' reflection on method as a critical foil, so Habermas, in his inaugural address, uses Husserl's *Crisis* to gain an initial picture of theory as traditionally conceived. Of course, *The Crisis of the European Science and Transcendental Phenomenology* (which Husserl worked on from 1934 through 1937) itself already represents the attempt to overcome the history of the scientistic model of science that in a certain sense began with the writings of Descartes. In his work Husserl began with the view that the project of modern science, originating with the Renaissance, had fallen into a global crisis because an objectivistic self-understanding, which in principle blocked the view of the origin of scientific analyses in the lifeworld, had in the meantime gained the upper hand in the particular scientific disciplines. Husserl regards this regression of the sciences, initially born of an ancient ideal of reason, in the factual sciences of the nineteenth century as the "positivistic reduction of the idea of science."[2] It has allowed the reality of the prescientific generation of scientific phenomena to be forgotten, and thereby rendered ineffective the "life-significance" of the sciences in general. In contrast to this positivistic self-forgetfulness, Husserl now offers the path of a transcendental self-reflection, namely, phenomenology, which, through the systematic clarification of the origin of the sciences in the lifeworld, at the same time emancipates itself from the network of prescientific conditions of interest. Since it sufficiently extricates itself from the self-understanding of the primary lifeworld, phenomenological reflection again finds a connection with the ancient ideal of contemplative knowledge and, precisely in this connection, finds meaning for the practical life (which was left behind by the sciences as well).[3] Husserl feels justified in reaching such a paradoxical conclusion because he makes recourse to the concept of theory in the Greek philosophical tradition wherein only those theoretical achievements of the mind that have completely freed themselves from the context of everyday concerns are able to achieve power for orienting action. In this way, phenomenology, in the transcendental reflection on the constitutive context of science in the lifeworld, also frees itself from that context and retrieves for itself the normative-practical moment that was lost along the path of the objectivistic self-restriction of the sciences. At this point in Husserl's argumentation, Habermas introduces the goal of his critique of traditional theory. He wants to show that the therapeutic proposal of a contemplative, pure theory, with which Husserl hopes to overcome the crisis of the European sciences, allows a revival of precisely that fiction of an interest-free knowledge which has always belonged to the traditional concept of theory. In contrast to this, Habermas, as well as Horkheimer, insists on an indissoluble connection between knowledge and interests.

The argument with which Habermas opens his objection to the phenomenological program of the *Crisis* is of a philosophical-historical nature. He is convinced that Husserl, in calling for a contemplative ideal of knowledge, falsely neglected the context of interests in which this ideal was originally introduced. Greek philosophy could expect power for orienting action from a pure, intuitive theory only insofar as it could at the same time also suppose a cosmological order which, so to speak, furnishes the ideal for human-social relations. Only because the ability of the cosmos to provide a social model is previously secured at the ontological level could directions for guiding action and practical recommendations be expected from a theory that observes the cosmological order of the world from a seemingly interest-free posture. Husserl, who leaves this constitutive connection out of consideration, therefore deceives himself when he places the same practical expectations in a phenomenology that Greek philosophy, under its ontological presuppositions, could rightly place in a contemplative theory:

Theory in the sense of the classical tradition only had an impact on life because it was thought to have discovered in the cosmic order an ideal world structure, including the prototype for the order of the human world. Only as cosmology was theory also capable of orienting human action. Thus Husserl cannot expect self-formation processes to originate in a phenomenology that, as transcendental philosophy, purifies the classical theory of its cosmological contents, conserving something like the theoretical attitude only in an abstract manner. Theory had educational and cultural implications not because it had freed knowledge from interest. To the contrary, it did so because it derived *pseudonormative power from the concealment of its actual interests.*[4]

In a brief recollection of the origin of Greek philosophy, Habermas supports the claim that at the basis of traditional theory in the Greek sense there is also a knowledge-constituitive interest, the denial of which was constitutive for it. Its origin is conceived as the emancipatory product of a process of will-formation in which the superhuman powers of a sovereign world of the gods become the weakened, inner-worldly forces of the human emotions and passions. But because the identity of individuals, under the conditions created by the demythologization of worldviews, became, in precarious ways, independent of the old originary powers, it now requires the fiction of a stable and exemplary cosmos in whose fixed laws subjects are once again progressively able to find a normative support. Insofar as theory in Greek philosophy was viewed precisely as an undertaking which, in an interest-free attitude, investigates the cosmos in its eternal order, it assumed exactly the function that was necessary for stabilizing the emancipated consciousness of individuals. Of course, it could fulfill its social task only by continuously denying its own emancipatory interest in the objectivistic fiction of an independently given cosmos. That is, "had it been possible . . . to detect that the identity of pure Being was an objectivistic illusion, ego identity would not have been able to take shape on its basis."[5]

Habermas recalls this origin of Greek philosophy only in order to insist, against Husserl, on the discreet connection between interests and the type of a pure theory which Husserl had taken up in his own program of overcoming the positivistic age. Husserl not only misunderstands that without cosmological presuppositions a purely contemplative theory could not achieve any action-guiding insights, but he himself, as this philosophical-historical review shows, relies on the illusion of pure theory that Greek philosophy must necessarily have given to theoretical knowledge if it wanted to protect the achieved state of consciousness from falling back into a mythological interpretation of the world. Accordingly, Husserl draws the wrong consequences from his critique of the objectivistic self-understanding of the modern sciences. Instead of also applying the phenomenological insight into the prescientific lifeworld of scientific theory to its own philosophical theory-construction, and therefore determining the knowledge-constitutive interest of his own critique of science, he insists precisely upon the status of an interest-free knowledge for his critique. He thereby only repeats once again at a higher level the objectivistic misunderstanding for which, in his critique, he had just reproached the modern sciences. In contrast to this, Habermas, having shown the unaddressed lifeworld of traditional theory in Husserl, can now insist on a connection in principle between scientific theory-construction and prescientific interests. The image of a pure theory, on which Husserl had concentrated his hopes, is therefore futile: "Our reason for suspecting the presence of an unacknowledged connection between knowledge and interest is not [like Husserl's—A.H.] that the sciences have abandoned the classical concept of theory, but that they have not completely abandoned it. The suspicion of objectivism exists because of the ontological illusion of pure theory that the sciences still deceptively share with the philosophical tradition after casting off its practical content."[6]

With the assertion that the positivistic sciences share with the philosophical tradition the self-misunderstanding of an interest-free form of knowledge, Habermas has addressed, in the specific context of his critique of Husserl, the theoretical presupposition with which Horkheimer began his classical study "Traditional and Critical Theory": Both are convinced that every form of scientific knowledge is invariably bound to a prescientific interest. Therefore, like Horkheimer, Habermas must now also determine more precisely, from an epistemological point of view, the interest-context of the traditional type of theory, as he conceives it, in order to be able to retrieve from it the specific tie to interests of a critical social theory. But the fact that he imputes to traditional theory (in the sense of the Greek philosophical tradition) an emancipatory cognitive interest already indicates that he is not content to leave it, like Horkheimer, with a simple separation into two possible types of theories: traditional theory and critical social theory. Habermas is more complex in his epistemological considerations: Alongside the positivistic sciences (captured above all in Horkheimer's concept of "traditional theory") and the critically oriented sciences (which above all Horkheimer wanted to understand in terms of the conception of a critical social theory reaching back to Marx), Habermas considers the tradition of hermeneutics, to which Adorno and Horkheimer had always remained closed. His programmatic thesis, in which the basic premises of the original approach of Habermas' theory come together, reads:

There are three categories of processes of inquiry for which a specific connection between logical-methodological rules and knowledge-constitutive interests can be demonstrated. This demonstration is the task of a critical philosophy of science that escapes the snares of positivism. The approach of the empirical-analytic sciences incorporates a *technical* cognitive interest; that of the historical-hermeneutic sciences incorporates a *practical* one; and the approach of critically oriented sciences incorporates the *emancipatory* cognitive interest that, as we saw, was at the root of traditional theories.[7]

The epistemological analysis of these three types of knowledge makes up the center of a first phase of Habermas' work.[8] In it the epistemological investigations take over not only the task of clarifying the scientific status of a critical social theory but also the task of furnishing directly the framework for the construction of social theory. In the beginning Habermas attempts to portray epistemology itself as a form of social theory in which he conceives the different forms of knowledge as universal components in the reproduction of societies. From this there emerges the idea of an analysis of society, sketched as a critique of positivism, which justifies his original approach. It is based on the epistemological analysis of the relations between anthropologically deep-seated models of action, knowledge-constitutive interests, and social types of rationality.

For Habermas the concept of "knowledge-constitutive interest" is already quite early the key for the epistemological justification of a critical social theory. With it he offers the bridge between the theory of human action, initially set forth in anthropological terms, and the analytic of social rationality that together will produce the categorial framework for social the-

ory. If, as Habermas has attempted to show in contrast to
Husserl, all scientific knowledge is supposed to proceed from
a prescientific connection to experience—so that the idea of
"pure" theory-construction shows itself to be an objectivistic
illusion—then it is the task of epistemology to demonstrate that
practical constitutive connection for every form of science as
well as for itself. Habermas calls "interests" the prescientific
patterns of orientation, which are supposed to produce the
perspectives from which reality is first constituted as an object
of experience for humans. Thereby the category apparently
fulfills the same epistemological function that the unsystemat-
ically applied category of "relation to conduct" had taken
in Horkheimer's text. But it is not indebted, as in the case
of Horkheimer, to a direct application of the epistemological
intuitions of the young Marx, but rather to an early and
deep-seated reception of philosophical anthropology and to a
subsequent appropriation of American pragmatism and philosophical hermeneutics.

The first motivation for the introduction of the concept of
"knowledge-constitutive interest" probably arose for Habermas
from the theory of Arnold Gehlen. In support of this, the
epistemological idea in this sense first finds mention in remarks
about philosophical anthropology. Gehlen was able to show that
humans, as indeterminate beings by nature, are oriented to a
practical mastery of their environment. Therefore, as Habermas states in connection with Gehlen, "world-orientation and
action-conduct are one" for humans.[9] Humans construct, so to
speak, their experiential space according to the model of action
through which they learn to maintain themselves within nature.
Habermas held this line of thought when he still operated
within the context of his philosophical beginnings, which were
tied to the results of Heidegger's analytic of *Dasein*.[10] There
the demonstration, introduced at the phenomenological level,
corresponds to the anthropological finding that humans first
sketch the world in which they find themselves according to
their manner of "being-in-the-world."[11] From an epistemological point of view, Heidegger's existential ontology could, therefore, confirm the conclusion that Gehlen had drawn at the
anthropological level from the biological fact of human unspec-

ifiability. Both explained the "world-orientations" in which humans always already move in terms of the unique compulsion toward a bodily-practical engagement through which humans are existentially or biologically characterized. It is from this common background with philosophical anthropology that Habermas, at this time, views the epistemological significance of Heidegger's early work. Hence, in his presentation of the basic thought of the analytic of *Dasein* in *Being and Time*, Gehlen's anthropology always audibly rings through: "As humans produce and maintain themselves through labor, Being bursts forth round about them in its significance."[12] Now, to be sure, with the reception of Gehlen's or the early Heidegger's epistemological motives, the perspective of an anthropologically or existential-philosophically altered transcendentalism, in which the practical world-orientations of humans appear as conditions of the possibility of experience, is already achieved. But this result is still not fully satisfactory for a differentiated logic of science, since at least two further steps are required in order to be able to trace the different forms of scientific knowledge back to the prescientific lifeworlds. On the other hand, the discussion, completely unspecified until now, of the practical world-orientation as the horizon from which reality is opened up to humans, must be converted from the singular to the plural so that it might become clear why it should finally permit different models of scientific knowledge to be derived from the specifically human compulsion toward the practical enclosure of the world. For this it was necessary to distinguish within the natural or existential basic situation of humans different modes of action, practice, or "Being-in-the-world." Then, as an analogue to these, different models of the construction of human experience, and thereby different models of object-constitution, could be observed. On the other hand, the different models of the prescientific experience of the world, if they could actually be plausibly drawn out from particular modes of human action, must be shown to be determinants of the logical-methodological procedure of different types of scientific knowledge, because only in this way was proof for the scientific-constitutive role of world-orientations to be furnished. For this it was necessary, in an immanent exposition of the factually given logic of science, to push forward to that dimension in which the logical methodological differences between the separate types of science appeared as differences in the constituting world-orientation. From these considerations, which resulted from the initially still vague idea of an anthropologically altered transcendentalism and with which Habermas will answer both of these tasks, emerges the concept of "knowledge-constitutive interests." At the conceptual level the concept first appeared in the essay Habermas published in connection with the "positivist dispute" at the beginning of the 1960s.

Habermas' contributions to this epistemological debate grew out of the controversy between Karl Popper and Theodor Adorno over the validity and range of methods in the social sciences and, in the "positivist dispute," finally exerted a lasting influence upon the discussion about methods in the social sciences.[13] These essays are almost completely free of the terminology of philosophical anthropology and, even more, Heidegger's analytic of *Dasein*. In their place a language now emerges that, in addition to analytical theory of science, derives from American pragmatism and hermeneutic philosophy. But in this new conceptual world the original idea still exists in which what was previously characterized as "practical orientations to the world" is now viewed under an altered title as a prescientific interest within whose horizon scientific experiences in general are first able to be formed.

In a manner different than Adorno, Habermas sets out immanently with his attempt to ground epistemologically the proper place of a critical sociology in opposition to critical rationalism's methodological claim to universality. He undertakes this by showing the connection between the methodological rules of procedure that Popper would like to make obligatory for all the sciences and a type of scientific task drastically distinguished from that of a critically social science. Habermas's principle area of proof is the methodological discussion concerning the so-called basis problem posed by the clarification of the possibility of an empirical verification of theoretical hypotheses. Logical empiricism saw the solution to the problem as lying in the verification of the empirical correctness of logically well-constructed hypotheses by reference to elementary protocol sentences in which the results of controlled observations were directly retained. Against this conception Popper offered the refutation (which today, after the postempirical turn of philosophy of science, sounds trivial) that even the most simple protocol sentences do not merely represent sense perceptions, since theoretical generalizations unavoidably enter into them. As is well known, Popper then wanted to lead the way out of the methodological dilemma presented by his objections against the possibility of an empirical verification of theoretical hypotheses by means of a general conception of falsification.[14] In this way it is seen that lawlike hypotheses are indirectly tested through systematically induced attempts at contradiction instead of directly in an inductive verification in empirical test situations. Of course, the same problem that Popper had worked out in reference to the model of verification of logical empiricism occurs here again within the altered context of the concept of falsification. Observation sentences, with whose help lawlike assumptions can be falsified by contradicting existential assertions, cannot simply be justified by the certainty of sense perceptions. Thus, in a last turn in his argument, Popper finally makes the decision about whether a specific observation sentence subjected to falsification ought to be considered empirically true dependent upon an agreement among scientists conducting research. Consequently, the last instance before any given lawlike hypothesis is indirectly confirmed is the agreement of the investigator to regard a basic proposition as a sufficiently established observation statement.

This surprising concession of Popper concerning the constitutive role of the research community now serves as an entrance into Habermas's own argument. In a first step he shows that Popper unintentionally draws a consequence from this line of thought to which the quite different tradition of hermeneutic philosophy has already drawn attention. To the extent that Popper reconnects the empirical testing of theoretical statements to the judgment of the engaged scientist, the research process is interpreted as a communicative relation in which the inquiring subjects must have already acquired a common preunderstanding about the meaning of their investigation in order to be able to reach a consensus about the empirical validity of observation statements. Hence the process of scientific research is also embedded within the horizon of a prior interpretation of meaning in which, moreover, from the view of hermeneutics, every act of reciprocal understanding is realized in social praxis:

Research is an institution composed of people who act together and communicate with one another; as such it determines, through the communication of the researchers, that which can theoretically lay claim to validity. The demand for controlled observation, as the basis for decisions concerning the empirical plausibility of law-like hypotheses, already presupposed a preunderstanding of certain social norms. It is certainly not sufficient to know the specific aim of an investigation and the relevance of an observation for certain assumptions. Instead, the meaning of the research process as a whole must be understood before I can know to what the empirical validity of basic statements is related.[15]

Habermas makes use of the basic ideas of hermeneutics, which he introduces with reference to the studies of Gadamer, in order to emphasize the insight, as an unintended consequence of Popper's argument, into the structure of understanding of all scientific processes of investigation. That is, the question now put to critical rationalism is: What kind of "socially normed behavioral expectations"[16] can be provided that support the agreement of the research community about the empirical validity of basic propositions? Popper could only be satisfied with a decisionistic solution for his argument because he had not explicitly considered the embeddedness of research processes in a prior horizon of interpretation. However, the moment when that happens, that is, when the dependency of scientific research upon a communicative preunderstanding is hermeneutically brought to consciousness, the question of the character of this preunderstanding can no longer remain unanswered.

Thus it is not hard to see that Habermas again introduced at a hermeneutic level the epistemological perspective that Gehlen's philosophical anthropology and Heidegger's existential ontology had opened up to him. Initially the thesis that all scientific research processes are so embedded in an interpretive horizon that a kind of preunderstanding concerning the meaning of their application as a whole always already exists said little more than that scientific knowledge is contained within the framework of a prescientific, knowledge-constitutive orientation to the world. But with the second step in the dispute with critical rationalism, Habermas goes beyond this elementary identification; he now sets out to clarify the character of the preunderstanding by which the scientists who participate in a scientific research process are commonly governed in their joint activity. For this Habermas relies upon the epistemology of American pragmatism. His explication aims at tracing the conditions of validity of the research methods described by Popper back to the criteria of success that are naturally built into the process of social labor.

Pragmatism's fundamental thesis that our scientific activity is guided by practically established convictions until particular elements from this horizon of latent certainties become problematic and thereby first assume the character of scientific hypotheses in general serves as an introduction to the argument with which Habermas grounds his thesis. If we can conceive scientific assumptions as the cognitive products of the disturbance of a practically well-coordinated behavior—in a sense, as temporarily unsuccessful certainties about action that, because of their failure, become conscious—then we can conclude that the scientific tests to which we submit our problematized convictions for the purpose of proof in principle reconstruct the same test procedures that already continuously underlie our actions in everyday life and the certainty that accompanies them. Now, insofar as our well-coordinated behavior, from which Habermas initially begins, is confirmed by the technical success of our plans of action, we can justifiably assume a knowledge-constitutive interest that is found in the increase of technically utilizable knowledge to be the preunderstanding of empirical-analytic research processes:

In the last instance, therefore, the empirical validity of basic statements, and thereby the plausibility of law-like hypotheses and empirical scientific theories as a whole, is related to the criteria for assessing the results of action which have been socially adopted in the necessarily intersubjective context of working groups. It is here that the hermeneutic pre-understanding concealed by the analytically theory of science, is formed, a pre-understanding which first makes possible the application of rules for the acceptance of basic statements. The so-called basis-problem simply does not appear if we regard the research process as part of a comprehensive process of socially institutionalized actions, through which social groups sustain their naturally precarious life. For the basic statement no longer draws empirical validity solely from the motives of an individual observation, but also from the previous integration of individual perceptions into the realm of convictions which are unproblematic, and have proved themselves on a broad basis. This occurs under experimental conditions which, as such, imitate the control of the results of action which is naturally built into systems of societal labor.[17]

As a criterion for the demarcation of the preunderstanding that is supposed to support the empirical-analytical sciences as a whole, Habermas chooses the kinds of test procedures that experimental hypotheses display in the process of research. Because the experimental conditions under which scientific tests take place simply reconstruct artificially the confirmation procedures that are more or less introduced into every act of social labor, we can assume that the sciences are embedded in the same interpretive horizon, or, as we can also say, in the same orientation to the world, within which humans prescientifically master nature.[18] This practical preunderstanding finds the unproblematic agreement it apparently enjoys throughout the different epochs and cultures because humanity is universally subjected to the constraint of the technical control over natural processes and, hence, to the constraint of a technical orientation to the world:

The interest in the sustenance of life through societal labor under the constraint of natural circumstances seems to have been virtually constant throughout the previous stages in the development of the human race. For this reason, a consensus concerning the meaning of technical domination can be achieved without difficulty, in principle, within historical and cultural boundaries; the intersubjective validity of empirical-scientific statements that follows the criteria of this preunderstanding is therefore secured.[19]

Thus, Habermas turns into an anthropological argument the
epistemological argument in which the empirical-analytical research procedures are plausibly described as the methodologically reflected continuation of an activity of labor that has been
disrupted in everyday life. He maintains that the technical
preunderstandings that support the sciences have universal
significance insofar as they reconstruct in their validity conditions the criteria of success of technical action, since humanity
can guarantee its survival only through the technically successful appropriation of nature. However, in the cited passage, he
further assumes that different human cultures have in fact also
ascribed the same meaning to the labor that is unavoidable for
all. He will later replace this incautious formulation with the
weaker thesis that in every form of social labor, quite independent of the cultural meaning that the different epochs and
societies attribute to it at any given time, a basic attitude of
orientation to success must necessarily always come into play.
The theoretical line of thought formulated in this version now
becomes a firm component in Habermas' theory. It provides
the theoretical basis for the perspective of an anthropologically
transformed transcendentalism that, as we have seen, Habermas already held firmly in view in his earliest writings. Now,
from a general perspective, Habermas views the orientations
to the world-horizons of interpretation that were introduced
as conditions for the possibility of scientific experience as cognitive attitudes that are connected to anthropologically fundamental forms of action. In those modes of action that they
are compelled to fulfill in order to maintain their life, humans
take up specific attitudes to the world that, as communicatively
shared interpretive horizons or orientations to the world, determine what can be scientifically learned by them. The cognitive conditions for the empirical-analytic sciences that Popper
had grasped from the perspective of the theory of science are
"transcendentally" defined by the attitude that humans are
then compelled to take up when they appropriate nature for
the purpose of securing their lives. The sciences let themselves
be guided by a "technical cognitive interest,"[20] as it is now
expressly called.

So far the line of thought that Habermas follows in his

contributions to the "positivist dispute" still corresponds for the most part to the direction of argument that Horkheimer had adopted in his epistemological sketch of traditional theory. Of course, Habermas' pragmatic methodology differs from the crude instrumentalism Horkheimer took over from the young Marx. But, as a result of their reflections, both view positivistic science as the methodical completion of the process of the appropriation of nature by which the human species secures its material life. Similarly, in this connection, both are confronted with the same epistemological task of needing to retrieve from the technical interest of the empirical-analytic sciences the interest by which a critical theory of society is itself defined. As I have shown, Horkheimer, in claiming a "critical attitude" alongside the "technical attitude" that was admittedly not justifiable within the context of his philosophy of history, directly approaches this decisive question from a social-theoretic perspective. Habermas approaches the same problem in another way. He initially insists upon the existence of alternative forms of theory construction only indirectly, in that he shows how positivism has systematically obstructed the view to all further cognitive interests with the generalization of the empirical-analytic form of research as the only scientific method.

Only in this next step of his reply to Popper does Habermas first develop the basic moves of a critique of positivism. Up to this point his argument still does not include the attempt to make an epistemological critique of the empirical-analytic sciences; it presents only the path of an immanent tracing back of these sciences to a prescientific connection to interests. In contrast, the mode of research of the sciences expressly grasped by Popper is first found to be epistemologically justified in that it is connected, in a transcendental manner, to the process of social labor. In principle Habermas has no objections to the well-coordinated procedures of the exact natural sciences as these are methodologically defined by modern philosophy of science, so long as they are employed only for the scientific solution of questions that result directly from the task of the technical control over the processes of nature. This consequence, which follows necessarily from the approach of an anthropologically transformed transcendentalism, is the source of Habermas' dogmatism with respect to methodological questions of the natural sciences against which today an ecologically motivated critique, supported by postempiricist developments in the theory of science, raises significant objections.[21] However, the same epistemological conclusion that leads Habermas to a methodological dogmatism with respect to the natural sciences now equally serves him as a presupposition for the critique he develops against the positivism of modern theory of science, represented by Popper. That is, if the empirical-analytic methods of procedure are valid only with respect to scientific questions of the technical control over the process of nature, then they of course lose their theoretical validity where scientific research deals with questions other than technical ones. However, since analytic theory of science believes itself to have freed the scientific process of research from any connection to a prescientific lifeworld, it cannot pose the question about the specific domain of validity of the methods of research put forward by it. It must clarify the methodical procedures it actually encounters in the prevailing forms of the exact sciences as a universally valid logic of research, although the constitution of the scientific object domains are already indebted to their connection with a specific, namely technical, cognitive interest.

For Habermas, the positivism of modern theory of science begins where epistemological reflection upon the universal conditions of the possibility of scientific experience is lost and, hence, when, beyond the boundaries of its legitimate domain of application, the particular research methods of the natural sciences claim validity for all forms of knowledge. Accordingly, positivistic thought can be conceived, as is stated in a passage with a paradoxical reference to Marx's critique of ideology, as "the false consciousness of a correct praxis," namely, the research process guided by a technical cognitive interest:

My criticism is not aimed at research practices in the exact empirical sciences. . . . My critique is exclusively directed at the positivistic interpretation of such research processes. For the false consciousness of a correct practice affects the latter. I do not dispute that the analytical theory of science has stimulated actual research and has helped to elucidate methodological judgments. At the same time, however, the positivistic self-understanding has restrictive effects; it silences any binding reflection beyond the boundaries of the empirical-analytical (and formal) sciences.[22]

Habermas turns against positivistic thought because it theoretically raises the research methods of the exact sciences that have proceeded from the specific action context of labor to the sole form of human rationality, so that all socially important questions finally appear under the perspective of questions to be treated technically. However, in order to be able to characterize the exclusive completion of a technically defined interpretation of science as an "incomplete rationalization," as Habermas already does here, it is necessary to demonstrate epistemologically another form of scientific rationalization. Habermas undertakes this by making explicit the type of knowledge that so far was thematized in the indirect form of a limiting condition of positivism as a principle of knowledge that is connected to a second practical interest. Thus, in his controversy with Popper he enters the dimension that from now on will characterize the proper domain of his theory.

In an earlier context Habermas already viewed the communicative self-understanding of the subjects involved in a research process as an unavoidable presupposition of the sciences. In the next step of his argument he now frees this phenomenon from the context of the theory of science in which it was initially developed and presents it as a characteristic of the socio-cultural *Dasein* of humans generally. Thus, alongside the anthropological dimension of labor in terms of which the technical cognitive interest was initially defined, a second dimension of action, regarded as equally fundamental, is introduced that, accordingly, justifies the recognition of a second cognitive interest.

The line of argument that leads Habermas to this result begins with a consideration that was already significant in connection with the original controversy with Gehlen's anthropology. Against the tendency he finds in Gehlen's early writings to limit the peculiar capacities of human action to the one ability for the "practical mastery of life" (that is, labor), Habermas advances the related thesis that human expressions of action "precisely break open the circle of the mere reproduction of life"[23]: "A blind reproduction of life solely for its own sake is indifferent to barbarism and humanism, to the definition of an existence that is posed simply by nature on the threshold of risk between truth and falsehood."[24] The objection (which is not completely fair to Gehlen's early anthropological work, since it does not consider its emphasis on the creative capacities of human action) is of immense significance for the development of Habermas' theory[25]; directly connected with it is the question of what other forms of expressions of life and capacities of action there are that, beyond the ability for instrumental action, are uniquely human. In the earlier text from which the cited objection is taken, a clear answer to this question is not found. With reference to Gehlen's later writings, Habermas emphasizes the mimetic-representative action of the human mode of life, but the argument in no way leads to the assertion of a second action-potential of humans that is equally comparable to labor. As is also the case with his interpretation of Marx from the same time, Habermas is still so shaped by a philosophy of history influenced by Heideggerian Marxism that he is not yet able to replace the idea, already authoritative for Adorno and Horkheimer, of a production of history through human labor alone.[26] Thus we first find a new kind of answer to the proposed problem, stimulated not least by Hannah Arendt's praxis-philosophy, after Habermas becomes determined to find a second form of human action, at the anthropological level, within the dimension of communicative understanding brought to light by hermeneutic philosophy.

In connection with his controversy with Popper, Habermas completes the step that, together with the recognition of a second form of human action, leads to the identification of a further cognitive interest. He does this by interpreting the understanding of the scientist, regarded as a necessary condition for the research process, as a fundamental principle of human socialization in general. Thereby, Habermas is guided by a consideration that throughout can be understood as a concretization of his objections to Gehlen. The formulation for the state of affairs that has so far been established only vaguely in contrast to Gehlen now maintains that individuals united within societies are capable of maintaining their lives only when, beyond the reproduction of their material existence, they also continuously contribute to a renewal of their social lifeworld. Just as the research community must reach an understanding about the meaning and the goal of scientific undertaking, a society as a whole must produce a kind of elementary consensus about the meaning and the goal of social life. Thus, in human history, the requirement of social labor is peculiarly limited by the task of communicative self-understanding:

Socialized individuals are only sustained through group identity which contrasts with animal societies which must be constantly built up, destroyed and formed anew. They can only secure their existence through processes of adaptation to their natural environment, and through readaptation to the system of social labor in so far as they mediate their metabolism with nature by means of an extremely precarious equilibrium of the individuals amongst themselves. The material conditions of survival are most closely bound up with the most sublime conditions; organic equilibrium is bound up with the distorted balance between separation and unification. Only in this balance, through communication with others, is the identity of each ego established.[27]

With this statement Habermas not only formulates the basis of his criticism of positivism; he also inconspicuously separates himself from the basic assumptions of a philosophy of history that for so long were decisive for the tradition of critical theory. In a certain sense the quoted passage sets out the touchstone of the communication-theoretic turn of critical Marxism, as the whole of Habermas' social theory may now be conceived. Habermas no longer views the process of human socialization only in terms of the process of a continually expanding appropriation of nature. For him its significance consists much more in the fact that the collective securing of material existence, which is guaranteed by social labor, is from the beginning dependent upon the simultaneous preservation of a communicative agreement. Since generally humans are able to develop personal identities only so long as they can grow up in the intersubjectively shared world of a social group and operate within it, the disruption of the communicative process of understanding

damages a presupposition of human survival that is as fundamental as the presupposition of the collective appropriation of
nature. Linguistic communication is the medium in which individuals are able to secure the commonality of their action
orientations and world-representations necessary for mastering
the collective task of material reproduction. Thus intersubjective understanding is the ground upon which societies must be
anchored in order to be able to secure their material survival.

From an epistemological perspective, what is unique about
the communicatively established commonality is that the distortions and disturbances that emerge within it cannot be eliminated through those technical interventions which scientific
research, in connection with its cognitive interest, invariably
recommends as a solution. The exact sciences do not extend
to the sphere of communicative understanding; with their assertions and prognoses, they do not touch upon the self-understanding of acting subjects, but only upon the unintentional
course of events of a reality objectified from the perspective of
control. Thus, too, no conclusions can be gained from theoretical results about how a process of social communication
interrupted in its everyday flow could again be set in motion
by scientific means. Therefore, it can be said that positivism
misrepresents the peculiarity of human socialization when it
offers the procedures of modern science as the methodological
principle of scientific rationalization for the solution to problems in general, since precisely those tasks that grow out of the
social need for communicative understanding cannot be solved
with the help of the scientific results of empirical-analytic research. Habermas illustrates this conclusion with the example
of a naturalistic sociology:

A sociology which restricted itself in its critical intention to empirical-
analytical research would only be in a position to examine the self-
preservation and self-destruction of social systems in the sphere of
pragmatically successful adjustment processes, and would have to
deny other dimensions. Within sociology as a strict behavioral science,
questions relating to the self-understanding of social groups cannot
be formulated. Yet they are not meaningless on that count, nor are
they beyond binding discussion. They arise objectively from the fact
that the reproduction of social life not only poses technically soluble

questions; instead, it includes more than the processes of adaptation along the lines of the purposive-rational use of means.[28]

Admittedly, what still appears here negatively as a limit upon a type of scientific thinking positively signifies the recognition of an independent region of scientific knowledge. After Habermas has introduced communicative understanding as a dimension of a social learning process that in its universal significance is comparable to that of production, he is quite consistent to also find within it the condition for the possibility of scientific experience. He does not hesitate for long to speak of a second type of knowledge that is "aided by the hermeneutic clarification of the self-understanding of acting subjects."[29] In the same way that the empirical-analytic sciences are embedded in a practical understanding of the world to which humans are compelled under the constraint of the appropriation of nature, these hermeneutic sciences are embedded in a practical understanding of the world in which humans, under the continual constraint of intersubjective understanding, know themselves to be placed. While in the former reality is experienced under the guiding preunderstanding of technical control, under the latter reality is constituted under the guiding preunderstanding of the guarantee and expansion of communicative agreement. The interpretive understanding of a handed-down or contemporary context of meanings corresponds to the procedure of the nomological explanation of connections between events.

In the context of his contributions to the "positivist dispute," Habermas is initially only groping for these epistemological distinctions. But the arguments he produces already show that, along the path of his transcendental-anthropological reconsideration of the universal conditions of the possibility of scientific experience, he succeeds in a critical reevaluation of the understanding of meaning on a material basis. Hermeneutics was unimportant for the critique of science in the critical theory presented by Adorno and Horkheimer. It may be that Adorno considered the hermeneutic method of understanding meaning as a possibility of unreified knowledge, but systematic significance could not be attributed to it in the context of his

conception of science since, from the perspective of the philosophy of history, he conceived the act of knowledge in general only as the cognitive relation of a subject to an object, not
as an interpretive relationship between subjects.[30] By contrast,
Foucault, in *The Archeology of Knowledge,* agrees with semiological structuralism in its criticism, in principle, of the epistemological understanding of meaning. For him hermeneutics,
like phenomenology, represents a misleading tradition of
thought because it regards the production of socially shared
meaning as the accomplishment of meaning-projecting subjects, whereas the constitution of meaning seems to be the work
of subjectless rules of the individual or social unconscious.[31]
Thus, in the theoretical development we have observed, Habermas is the first to attempt to take up positively, in the context
of his own theory, the method of the understanding of meaning investigated by the hermeneutic tradition. The reasons that
drive him to this are connected with the particular way in
which, in contrast to Adorno and Foucault, he defines the
structure of human socialization: The mutual understanding
of subjectively intended meanings, and thus the understanding
of meaning, must be built in as an element in the process of
social development, if the members of a society are among
themselves directed to a social agreement that cannot be artificially produced in administrative ways (Adorno) or cognitively
secured in anonymous ways (Foucault), but can only be
achieved communicatively in a continuously renewed
understanding.

Habermas regards interpretive understanding as an elementary component of social life. As a cognitive operation it is, for
him, of the same significance as the cognitive achievement
associated with the appropriation of nature. Adorno and Foucault represent the same tradition of thought in that they are
unable to take into consideration the specific cognitive ability
of the understanding of meaning only because they are unable
to recognize in human socialization a need for communicatively
achieved understanding. By contrast, Habermas must make
explicit the hermeneutic method of understanding, since he
sees human socialization to be oriented not only to products of
the appropriation of nature but also, at least minimally, to a

social consensus. As a consequence of this view, a practical interest lies at the basis of the hermeneutic sciences just as a technical interest lies at the basis of the empirical-analytic sciences. This practical interest guarantees the process of communicative understanding within the social community through the interpretation of culturally objectified meanings.

With the transcendental-anthropological renewal of the understanding of meaning, Habermas works out the theoretical presuppositions necessary to be able to fundamentally characterize the positivistic mode of thinking as a "truncated rationalism." But the demonstration thereby achieved of a second form of human rationality rooted in the sphere of intersubjective understanding—and misunderstood by positivism—apparently does not extend far enough to justify epistemologically the interest of a critical theory in an emancipation of society. As Horkheimer did before him, Habermas conceives the central concern of his critical theory of society to be the overcoming of those relations of force that proceed, not from the unalterable givens of social life, but from ideologically concealed interests in domination. The arguments that we have followed from the beginning serve the epistemological justification of this emancipatory goal of social theory. However, the interpretation of the hermeneutic sciences that Habermas develops exposes a conservative tendency that evidently contradicts the particular goals of a critical social theory: If the practical interest of hermeneutic knowledge is actually directed only to the goal of preserving an existing agreement among members of society, then it must refer indifferently to the normative implications of that agreement. Neither the conditions under which a social consensus has come about nor the degree to which the members' freedom is preserved can be tested within the limits methodologically imposed by the hermeneutic sciences. Habermas first explicitly confronts this difficulty (which admittedly emerges for hermeneutics only when it is measured against the goal of a normative evaluation of different forms of agreement and, hence, is supposed to be applied with a view to social criticism) later in his controversy with Gadamer.[32] But in the context of the positivist dispute it already leads him to the conviction that, although along the path of a transcendental-anthropological reconstruction of the hermeneutic sciences a dimension of human rationality ignored by positivism is opened up, a further interest in the "emancipation from nature-like force"[33] cannot be justified. Thus, even after the introduction of a second interest attributed to hermeneutics, the normatively decisive question as to how the emancipatory cognitive intention of a critical theory of society is demonstrated remains basically unanswered.

However, the expression "normative" is, in a certain sense, misleading with respect to the theoretical considerations that Habermas initially offered to justify the idea of a critical social theory. In the essays on Marxism that appeared just prior to the period of the "positivist dispute," he had still attempted to ground the emancipatory intention of his critical theory in a way that was supposed to come about without the distinctions usually encountered between empirical and normative questions, or between "descriptive" and "prescriptive" statements.[34] The methodological solution with which Habermas at that time had hoped to fulfill such a claim was derived from the Hegelian-Marxist model of the critique of ideology and consisted in a specific process of "determinate negation": In it empirical reality is supposed to be confronted with those normative-practical goals that human history reveals to itself as soon as it is considered from the hermeneutic perspective of overcoming existing injustice. Thus, the normative standard by which present relations were supposed to be critically measured was immanent in the historical process only under the hypothetical proviso that in the future, in the process of its realization, it could be demonstrated as an actual goal of history.[35] To be sure, in his epistemological contributions to the "positivist dispute" Habermas had already virtually abandoned the conceptual framework of the philosophy of history, to which the process of "determinate negation," in its older conception, was obviously still tailored. The idea (taken over from Merleau-Ponty) that the validity of a meaning hypothetically attributed to history can first be justified according to the degree of its successful realization is no longer of great importance for the argument developed there.[36] But the idea of a critique of society originally contained in the philosophy of history, initiated

in a historically immanent fashion, is also preserved as a methodological paradigm in the altered context. It arises here again
in the theoretically revised form of a social science that proceeds in an objective-hermeneutic manner—but now it suddenly comes into direct competition with a second normative
model of thought, to which Habermas first makes reference in
the same context.

In his controversy with Popper, Habermas surprisingly offers two conflicting answers to the problem—central to any
approach to a critical social theory—of how to justify critical
claims theoretically. The first proposal for a solution, which
admittedly remains just as vaguely sketched as the second, is
apparently understood as a version, made epistemologically
more precise, of the original concept of a critique that proceeds
in an historically immanent fashion. The old line of thought,
the Hegelian-Marxist model of the critique of ideology, is now
translated into the new philosophical context of a transcendental-anthropological theory of knowledge by being interpreted
as a systematic combination of the two procedures of the empirical-analytic and the hermeneutic sciences, transcendentally
contrasted to one another.[37] The view from which this proposal
proceeds begins with objections to the hermeneutic method of
understanding meaning that we have already encountered.
After this, a critical theory of society cannot be satisfied with
simply taking over the procedures for interpreting the symbolic
contexts of meaning practiced in the social sciences, since it
would then abstract from all the social conditions under which
the self-understanding of individuals recorded in the interpreted contexts of meaning comes about. The understanding
of meaning that initially recommends itself as a methodological
counterweight to the application of empirical-analytic procedures in the social sciences therefore cannot itself be comprehended as the last step in the procurement of a critical theory
of society: "Just as dialectics eludes the objectivism under which
societal relations of historically acting people are analyzed as
law-like relations between things, so too it resists the danger of
ideologizing which exists as long as hermeneutics naively measures the relationships solely in terms of that which they subjectively regard themselves to be. The theory will adhere to

this meaning, but only in order to measure it—behind the back of subjects and institutions—against what they really are."[38]

In order to avoid the theoretical illusions that in the social sciences are associated with the methods of the humanistic sciences since the self-understanding of acting individuals disclosed in the interpretation of meaning can no longer inquire into the social conditions of its genesis—that is, in order to avoid the "idealism of hermeneutics"—Habermas proposes a kind of continual revision of hermeneutic interpretation through the traditional methods of an objective analysis of social facts. In this way the hermeneutically interpreted action orientations and guiding ideas to which subjects attest in their symbolic utterances are measured against what the individuals, as he puts it, "really are." The theoretical result that Habermas expects from this kind of combination of the understanding of meaning and scientific methods is indicated in the program of a critique of ideology that achieves a hypothetical insight into the "objective meaning of a historical life context" in the confrontation of the subjective consciousness of the situation by acting individuals with the empirical social conditions under which they have to live:

Dialectical thought does not simply eliminate the dogmatics of the lived situation through formalization, in fact it retains the subjectively intended meaning in its examination of the prevailing traditions and breaks this meaning up. For the dependence of these ideas and interpretations upon the interests of an objective configuration of societal reproduction makes it impossible to remain at the level of subjective-meaning-comprehending hermeneutics; an objective meaning-comprehending theory must also account for that moment of reification which the objectifying procedures exclusively have in mind.[39]

This line of thought, which is still indebted to Adorno not only in its language but also in its theoretical points, admittedly offers only a first impression of the methodological construction through which Habermas characterizes a critical social science. However, an argumentative possibility of justifying its critical claim is not thereby opened up. In general, along the path that Habermas adopts with the proposal of an objective theory for interpreting meaning, it is difficult to discover the place that is supposed to be able to lead to a kind of justification of normative standards without further assumptions; that is, if the viewpoints under which social relations appear in a critical light are supposed to be "legitimated dialectically from the objective situation,"[40] as Habermas requires, then such a justification is possible only under the additional hypothesis that the viewpoints referred to in the goal of social critique already in some way dwell within the relations criticized. The classical critique of ideology found in Marxism also consistently proceeded from such a presupposition in that it supposed that, in the ideological self-understanding of bourgeois society, its culturally proclaimed goals and legitimations, normative principles are already presented that contain the standards by which the actual social regulation even of this society can be morally criticized. However, Habermas appears to want generally to renounce presuppositions of a comparable kind in the methodological considerations he develops in his reply to Popper. He does not make the assertion that in the subjective consciousness of situations of individuals or in the ideological claims of institutions—for both of which a critical social science must inquire about their factual presuppositions—those moral values are already contained upon which the critique itself can then be supported. Hence the theoretical element, which first granted to the traditional critique of ideology its normative importance, is hollow in its conception and, correspondingly, also nullifies the attempt to justify the model of an immanently applied social critique in the form of an objective-interpretive social science.

However, that does not mean that, conversely, the methodological idea of an objective-hermeneutical social theory must, for its own part, already be abandoned. On the contrary, Habermas will pursue further the basic ideas opened up by his proposal, and finally make it a guide, in his book *On the Logic of the Social Sciences.* But this methodological proposal offers no satisfactory answer to the particular problem that was presented to him with the task of the grounding of an emancipatory knowledge-claim according to which he had distinguished, in a transcendental-anthropological fashion, between empirical analytic and hermeneutic knowledge. It alone is not sufficiently able to develop in a theoretically convincing way the model of a historically and immanently applied social criticism that Habermas originally had in mind as his methodological solution to the problem of justification. Thus, Habermas implicitly breaks with this proposal before he has in fact transformed it. In the same context of his controversy with Popper, a second model of justification emerges in its place that is supposed to solve the same task with new means. Instead of looking for the moment of critique in the historical process of the socialization of humans, it now looks for it in the basic, invariant conditions of its socio-cultural existence.

With this second model of justification a theoretical line of thought takes shape in Habermas' work that first finds an appropriate clarification in his inaugural address at Frankfurt. In order to be able to justify the particular scientific claim of a critical social theory in the midst of the empirical-analytic and hermeneutic sciences, Habermas now undertakes to ground in a transcendental way a third form of knowledge. He is no longer satisfied with attempting to make plausible the specific achievement of social criticism from a "dialectical" combination of the two encountered modes of research; now he traces it back to a particular capacity of human rationality. However, the consideration that leads to this bold undertaking is mentioned in only one place in his reply to Popper, when Habermas appeals to a reflective power that seems to be contained within every discussion concerned with the critical assessment of arguments: "As a makeshift, we can conceive of criticism—which cannot be defined because the standards of rationality can only be explained within criticism itself—as a process which, in a domination-free discussion, includes a progressive resolution of disagreement. Such a discussion is guided by the idea of a general and unconstrained consensus amongst those who participate in it."[41]

Here Habermas mentions the "idea of an uncoerced consensus" only in a preliminary way in order to remind his theoretical opponent in the "positivist dispute" about a specific dimension of rationality within which he already moves as soon as he enters into a scientific discussion. That is, since every participant in a theoretical controversy must necessarily suppose that the arguments introduced by him, just as the arguments of every other participant, can be recognized or rejected without force, it must be the mutually supposed goal of every common discussion to produce an "uncoerced consensus." But so long as this supposition is empirically effective, sound arguments can produce from within themselves the power to shake opinions that have been handed down and produce new convictions. Thus the peculiar capacity that belongs to insights argumentatively produced breaks the hold of false attitudes by virtue of logical force alone. Therefore, not only must a hermeneutic of technical preunderstanding exist in scientific discussions; in addition, an ability of reason which overarches both must be at work that is capable of breaking up the "power of the unpenetrated" by rendering it conscious.[42] Not far from the cited passage, Habermas calls this emancipatory process of consciousness a "movement of reflection." Of course, what is meant with this Hegelian phrase, as is already clear from what has been said, is not a monological act of thought but rather a particular form of self-reflection that, in the course of an intersubjective dialogue, gradually liberates self-incurred but as yet unrecognized deceptions.

However, Habermas now seems to be unsatisfied with a simple methodological characterization of the particular abilities of reason that inhabit the procedures of scientific discussions. To be sure, the presented line of thought also has the function of recalling to critical rationalism an overarching dimension of knowledge that it itself is not able to bring into view let alone to justify, although it is just this dimension that first guarantees the progress of theoretical debates in general. But Habermas primarily links the analysis of the self-reflective character of discussion to the additional aim of justifying those norms that is able to serve as a measure for a critical science. To attain this, however, requires a final transformation of scientific definitions into normative ones. The conditions of freedom from domination that the participants in a scientific discussion must always already presuppose if they want to participate in the common process of self-enlightenment can then be grasped as the moral norms upon which the critique can legitimately be supported. A clarification of the normative implications that lie at the basis of a debate would then reveal to the participants that they already continually claim as a critical standard of their own procedure the conditions of a discussion without domination. It is this idea that Habermas seems to have in mind when he states in the quoted passage that the "standards of rationality" can be explicated only in the process of criticism itself. But the line of thought thereby sketched out remains too undeveloped in the context in which it now appears to be able to represent a sufficiently justified alternative to the model of the critique of ideology. Habermas still hesitates to bring the concept of self-reflection together with the assumption of a third cognitive interest and, hence, to adopt the way of a transcendental-anthropological grounding of social criticism. For this step a further assumption would have been required that would have finally burst open the epistemological framework of his critique of Popper.

Nevertheless, if the outlined train of thought leaves unclear how the process of an ongoing dialogical self-reflection is supposed to be set in relation to the previously developed dimension of communicative understanding, this difficulty becomes even more important with the move to a third knowledge-constitutive interest. Habermas first generally makes the step to the claim of a third, emancipatory cognitive interest after he has demonstrated for "self-reflection," beyond the functional connection presented so far, a fundamental importance for the reproduction process of the human species as a whole. That is, only then, when the intersubjective "movement of reflection" can be claimed as a form of knowledge to which humans are as basically oriented in their development as to the objectifying knowledge of nature and to hermeneutic understanding, can it correctly be traced back to a further cognitive interest and, hence, placed on the same transcendental-anthropological level as the other two modes of knowledge. Habermas attempts to produce evidence for this decisive thesis for the first time in his inaugural address. Later, in *Knowledge and Human Interests,* he further worked out this line of thought and made it more precise without essentially altering it.

In his inaugural address Habermas proceeds from an expanded definition of the social reproduction process. He no longer only distinguishes the task of social labor from the problem of communicative understanding; now he also introduces the ego-development of the subject as a third class of tasks of social reproduction. Accordingly, the human species is not only oriented to an intelligent mastery of the tasks presented it by the requirement of appropriating nature, and to symbolically mediated interaction; it is additionally confronted with problems that arise from the enduring requirement of individual identity formation:

> The human species secures its existence in systems of social labor and self-assertion through violence, through tradition-bound social life in ordinary-language communication, and with the aid of ego identities that at every level of individuation reconsolidate the consciousness of the individual in relation to the norms of the group. Accordingly the interests constitutive of knowledge are linked to the functions of an ego that adapts itself to its external conditions through learning processes, is initiated into the communication system of a social lifeworld by means of self-formation processes, and constructs an identity in the conflict between instinctual aims and social constraints.[43]

Whereas Habermas had so far simply attributed the formation of individual identity to the social accomplishments that result from the process of communicative understanding, from now on he separates the development of identity from interaction as a special problem of the social production of life. Therefore, as the cited passage shows, he has already associated an enlargement of the two previously introduced cognitive interests with a third knowledge-constitutive interest. He departs from the assumption that with the process of the formation of identity a transcendental framework for the apprehension of the world is posited just as with the processes of labor and interaction which are necessary for reproduction. However, this is valid only if he is able not only to show the particular cognitive achievement that is required in the process of identity formation but also to demonstrate its socially constitutive function. With the problems associated with this task, the difficulties into which Habermas falls with his attempt to reinstate social criticism upon an independent cognitive interest become clear.

The decisive presupposition for an epistemological analysis of this newly emerged system of reference is initially a definition of the cognitive process that moves along with the formation of ego identity. Habermas brings into the center of his description the dimension of identity formation that is defined by the task of the gradual overcoming of self-alienating norms and convictions. Only with such a definitive point can he analytically distinguish the process of "training in a context of communication"—that is, socializing interaction. In contrast to the conservative function that the process of symbolically mediated interaction appears to serve for the development of personality by allowing the individual to grow up within an existing horizon of tradition, the process of identity formation is characterized by a critical function: in the construction of its identity, the individual gradually learns to free itself from the power of unrecognized fixations and dependencies until it finally autonomously learns to integrate the claims of its own needs (which have become transparent) with the demands of society. But when the process of identity formation is defined in this way, it is only consistent to coordinate with it a particular form of knowledge. In contrast to the two types of technical knowledge and intersubjective understanding, the cognitive acts that are performed in the process of the autonomization of the ego are not directed to the alien object of nature or the social world, but are reflexively related to the ego's own self. Here a practical self-relation, through which the ego acquires insights into unintended constraints and is thereby emancipated from them, corresponds here to the activities of labor and interaction. Habermas calls "self-reflection" this third type of cognitive achievement, to which individual identity-formation seems to be as connected as social labor is to technical knowledge and as the intersubjective act of coming to an understanding is to hermeneutic understanding. Thus he already raises to the universal level of a necessary cognitive faculty what he had still more cautiously introduced in his reply to Popper as the particular accomplishment of scientific discourses.

Of course, with this step nothing more is initially gained than a more precise definition of the specific cognitive faculty that humans employ in the construction of their identity. But why in general is the knowledge that is acquired in the completion of identity formation supposed to be able to assume the form of a science just as technical knowledge had assumed in the natural sciences and communicative understanding in the social sciences? And how can a form of knowledge that is supposed to be characteristic for the process of the individual acquisition of identity function as the transcendental framework for the theory whose object is the global life of a society?

In order to be able to derive the claim to knowledge of a critical theory of society from the accomplishments of self-reflection, Habermas must answer these questions within the frame of reference that he has so far laid out. In this, according to the paradigm of pragmatism, the logic of research of the various sciences was conceived as the methodologically objectified expression of attitudes that had originated in the functional arena of prescientifically exercised activities. If in the same way the self-reflection that moves along with identity-formation is also supposed to be viewed as the practical anticipation of a particular science, then those criteria must initially be found for it that permit its performance to be so broadly objectified that it can in general be brought into the methodological form of an intersubjectively testable procedure. Such criteria, in the other two cases of the empirical-analytic and hermeneutic sciences, result from the kind of tests that underlie the prescientific cognitive activity in everyday routines of action: The empirical-analytic sciences construct in their methodical procedures the controls of success that are continually embedded in technical action, just as the hermeneutic sciences do for the interpretive operations that are effective in every process of communication. But the success of a process of identity-formation is measured by the degree to which a subject is able to acquire individual autonomy. Thus a scientific theory that is supposed to appear as the methodically objectified form of self-reflection must, at least initially, be understood as an attempt to help the individual process of will-formation to attain autonomy by virtue of its theoretical efforts if its "naturelike" development is disturbed. The methodological context in which such a theory could attain its knowledge would, correspondingly, be defined by the intention to "free conscious-ness from its dependence on hypostatized powers."[44]

Nevertheless, in order to be able to assume an intersubjec-tively testable form, the theory supported by this intention still requires a standard that would permit it to determine the goal of the process of reflection set in motion, that is, the condition of realized autonomy. Only against the background of this kind of preliminary notion would it be in the position to identify in any given process of will-formation the "hypostatized powers," the unrecognized constraints upon action and self-incurred deceptions that could be overcome through the reflective achievement encountered by it. A theory that is supposed to reconstruct the prescientific process of self-reflection would be directed to criteria of a normative kind in a different way than in the cases of empirical-analytic and hermeneutic sciences. It could not simply derive the perspectives under which it oper-ates from the immanent rules of verification of a well-coordi-nated life-practice; rather, it must first attain them from the anticipation of the general condition that it seeks to clarify by virtue of its methodical efforts. In a surprising turn, Habermas describes this condition, which is to be normatively defined, as a situation of "uncoerced consensus." In a well-known formu-lation, he claims theoretical certainty for it:

It is no accident that the standards of self-reflection are exempted from the singular state of suspension in which those of all other cognitive processes require critical evaluation. They possess theoret-ical certainty. The human interest in autonomy and responsibility is not mere fancy, for it can be apprehended *a priori*. What raises us out of nature is the only thing whose nature we can know: *language*. Through its structure, autonomy and responsibility are posited for us. Our first sentence expresses unequivocally the intention of uni-versal and unconstrained consensus.[45]

Habermas has already insisted upon a dialogue situation free of domination as a necessary presupposition for scientific dis-cussions. Now he gives this reflection an anthropological turn in which he relates it to the structure of human language as a whole. A prior conception of the conditions of communication free of domination already dwells within linguistic understand-ing, as a medium in which humans distinguish themselves from the animal world, because every speaker unavoidably acknowledges, with the utterance of a sentence, the opportunity for an uncoerced evaluation of the assertions raised by him. This is the first place in which Habermas explicitly makes use of the thought of a normative internal structure of human language. The related idea of an uncoerced dialogue, which he will later justify with the help of universal pragmatics and which he will make the foundation of an ethics of discourse, accompanies the development of his theory from now on.

However, at this point it is not clear what connection such an ethical concept of freedom from domination is supposed to have with the question of the theoretical standards of a methodically trained self-reflection—the question that now interests us. Habermas is ambiguous to the extent that earlier he strictly distinguished between the processes of identity-formation and social interaction, between the acquisition of ego-autonomy and training in a communicative relation. A connection first comes about theoretically when the process of identity-formation, in contrast to such a sharp distinction, is viewed directly as a process of the symbolization of motivation-potential, that is, as a process of will-formation in which an ego progresses along the path of the gradual articulation of its own needs within the universal context of a public language game to the experience of its own particular identity. "Dialogue without domination" is then the title for the ideal condition, achieved through the uncoercive "linguistification" of individual need-potential, of subjects who are transparent to one another and who are, to that degree, autonomous. Conversely, a disturbance of the process of identity-formation can be conceived as the result of a communication marked by domination and determined by force. Now, with the background of these definitions, it becomes clear why Habermas can regard the reference to the language-immanent ideal of freedom from domination as an answer to the question of the standards of self-reflection. If the accomplishments of reflection, by virtue of which an individual develops into an autonomous subject, are acts of the "linguistification" of naturally instilled motivation-potential, then a state of uncoerced discussion must be viewed as the immanent goal of individual processes of will-formation.

Therefore a science that attempts, through theoretical efforts, to once again set in motion a disrupted process of will-formation can only be guided from the perspective of overcoming the obstructions to communication that systematically block the free articulation of motivation potential. The standards of a theory that has the movement of self-reflection as its paradigm are identical with the ideal of an uncoerced and universal communication.

It does not follow from all this that Habermas can trace emancipatory knowledge back to a third, independent cognitive interest in the same way as can be done for technical or practical knowledge. Rather, like the hermeneutic sciences, critical science is transcendentally anchored in the practical contexts of everyday communication. But its particular accomplishment of reflection first arises with the distortions and obstructions with which this prescientific process of communication is concerned in a way inaccessible to hermeneutics. Thus, Habermas will later grant only a derivative status to the critical cognitive interest and, finally, let it converge with the practical interest in the expansion of linguistic interaction as a whole.[46] But what is clear from our comments is that Habermas must have in mind the example of a linguistically interpreted psychoanalysis when he initially illustrates the methodological structure of a critical theory of society in connection with the reflective accomplishments of the process of individual will-formation. As a science, psychoanalysis responds to disturbances in this process of will-formation. Its goal is to initiate, in a certain sense from without, the emancipatory powers of "linguistification," through which the individual normally learns to develop but which, in the specific case of a disturbance, are rejected. It does this by seeking interpretations for the social causes of constraints to communication. When, with the aid of an appropriate interpretation of the original experience, it finally succeeds in simultaneously bringing about an act of recollection and a process of linguistification within the patient, it also frees him at the same time from the force of unperceived conflicts. Admittedly this is only a methodologically diluted outline of a linguistic interpretation of psychoanalysis for which Habermas first offered the interpretive illustrations and scientific justification in *Knowledge and Human Interests*. But these few indications already suffice to show the epistemological context in which he attempts to ground the third category of sciences, and the particular type of a critical theory. Habermas sees in psychoanalysis the methodological paradigm for a critical social theory: Just as psychoanalysis analyzes the individual process of will-formation from the perspective of an emancipatory cognitive interest in order to free a subject from the force of unrecognized constraints upon action, so a critical social theory correspondingly analyzes the process of species will-formation in order to free it from the force of uncomprehended dependencies. But how is the history of human society to be construed so that in it the phylogenetic equivalence for the individual process of identity-formation can be found? And why must the actual history of the species be understood, against this background, as a disturbed process of will-formation?

Two Competing Models of the History of the Species: Understanding as the Paradigm of the Social

In his critique of positivism, Habermas already finds himself within the parameters of social theory. Since from the outset he addresses the epistemological question concerning the validity basis of positivism from the perspective of an anthropologically transformed transcendentalism, in his methodological treatise he is occupied with the basic questions of social theory. The prescientific context of interests to which he wants to trace back the different research methods can be viewed as transcendental conditions for scientific knowledge only if it can be shown that they are unalterably connected to the social life of the human species. Therefore, the different forms of social action, to which the knowledge-constitutive interests are themselves supposed to be connected, must be capable of being comprehended as the universal constituents of societies. In this sense, the doctrine of knowledge-constitutive interests that Habermas develops in the context of his critique of positivism refers, additionally, to a material concept of society. In its frame of reference, the different types of knowledge-mediating action encountered in the theory of knowledge appear as those social achievements through which a social lifeworld is constituted and historically developed.

Social labor was initially disclosed as the first form of a praxis that, together with the factual presuppositions of social reproduction, creates the transcendental conditions for the constitution of reality. It appears as the kind of activity in whose framework of orientation the empirical-analytic sciences are transcendentally anchored. Habermas introduces the activity of labor simply as instrumental action. He abstracts from all the expressive and personality-forming elements that the early Marx, along with Hegel and the romanticists, had also included within the concept of labor, and he posits only the perspective of purposive-rational control over natural processes[1]: "By 'work' or *purposive-rational action* I understand either instrumental action or rational choice or their conjunction. Instrumental action is governed by *technical rules* based on empirical knowledge. In every case they imply conditional predictions about observable events, physical of social. These predictions can prove correct of incorrect."[2]

Of course, Habermas does not accept the emphatic characterization of labor as an expressive event. Rather, in supplementing the elementary concept of social labor as a universal process of the appropriation of nature, a concept he shares with the tradition of social theory extending back to Marx, he moves beyond the classical framework of Marxism by claiming that a second type of action is necessary for social reproduction. In the critique of positivism, communicative understanding was shown to be a second form of social praxis that is as unconditionally connected to the social reproduction of the species as is labor. It appears as the mode of action within whose cognitive framework of orientation the historical-hermeneutic sciences are rooted. The epistemological reinstatement of the understanding of meaning that results from the critique of positivism goes hand in hand with the reinstatement of interaction. Together with hermeneutic knowledge, the prescientific act which it represents in a methodically systematized fashion must also be recognized over against the positivistic reduction of human praxis to technical conduct. Habermas views this other mode of action that underlies the understanding of meaning as the kind of interpretive activity through which subjects reciprocally come to an understanding about a social system of norms and subsequently actualize it in specific situations. Initially this aspect of the communicative observance of norms stands in the forefront of the definition:

By "interaction," on the other hand, I understand *communicative action,* symbolic interaction. It is governed by binding *consensual norms,* which define reciprocal expectations about behavior and which must be understood and recognized by at least two acting subjects. Social norms are enforced through sanctions. Their meaning is objectified in ordinary language communication. While the acceptance of technical rules and strategies depends upon the validity of empirically true or analytically correct statements, the validity of social norms is grounded only in the intersubjectivity of mutual understanding of intentions and secured by the general recognition of obligations.[3]

With the two concepts of instrumental and communicative action, the elementary presuppositions for a theory of society are already in hand. Together they supply guidelines for a comprehensive concept of society in which the process of material reproduction is seen as dependent upon a process of intersubjective understanding mediated by social norms. Social labor is included within an overarching framework of social interaction, since only within it can the members of society reach an understanding with one another about obligatory norms that make it possible to regulate the organization of social life in general and the labor process in particular. As we can already gather from these few indications, on the basis of this normative concept of society the action-theoretic problems that hindred Adorno and Foucault from bringing the results of their critical diagnosis of the times into a convincing social theory are solved. Along with material reproduction realized through instrumental activity, Habermas' social theory also takes up the communicative dimension of normative integration—symbolic reproduction. It does not ignore in social praxis the element of a normatively regulated agreement from which power and domination can alone be comprehended as social phenomena. Rather, with the concept of "communicative action" Habermas places the process of intersubjective understanding in the central position that had been occupied by social labor in social theory reaching back to Marx and by the theory of power in the struggle of conflicting actors going back to Nietzsche. In this way he helps to bring the central motive of Durkheim into the tradition of critical Marxism, as only Antonio Gramsci had previously done.[4]

The concept of symbolically mediated interaction thus determines the special place occupied by Habermas' theoretical approach in the tradition of a critical social theory going back to Marx. In a turn stimulated by the encounter with hermeneutics, Habermas takes up normative and linguistic currents within sociological thought.[5] In this way he is, from the beginning, on the watch for a reductionism that interprets society as a norm-free relation of instrumental or strategic action. Everyday linguistic understanding about action-guiding norms is recognized as the supporting dimension of societies. For the first time in the history of Marxism, communicative understanding is treated systematically as the paradigm of the social. Of course, this foundation achieved in an epistemological fashion is not sufficient for grounding a communication-theoretic concept of society, or for opposing a reductionistic interpretation of the history of the species with a convincing alternative. The model of society to which the transcendental-anthropological argument of Habermas' critique of positivism leads initially indicates only a greatly simplified and rough picture of the social lifeworld. Moreover, the model is still static and free of any internal conflict. So far we know only that the process of social reproduction is to be interpreted as a process of communication that extends over groups and in which the tasks of material reproduction are organized on the basis of socially recognized norms. But it remains open how the inner dynamic of the normatively integrated relation to action can be grasped as a process of the will-formation of the human species.

If he wants to advance from the communication-theoretic insights of his critique of positivism to a new understanding of the history of the species, Habermas must be able to answer questions that are connected to his model of social theory at a very basic level. A clarification of the historical development of societies is initially crucial for this. With the conceptual expansion of social reproduction to the dimension of intersubjective understanding, the historical movement of societies is represented in another light. Social evolution is determined by the forms and the content of symbolically mediated interaction rather than only by the stages of material production. It is no longer the social consequences of the economic processes of development but the dynamic interrelations between social labor and the overarching process of understanding that now constitute the phenomenon in need of explanation. Within the vicinity of the general problem that arises from this model, the second question that was extremely important for previous social theory and that especially interests us—namely, the question of the establishment of domination and hence the legitimation of power—is, in some ways, already settled. This old problem arises for Habermas in the specific context defined by the key concept of intersubjective understanding. With the introduction of the theory of interaction, the origin and exercise of social power is represented differently than in the social theory of Adorno and Foucault: It is represented as a normative event. The establishment of domination is regarded as a process that assumes the form of an intersubjective agreement about social norms, that is, as a process of the formation of a moral consensus. Therefore, the mechanisms or motivating factors that are able to influence the intersubjective process of agreement in such a way that the disadvantaged groups are also willing to accept the established system of power and privilege have to be investigated. Only by satisfactorily clarifying this connection will it be possible to explain how the asymmetrical distribution of burdens and advantages has been able to find the degree of moral agreement presupposed by the guiding theoretical concept.[6]

A treatment of these two sets of problems is no longer possible along the indirect path of a transcendental-anthropological theory of knowledge; it is possible only from the direct perspective of a theory of society. Thus we find collected in the social-theoretical writings that are joined to this phase of his early critique of positivism the answers that Habermas attempts to give to the two questions regarding the historical development and organization of societies. In this connection we can consider above all the collection of essays in *Toward A Rational Society*, as well as the corresponding chapters of *Knowledge and Human Interests*.[7] Of course, Habermas' model of a social theory did not arise from nowhere. The direction of a communication-theoretic model of society is already indicated in the sociological studies that were introduced in his

Habilitationsschrift, entitled *The Structural Transformation of the Public Sphere,* and developed in several essays in his collection *Theory and Practice.*[8]

Habermas already makes use of a communication-theoretic interpretation of social reality in his book on the public sphere. But here the basic idea of his critical theory initially assumes only the implicit form of systematic historical writing. Habermas reconstructs the structural transformation of the bourgeois public sphere as a process of the contradictory formation and institutionalization of a normative idea. In the context of a historical analysis of institutions, he follows the moral process of enlightenment in which the emancipated bourgeoisie learned to see the practical necessity of a transformation of arbitrary domination to rational action.[8] Habermas considers the liberal idea of an uncoerced public sphere of discussion to be the result of this learning process of communication among citizens gathered into discussion groups.[10] Of course, in contrast to this, the structures of a bourgeois class society, the early-capitalist forms of the organization and domination of labor, were effective limiting conditions. Therefore, the normative idea could only be realized in a contradictory form, although it shaped the moral self-understanding of the rising bourgeoisie and was thus able to achieve the power of a principle that governs action. From the outset Habermas conceives the institutionalization of normative principles which are embodied in the liberal model of the public sphere as a limited process of moral progress. But the emancipatory potential contained in this idea could not be institutionally developed in an unhindered manner, since the capitalist presuppositions of an unequal distribution of power and property function as a social limitation against it.

In his study Habermas further pursues the developmental history of the bourgeois public sphere through the historical stage at which it threatens, with the forced construction of the social-welfare state and the emergence of the opinion-forming mass media, to dissolve the institutional conditions that were originally constitutive for the normative idea of a public sphere of discussion free from domination.[11] Thereby the distant view of the historian gradually yields in the course of the description to the practically engaged view of the social theoretician. Habermas is interested not only in a social presentation of the developmental path of the liberal public sphere but also in an action-theoretic clarification of the configuration of the institutions of late capitalism. He investigates the dangers that arise for the principle of the discursive public sphere from the social-welfare state's transformation of capitalism in order to gain information about how today it orders the chances for a practical realization of the ideal initially associated with the liberal model. In the end the historical analysis is transformed into a sociological diagnosis of the times that informs the institutional spaces for a repoliticization of the public sphere. In this turn a practical-political motive is revealed—we shall later see the extent to which, as an internal impetus, this guides the structure of Habermas' social theory.

However, the systematic connection that exists between the interpretive approach of the book on the public sphere and the basic idea of social theory that has since come to light is already not difficult to perceive. It can be seen in the fact that, in his historical analysis, Habermas already directs his attention to the social accomplishments of communicative action which then appear in the epistemological reflections as the elementary dimensions of human socialization. Since he regards the institutions of the liberal public sphere as a product of the formation of a moral consensus within the bourgeoisie, in certain ways he already anticipates the basic communication-theoretic insight of his social theory. He treats the intersubjective learning process that leads to the normative principle of an uncoerced discussion about all public affairs as a concrete historical-empirical form of the type of social practice which he introduced conceptually as "symbolically meditated interaction." That is why, already in the book on the public sphere, a social efficacy falls to the moral idea that goes far beyond the standard represented in the tradition of critical theory and, earlier still, historical materialism. Habermas views an intersubjective understanding about social norms as a motivating power that is able to drive historical development up to those boundaries that are drawn at a given time by the objective conditions of the social relations of labor and domination.

However, the thesis in which a historically constructed conflict between the emancipatory potential of communicative action and the limiting conditions of established forms of domination is so far maintained is only implicitly contained in the perspective from which Habermas follows the developmental history of the bourgeois public sphere. The decisive line of thought is still too deeply entwined with the representation of a historical process to be reflected in its universal scope and to be made fruitful for a model of the history of the species.

But Habermas soon takes this step of universalization. The course that the elaboration of a social theory takes with him can be understood as a process of the gradual generalization of the moment of conflict introduced in the book on the public sphere. Habermas attempts to take the temporally and spatially localized processes of development that he had studied in the contradictory institutionalization of the bourgeois public sphere as a model for the logic that controls the dynamic of social evolution as a whole. He removes the conflict he could observe earlier between the moral process of will-formation of citizens who communicate with one another and the historically realized conditions of capitalist class society from its historically determined context and, at a higher level of abstraction, makes it the driving power of the process of civilization. However, before this course of a systematic generalization of a historically fixed event can be adopted and the step to a universal theory of society thereby realized, a relevant ambiguity must first be eliminated: The course of conflict that was the object of the historical investigation permits a generalized interpretation in two directions.

On the one hand, we can conceive the practical process of will-formation that issues from the experiences of communicative action as an independent process that emerges as something foreign to the relations of labor and domination; on the other hand, we can understand the same process of will-formation not only as a process in which the relations of labor and domination intervene but also as a process which in turn molds the institutional conditions of these relations. Then the social conflict that it concerns no longer develops, as in the first case, between the developmental dynamic of symbolically mediated interaction and the systemic conditions prevailing at the time; rather, it already dwells within the process of communicative action as such. The historical investigation that Habermas provides offers sufficient points of reference and examples for both interpretations, but according to the preferred version the connection between the process of social interaction and the encountered social structure, the process of social integration, and finally the logic of the history of the species are portrayed differently. However, when he turns to the elaboration of his social theory, Habermas does not offer a sufficient account of the difference between these two models. Rather, as we will see, he strongly favors, at different times and places in his writings, one of the two possibilities of interpretation, and converts it into a universal proposal for the logic of social evolution. But for this reason a peculiar discord between two different models of the history of the species emerges in Habermas' social theory. Both start from the same communication-theoretic premises, but they develop different conceptions of the historical interdependence of instrumental and communicative action, of labor and interaction.

The theoretical context from which the first of the two versions proceeds is conditioned by the discussion concerning the "technocracy thesis." The concept embraced in this formula emerged in the 1950s and the 1960s as the result of a series of sociological investigations into the social and political consequences of technological progress. From the empirical development tendencies that resulted, Schelsky, Freyer, and Gehlen drew the consequence of an irresistible autonomization of technology and, hence, of a necessary subordination of social evolution to the causal constraints of technical operations. Objections and considerations were soon raised from within the theoretical parameter of the student movement against this thesis, whose central content was concisely summarized in the concept of "technocracy."[12] Among these, the reservations that Habermas formulated in his essays in *Technology and Sciences as "Ideology"* occupy a special place because they treat the theme within the comprehensive perspective of a theory of social development.

From the beginning the technocracy thesis signifies a special challenge for Habermas. In large part he adopts the picture that it offers of the processes of social evolution in advanced societies. Like Hans Freyer, he sees a decisive contemporary tendency disclosed in "The Dominance of Technical Categories Within the Lifeworld of Industrial Society."[13] Accordingly, Habermas wants to achieve something more with his critique of the technocracy thesis than the mere rejection of a conservative diagnosis of the times. He must be able to attain, along this path, the basic assumptions of a critical analysis of society. If it offers something more than empirical intuitions, the technocracy thesis simply represents the false consciousness of a correctly apprehended state of affairs. Habermas is able to bring into question not the social tendencies of development on which it stands, but the sociological significance that is drawn from it. Thus, as a critique of ideology he makes it his task to refute the technocracy thesis in order to attain along the path of a theoretically immanent critique—analogous to Marx in his critique of political economy—the correct interpretation of the developmental tendencies that socially define the present.

For the justification and closer determination of the approach via the critique of ideology that Habermas thus chooses, an argument is used that arises with a reference from the sociological back to the epistemological context. From the beginning Habermas perceives the technocracy thesis from the perspective of his epistemological definitions. It represents for him the sociological complement to the methodological position of positivism, and it is, to the same extent as the former, the "false consciousness of a correct praxis."[14] With this interpretation Habermas not only justifies the ideological suspicion that has been raised against the technocracy thesis, but also already determines the steps he will follow for its proof. Since the technocracy thesis represents positivistic consciousness in the field of sociology, it must be characterized by the same "truncated rationalism" that had also characterized epistemological positivism. Whereas there positivism indicated the inappropriate generalization of the methods of research of the natural sciences to an exclusive form of knowledge, it must now mean for the concept of technocracy that it can achieve an affirmative interpretation of the tendency toward technical autonomization only because it had not correctly considered the possibility of processes of social rationalization in other directions. In this way the theme and the task of a critique of the technocracy thesis are defined. Habermas must be able to show that this sociological theory falsely estimates in its conceptual framework what it correctly describes for the present as a dominance of technical action-performances. In order to be able to demonstrate this it is necessary to prove, as in the critique of positivism, that those other forms of scientific knowledge, through whose epistemological reconstruction positivism was criticized as a "truncated rationalism," have also become embodied in particular processes of social rationalization and have thereby taken form in social institutions. For only if it is possible to discover the necessary complementary processes for the positivisitically suppressed forms of hermeneutic or critical knowledge in the evolution of societies can one correctly maintain that the technocracy thesis offers an incomplete, even "truncated," picture of social rationalization so long as it concentrates on the one-sided process of the expansion of technical action. Therefore, Habermas is compelled to go beyond the communication-theoretic model of society that he has developed so far in the direction of a corresponding theory of social development.

Habermas takes this step by making the epistemologically acquired distinction between "labor" and "interaction" fruitful for an expanded conception of social rationalization. A controversy with Marcuse's critique of technocracy provides the immediate motivation for this undertaking, but the theoretical starting point is provided by Max Weber's concept of rationality.[15] It provides a point of entry since in it the problem that interests Habermas in the technocracy thesis is already anticipated in a conceptually different manner. With the help of the concept of "rationalization" Weber had investigated the historical process of the expansion of the purposive-rational paradigm of action that in the technocracy model is thought through to the conclusion of a technically administered society. Under this concept he understood, roughly stated, the institutional transformation of traditionally defined spheres of life into purposive-rationally organized domains of action. Thus, for Habermas, with a view to the technocracy thesis, the problem is how this process of social rationalization must then be newly defined if not only the accomplishments of purposive-rational action but, in addition, the practice of communicative action is viewed as constitutive for societies. Since the difficulty is to determine precisely the meaning of the expansion of "the rationality embodied in systems of purposive action to the proportions of a life form, of the 'historical totality' of a life-world,"[16] the question as to what is regarded as a necessary dimension of the social processes of rationalization must, accordingly, be answered in a different way. Habermas begins the argument that is supposed to lead to the clarification of the stated problem with a distinction delineated earlier on the level of social domains of action by the structural difference between "labor" and "interaction." In this way he makes a prior judgment that already represents a basic presupposition for the version of a construction of the history of the species that we shall first follow:

In terms of the two types of action we can distinguish between social systems according to whether purposive-rational action or interaction predominates. The institutional framework of a society consists of norms that guide symbolic interaction. But there are subsystems such as (to keep to Weber's examples) the economic system or the state apparatus, in which primarily sets of purposive-rational action are institutionalized. These contrast with subsystems such as the family and kinship structures, which, although linked to a number of tasks and skills, are primarily based on moral rules of interaction. So I shall distinguish generally at the analytic level between (1) the *institutional framework* of a society or the sociocultural life-world and (2) the *subsystems of purposive-rational action* that are "embedded" in it.[17]

Of course, this distinction is not as unmediated as it initially appears here. Both of its components possess an earlier conceptual history in Habermas' work that is not exhausted in the distinction between the two types of action. Habermas had already used the concept of the social lifeworld in earlier essays to describe the horizon of the norms articulated in everyday speech which shape the practical self-understanding of social groups.[18] In the present context, however, the same concept characterizes not the normative action orientations of a particular group, but those of an entire society insofar as they have taken shape in social institutions. Accordingly, the concept of the socio-cultural lifeworld no longer possesses a hermeneutic character; it possesses an institution-theoretic one. It separates out from all the normative convictions and orientations that exist alongside one another in society those that have acquired institutional validity. Now Habermas conceives the totality of these institutional norms as the comprehensive system of a society in which all remaining social domains of action are embedded as in a framework. Thus he obviously relies on Talcott Parsons, who defined the social system as a functional connection of institutions in which culturally transmitted values have assumed the action-steering power of obligatory norms. However, in contrast to Parsons, Habermas derives the norms which make up the institutional framework of a society not from the unquestioned validity of a cultural tradition but from the process of symbolically mediated interaction. But this decisive difference is immediately blotted out again, since Habermas also characterizes the totality of all institutionalized norms as a "system." The concept of system is not able to grant an appropriate expression to the interpretive and thus fragile character that the process of the production and observance of norms still held in the model of communicative action.

The same systems-theoretic conceptual choice, in which the institutional construction of society appears as a system, now also enables Habermas to construct the concept of the "subsystems of purposive-rational action." This concept designates those social domains of action that are distinguished from the normatively regulated meta-system, since in them only the maxims of purposive-rational action have an obligatory character. In line with Weber, Habermas assigns the organizational domains of economic and state-administrative action to those social sectors that are supposed to be characterized by such a norm-free regulation. The train of thought that leads to this conceptual determination is not very convincing, but proves to be unavoidable given the distinction that Habermas draws. As in the case of the category of the "social lifeworld," the newly introduced concept is anticipated by considerations in the earlier writings.

Specifically, as we have seen, in his initial controversy with hermeneutics, Habermas already opposed to the dimension of cultural tradition (on which hermeneutic understanding concentrates) the relations of power and domination as a second dimension. Thus he wanted to draw attention to social conditions which the hermeneutic process was not able to take into account, although they distortively affect the event of tradition to be interpreted. In *On The Logic of the Social Sciences,* which again takes up the thread of the hermeneutic critique and develops in the direction of the methodology of a critical sociology, these social conditions, as "non-normative forces," "enter into language as a metainstitution."[19] Habermas now includes in these the "system of domination" as well as the "system of social labor."[20]

At this point the extent to which the social relations of domination and labor could be conceived as norm-free zones was already unclear, since the social institutions of the organization of labor or the distribution of power apparently consist not only of the morally neutral definitions of purposive-rational action but also of political-practical goals. Still, from now on the dualism of normatively regulated and non-normative spheres of action accompanies the development of Habermas' social theory. As will immediately become clear, a reifying transfer of both types of action—purposive-rational and communicative—to concrete spheres of societal reproduction is indebted to it.

The path that finally leads to the model of the "subsystems of purposive-rational action" also passes through the stages outlined in the critique of hermeneutics. In this model Habermas comprehends positively in the language of systems theory what he had before conceived only negatively as the non-normative conditions of the communicative process excluded by hermeneutics. "Non-normative" now means all those societal spheres of action whose internal organization and praxis are primarily determined by the rules of purposive-rational action. These spheres of action are considered "subsystems," since their boundaries and functions are fixed by the encompassing system of institutionalized norms. However, the problems that are already raised by the concept of "non-normative forces" are not eliminated by the reformulation in terms of systems theory. Rather, they reappear in the question of what it might mean to say that there are social subsystems, such as the "economic system" or the "state apparatus," in which "primarily sets of purposive-rational action are institutionalized."[21] The assertion contained in this systems-theoretic formulation no more removes the difficulties than does the misleading image of "non-normative forces." It is plausible only in the one respect that the fulfillment of societal tasks posed by the constraints of economic production or state administration also always requires adherence to rules against which the purposive achievement of pregiven ends under specific conditions are measured.

But the form for using such purposive-rational rules, their organizational transposition into the praxis of a social community of organization, already requires the additional application of rules of practical-political action.[22] The practical indeterminacy of maxims of purposive-rational action accounts for a wide spectrum of alternatives associated with their social application. Technical rules incompletely prescribe the respective form of their transposition into concrete actions. Possibilities for action are closed not by a repeated recourse to purposive-rational considerations but only through the additional application of normative or political viewpoints—Cornelius Castoriadis has typically shown this for technology[23]; and for the organizational forms of labor it is demonstrated today by the discussion connected with Harry Braverman's investigation of Taylorism, which attempts to make room for political factors in the formation of social labor through the concept of "productive politics."[24]

Of course these considerations provide only one reason for making it seem questionable to speak of the spheres of social labor or political domination as "subsystems of purposive-rational action." A second objection results from considerations for which Habermas already laid the ground with his communication-theoretic foundation of the social sciences. So far this approach means that the process of the social reproduction is always directed to a communicative praxis in whose framework the members of society reach an understanding about the validity of social norms. However, with the systems-theoretic model we are pursuing at the moment, this basic thesis is limited in the sense that for certain spheres of action the possibility is now furnished for an exoneration from the accomplishments of intersubjective understanding. Of course, such a capacity of the social system is at first only a manner of speaking. Habermas does not claim that in the organizational domains of the economy and the state social praxis actually takes place without communicative understanding (that is, through the exclusive observance of purposive-rational rules); he claims only that it is primarily rules of purposive-rational action that are institutionalized in those domains. But even this weaker formulation, which refers only to action-orientation imposed in an obligatory manner rather than being actually realized, permits an interpretation according to which purposive-rationally organized domains of action can be uncoupled from those internal consensual requirements that can only be fulfilled through the process of communicative agreement about social norms. If Habermas thinks this (that is, if he supports the possibility of an organizational exoneration of intersubjective processes of understanding for a specific type of social spheres of life so that, in principle, the activity of individuals can be conceived "without communication"), then, against that, the intuitions of his early approach which show that there are no spheres of social life in which a process of intersubjective understanding does not ensure that a normatively accepted consensus about the organizational forms of social action have to be maintained. Similarly, however, one must also insist that, accordingly, there is no place or time in social life in which this moral consensus, because it is directed to continual renewal in social processes of communication, could not also suddenly break down.

However roughly they have provisionally been formulated, the two objections taken together support the conjecture that Habermas allows himself to be misled into a falsely placed concretization by the plausibility of his own action-theoretic distinctions. The structural differences that he has drawn conceptually between communicative and purposive-rational action he now repeats at the level of the social process of reproduction to the extent that he distinguishes between social spheres according to which of the two types of action predominates within them. He thus unintentionally lets the analytical distinction pass over into a difference between empirical domains of phenomena so that in the end the fiction is produced of a society divided into communicatively and purposive-rationally organized domains of action. Instead of asking about the specific organizational form of the processes of communication that contribute to the purposive-rational mastery of the respectively posed tasks, the image arises of a mastery of tasks that is at one time purposive-rational and at another time communicative.

Now, such a suspicion concerning the texts that we are currently considering is still not fully grounded. Here Habermas has at first only vaguely sketched, and barely shown theoretically, the systems-theoretic perspective to which the conceptual model of the "subsystems of purposive-rational action" leads. The problematic distinction between the two action spheres presents the terminological entrance into a model of the history of the species whose particular task is to find the appropriate meaning for the evolutionary tendencies correctly recognized but falsely understood by the technocracy thesis. The theoretical step essentially followed by the differentiation between the two social spheres deals directly with this goal. It consists in the attempt, with the help of this distinction, to so conceive sociocultural development that in it the present tendencies toward an autonomization of technocracy can be grasped as a one-sided form of social rationalization.

Habermas derives the model that is supposed to lie at the basis of the civilizing development of the relation between institutional framework and purposive-rationally organized subsystems from a specific version of historical materialism. The productive forces are conceived as the motor of historical progress to which so far productive relations have always been subsequently able to adapt. If this "dialectic" between productive forces and relations of production is translated into the abstract conceptual framework provided by the distinction between the two action spheres, then the gradual adaptation of the institutional framework to the permanent expansion of purposive-rationally organized domains of action proves to be the mechanism for the historical development of the species:

> From the very beginning the pattern of human socio-cultural development has been determined by a growing power of technical control over the external conditions of existence, on the one hand, and a more or less passive adaptation to the expanded subsystems of purposive-rational action on the other. Purposive-rational action represents the form of *active* adaptation, which distinguishes the collective *self*-preservation of societal subjects from the preservation of the species characteristic of other animanls. We know how to bring the relevant conditions of life under control, that is, we know how to adapt the environment to our needs culturally rather than adapting ourselves to external nature. In contrast, changes of the institutional framework, to the extent that they are derived immediately or mediately from new technologies or improved strategies . . . have not taken the same form of active adaptation. In general such modifications follow the pattern of *passive* adaptation. They are not the result of planned purposive-rational action geared to its own consequences, but the product of fortuitous, undirected development.[25]

Purposive-rational action emerges here as the reproductive core of society. Its gradual productive increase results in "new technologies" and "improved strategies" for the control of the environment. In contrast to this, the institutions that normatively regulate social intercourse are so far only passively changed in that they successively reproduce the evolutionary advances of purposive-rationally organized action spheres. Admittedly, Habermas retains this traditional concept of history only for a short time. He abandons it the moment he no longer conceives the change of socially integrated norms as a passive process but rather traces it back to an active learning process tied to the moral experiences of symbolically mediated interaction.[26] But at this point it is not yet communicative action but purposive-rational action that represents the force propelling social evolution forward. The mechanism of the history of the species is characterized in such a way that "structural modification is necessitated under the pressure of relatively developed productive forces."[27]

With this scheme of universal development Habermas now arranges in a new way what Weber understood as "social rationalization." He is thus able to profit from the advantages acquired by the translation of basic Marxist concepts into the language of his action theory. The two conceptual models in which he transformed the distinction between "productive forces" and "relations of production" are laid out in such a way that they can be easily connected to the concept of rationalization. For the action concepts, with whose help institutionalized norms as a system of communicative action are distinguished from the "subsystem of purposive-rational action," are intended to characterize not only specific forms of activity but particular achievements of knowledge as well. To that extent, the two spheres of social action must also be distinguished by their own form of the production of knowledge and a specific type of "rationality." The cognitive process in the course of which knowledge produced in the respective action spheres systematically accumulates may then be referred to as a process of "rationalization." This can be unproblematically demonstrated in the case of the "subsystem of purposive-rational action." Habermas need only tie into Weber's analyses and bring them within his Parsonian concept in order to be able to understand as "rationalization" the increase in purposive-rational achievements produced in this domain of action. The process of the development of productive forces from which historical materialism unfolds is thus conceived as a process of rationalization that permits the purposive-rational control of society over external nature and internal relations to steadily accumulate. However, the attempt to apply the Weberian concept of rationalization to the second action sphere, that is, to the institutionalized norms of society, is more problematic. With this step Habermas must necessarily leave behind the firm ground that Max Weber had prepared when he aligned the concept of rationalization with the clearly defined criterion of purposive rationality and push forward into new social-theoretic terrain.

With respect to the evolution of social norms, in order to be able to speak of a process of rationalization it is necessary to determine the criteria in connection with which the rationality of norms can be tested and an increase in their rationality measured. For Habermas the possibility arises of introducing criteria of this kind as a consequence of the epistemological analyses with which he had earlier characterized the cognitive accomplishments of communicative action. Of course, he cannot return to the original version of his epistemology, which proceeded from the three forms of prescientific knowledge, but must rely upon that conception in which he overcame the noted difficulties by anchoring the emancipatory knowledge directly in the process of symbolically mediated interaction.[28] With this background, he can now argue in the following manner: Social norms have the task of regulating the social intercourse between the members of society. They develop and reproduce in the same process of symbolically mediated interaction which they must also institutionally organize. But the realization of the conditions of freedom from domination is inherent in this process of communicative understanding as a goal. The process can succeed only to the degree that all the members of society are able to participate freely in it. Hence, at each advanced stage of socially regulated interaction a knowledge about the present limitations upon the freedom from domination again grows up. The social norms can be interpreted as the institutional embodiments of this communicatively produced knowledge. To that extent, the degree of its rationality is measured by the degree to which it succeeds in organizing social intercourse without domination. Habermas can conclude from this that "*rationalization at the level of the institutional framework* can occur only in the medium of symbolic interaction itself, that is, *through removing restrictions on communication.*"[29] From this basic definition a series of normative criteria can then be derived that permit the increase in rationality of social institutions to be measured just as the criterion of purposive rationality previously permitted the increase in rationality of the economic and political sectors to be determined:

A rationalization of social norms would, in fact, be characterized by a decreasing degree of repressiveness . . . , a decreasing degree of rigidity . . . , and approximation to a type of behavioral control that would allow role distance and the flexible application of norms that, while well-internalized, would be accessible to reflection. Rationalization measured by changes in these three dimensions does not lead, as does the rationalization of purposive-rational subsystems, to an increase in technical control over objectified processes of nature and society. It does not lead *per se* to the better functioning of social systems, but would furnish the members of society with the opportunity for further emancipation and progressive individuation.[30]

As we see, Habermas is able to rely upon a second dimension of social rationalization because he can indicate a standard for the rational development of social norms that is not simply brought to these norms from without but is supposed to be inferred from the process of their production. The basic thought that entitles him to this arises from his recourse to the linguistic concept of freedom from domination, whose epistemological formation we have already followed. In it the ethical principle of communication without domination was regarded above all as a goal that lies from the beginning at the basis of the species-evolutionary process of symbolically mediated interaction, so that the degree to which they guarantee freedom from domination can now be considered as a criterion for the degree of the rationality of moral norms that regulate the processes of communication within society. From this universal standard the detailed criteria that Habermas presents in the cited passage can be deduced as those properties possessed by acting subjects who are supposed to be capable of communication without force.[31]

If for the "institutional framework" of a society the possibility of a rationalization that is measured not by the criterion of purposive-rational success but by the criterion of communicative freedom is to be established, then the form of what Weber understood under "social rationalization" must also be altered. Habermas proceeds from a reciprocal relation between two processes of rationalization. He must take into consideration a reaction of the technical progress, of the "rationalization of purposive-rational systems," not simply upon traditionally defined relations of life but also upon the process of communicative rationalization. By means of the application of the evolutionary scheme that he has taken from historical materialism, he can thus assume that the development of the relations of production comes about as a process of moral emancipation that at every historical stage is again impinged upon by the advances in the development of productive forces. With this conception of the history of the species, the theoretical framework is already created which Habermas must presuppose in order to be able to carry out the intended critique of the technocracy thesis. What was revealed in the critique of positivism at the level of the logic of science as a suppressed form of human rationality is therefore shown to be an internal, dynamic element of the process of history.

The concept of communicative rationalization assumes the same place in Habermas' social theory that the conception of the hermeneutic and critical sciences had taken in his epistemology and provides the possibility for a critical reinterpretation of the technocracy thesis. However, for such a reinterpretation a decisive presupposition is represented by the more precise analysis of the social and political conditions that have been created by the developmental tendencies asserted in the technocracy thesis. Habermas relies upon Weber's interpretation of capitalism in order to be able to undertake this analysis, but he confers on it the specific turn that results when one proceeds with two forms of social rationalization instead of one. The passage to "modern societies" that Weber had in mind when he spoke of "rationalization" in the narrower sense is interpreted as a process that forced a twofold adaptation of the institutional framework of premodern societies to the dynamic of the productive forces set free in capitalism. With capitalism the forces of production attain a state of development that "makes permanent the extension of subsystem and thereby calls into question the traditional form of the legitimation of power."[32] The establishment and the expansion of purposive-rational organizations, which must endanger an infrastructure adapted to the accelerated economic growth and the replacement of traditional forms of the legitimation of power by forms of justification satisfying secularized, scientific claims, are the two transformations that social life undergoes with the explosive development of productive forces at the beginning of capitalism. Along the way, for the first time in the course of socio-cultural evolution, a society emerges whose institutional framework, "the rationality of language games associated with communicative action,"[33] is threatened by the subsystem of purposive-rational action, that is, by the "rationality of means-end relations."[34] The social core of society, which so far was thoroughly reproduced by the medium of symbolic interaction, comes under pressure from organizations that "train the individual to be able to 'switch over' at any moment from an interaction context to purposive-rational action."[35]

Habermas is consistent when in this abstract way he describes the organizational form of liberal capitalism as a specific conflictual relation between the two different patterns of social rationalization. He is thus systematically encouraged, if not compelled, by the dualistic approach grounded in his distinction between two action spheres in such a way that, for him, the theoretical problems implied by this approach must be repeated here at the level of empirical-historical claims. The assumption that with the emergence of capitalism "traditional structures are first increasingly subordinated to conditions of instrumental of strategic rationality"[36] cannot be considered self-evident, since the everyday social life of the lower classes in precapitalist societies is accomplished largely through the force of the purposive-rational organization of the mastery of life; nor can the social institutions that prepared the social conditions for the process of capital accumulation—the education system, the commerce system, legal institutions, and the state bureaucracy—be regarded, in the way Habermas supposed, as normatively neutral instances that operate in a merely purposive-rational manner, since beyond their particular task they have been political mechanisms of control as well as mechanisms of moral socialization. These institutions have confronted people not only with the "rationality of means-ends relations" but also with new maxims of cultural, moral, and physical behavior, because in them, alongside the goals of success-oriented action, specific norms of communicative action were also institutionalized. So conceived, it is not so much the theoretical element in particular, or the high degree of abstraction as such, that is questionable in Habermas' description of the structural principles, but the general model with which the totality of an intersubjectively achieved society becomes so cut up into a communicative and a purposive-rational side that the emergence of capitalism must be grasped as a breakthrough of purposive-rational principles into a lifeworld previously organized communicatively.

But now this structural description represents only the theoretical precondition for a communication-theoretic analysis of the phenomenon that primarily interests Habermas: the trend, introduced with late capitalism, toward the autonomization of technology—a trend that was interpreted one-sidedly by the technocracy thesis. Habermas lays out two processes of development that led from the liberal organizational form of capitalism to the advanced stage of late capitalism and thereby to those institutional transformations that, in a certain sense, allowed technology to become dominant. He supports this with the interpretation in which he had already attempted to explain the structural transformation of capitalism in the earlier context of his interpretation.[37]

On the one hand, in the same way as Pollock, Habermas assumes an increase in the interventionist activity of the state: Under the constraint of avoiding economic crises, the capitalist state, whose performances were originally limited to the guarantee of social and legal presuppositions, must expand its activities so far that today it is in the position to steer the course of the economy by social and political means. But through this the institutional framework, which under the conditions of liberal capitalism was autonomously organized for the first time, insofar as the exchange of goods and labor power was regulated by the market, is repoliticized. The repoliticization of the social sphere has destructive consequences for the ideological construction under which capitalism in its early phase was justified. The ideology of free exchange that had legitimated the capitalist system of domination through the rationality of the market must necessarily break down the moment when the state, before everyone's eyes, supportively intervenes in the economic process. However, the other developmental process from which Habermas proceeds compensates for the destruction of legitimation that threatens late capitalism. Like Marcuse, Habermas assumes, as a second trend in late-capitalist societies, a growth of technology into the role of a new ideology: With the scientization of industrial production since the end of the nineteenth century, technical progress has attained such importance for the reproduction of the entire society that today the decisions of the state sector can by justified by the demonstrative indication to its internal lawfulness. The technocratic ideology that is expressed in this new form of political legitimation produces the appearance of progress in society, dictated by the force of things [*Sachzwänge*]. Its singular achievement consists in its ability to "detach society's self-understanding from the frame of reference of communicative action and from the concepts of symbolic interaction and replace it with a scientific model."[38]

Taken together, the two processes of development that can be imputed to late capitalism produce the picture of a twofold threat to communicative praxis: Through the formal change of the state's activity, in which political action is oriented to "the solution of technical questions" instead of to "the realization of practical goals,"[39] as well as through the cultural change of consciousness that lets the development of society become detached from the frame of reference of normatively guided action, a process is set in motion that gradually begins to undermine the sphere of the social (that is, of communicative understanding). Because the technocracy thesis affirmatively expresses this development (which threatens the society it represents) as the false interpretation of a correctly perceived tendency, it represents the dominant ideology of the age:

Of course this technocratic intention has not been realized anywhere even in its beginnings. But it serves as an ideology for the new politics, which is adapted to technical problems and brackets out practical questions. Furthermore it does correspond to certain developmental tendencies that could lead to a creeping erosion of what we have called the institutional framework. The manifest domination of the authoritarian state gives way to the manipulative compulsions of technical-operations administration. The moral realization of a normative order is a function of communicative action oriented to shared cultural meaning and presupposing the internalization of values. It is increasingly patterned after the structure of purposive rational action. The industrially most advanced societies seem to approximate the model of behavioral control steered by external stimuli rather than guided by norms.[40]

Viewed from this perspective, the developmental tendencies which the technocracy thesis helped to present in an ideological form are presented not merely as a danger for a specific formation of society but as a disturbance in the entire process of the history of the species: With the disintegration of the institutional framework, the process of communicative understanding, on whose existence social reproduction is constitutively based from the beginning, is threatened with destruction. Societies are reproduced, as we have seen, in dependence upon a process of intersubjective understanding mediated by social norms. In the historical moment in which the process of communicative rationalization laid out within it begins to be taken over by "systems of purposive-rational action that have taken on a life of their own," so that the "distinction between the practical and the technical" threatens to disappear completely from the consciousness of the age, the process of will-formation of the species as a whole is destroyed.[41] Therefore, in this situation, it is the task of a critical theory of society to "disclose the fundamental interests of a mankind as such, engaged in the process of self-constitution":

The new ideology consequently violates an interest grounded in one of the two foundational conditions of our cultural existence: in language, or more precisely, in the form of socialization and individuation determined by communication in ordinary language. This interest extends to the maintenance of intersubjectivity of mutual understanding as well as to the creation of communication without domination. Technocratic consciousness makes this practical interest disappear behind the interest in the expansion of our power of technical control. Thus the reflection that the new ideology calls for must penetrate beyond the level of particular historical class intentions to disclose the fundamental interests of mankind as such, engaged in the process of self-constitution.[42]

I have followed Habermas' argument to this point because the conception of the history of the species that lies at the basis of his critique of the technocracy thesis can now be seen from this point of view. Accordingly, we also find here a first answer to the question posed earlier: How can the actual course of socio-cultural history be understood as a distorted process of will-formation so that critical social theory can emerge over against it in the same methodological role that psychoanalysis had assumed over against the individual process of will-formation? In this connection, the increasingly unequal importance of the processes of rationalization anchored in the different action spheres is regarded as the basic conflict of the history of the species and is also presented as the cause of its "disturbance." As a practical motive, the experience that lies at the basis of this model of the history of the species is tied to the same perception of the present that also shaped the technocracy thesis, albeit with opposing intentions.

Habermas does not develop the theoretical conception we are now considering with the simple aim of criticizing the technocracy thesis. Rather, he also lets himself be so deeply influenced by its perspective on the diagnosis of the times that he too locates the dominant developmental tendencies of the present in the autonomization of technocracy. Of course, as we have seen, he does not simply accept this process unproblematically. Rather, he arranges it within the context of an anthropology of knowledge. Thus the same process that the technocracy thesis describes affirmatively is presented as a process of the draining off of communicatively achieved relations of life through purposive-rationally determined action accomplishments, through a "dominance of technology." Habermas' theory is so deeply shaped by this experience that it appears in the background of all other crisis phenomena and current problems. This is, of course, not self-evident, since a critical theory of society can also be theoretically motivated by other crisis phenomena of the present that are taken to be central. For Habermas, however, the experience of an autonomization of technocracy is so central that he also lets the basic concepts of his model of the history of the species be shaped from the task of a clarification of this *one* developmental tendency. He views the species' history as a process of will-formation that takes place in two dimensions of social rationalization: Whereas in the subsystems of purposive-rational action (in which the tasks of social labor and political administration are organized) the species progresses through the accumulation of technical and strategic knowledge, within the institutional framework in which norms for social integration are reproduced the species further develops through liberation from forces that inhibit communication. The concept of "framework" that Habermas applies to social institutions makes it clear how the socio-cultural beginnings of the species are created: The rationalization of purposive-rational action initially still takes place under the direction of those social norms that regulate social commerce as a whole; but whereas the formation of technical productive forces is from now on actively propelled forward by the species, the process of communicative rationalization is at the same time only passively realized as a consequence. Thus the logic of the history of the species can be conceived as a gradual shifting of importance between the two spheres of social action. That is, the more the achievement of technical scientific progress increases and the perimeters of the subsystem of purposive-rational action gradually expand, the more the institutional framework diminishes, since more actions constantly come together under the organizational principles of purposive rationality. This process comes to a crisis that threatens society with the institutional transformation that takes place in the passage from liberal to late capitalism. From now on the form of political domination and the type of its ideological justification, the politics of administrative steering and technocratic ideology, permit the elementary distinction that once existed between communicative praxis and technical action to be forgotten. In the face of such a crisis it is the task of a critical social theory first to make apparent once again the general dimension of communicative rationalization that has been overwhelmed. Only progress at this second level—that is, a further "removing of restrictions to communication"—can overcome the risk that arises with the autonomization of technocracy. Such a removal of restrictions to communication brings about a "public, unrestricted discussion, free from domination, of the suitability and desirability of action-orienting principles and norms in the light of the socio-cultural repercussions of developing subsystems of purposive-rational action."[43]

Processes of social domination—indeed, the problem of the social formation of power in general—are secondary for the model of the history of the species that leads to this practical conclusion. To be sure, the institutional framework is each time thought of as a communicatively built and, accordingly, normatively achieved system of social order, that is, as a specific stage in the overcoming of limitations to communication. But power or domination that disruptively influences the species' process of will-formation results not from the administrative control of socially privileged groups but also from the pressure for adaptation that purposive-rational organizations socially exercise. To this extent, the basic conflict that distinguishes social evolution does not dwell within the process of social understanding as an opposition between social groups or classes, but is set out in the field of opposition between purposive-rational and communicatively organized action spheres. The movement that historically unfolds with this basic conflict is not mediated through the struggle of social groups or classes but takes place as a process of rationalization extending beyond classes and lets purposive-rational actions initially emerge from the framework of intersubjectively valid norms and, finally, as systems react destructively for their part upon the morally developed relations of interaction.

Not an internal, but only an external connection exists between the two processes of rationalization, in which, as a result of the basic conflict in the history of the species, a growing tension is anchored. The social processes of communication, from their level of development, do not formatively influence the organizational form of purposive-rational action; nor do the purposive-rational organizations, from their level of rationalization, react other than destructively upon the forms of social understanding. To be sure, at every level of social development the achievement of technical knowledge is again supposed to run up against the process of communicative rationalization, but work and interaction are not thereby intertwined with one another in the history of the species. Habermas is hindered from introducing at a basic conceptual level another conception of the social interdependence of the two forms of action, as we have seen, by reifying the distinction between the two social spheres of action and, at the level of a diagnosis of the times, by an unintended connection to the technocracy thesis. But he could have found such an alternative

conception if he had consistently followed one of his own interpretive proposals and had understood social interaction also
as a *struggle* between social groups for the *organizational form* of
purposive-rational action. The approach to this second model
of the history of the species is found in the interpretation of
Marx contained in *Knowledge and Human Interests.* Of course,
this alternative conception is not developed further than a
preliminary sketch, but it still exhibits the contours of a social
theory that Habermas could have achieved on the basis of the
same communication-theoretic premises.

The Marxist dialectic of productive forces and relations of
production presented the frame of reference for the first
model in which Habermas attempted to grasp the logic of the
history of the species. This earlier mechanical model of history
is already contradicted within Marxian theory by another
model that proceeds from the dynamic of class struggle, instead
of from a supraindividual evolutionary mechanism. In the
place that had been occupied by the process of a gradual
adaptation of the relations of production to the development
of productive forces, the struggle between social classes
emerges as the event that is supposed to explain the reproduction and renewal of societies.[44] This alternative model of
interpretation, which admittedly Marx applied consistently
only in his historical investigations, now offers the model for
a second conception within Habermas' theory. In it the attempt
is undertaken to reconstruct the logic of the species' evolution
from the moral dynamic that is found in the struggle between
social classes. The conceptual framework that Habermas
thereby takes as a basis is also again provided by the action-
theoretic distinction between "labor" and "interaction," but the
particular approach from which the construction of the species'
history begins this time is grounded on the thesis that social
interaction under the conditions of class relations possesses the
form of a struggle between social classes.

Habermas again begins with the portrayal of the social significance of communicative action. However, the explication of
this universal claim is now connected with an answer to the
additional question of how the process of intersubjective understanding is then constituted "if the institutional framework

does not subject all members of society to the same repressions."[45] With the formation of social classes posed by the division of labor in the socio-cultural evolution, the species subject, which until then was discussed in the singular, loses its fictive unity: To be sure, "in principle, the members of a society all live at the same level of mastery of nature which in each case is given with the available technical knowledge," but they share in unequal degrees the burdens of labor and social advantages.[46] However, subjects divided among classes could not have agreed in the form of a peaceful process of understanding to social norms that in this way asymmetrically regulate social commerce. So long as social subjects profit unequally from the institutionalized norms, communicative action must be carried out in a practical opposition between social classes. Correspondingly, under the conditions of a class society, the process of social understanding, as Habermas puts it, is "mediated" through an interaction of class subjects, be it through integrated force or open rivalry with one another.[47]

Social struggle, which Foucault had unconditionally introduced as a basic phenomena of social relationships and had made the conceptual basis of his theory of power, is thus perceived as a distorted form of intersubjective understandings[48]: Under conditions characterized by an unequal division of burdens and privileges, communicative action assumes the form of a struggle that the concerned subjects conduct over ways of organizing their common praxis. This social conflict does not simply assume the form of a strategic conflict over the attainment of a good; rather, the object on account of which the fight comes about is an institutionalized norm so that the struggle takes place as a practical conflict about the legitimacy of existing social norms and the introduction of new ones. But if the normative rules that support social commerce develop according to the measure of a moral struggle among the social classes, then we must correct the understanding that we have held so far about the process of the will-formation of the species: We are compelled to conceive the modification of institutional frameworks (that is, what we have characterized as "communicative rationalization") as a process of repression and liberation.

The conceptual model in which class struggle is presented as a form of socially distorted communication lets the entire process of the formation and institutionalization of social norms appear in a new light. Whereas in the first version we encountered this process was abstractly conceived as a moral advance in learning that the human species realizes as a whole, the same process is now conceived as a process of will-formation that takes place between two social groups in the form of a struggle over the basis of validity of moral norms. Thus, now it is no longer universal knowledge about the conditions of communication without domination but rather the concrete knowledge of suffered domination and experienced injustice that summons up the insight into the limitations of a social interaction. And the path that leads to the institutionalization of justified norms is prepared by the practical struggle of social groups and not by linguistic understanding alone. Of course, in order to be able to rise from such preliminary definitions to a new conception of the logic of species evolution, what is first required is a reconstruction of the stage sequence, as a universal pattern of evolution, that lies at the basis of the moral process of the will-formation of class struggle. For this goal Habermas makes use of Hegel's model of a "dialectic of moral life."[48] With this the process of will-formation that leads to a clarification of ethical relations is described as an intersubjective process that begins with the destruction of reciprocal conditions of communication, continues through the practical resistance of morally injured subjects, and finally comes to rest in the communicative renewal of a situation of mutual recognition. But since, as we have seen, Habermas describes the emergence of social classes as a "distortion of the dialogic relation"[50] (that is, as an institutional destruction of the conditions of reciprocal recognition), he can now, in the same way, conceive class struggle, in the course of which this moral injury comes about, as a dialectical movement of moral life. The practical conflict of social classes then takes place through the same stages of moral will-formation that Hegel had outlined for the process of the destruction and restoration of an ethical community:

It is those who establish such domination and defend positions of power of this sort who set in motion the causality of fate, divide society into classes, suppress justified interests, call forth the reactions of suppressed life, and finally experience their just fate in revolution. They are compelled by the revolutionary class to recognize themselves in it and thereby to overcome the alienation of the existence of *both* classes. As long as the constraint of external nature persists in the form of economic scarcity, every revolutionary class is induced, after its victory, to a new "injustice," namely the establishment of a new class rule. Therefore, the dialectic of the moral life must repeat itself until the materialist spell that is cast upon the reproduction of social life, the Biblical curse of necessary labor, is broken technologically.[51]

At the same time, this passage provides an answer to the question of how the evolution of the species is presented within the altered frame of reference. The dialectical movement of the suppression and restoration of a communication that concerns mutual recognition characterizes the universal pattern according to which the species' evolution always proceeds again at each established stage. Initially the unequal relations of life that emerge with the formation of social classes permit the experienced disunity of a social interaction situation to come to consciousness in the suppressed class. In the practical conflict that breaks out with this, the enemy parties fight over the norms that institutionally determine the organization of production and, hence, the distribution of life-chances. The social struggle finally first comes to rest when the ruling class—through force or from insight—recognizes the alienated dialogue partner in the suppressed class and has agreed to an institutional organization of society in which the conditions of mutual recognition are initially again restored on a more just level of development. But so long as the newly negotiated system of institutions again prescribes normatively an unequal distribution of burdens and advantages, the struggle between the classes for social recognition is continually set in motion again. To this extent the evolution of the species takes place as a dialectic of class antagonism that proceeds in moral stages of will-formation. This intersubjective process of the will-formation of social classes is tied to the developmental level of productive forces in that the degree of class domination can always be measured only by the economic possibilities that are held out by the entire social output of economic production at the time: "That is why the relative destruction of the moral relation can be measured only by the difference between the *actual* degree of institutionally *demanded* repression and the degree of repression that is *necessary* at a given level of the forces of production. This difference is a measure of objectively superfluous domination."[52]

Two things follow from these considerations for the model of the history of the species. On the one hand, with the materialistic reinterpretation of Hegel's model of will-formation, the basic conflict through which the developmental process of the species is upset and at the same time driven forward is itself displaced in the process of communicative understanding. As in the tradition of Marxism reaching back to Gramsci and Sorel, in which class struggle is always conceived as social struggle over the integrating values and norms of a society (that is, as a moral conflict), Habermas now also reconstructs the species' history from the dynamic of a struggle between social classes conceived as moral conflict. He views the separation of society into social classes as an institutionally fixed distortion of linguistic interaction. With the distortion of social communication, which finds its visible expression in the unequal distribution of life-chances but which has its institutional origin in the unequal distribution of the exercise of power, a process of reflection moves along that lets the suppressed class experience the communicative distortion as injustice and strive for practical resistance. It is this process of crisis, of a forceful suppression and a practical restoration of social understanding, from which the logic of the species history can then be reconstructed: The basic conflict of socio-cultural development dwells within the process of communicative action itself as an opposition of social classes brought forth by social domination. This conflict always drives the process of development beyond each established level of an institutionally regulated interaction.

On the other hand, with the theoretical considerations that we have followed, not only the construction of the history of the species but also the social-theoretic frame of reference in which it is embedded has changed. Habermas no longer analyzes society as an action system separated into purposive-rational and communicative spheres. In the place that this proposed systems-theoretic dualism had occupied so far, the presentation of a society differentiated into social classes and groups now appears. The perspective from which the social regulation of societies is observed is therefore altered as a whole: Now the model according to which the integration of societies is conceived is represented not by the embeddedness of purposive-rational organizations in a communicatively reproduced framework of institutionalized norms but by the institutionally mediated relationship of morally integrated classes. The social interaction that occurs between social groups in the different forms of understanding or in the distorted forms of struggle thereby becomes the overarching action mechanism that regulates the institutional organization of all social domains of tasks. The results of "this class struggle," so it is stated in the context of the considerations we have dealt with, become "sedimented in the institutional framework of society, in social *form.*"[53] Habermas does not expressly draw the conclusion, but it is nevertheless a result that follows from his arguments. If the organization of social praxis as a whole is understood as a temporary product of a process of interaction in which the social classes have introduced their differing action orientations, then the theoretical idea that lies at the basis of the concept of the "subsystem of purposive-rational action" becomes untenable. The institutional forms in which social labor or political administration is organized must then be grasped as the embodiments of a moral consensus formation that the social groups, in their interaction, have (as always) attained through compromise. That is, the apparently purposive-rational organizations are also codetermined by moral-practical viewpoints that must be conceived as results of communicative action.

Of course, if he conceives the social regulation of societies in this altered way, Habermas must claim a conceptual presupposition that is already present in his argument but which is not compatible, without further argument, with the conceptual framework of his theory developed so far. Conceptually linked with the interpretation of the class struggle as a distorted form of social understanding is the necessity of admitting collective as well as individual actors as the bearers of communicative action. So far it was an implicit assumption of Habermas' theory of action that it is primarily only individuals that reciprocally come to agreement in interaction about the meaning of their situation and adjust their interests to one another. But the social struggle over the legitimacy of valid norms unambiguously represents a form of interaction that is realized not only between particular subjects but also between social groups. In social conflicts, for which we find extensive examples in negotiations, strikes, and boycotts, in silent disobedience and in open struggle, it becomes clear that organized or unorganized groups are also able to relate to one another communicatively. The members of these groups share so many values and action orientations with one another that they are capable of collective action; that is, they can emerge as actors.

However, this conceptual expansion of action theory easily leads to the well-known errors that result when supra-individual unities are secretly explained as subjects and treated as bearers of cognitive and practical achievements: social groups (and also institutional organizations) are then presented in the same way as homogeneously acting and thinking beings, a manner in which only individual subjects can be meaningfully conceived. Habermas also does not avoid the errors associated with this idea when he interprets class struggle from the perspective of the philosophy of history, as a process of reflection on the part of social classes.[54] But this problematic bias is not necessarily connected with the social-theoretic model that he develops with his interpretation of class struggle as a distorted form of understanding. That is, as already indicated, as soon as the identity of social groups of classes is reconstructed from the relation of the intersubjectivity of subjects who communicate with one another, the conceptual necessity of a philosophy of history that underlies his arguments falls away. The collective actors that relate communicatively to one another need not be understood as macro-subjects; they can be understood as social groups whose collective identity itself is the fragile and always threatened product of a process of socialization carried out between individuals. Hints for such a concept can be gained from such varied theories as Lucien Goldman's genetic structuralism, Karl Mannheim's sociology of knowledge, and more recent English sociology of culture, all of which have continuously understood the formation of the identity of social groups as a process of the communicative elaboration of class-specific experiences.[55]

Now, Habermas himself, as the philosophy-of-consciousness turn of his concept of class shows, neither theoretically explicated nor conceptually thought out all these sociological conclusions that can be derived from his interpretation of Marx's work. But the few indications allow us to perceive at least the contours of a second model of the history of the species, in which the basic communication-theoretic concepts are entered upon in a different form than in the model that proceeded from a criticism of the technocracy thesis. Both versions that we have followed make clear alternatives that stand at the point of transformation of the action-theoretic approach in a theory of society. In the first approach, Habermas takes the basic concepts of communicative and purposive-rational action as indicators for different forms of organization of social domains of action. He contrasts the communicatively reproduced sphere of institutionalized norms against the purposive-rational sphere so that he can analyze the development of the history of the species as a two-track process of social rationalization. He can then conceive the growing disproportion between these two processes of rationalization which are carried out in independence from one another as the basic conflict of the history of the species. Critical social theory becomes the critique of the power of purposive-rationally organized action systems that are exempted from communicative arrangement and have become independent of social understanding. On the other hand, in the second version of the species' history, Habermas takes the concept of communicative action as an indicator for the action mechanism through which the organization of *all* social domains of action is regulated. The development of the species' history takes place as an interaction between communicatively integrated groups in which the organization of social reproduction is socially "negotiated."[58] But this interaction so far stands under the norms that, with the force of institutions, asymmetrically distributed the social exercise of power and separate groups into social classes. Thus the intersubjective process of understanding is developed until today in the distorted form of a moral struggle between social classes which, as the "recurring dialectic of ethical life," gradually removes the superfluous forms of social domination and enlarges the possibility of an undistorted communication. This conflictual process of communicative rationalization also underlies the process of the rationalization of purposive-rational action (that is, the development of productive forces), since the institutional organization of all social domains of tasks is regulated in the interaction of social groups.

As is not difficult to see, the tasks of a critical social theory change with this second model of the history of the species. Because the distortion of social action produced by class domination is taken as the basic conflict of socio-cultural evolution, it is the goal of a critically applied theory to expand our knowledge about the particular forms of class domination at the moment and, hence, to again set in motion the suspended process of will-formation that could be freed from the socially rooted barriers and limitations to communication. Admittedly, Habermas has not followed this alternative of a critical social theory from its communication-theoretic foundation. He is too deeply impressed by the contemporary analysis of a technology that has taken on a life of its own, and too deeply influenced by the sociological diagnosis of a class conflict that resolves itself, to have been able to find the traces of a moral "dialectics of class antagonism" in the present societies of late capitalism.[57] Instead of this he proceeds to work out the approach of a critical social theory that was laid out in the first model of the history of the species, initially through an evolution-theoretic foundation and finally through an expansion and differentiation of the basic concepts of action theory. The result is one, but only *one*, communication-theoretic transformation of the philosophy of history first formulated by Adorno and Horkheimer in the *Dialectic of Enlightenment*.

9

Habermas' Theory of Society: A Transformation of the *Dialectic of Enlightenment* in Light of the Theory of Communication

Habermas converts the insights from the theory of communication underlying his theory of knowledge into two competing conceptions of the organization of society. Although this tension is not obvious, the writings from the late 1960s in which he attempts to transform his epistemological considerations into a theory of society contain two tendencies: On the one hand, there is the model of a two-tiered reproduction of society within instrumental-rational and communicative spheres of action. This model arose in connection with his criticisms of the technocracy thesis. On the other hand, there is the model of a maintenance of the social order through institutionally mediated communicative relations between morally integrated groups, which arose in connection with his critique of Marx. These two constructions of the social order suggest quite different conceptions of the developmental path of the history of the species as well as, in the end, competing diagnoses of social crisis. Of course, a critique of the first, systems-theoretic version of a theory of society can, as indicated, be joined to the line of argument that is found in the second version of the history of the species: The conceptual construction of a system of action organized in terms of purposive rationality, which is the central theoretical perspective in the first approach, is called into question and surpassed by the notion that lies at the basis of the second approach, namely the idea of a moral consensus formation encompassing all of society and organizing all domains of actions. But Habermas did not pursue further the basic idea of a social theory latent in the philosophical-historical idea of a moral "dialectic of class conflict." On the contrary, in the 1970s his social theory elaborates, in several steps, the approach formulated in his criticism of the technocracy thesis. This development culminates in the two-volume work *The Theory of Communicative Action* (1981). Along the path toward it, the traces of an alternative model of society are gradually lost.

Of course, the path from the first sketch to the mature theory, from the essay "Technology and Science as 'Ideology' " to *The Theory of Communicative Action*, is not straightforward. The development of Habermas' theory is marked by revisions and expansions in which he responds to problems in his original approach to a critical theory. In *Knowledge and Human Interests* Habermas had characterized the methodological structure of a critical social theory through an analogy to psychoanalysis. Just as the aim of psychoanalysis in the theoretically guided interpretation of a life history is to liberate the individual from an unperceived pathology, critical social theory, along the way toward an enlightened interpretation of the history of civilization, is supposed to liberate the species from a disturbance, a "pathology" in its process of self-formation.[1] However, Habermas altered the significance of what was taken to be the cause of the distortion in the collective process of self-formation according to his specific construction of the history of the species. In the one case, unintentionally indebted to the technocracy thesis, he regarded the naturelike process in which purposive-rational organizations become autonomous as the central disturbance to social development. In the other case, by taking up the basic intention of Marx's work, he introduced the asymmetrical distribution of the exercise of power as this central disturbance. Nevertheless, both constructions remained tied in their methodological perspective to the same presuppositions: Since he attempted to understand them by appealing to psychoanalysis, Habermas viewed the constructions as self-reflections of the species upon its self-incurred pathologies. Two problems arose in giving the theory this sort of status. Habermas worked on their solution in the development of his theory, and the analytic steps that led to *The Theory of Communicative Action* can be viewed in their light.

First, so long as he attempted to construct the history of the species methodologically according to the paradigm of psychoanalysis, Habermas identified "self-reflection" with "reconstruction" in an ambiguous manner. In the concept of "self-reflection" the problems of a critique of ideology that aids the critical and reflective solution of the self-misunderstanding of an individual or collective subject were conflated with the problems of a transcendental analysis aimed at clarifying the universal presuppositions of knowledge and action. Only in this way, as Habermas later acknowledged,[2] could he, in *Knowledge and Human Interests,* directly equate the transcendental-pragmatic analysis of the universal conditions of possible knowledge with a process of self-reflection, that is, with an act of reflective clarification of "unconsciously produced constraints."[3] Second, so long as he attempted to define critical social theory methodologically as "self-reflection," he made use of the unclarified presupposition of a unified species-subject. A theory understood as self-reflection upon the process of self-formation within the history of the species already presupposes in the concept of the "species" the undivided bearer of social learning processes ideally forming itself through the work of critical enlightenment. The revisions and expansions that Habermas undertakes in his theory during the 1970s can be clarified with reference to both of these difficulties. They take the form of a gradual derelativization of the hermeneutic point of view and lead to three constructive decisions that, taken together, produce the theoretical framework within which Habermas once again takes up on a higher level his original theme of a critique of the technocracy thesis.[4]

(1) From the beginning of the 1970s, Habermas was no longer content with a hermeneutic interpretation of his scientific claims for the elaboration of his theory. Whereas in *Knowledge and Human Interests* he had reconnected critical social theory to the practical frame of reference for a historically unique context of experience and, hence, had given theoretical critique the status of a temporally limited and practically engaged project, in his debate with Gadamer he develops for the first time

the idea of a theory of linguistic communication that is situation-independent and contextually neutral. In this way the process of communicative action, in which Habermas had from the outset social-scientifically and normatively grounded his conception of a critical theory, becomes the object of an investigation with universalistic truth claims. A transcendental analysis that reconstructs the universal conditions of the possibility of practical processes of understanding replaces a hermeneutic explication of the communicative experience.[5] Of course, with this step Habermas' theory leaves behind the framework in which it had originally been grounded as an anthropology of knowledge. The investigation of the basic structures of intersubjectivity is directed exclusively to an analysis of rules of speech so that the bodily and physical dimension of social action no longer comes into view. As a result, the human body, whose historical fate both Adorno and Foucault had drawn into the center of their investigation (though admittedly with theoretically insufficient means), loses all value within a critical social theory.[6]

As Thomas McCarthy has convincingly shown,[7] the methodological separation of the moments of ideology critique and reconstruction, which had not yet been distinguished within the initial concept of self-reflection, is the most important step in this decisive break with hermeneutics. The foundations of the theory are no longer achieved through a hermeneutic self-reflection on the unconscious presuppositions of actualized achievements of human action; they are now achieved through the rational reconstruction of universal conditions of human communication. Habermas initially develops this radicalized version of his theory of action in the form of a universal pragmatics.[8] Its specific goal consists in demonstrating that in the process of speech oriented to understanding interacting subjects raise reciprocal validity claims and necessarily assume the obligation of redeeming them in discourse. With the claim of such a "validity basis" in speech Habermas attempts to show that universal standards of rationality enter into the exercise of communicative action. These standards of rationality possess conclusive validity regardless of the accompanying consciousness of the participating subjects. Accordingly, the universal pragmatic analysis of the rules of linguistic understanding not only provides a renewed foundation for a communicative ethics with which Habermas, since his inaugural address, has attempted to justify the normative claims of a critical social theory; it also represents the extended foundation for the concept of social rationalization with which he attempts to investigate the reproduction of societies. With the reconstruction of the rational validity claims supposedly inherent in communicative action, the aspects are exposed under which social action in general is "capable of rationalization." We shall see how for Habermas, as a consequence of a universal-pragmatic analysis of the implications of communicative understanding for rationality, the spectrum of social rationalization extends to include a third component, namely, the aesthetic-expressive.

(2) Whereas universal pragmatics is the theory in which Habermas develops his insights concerning the internal structure of communicative action on the methodologically clarified foundation of a reconstructive procedure, its systematic completion is contained in a theory of social evolution in which the development of societies is investigated from the perspective of their universal logic. Habermas has been engaged in the elaboration of the theory of evolution since the beginning of the 1970s. It appears as the diachronic counterpart to the synchronically-laid-out theory of communicative action. Whereas the latter reconstructs the implicit rule systems of social action in the form of a universal pragmatics, the former is supposed to analyze its stage-like development in the phylogenetic dimension of the history of the species. Habermas considers the idea of a reconstruction of the internal logic of social evolution for the first time in his controversy with Luhmann's systems theory: The "attempts at reconstruction, as it were, in the vertical dimension, are theories which must presuppose, to use Hegel's language, the logic of the concept, namely, the reconstruction of abstract systems of rules, in order, for its own part, to be able to clarify the logic of evolution and, therefore, the necessary sequences of the development, the acquisition, or the completion of those systems of rules

under empirical conditions."[9] Habermas adapts Piaget's onto-genetic developmental logic to the process of the history of the species in order to be able to describe the evolution of societies as a sequence of necessary stages of the rationality of human action. Of course, he contrasts this logical dimension of the development of societies with the factual process of social change which, as a dimension of the dynamic of evolution, takes place under empirically unique conditions.[10] However, whereas in the essays collected in *Toward the Reconstruction of Historical Materialism* (1976) he initially limits himself to the description of the process of the species' history corresponding to the distinction between communicative and instrumental action as a process of the gradual completion of moral-practical and technical-instrumental models of rationality, later the spectrum of the components of social evolution comprehended in a developmental logic is broadened by the universal pragmatic expansion of the concept of rationality.[11] As we shall see, next to the increase in the purposive-rational steering capacity and the structural change of the moral system, the expansion of the realm of individual autonomy appears as a third dimension in which Habermas attempts to define the history of the species as a process of the stage-like development of human rationality.

(3) The clarification of a concept of system, only vaguely used up to the end of the 1960s, is the third important decision for the development of Habermas's theory. Of course, as I have shown, the category of system had already played a central role in the essay "Technology and Science as 'Ideology.'" There it was introduced as an alternative concept to the world of interaction mediated by everyday language, and it was to characterize the "norm-free" organization of purposive-rational action. But this initial concept of system was neither systematically developed from the basic categories of the theory of action nor theoretically defined within the tradition of structural-functionalism. Further, at that time, the concept of system did not readily fit into the general philosophical framework of Habermas' theory, in which, until *Knowledge and Human Interests,* the human species was conceived as the subject of a historical process of evolution. That changed the moment

Habermas responded to the critical objections against the ideal-istic implications of his philosophy of history and dropped the notion of a unified subject of history.[12] From then on he no longer interprets the processes of rationalization, in which he attempts to conceive the evolution of societies, as a process of the will-formation of the human species; rather, he under-stands them as supra-subjective learning processes carried by the social system. With this step in the abandonment of ideal-istic premises, which he again adopts in his controversy with Luhmann, Habermas bestows on the concept of system a sys-tematic value within the conceptual framework of his model of history: "Since the collective subject of a meaningfully consti-tuted lifeworld, borrowed from transcendental philosophy, has been shown, at least in sociology, to be a misleading fiction, the concept of system is proposed. Social systems are unities that can solve objectively posed problems through supra-subjective learning processes."[13]

Of course the conceptual retreats that Habermas makes with this are of greater significance than his formulation suggests. That is, since he now attributes the evolutionarily important learning processes to social systems of action in which processes of rationalization are supposed to take place "supra-subjec-tively," in important ways he rules out the conceptual alterna-tive that we encountered in the reconstruction of the second version of his communication-theoretic model of society. Then, instead of switching over directly to the concept of "social system" he could also have made use of the idea of collective actors in order to avoid the misleading notion of a unified species-subject. The social learning processes that proceed within societies would then be attributable neither to a macro-subject nor to anonymous action systems, but to social groups which along the way of the communicative processing of group-specific experiences attain new insights and convictions. This theoretical approach would have opened up the possibility of interpreting the process of social rationalization as a process in which social groups struggle over the type and manner of the development and formation of social institutions. At the same time, a practically decisive role in the process of repro-duction of societies would thereby have been assigned to the action orientations and value-representations specific to groups. But Habermas does not give acting groups a conceptual role in his social theory. Instead, when it concerns the bearer of social activities, he links the level of systemically constituted systems of action directly to the level of individual acting subjects without taking into consideration the intermediate stage of a praxis of socially integrated groups.[14] Accordingly, in the writings that follow the controversy with Luhmann he systematically develops in consistent ways the concept of system which, with the help of Parsons's concept of media, he derives from the theory of action and raises to a key element in his new theory of society.

With the theory of communication outlined in connection with a universal pragmatics, the theory of social evolution, and the assimilation of the basic assumptions of systems theory, the theoretical decisions that mark the path from Habermas' original criticism of the technocracy thesis to *The Theory of Communicative Action* are defined. Together these three concepts provide the theoretical presuppositions with which Habermas again attempts to solve the problems that were already specified in the early essay. *The Theory of Communicative Action* also pursues the goal of elaborating a concept of social rationalization that is comprehensive enough to permit a normatively and social-theoretically developed critique of the one-sided forms of social rationalization, namely those dominated by purposive-rationality. Now, however, Habermas opposes not only the Marxist analysis of capitalism and the Weberian concept of rationalization but also Adorno and Horkheimer's diagnosis of history in order to ground his own approach in a critique of the classical theories of social rationalization. As he had done earlier with respect to Marx and Weber, he now attempts with respect to critical theory to work out the action-theoretic bottlenecks that stand in the way of the goal of a comprehensive and grounded critique of the one-sided, purposive-rational form of socialization. To this extent, the new work can also be understood as an attempt to give a communication-theoretic turn to the diagnosis that in the *Dialectic of Enlightenment* took the form of a philosophy of history.[15]

Admittedly, Habermas no longer attains the comprehensive concept of rationality necessary for this goal from the simple opposition of "labor" and "interaction," of "instrumental" and "communicative" rationality. Rather, he places at the basis of his theory a systematic analysis in which what is rational is defined solely from the internal perspective of communicative action.[16] Habermas resumes the preliminary studies on universal pragmatics in which he had given his theory of communication a linguistic direction in order to distinguish within communicative speech acts the different dimensions in which a claim to the rational validity of utterances is implicitly raised. This analysis leads to the claim that there are three forms of rationality inherent within linguistic understanding, since a speaker does not make a claim only about the "truth" of his utterances. While the truth of his utterances is measured against the objective world of existing states of affairs, their rightness is judged against the social world of moral norms and their truthfulness against the world of inner experience, which is accessible only to the individual. When he now speaks of the possibility of a rationalization of human action in three dimensions, Habermas proceeds from these three "relations to the world" clarified in relation to Popper's three-world theory[17] and supported with reference to Karl Bühler's linguistic theory.[18] Thus, in the form of learning processes we can increase our knowledge not only of the physical environment but also of the world of social norms and the world of subjective experiences and, thereby, gradually develop the rationality of our actions. However, whereas in everyday praxis we make intuitive use of those stocks of knowledge and, in the different forms of action, relate directly to the world, only in communicative action do we apply our knowledge reflexively. In a different and more precise way than before, Habermas now views the process of coordinating individual plans of action within the specific praxis of communicative action as an act of linguistic understanding in which the participants come to an agreement about a common interpretation of their action situation through the conscious use of their intuitive knowledge.[19]

As these brief indications show, the communicative model of action that lies at the basis of Habermas' social theory has changed considerably in comparison with his previous approaches. The process of communication is now no longer simply set over against purposive-rational action; rather, it is conceived as a process of understanding that includes all aspects of human rationality as internal points of reference. At the same time, the dimensions of communicative and instrumental rationality, which Habermas had previously distinguished, are extended by the third dimension of aesthetic-expressive rationality, which is supposed to be set forth in the authentic relationship of the subject to the world of his internal perceptions and experiences.[20] From this Habermas derives a view of aesthetics that, in problematic ways, attempts to connect the rationality of a work of art to the truthfulness of expressions formed within it.[21] Not only is the internal structure of communicative action now specified differently; so is its social role: It now defines not a specific form of social action that can be separated from other modes of action but a special form of the coordination of goal-directed action. Henceforth, Habermas proceeds from the problematic presupposition of a teleological, internal structure of all individual action[22]: "Concepts of *social action* are distinguished . . . according to how they specify the *coordination* among the goal-directed actions of different participants. . . . In the case of communicative action the interpretive accomplishments on which cooperative processes of interpretation are based represent the mechanism for *coordinating* action; communicative action is *not exhausted* by the act of reaching understanding in an interpretive manner."[23]

If, however, linguistic understanding represents the particular form of a coordination of goal-directed actions that comes about by virtue of the mutual accomplishments of interpretation, it may be asked how all the processes of coordinating action that exist in the physical or psychological, moral or cognitive relations between a subject and its object are to be characterized. To be sure, in the section of his work on speech-act theory Habermas attempts to demarcate forms of strategic action from forms of action oriented to understanding, but the former do not systematically appear in his argument as ways for coordinating action.[24] The conceptual gap that thus emerges in the system of basic action-theoretic concepts finally has a repressive effect in the construction of his social theory: Habermas is no longer able to introduce the concept of power from an action-theoretic perspective; he now can introduce it only from a systems-theoretic perspective.

Habermas initially achieves the transformation of his communication-theoretic premises through the introduction of the concept of the "lifeworld." This category had already performed a decisive role in his original critique of the technocracy thesis. But now Habermas systematically develops the concept that he had defined only vaguely before. He introduces it as a concept that complements the concept of communicative action; thereby, he attempts to distinguish it from phenomenological modes of its employment.[25] The view that every act of linguistic understanding always occurs within an intersubjectively recognized framework furnishes the background for this train of thought. The cooperative accomplishments of interpretation produced in the process of understanding do not always begin anew with a definition of all the components of a situation. Rather, they are, for their own part, connected to innumerable already-established convictions. Habermas now calls "lifeworld" such a horizon of intersubjectively shared background assumptions in which every process of communication is already embedded. He views it as the congealed result of the act of communication for stabilizing convictions, that is, as the historical product of the interpretive efforts of preceding generations. The lifeworld furnishes the channel of everyday knowledge for orientation in which the flow of social processes of communication can continue without the threat of interruption:

Subjects acting communicatively always come to an understanding in the horizon of a lifeworld. Their lifeworld is formed from more or less diffuse, always unproblematic, background convictions. This lifeworld background serves as a source of situation definitions that are presupposed by participants as unproblematic. . . . The lifeworld also stores the interpretive work of preceding generations. It is the conservative counterweight to the risk of disagreement that arises with every actual process of reaching understanding.[26]

With the concept of the lifeworld the first stage of Habermas' social theory is already outlined, since within the horizon of the intersubjectively shared convictions and values that furnish the stable background of all everyday processes of communication we are able to discern the social core of societies and, within this, the "institutional framework" that Habermas had spoken of in his initial approach. Accordingly, societies reproduce themselves by way of their members' continuing the interpretive activity of preceding generations in which the members intersubjectively exchange the world orientations and situational definitions stored up in the lifeworld. This process of the symbolic reproduction of a society occurs within the three dimensions of cultural tradition, social integration, and individual socialization.

Of course, the members of a society do not simply pass on their common background assumptions; rather, at the same time, they extend their lifeworld knowledge in relation to collective learning processes. Habermas derives from this the notion of a rationalization of the social lifeworld through which he extends the basic theory of action rationality into a dynamic concept. Its basic concept is that along the path of cognitive learning processes the lifeworld knowledge for orientation differentiates itself at an ontological level so widely that the three fundamental relations to the world separate out from one another and become intelligible as distinct aspects of rationality. Habermas again makes use of an adaptation of Piaget's developmental psychology to the history of the species' consciousness in order to clarify the logic of these overarching learning processes. That is, he regards the same process of a cognitive decentration that Piaget had claimed for the intellectual development of the child as the mechanism that leads to the differentiation of systems of meaning in the lifeworld. The formal differentiation of the universe into three dimensions of rationality that represents the presupposition of a reflective acquaintance with reality (and, hence, the condition of linguistic processes of understanding) takes place at the level of the lifeworld as a process of the gradual decentration of an initially socio-centrically formed understanding of the world:

The more the world view that furnishes the cultural stock of knowledge is decentered, the less the need for understanding is covered *in advance* by an interpreted lifeworld immune from critique, and the more this need has to be met by the interpretive accomplishments of the participants themselves, that is, by way of risky (because rationally motivated) agreement, the more frequently we can expect rational action orientations. Thus for the time being we can characterize the rationalization of the lifeworld in the dimension "normatively as-cribed agreement" *versus* "communicatively achieved understanding." The more cultural traditions predecide which validity claims, when, where, for what, from whom, and to whom must be accepted, the less the participants themselves have the possibility of making explicit and examining the potential grounds on which their yes/no positions are based.[27]

The rationalization that now takes place in the form of the decentration of the implicit structures of knowledge in the lifeworld can be made socially effective only when their intellectual results penetrate the institutions of a society and, in this way, attain objective validity. Thus, the model according to which this transformation of culturally rationalized forms of consciousness proceeds must be clarified if the process of social rationalization as a whole is to be investigated. In order to be able to answer this question, Habermas relies upon Weber's theory of rationalization. From the sociology of religion, in which Weber analyzed the formation of Western rationalism, Habermas acquires the notion that cognitive rationalizations provide for the emergence of institutional complexes that are specialized for the processing of various aspects of rationalization. Thus, the process of social rationalization is represented as a process in which the dimensions of rationality, at first differentiated at the cultural level, gradually become embodied in separate spheres of action and thereby rearrange the social order of life.

So far the reproduction of a society is admittedly represented only as a process of the symbolic renewal of its socio-cultural lifeworld. The rationalization of this social domain that occurs in the form of a gradual decentration of cultural worldviews frees communicative action from traditionally defined orientations and thereby expands the domain for linguistic processes of understanding. However, the development of societies is admittedly not exhausted in the symbolic renewal of social lifeworlds. Social reproduction is just as fundamentally dependent upon the appropriation of natural resources in which the material conditions of social life are maintained. Correspondingly, Habermas distinguishes the task of symbolic reproduction from the requirement of material reproduction, which includes the exercise of political administration as well as social labor: "Whereas the aspect of social action most relevant to the symbolic reproduction of the lifeworld is that of mutual understanding, the aspect of purposive activity is important for material reproduction, which takes place through the medium of goal-directed interventions into the objective world."[28]

The old distinction between "labor" and "interaction" reappears here initially in the difference between the two dimensions of social reproduction. In this way the possibility of examining socio-cultural evolution as a whole is opened up. However, Habermas is now less interested in the contrast between communicative and purposive-rational action orientations as such than in the contrast that exists between the forms of organization of these two modes of action. He enters upon the second stage of his social theory with the assertion that, in contrast to communicative action, purposive-rational activity which contributes to the material reproduction of society is permitted to govern only functional mechanisms. The distinction that Habermas finds in this is, therefore, of great significance, since with its help he will justify the introduction of systems theory from an action-theoretic perspective:

To be sure, the material reproduction of the lifeworld does not, even in limiting cases, shrink down to surveyable dimensions such that it might be represented as the intended outcome of collective cooperation. Normally it takes place as the fulfillment of latent functions going beyond the action orientations of those involved. Insofar as the aggregate effects of cooperative actions fulfill the imperative of maintaining the material substratum, these complexes of action can be stabilized functionally, that is, through feedback from functional side effects.[29]

This first step along the path that will lead to an expansion of the action-theoretic approach through a concept of system is already not wholly convincing, since it does not account for the fact that even the symbolic reproduction of a society through communicative action cannot be represented as the "intended result of a collective cooperation" but rather is to be conceived only as an unintended fulfillment of latent functions. The cultural integration of social groups takes place through an entire complex of communicative actions which are not able to be surveyed as such by members of groups. Nevertheless, Habermas presupposes this provisional distinction when he proposes a methodological change of perspective within the theory for the analysis of material processes of reproduction:

> With respect to these "metabolic processes" (Marx), it makes sense to objectify the lifeworld as a boundary-maintaining system, for functional interdependencies come into play here that cannot be gotten at adequately via members' intuitive knowledge of lifeworld contexts. Survival imperatives require a junctional integration of the lifeworld, which reaches right through the symbolic structures of the lifeworld and therefore cannot be grasped without further ado from the perspective of participants.[30]

The material reproduction of the social lifeworld is supposed to be conceived as a process of system maintenance, since only within its framework can the necessary purposive activities of subjects be functionally coordinated. Therefore, the change of perspective that Habermas recommends is to be understood not as a simple transition from one theoretical viewpoint to another equally meaningful viewpoint but rather as a change demanded by the structural properties of social reality itself. The conceptual boundary line with which Habermas distinguishes between social integration and system-integration refers not to possible attitudes of theory with respect to its object but to an actual distinction within the social organization of societies: "In one case the action system is integrated through consensus, whether normatively guaranteed or communicatively achieved; in the other case it is integrated through the nonnormative steering of individual decisions not subjectively coordinated."[31]

The reifying tendency that we could already discover in the dualism of "purposive-rational subsystems" and "institutional frameworks" in Habermas' critique of the technocracy thesis is repeated in this distinction at a higher level of reflection. To be sure, Habermas now no longer simply illustrates the difference between purposive-rational and communicative action types with entire spheres of social life. In the approach of his reformulated theory of action, "labor" and "interaction" no longer directly oppose one another as two forms of action. Rather, social actions are distinguished by the mechanism through which they are socially coordinated. Thus on a first-order level such a reification is already ruled out for conceptual reasons. But with the rigid coordination of the two dimensions of symbolic and material reproduction with the analytically distinguished mechanisms of social integration and system integration, the same fictions are in principle introduced that were already present in the initial approach. That is, this division introduces a distinction within the process of social reproduction for which it is extremely difficult to find actual correspondences. Neither the symbolic nor the material reproduction of societies can be conceived as such normally transparent relations of actions that they "may be represented as the intended result of a collective cooperation." For this both spheres of reproduction require mechanisms that so unite the particular processes of communication or cooperation in a complex that together they are able to fulfill the corresponding functions of symbolic reproduction or material reproduction. In both cases, mechanisms of this kind represent institutions in which the respective accomplishments of action are normatively institutionalized, that is, under the constraint of the action orientations of subjects that are stored up in the lifeworld, while their execution is sanctioned by the degree of autonomy of a society found in democratic agreements or under authoritatively bound orders. If we explain the coordination of social action from the elementary mechanism of the construction of institutions in this manner, the distinction with which Habermas operates will be untenable, since in the case of both symbolic and material reproduction the integration of the accomplishments of action then takes place on the way toward the formation of normatively constructed institutions. This formation is the result of a process of communication realized in the form of understanding of struggle between social groups.

However, Habermas now uses the distinction between two forms of integrating social action to describe the evolution of societies from the twofold perspective of the rationalization of the lifeworld and the increase in system complexity. The distinction he had attempted to justify with a view to the factual differences in the forms of coordination of symbolic and material reproduction, he again immediately reduces to a mere methodological distinction between the perspective of the participant and the observer in order to be able to develop the particular point of his two-level concept of society. This consists in the claim that only in the course of socio-cultural evolution are the mechanisms of system integration first so strongly separated out from the horizon of the social lifeworld that they appear as self-sufficient forms of coordination of social action and create autonomous spheres of action. The methodological dualism of "system integration" and "social integration" that was initially only supposed to describe two complimentary perspectives in the analysis of one and the same process of evolution is transformed along the path toward the rationalization of social action into the factual dualism of "system" and "lifeworld":

System and lifeworld are differentiated in the sense that the complexity of the one and the rationality of the other grow. But it is not only qua system and qua lifeworld that they are differentiated; they get differentiated from one another at the same time. . . . Modern societies attain a level of system differentiation at which increasingly autonomous organizations are connected with one another via delinguistified media of communication: these systemic mechanisms—for example, money—steer a social intercourse that has been largely disconnected from the norms and values, above all in those subsystems of purposive rational economic and administrative action, that, on Weber's diagnosis, have become independent of their moral-political foundations.[32]

With this line of thought Habermas henceforth attempts to view the two action spheres of "system" and "lifeworld," which in his initial approach he had still understood as universal components in social evolution, as the historical results of a process of differentiation in which socio-cultural evolution is characterized as a whole. To be sure, the change he thereby assumes in the basic assumptions of his social theory produces an internal contradiction by introducing a factual difference justified from the perspective of a universal history (a difference I have already mentioned), but it also brings with it the advantage of an historically relativized use of the concept of system. Habermas views the evolutionary process of differentiation, which has led to the formation of autonomous systems of purposive-rational action and which, thus, is now supposed to justify the application of systems theory, as a process that follows the rationalization of communicative action.[33] Thus, he proceeds from the general thesis that higher forms of organization of material reproduction, and therefore new levels of system differentiation, can become established evolutionarily only if the institutional presuppositions within the lifeworld have already been achieved by corresponding advances in forms of communication. Thus, the increase in system complexity that is realized in the course of a development in the integrative mechanisms of material reproduction must be comprehended as an evolutionary process that depends upon the process of the rationalization of communicative action accompanying the formation of institutions. Finally, the particular level of communicative rationality, in which the mechanisms of system integration can at last be separated out from the normative horizon of the lifeworld and in which the form of purposive-rationally organized systems of action can be assumed, is then accounted for so long as the aspects of orientation to success and orientation to understanding are also separated from one another in the course of decoupling communicative action from particular value orientations:

The trend toward value generalization gives rise to two tendencies on the plane of interaction. The further motive and value generalization advance, the more communicative action gets detached from concrete and traditional normative behavior patterns. This uncoupling shifts the burden of social integration more and more from religiously anchored consensus to processes of consensus formation in language. . . . On the other hand, freeing communicative action from particular value orientations also forces the separation of action oriented to success from action oriented to mutual understanding. With the generalization of motives and values, space opens up for subsystems of purposive rational action. The coordination of action can be transferred over to delinguistified media of communication only when contexts of strategic action get differentiated out.[34]

As the last quotation shows, Habermas introduces the concept of system via the concept of "delinguistified media of communication." Concealed behind this concept is the idea, borrowed from Parsons, that social actions can also be coordinated with the help of expense-saving media that are supported by generalized consent, instead of along the demanding path of linguistic communication alone. Such media relieve social reproduction from the growing demands of coordination that originate with the release of communicative action from cultural traditions. They are able to motivate social actions apart from the requirements of interpretation. Habermas distinguishes two types of mechanisms that relieve burdens in this way, in the form of "communication media that either condense or replace mutual understanding in language."[35] Of course, the delinguistified media of communication participate only in the formation of purposive-rational action systems. With the development of money and the establishment of state-organized power, two steering media arise in social evolution that are able to coordinate the purposive-rational actions that contribute to the mastery of material reproduction while avoiding the demand of linguistic communication:

Media such as money and power attach to empirical [as opposed to rational—A.H.] ties; they encode a purposive-rational attitude toward calculable amounts of value and make it possible to exert generalized, strategic influence on the decisions of other participants while *bypassing* processes of consensus-oriented communication. Inasmuch as they do not merely simplify linguistic communication, but *replace* it with a symbolic generalization of rewards and punishments, the lifeworld contexts in which processes of reaching understanding are always embedded are devalued in favor of media-steered interactions; the lifeworld is no longer needed for the coordination of action.[36]

Habermas finds in the capitalist economic system the first action sphere that was historically separated out from the lifeworld as a result of the institutionalization of a delinguistified medium of communication and was established as a norm-free subsystem. With the generalization of money as a universal exchange medium, the possibility arises for the first time of organizing social production in a separate action system capable of directing the recruitment of labor power as well as the circulation of commodities through the channels of a delinguistified medium of communication. Thus, with the completion of the capitalist economy, which is bound to the lifeworld presupposition of a release of success-oriented attitudes institutionalized in bourgeois law, a purposive-rationally organized domain of action develops that is no longer tied to the mechanism of communication.[37] A state apparatus that looks after the social presuppositions of economic production completes this development. Since under capitalist conditions it becomes dependent on the media-steered economic system, the state apparatus is forced to reorganize its own activities "in such a way that political power takes on the structure of a steering medium—it is assimilated to money."[38] To be sure, as a medium of communication, state-organized power, as Habermas emphasizes, remains tied to goals capable of legitimation and, therefore, is still indirectly dependent on a normative consensus among the members of society. But the state's decisions, so long as they are made under the modern conditions of legalized domination, function like exchange values, since they are able to steer instrumental action accomplishments for the purpose of realizing collective goals.[39]

Thus, Habermas sees a level of system differentiation attained in modern societies in which the autonomous action systems of the economy and the state organize material reproduction through delinguistified communication media. The power of the lifeworld is finally withdrawn from these spheres of life because, as norm-free domains of social action, they are no longer directed to the practices of moral understanding:

Via the media of money and power, the subsystems of economy and the state are differentiated out of an institutional complex set within the horizon of the lifeworld; *formally organized domains of action* emerge that—in the final analysis—are no longer integrated through the mechanism of mutual understanding, that shear off from lifeworld contexts and congeal into a kind of norm-free sociality.[40]

The problems and difficulties that Habermas falls into with this conclusion emerge still more clearly a little later on in a formulation in which he poignantly repeats the same line of thought:

> The social [as it is expressed here, in what is our guiding concept— A.H.] is not absorbed as such by organized action systems; rather, it is split up into spheres of action constituted as the lifeworld and spheres neutralized against the lifeworld. The former are communicatively structured, the latter formally organized. They do not stand in any *hierarchical* relationship between levels of interaction and organization; rather, they stand *opposite* one another as socially and systemically integrated spheres of action.[41]

If capitalist societies are conceived in this way as social orders in which system and lifeworld stand over against each other as autonomous spheres of action, two complementary fictions emerge: We then suppose (1) the existence of norm-free organizations of action and (2) the existence of power-free spheres of communication. In both of these fictions produced by the concept of system the theoretical errors that we have already recognized as reifications in Habermas's critique of the technocracy thesis reappear:

(1) The representation of purposive-rationally organized systems of action generates the double appearance that, first, the forms of organization of the economy and the administration of the state may still be conceived only as embodiments of purposive-rational rules of action and, second, the accomplishments of action within the organizations can take place independent of the processes of normative consensus formation. The view that arises with the first assumption contradicts the thesis, well demonstrated in the meantime, that the organizational structures of management and administration can be generally clarified only as institutional embodiments of both purposive-rational and political-practical principles.[42] The political-practical standards that at any time determine the normative conditions under which the corresponding organizational tasks are purposive-rationally fulfilled may be conceived as the result of a continuous process of communication among concerned actors. For this reason, the view that arises from the second assumption is also already shown to be a theoretical fiction. Actions produced in organizations such as

management and administration not only remain dependent upon practices of social understanding in the sense that they cannot be connected to a complex of functionally directed accomplishments without the mediation of direct, situation related decisions[43]; they are also bound to a process of normative consensus formation in the sense that their specific domain of operation and their particular form of organization are continuously being dealt with from a new perspective. Further, neither management nor administration can be made independent from the normative agreement of its members to the degree that the systems-theoretic sociology of organizations supposes.[44]

(2) Conversely, the image of communicatively integrated spheres of action suggests the independence of the lifeworld from practices of domination and processes of power. This second fiction results not only from Habermas' evolution-theoretic explanations of the emergence of modern societies in terms of the decoupling of system and lifeworld but also from the terminological constraints into which he falls with his distinction between two forms of integration of social action. As I have shown, Habermas has tied the formation of the subsystems of purposive-rational action to the presupposition of a cognitive separation of actions oriented to success and actions oriented to understanding. First, since the rationalization of the lifeworld has progressed so far that strategic attitudes become possible along the path toward the decentration of worldviews, the coordination of action can be transferred to the delinguistified media of communication (since only these are structurally suited for the steering of purposive-rational actions). Corresponding to the independence of purposive-rational systems of action, the autonomization of the lifeworld then appears as a process to be realized in which the potential for action oriented to understanding, released from all strategic impurities, is, so to speak, concentrated in specialized spheres of communication and only then undertakes the coordination action. Therefore, system and lifeworld are historically uncoupled, if we follow this explanation, in that the "social" becomes separated into purposive-rationally organized

systems of action and communicatively reproduced spheres of action. Then, of course, it must seem as if the social lifeworld is reproduced independent of the practices of strategic influences (that is, of the forms of the physical, psychological, or cognitive exercise of power). In other words, since only actions oriented to understanding look after the coordination of plans of action within the differentiated spheres of communication, which Habermas regards as primarily the family and the public sphere, all attempts at the success-oriented completion of interests are already excluded at the conceptual level. This theoretically produced fiction corresponds at the conceptual level to the difficulty of distinguishing between understanding-oriented and success-oriented models of the coordination of action in the process of social integration. Admittedly, Habermas subsequently undertook an attempt to distinguish "agreement" and "influence" as two mutually exclusive mechanisms for the linguistic coordination of social action and thereby already opened up the possibility of distinguishing, from within an action-theoretic perspective, forms of the exercise of power on the level of social integration.[45] But in *The Theory of Communicative Action* this differentiation does not play a decisive role, since forms of the external influence of acting subjects are first considered at the level of their embodiment in delinguistified media of communication and thus take over the functions of system integration. Thus the category of "social integration" lies closer to forms of coordinating action oriented to understanding, whereas the concept of "system integration" can only be thought of in reference to external (that is, success-oriented) forms of coordinating action. As a result of this suggestion, the social lifeworld already assumes at the conceptual level the character of a power-free sphere of communication, which will actually be attested to with the development of the evolution-theoretical arguments.[46]

It is clear that these two fictions have a complementary relationship. Whereas purposive-rational domains of action seem to be separated out from all processes of the integration of the lifeworld, the social lifeworld is represented as freed from all forms of the exercise of power. "Power," as a means for the coordination of social action, is considered only at the level of systems integration, so all presystemic processes of the constitution and reproduction of domination must fall out of view.[47] On the other hand, the socially integrative achievements of the lifeworld are observed in only those spheres of social action that aid the symbolic reproduction of a society, so all processes of moral consensus formation internal to an organization must fall out of view. The first fiction contradicts all that we have encountered as achievements of the action-theoretic approach, though not, of course, the systems-theoretic completion, of Foucault's theory of power: namely, the importance of pre-state, situationally bound forms of the exercise of everyday domination in the reproduction of a society. The second fiction contradicts all that is to be learned from the communication-theoretic critique of classical sociology of organizations: namely, the importance of processes of social interaction internal to an organization for the functioning of social organizations.

With this mutual exclusion, Habermas merely continues at an advanced level the social-theoretic dualism for which he had prepared the ground in his critique of the technocracy thesis. However, the fictions now yield a reifying picture not of two types of action, but of two forms of coordinating social action within whole spheres of social reproduction. The diagnosis of the times that results from this social-theoretically renewed dualism thus represents in principle only a more precise form of the previous analysis, in which Habermas had already viewed the independence of technology as a threat to communicative practice. Of course, he now presents the same social tendencies within the gradually developed framework so that a process of the *Dialectic of Enlightenment* is discernible in it: "When this tendency toward an uncoupling of system and lifeworld is depicted on the level of a systematic history of forms of mutual understanding, the irresistible irony of the world-historical process of enlightenment becomes evident: The rationalization of the lifeworld makes possible a heightening of systemic complexity, which becomes so hypertrophied that it unleashes system imperatives that burst the capacity of the lifeworld they instrumentalize."[48]

In the end it seems that, through the stages of the development of his social theory, Habermas has worked his way up to
a diagnosis of the times that, like Adorno's and Foucault's
analysis of the present, concentrates on the social consequences
of power complexes that have become autonomous. Habermas
locates the developmental tendencies of the present within the
dualism of system and lifeworld, as Adorno had within the
dualism of organization and individual and Foucault had
within the dualism of power apparatus and human body. The
penetration of systemic forms of steering into the previously
intact region of a communicative everyday practice represents
for Habermas the pathology of our society: "In the end, systemic mechanisms suppress forms of social integration even in
those areas where a consensus-dependent coordination of action cannot be replaced, that is, where the symbolic reproduction of the lifeworld is at stake. In these areas, the *mediatization*
of the lifeworld assumes the form of a *colonization*."[49]

Of course, the hypostatization of social spheres as systems
that also lies at the basis of the diagnoses of the times does not
arise for Habermas, as it does for Adorno and Foucault, from
a presupposed and unquestioned coercive model of the social
order in which the constitutive role of moral processes of understanding simply remain ignored. Rather—and this distinguishes him from all others within the tradition of a critical
social theory—Habermas views communicative action as the
fundamental mechanism of reproduction of all societies. His
critique of positivism and his critique of one-sided concepts of
rationality are the unique witnesses of a communicative theory
of society aspired to along the path of a theoretical argument
with competing tendencies. Only this approach puts him in the
position to interpret the phenomena of a dialectic of enlightenment, observed by Adorno and Foucault, in such a way that
they can be criticized as one-sided, purposive-rationality directed forms of social rationalization. He is no longer deprived
of the standards in connection with which a critique of the
capitalist model of socialization could be indicated. However,
Habermas is so wedded to the basic convictions of the technocracy thesis that he attempts to conceive the domain of
material reproduction as a norm-free, purely technically

organized sphere of action. Hence, he excludes it from the definitions of his own theory of communication. This ultimately pretheoretic decision lets him take hold of the means of systems theory in order to be able to analyze evolutionary processes within the historically differentiated spheres of the economy and politics as systemically steered processes of purposive-rational action. Thus, the action spheres in which material reproduction is today organized finally appear as domains of norm-free sociality that, as a closed universe, stand over against the sphere of communicative everyday praxis. With this dualism, the diagnosis of the times that is able to discern pathological distortions only where purposive-rational principles of organization invade from outside a lifeworld regarded as undamaged acquires its theoretical foothold. But therefore Habermas not only abandons within his social theory the normative orientation to another domain, namely the communicative organization of material reproduction which, under the title "self-administration," belongs to the productive part of the tradition of critical Marxism.[50] He not only gives up the possibility of a justified critique of concrete forms of organization of economic production and political administration. Habermas loses above all—and this again makes him heir to the tradition of critical social theory we have investigated here—the communication-theoretic approach he had initially opened up: the potential for an understanding of the social order as an institutionally mediated communicative relation between culturally integrated groups that, so long as the exercise of power is asymmetrically distributed, takes place through the medium of social struggle. Only a consistent elaboration of this alternative version of a communicative theory of society would make it possible to understand the social organizations that Adorno and Foucault mistook as power complexes functioning in a totalitarian manner as fragile constructions that remain dependent for their existence on the moral consensus of all participants.

Notes

Afterword (1988)

1. For further suggestions and insightful questions I am indebted to the reviews of Klaus Günther [*Zeitschrift für philosophische Forschung* 41 (1987), pp. 323–327], Rainer Rochlitz ["Des philosophes allemands face à la pensée française," *Critique* 464/465 (1986), p. 7ff.], Hans-Peter Müller [abbreviated in *Soziologische Revue* 10 (1987), p. 7ff.], Emil Angehrn ["Krise der Vernunft?," in *Philosophische Rundschau* 33 (1986), pp. 161–209], Slawomir Magala ["History and the Way Out of It," *Thesis Eleven* 20 (1988), p. 119ff.], and Benjamin Gregg [Review of *Kritik der Macht* in *New German Critique* 47 (1989), pp. 183–188].

2. See Axel Honneth, "Communication and Reconciliation: Habermas's Critique of Adorno," *Telos* 39 (1979), pp. 45–61.

3. On this idea of a transformation of the Marxist doctrine of class struggle, see Axel Honneth, "Domination and Servitude: The Philosophical Heritage of Marxism Reviewed," *Graduate Faculty Philosophy Journal* (1988).

4. I am thinking primarily of "The Fragmented World of Symbolic Forms: Reflections on Pierre Bourdieu's Sociology of Culture," *Theory, Culture & Society* 3 (1986), p. 55ff.; "An Ontological Redemption of the Revolution. On Cornelius Castoriadis' Theory of Society," *Thesis Eleven* 14 (1986), pp. 62–78; "Critical Theory," in *Social Theory Today*, ed. A. Giddens and J. Turner (Polity, 1987), p. 347ff. An older essay that also belongs to this thematic context is "Moral Consciousness and Class Domination," *Praxis International* 2:1 (1982), pp. 12–25.

5. Rolf Wiggershaus, *Die Frankfurter Schule* (Munich and Vienna, 1986). See also Josef Früchtl, "Die positive Entzauberung der Frankfurter Schule," *Philosophische Rundschau* 35 (1988), p. 33ff.

6. Rolf Wiggershaus, *Theodor W. Adorno* (Munich, 1987), chapter 2.

7. Martin Jay, *Adorno* (Harvard University Press, 1984). See also the chapter on Adorno in Jay's *Marxism and Totality: The Adventures of a Concept from Lukács to Habermas* (University of California Press, 1984).

8. Josef Früchtl, *Mimesis. Konstellationen eines Zentralbegriffs bei Adorno* (Würzburg, 1986).

9. Stefan Cochetti, *Mythos und 'Dialektik der Aufklärung'* (Königstein, 1985).

10. See the essays in his collection *The Persistence of Modernity: Essays on Aesthetics, Ethics & Postmodernism* (MIT Press, 1990). For an extremely interesting comparison of Adorno's aesthetics to deconstructionism, though one that is a sharp alternative to Wellmer's, see Christoph Menke-Eggers, *Die Souveränität der Kunst. Aesthetische Erfahrung nach Adorno und Derrida* (Frankfurt, 1988).

11. Albrecht Wellmer, "Die Bedeutung der Frankfurter Schule heute," in *Die Frankfurter Schule und die Folgen*, ed. Axel Honneth and Albrecht Wellmer (Berlin, 1986), p. 25ff., here p. 32.

12. See the arguments directed partly against me by Fritz Reusswig and Michel Scharpening in "Hegelsche Argumentationsfiguren in der Soziologie Adornos," in *Das Bellen des toten Hundes. Über Hegelsche Argumentationsfiguren im sozialwissenschaftlichen Kontext*, ed. Jürgen Ritsert (Frankfurt, 1988), p. 37ff.

13. See Axel Honneth, "Ein strukturalistischer Rousseau. Zur Anthropologie von Claude Lévi-Strauss," *Merkur* 10 (1987), p. 819ff.

14. I am thinking primarily of Johann P. Arnason's *Zwischen Natur und Gesellschaft* (Frankfurt, 1976).

15. Klaus Eder, *Die Vergesellschaftung der Natur. Studien zur sozialen Evolution der praktischen Vernunft* (Frankfurt, 1988), chapters 1 and 2. An interesting attempt at presenting the history of the human relationship to inner nature that makes use of Adorno's philosophy of history was presented by Rudolf zur Lippe with the example of dancing; see *Naturbeherrschung am Menschen*, volumes I and II (Frankfurt, 1974).

16. See the already dated bibliography by Michael Clark, *Michel Foucault: An Annotated Bibliography. Tool Kit for a New Age* (New York, 1983). An overview of a different perspective is offered by the following: Mike Gane, "The Form of Foucault," *Economy and Society* 15 (1986), p. 110ff.; Alan Megill, "The Reception of Foucault by Historians," *Journal of the History of Ideas* 48 (1987), p. 117ff.; Michael S. Roth, "Review Essay of Recent Literature on Foucault," *History and Theory* (1987), p. 7ff.; Ulrich Johannes Schneider, "Eine Philosophie der Kritik. Zur amerikanischen und französischen Rezeption Michel Foucaults," *Zeitschrift für philosophische Forschung* 42 (1988), p. 311ff.

17. Nancy Fraser, "Foucault on Modern Power: Empirical Insights and Normative Confusions," *Praxis International* 1 (1981), p. 272ff.

18. For an overview see Roth, "Review Essay" (note 16 above). David Couzens Hoy's edited collection *Foucault: A Critical Reader* (Blackwell, 1986) is representative here.

19. See Stefan Breuer, "Foucaults Theorie der Disziplinärgesellschaft. Eine Zwischenbilanz," *Leviathan* 3 (1987), p. 319ff. In this context the much more comprehensive study by Peter Dews, *Logics of Disintegration. Post-Structuralist Thought and the Claims of Critical Theory* (London, 1987), also seems to me to be important.

20. Hubert L. Dreyfus and Paul Rabinow, *Michel Foucault: Beyond Structuralism and Hermeneutics* (Chicago, 1982).

21. Ibid, p. 205ff.

22. Jürgen Habermas, *The Philosophical Discourse of Modernity*, tr. F. Lawrence (MIT Press, 1987), chapter 10.

23. See Roth, "Review Essay." The fronts also become clear in the exchange between William E. Connolly and Charles Taylor in *Political Theory* 13 (1985), p. 365ff.

24. John Rajchman, *Michel Foucault: The Freedom of Philosophy* (Columbia University Press, 1985).

25. See Richard Rorty, "Foucault and Epistemology" in *Foucault: A Critical Reader* (note 18 above), p. 41ff.

26. Charles Taylor, "Foucault on Freedom and Truth," in *Philosophical Papers* (Cambridge University Press, 1985), volume 2, pp. 152–184.

27. Michael Walzer, "The Politics of Michel Foucault," in *Foucault: A Critical Reader*, p. 51ff.

28. See Barry Smart, *Foucault, Marxism and Critique* (London, 1983), chapter 6; John O'Neill, "The Disciplinary Society: From Weber to Foucault," *British Journal of Sociology* 37 (1986), p. 42ff.; Bryan S. Turner, "The Rationalization of the Body: Reflections on Modernity and Discipline," in *Max Weber, Rationality and Modernity*, ed. S. Whimster and S. Lash (London, 1987), p. 222ff.; Colin Gordon, "The Soul and the Citizen: Max Weber and Michel Foucault on Rationality and Government," ibid., p. 293ff.; Stefan Breuer, "Sozialdisziplinierung. Probleme und Problemverlagerungen eines Konzeptes bei Max Weber, Gerhard Östreich und Michel Foucault," in *Soziale Sicherheit und soziale Disziplinierung*, ed. Christoph Sachsse and Florian Tennstedt (Frankfurt, 1986), p. 45ff.

29. Stefan Breuer undertakes this in his article "Foucault's Theorie der Diziplingesellschaft. Eine Zwischenbilanz." For a glance at Weberian Marxism, see also Peter Dews, *Logics of Disintegration*, chapter 5.

30. So far, attempts at philosophical interpretations of these later writings predominate; see especially the special issue of *Philosophy and Social Criticism* 12 (1987), titled *The Final Foucault*.

31. See especially Alois Hahn, "Zur Soziologie der Beichte und anderer Formen institutionalisierter Bekenntnisse," *Kölner Zeitschrift für Soziologie und Sozialpsychologie* 34 (1982), p. 408ff.

32. For a recent confirmation see "Max Weber und das Projekt der Moderne. Eine Diskussion mit Dieter Henrich, Claus Offe und Wolfgang Schluchter," in *Max Weber. Ein Symposium*, ed. Christian Greuss and Jürgen Kocka (Munich, 1988), p. 155ff.

33. Bryan S. Turner, "The Rationalization of the Body: Reflections on Modernity and Discipline," p. 233. With reference to this point I have also attempted to strengthen my own objections in "Foucault and Adorno: Two forms of the critique of modernity," *Thesis Eleven* 15 (1986), pp. 48–59.

34. See Jürgen Habermas, *Faktizität und Geltung. Beiträge zur Diskurstheorie der Recht und der Moral* (Frankfurt, forthcoming).

35. See the "Bibliographie zur *Theorie des kommunikativen Handelns*" by Rene Görzten, in *Kommunikatives Handeln. Beiträge zu Jürgen Habermas' 'Theorie des kommunikativen Handelns'*, ed. Axel Honneth and Hans Joans (Frankfurt, 1986), p. 406ff.

36. Especially indicative of this tendency are three more recent books: *Habermas and Modernity*, ed. Richard J. Bernstein (MIT Press, 1985), Stephen K. White, *The Recent Work of Jürgen Habermas: Reason, Justice and Modernity* (Cambridge University Press, 1988), and Kenneth Baynes, *The Normative Grounds of Social Criticism: Kant, Rawls, and Habermas* (SUNY Press, 1991).

37. Albrecht Wellmer, "Über Vernunft, Emanzipation und Utopie. Zur kommunikationsthᵉoretischen Begründung einer kritischen Gesellschaftstheorie," in *Ethik und Dialog* (Frankfurt, 1986), p. 175ff.

38. Ibid., p. 175ff.

39. See Johannes Berger, "Die Versprachlichung des Sakralen und die Entsprachlichung der Ökonomie," *Zeitschrift für Soziologie* 11 (1982), p. 353ff.

40. See J. P. Arnason, "Die Moderne als Projekt und Spannungsfeld," in *Kommunikatives Handeln*, p. 278ff; Hans Joas, "The Unhappy Marriage of Hermeneutics and Functionalism," *Praxis International* (1987); Thomas McCarthy, "Complexity and Democracy: The Enchantments of Systemstheory," *New German Critique* 35 (1985). See also Karl Bruckmeier, *Kritik der Organisationsgesellschaft. Wege der systemtheoretischen Auflösung der Gesellschaft von Weber, Parsons, Luhmann und Habermas* (Münster, 1988).

41. Jürgen Habermas, "Entgegnung," in *Kommunikatives Handeln*, p. 327ff.

42. Jürgen Habermas, "Theorie der Gesellschaft oder Sozialtechnologie. Eine Auseinandersetzung mit Niklas Luhmann," in *Theorie der Gesellschaft oder Sozialtechnologie*, ed. J. Habermas and N. Luhmann (Frankfurt, 1971), p. 142ff., esp. 172ff.

Chapter 1

1. Max Horkheimer, "Traditional and Critical Theory," in *Critical Theory*, pp. 188–243 (hereafter cited as TCT).

2. TCT, p. 193.

3. TCT, p. 194.

4. TCT, p. 196.

5. TCT, p. 200.

6. On the following, compare J. P. Arnason, *Von Marcuse zu Marx* (Neuwied and Berlin, 1971), p. 79ff.; Michael Theunissen, *Gesellschaft und Geschichte* (Berlin, 1969), p. 14ff.

7. TCT, pp. 203–204. In his "Notes" from the 1950s and the 1960s, Horkheimer once again reiterated this line of thought in a virtually structuralist version that abolishes the human species as the unified subject of synthetic achievements and replaces it with a subjectless process of structuring (see "A Kantian Sociology," in *Dawn and Decline*).

8. TCT, p. 205.

9. Compare Ernst Michael Lange, *Das Prinzip "Arbeit"* (Frankfurt, 1980).

10. TCT, p. 238.

11. TCT, p. 212.

12. TCT, p. 212.

13. Max Horkheimer, "Zum Problem der Voraussage in den Sozialwissenschaften," in *Kritische Theorie*, volume 1 (Frankfurt, 1968), p. 117.

14. TCT, p. 213.

15. TCT, p. 208.

16. TCT, pp. 206–207.

17. Compare Karl Marx, "Theses on Feuerbach," in *Marx: The Early Writings*.

18. TCT, p. 229.

19. TCT, p. 231 [translation modified]. On the understanding of theory within critical Marxism of the 1920s, compare Furio Cerutti, "Hegel, Lukacs, Korsch. Zum dialektischen Selbstverständnis des kritischen Marxismus," in *Aktualiktät und Folgen der Philosophie Hegels*, ed. O. Negt (Frankfurt, 1970), p. 195ff.

20. TCT, p. 229.

21. TCT, p. 219.

22. TCT, p. 219.

23. TCT, p. 241.

24. TCT, p. 215.

25. See Helmut Dubiel, *Theory and Politics: Studies on the Development of Critical Theory* (MIT Press, 1984).

26. Max Horkheimer, "Geschichte und Psychologie," *Zeitschrift für Sozialforschung* (Munich, 1980), volume 1, p. 66ff.

27. Max Horkheimer, "Die gegenwärtige Lage der Sozialphilosophie und die Aufgaben eines Instituts für Sozialforschung," in *Sozialphilosophische Studien*, ed. Werner Brede (Frankfurt, 1972), p. 40.

28. Horkheimer, "Geschichte und Psychologie," p. 131ff.

29. Ibid. p. 133.

30. Ibid.

31. Compare Friedrich Pollock, *Stadien des Kapitalismus*, ed. Helmut Dubiel (Munich, 1975).

32. Compare Alfons Söllner, *Geschichte und Herrschaft. Studien zur materialistischen Sozialwissenschaft, 1929–1942* (Frankfurt, 1979), chapter 3.

33. TCT, p. 238.

34. Compare Helmut Dahmer, *Libido und Gesellschaft. Studien über Freud und die Freudsche Linke* (Frankfurt, 1973), chapter II.2.

35. "Geschichte und Psychologie," p. 139.

36. Ibid., p. 136.

37. "Authority and the Family," in *Critical Theory*, pp. 54–55 (hereafter cited as AF).

38. Erich Fromm, "The Method and Function of an Analytic Social Psychology," in *The Crisis of Psychoanalysis* (Fawcett, 1970), p. 158 [originally published in *Zeitschrift*, vol. 1, 1932].

39. In addition to the essay cited in the previous note, see especially Fromm's "Psychoanalytic Characterology and Its Relevance for Social Psychology," in *The Crisis of Psychoanalysis* [originally published in *Zeitschrift*, vol. 1, 1932].

40. Compare Erich Fromm, "Sozialpsychologischer Teil," in *Studien über Autorität und Familie*, ed. M. Horkheimer (Paris, 1936), p. 77ff.

41. Helmut Dahmer, "Notizen zur antifaschistischen Sozialpsychologie," *Arbeiterbewegung, Theorie und Geschichte*, Jahrbuch 4 (Frankfurt, 1976), p. 66ff.

42. Horkheimer, "Die gegenwärtige Lage der Sozialphilosophie und die Aufgaben eines Instituts für Sozialforschung," p. 43.

43. Compare *Family and Inheritance: Rural Society in Western Europe: 1200–1800*, ed. E. P. Thompson, J. Goody, and J. Thirsk (Cambridge University Press, 1976); Raymond Williams, *Keywords: A Vocabulary of Culture and Society* (Oxford University Press, 1985). An earlier essay by Fritz Sack, which worked out the conceptual significance of such a concept of culture in relation to research on American subculture and which has remained largely unnoticed, is "Die Idee der Subkultur: Eine Berührung zwischen Anthropologie und Soziologie," *Kölner Zeitschrift für Soziologie und Sozialpsychologie* 23 (1971), p. 261ff.

44. AF, p. 54.

45. AF, p. 54.

46. "But if past and present coercion plays its part even in the sublimest movements of the human psyche, yet the psyche itself, like all the mediating institutions such as family, school, and church which form the psyche, has its own laws. (AF, p. 57.)

47. AF, p. 59.

Chapter 2

1. "Traditional and Critical Theory," in *Critical Theory*, pp. 235–237.

2. One of the theoretical inconsistencies of "Authority and the Family" is that the weakening of the father within the family, to which such high social-psychological

significance is attributed, is derived solely from the demise of the "average-income" family but is then extended to families within all social groups; compare chapter 3.

3. "Art and Mass Culture," in *Critical Theory*, pp. 273–290.

4. Ibid., p. 279.

5. "The End of Reason," *Zeitschrift für Sozialforschung* 9 (1941), p. 366ff.; reprinted in *The Essential Frankfurt School Reader*, ed. A. Arato and E. Gebhardt (Continuum, 1982), pp. 26–48.

6. Ibid., p. 38.

7. Ibid., p. 46.

8. On the attempt to outline the phases in Horkheimer's theoretical development, see Gerd-Walter, *Der Kritikbegriff der Kritisichen Theorie Max Horkheimers* (Frankfurt, 1980), p. 196, n. 1.

9. Helmut Dubiel has documented the influence of these historical experiences on the formation of critical theory in *Theory and Politics*, tr. B. Gregg (MIT Press, 1984).

10. See the biographical sketch by Peter von Haselbergs, "Wiesengrund-Adorno," in *Theodor Adorno. Sonderband 'Text und Kritik'* (Munich, 1977), p. 7ff.

11. "On the Social Character of Music," "Über Jazz," and "On the Fetischistic Character of Music and the Regression of the Listener," in *The Frankfurt School Reader*.

12. "The Actuality of Philosophy," *Telos* 31 (1977), pp. 20–142; "The Idea of a Natural History," *Telos* 60 (1984), pp. 111–124.

13. Susan Buck-Morss has traced Benjamin's influence on Adorno's early writings in *The Origins of Negative Dialectics* (New York, 1977).

14. *Dialectic of Enlightenment*, p. 231.

15. See Friedemann Grenz, *Adornos Philosophie in Grundbegriffen* (Frankfurt, 1974); Josef F. Schmucker, *Adorno—Loqik des Zerfalls* (Stuttgart, 1977).

16. See Georg Lukács, "Reification and the Consciousness of the Proletariat," in *History and Class Consciousness*, tr. R. Livingstone (MIT Press, 1971), pp. 83–222; A. Sohn-Rethel, *Geistige und körperliche Arbeit* (Frankfurt, 1970) and *Warenform und Denkform. Aufsätze* (Frankfurt, 1971).

17. One finds this epistemological motif only sporadically in Adorno; in *Negative Dialectics*, see especially p. 177. One of the few references in Sohn-Rethel is also found in this passage. Sohn-Rethel incorporated this structural comparison between commodity exchange and bourgeois forms of thought into his epistemological theory early on (see especially *Geistige und körperliche Arbeit*); see also Adorno, *Against Epistemology*, tr. Willis Domingo (MIT Press, 1983).

18. See the very careful reconstruction of this argument by J. F. Schucker, *Adorno—Logik des Zerfalls*, p. 21ff. For a critique, see R. W. Mueller, *Geld und Geist*, part II, section 5.

19. *Dialectic of Enlightenment*, p. 180. In the following I consciously attempt an interpretation that reduces this work to its essential content; in the process, the interpretive artistry and philosophical fantasy that rightly distinguish this text are lost.

20. *Dialectic of Enlightenment*, p. 39.

21. Arnold Gehlen, *Der Mensch*, second edition (Frankfurt, 1971), p. 46.

22. *Dialectic of Enlightenment*, p. 181.

23. Ibid., p. 9.

24. Schmucker speaks of a "meta-economical theory of domination" in characterizing the conception of domination in the *Dialectic of Enlightenment*.

25. *Dialectic of Enlightenment*, p. 234. From a biographical perspective, the influence of Ludwig Klages on Walter Benjamin makes such an indirect dependence of the *Dialectic of Enlightenment* on the basic ideas of the cultural criticism developed within "life philosophy" seem likely; see Werner Fuld, "Walter Benjamins Beziehung zu Ludwig Klages," *Akzente* 28:3 (1981), p. 274ff.; Axel Honneth, 'Der Geist und sein Gegenstand'. Anthropologische Berührungspunkte zwischen der Dialektik der Aufklärung und der lebensphilosophischen Kulturkritik (unpublished manuscript, 1983).

26. See Hermann Mörchen, *Macht und Herrschaft im Denken von Heidegger und Adorno* (Stuttgart, 1980); Reinhart Maurer, *Revolution und 'Kehre'. Studien zum Problem gesellschaftlicher Naturbeherrschung* (Frankfurt, 1975), esp. chapter 5; Alfred Schmidt, "Herrschaft des Subjekts. Über Heideggers Marx-Interpretation," in *Martin Heidegger. Fragen an sein Werk* (Stuttgart, 1977), p. 54ff.

27. *Dialectic of Enlightenment*, pp. 188–189.

28. Ibid., p. 189.

29. Ibid.; see also pp. 192–193.

30. *Against Epistemology*, p. 80.

31. See Jessica Benjamin, "The End of Internalization: Adorno's Social Psychology," *Telos* 32 (1977), pp. 42–64.

32. *Dialectic of Enlightenment*, p. 33.

33. Ibid., pp. 54–55.

34. See Schmucker, *Adorno-Logik des Zerfalls*, pp. 37ff. and 53ff.

35. For this reason the interpretations that completely miss a theory of social domination in the *Dialectic of Enlightenment* are misleading; see A. Söllner, *Geschichte und Herrschaft. Studien zur materialistischen sozialwissenschaft 1929–1942*, p. 190ff. As will be shown, the admittedly vague yet interconnected fragments of a conception of social domination are nevertheless extremely important for Adorno's social theory.

36. I take this phase from *Negative Dialectics* (p. 315 of the German edition), but it is completely appropriate for what is intended in the *Dialectic of Enlightenment*.

37. *Dialectic of Enlightenment*, p. 14.

38. Ibid., p. 34 [translation modified].

39. Ibid., p. 35.

40. Ibid., p. 56.

41. Ibid., p. 21.

42. Ibid., p. 57.

43. Ibid., p. 36.

44. Ibid., pp. 36–37.

45. Ibid., pp. 21–22.

46. Johan Galtung has rendered this concept systematically fruitful for the social sciences; see *Kapitalistische Grossmacht Europa oder Die Gemeinschaft der Konzerne* (Reinbek bei Hamburg, 1973), chapter 3 ("Allgemeines über den Begriff der Macht").

47. See Michael Theunissen, *Gesellschaft und Geschichte*, p. 15ff.

Chapter 3

1. *Dialectic of Enlightenment*, p. 221.

2. Ibid., p. xi.

3. Ibid., p. 222.

4. Ibid., p. 242.

5. Ibid., p. 243.

6. The phrase is from Burkhardt Lindner, "Il faut etre absolument moderne'. Adornos Aesthetik: Ihre Konstruktionsprinzip und ihre Historizität," in *Materialien zur aesthetischen Theorie Theodor W. Adornos*, ed. B. Lindner and W. M. Lüdke (Frankfurt, 1980), p. 261ff., here p. 282.

7. *Negative Dialectics*, p. 9 [translation modified].

8. *Dialectic of Enlightenment*, p. 227.

9. Walter Benjamin, "The Work of Art in the Age of Mechanical Reproduction," in *Illuminations* (Schocken, 1969), pp. 217–251; Herbert Marcuse, "The Affirmative Character of Culture," in *Negations* (Beacon, 1968), pp. 88–133. For the difference between these two approaches to the theory of culture, see Jürgen Habermas, "Consciousness-Raising or Redemptive Criticism—The Contemporaneity of Walter Benjamin," *New German Critique* 17 (1979), pp. 30–59.

10. On the place of the concept of mimesis in Adorno's aesthetics—and, thus, in contrast to Lukács'—see B. Lindner, "'Il faut etre absolument moderne'. Adornos Aesthetik: Ihre Konstruktionsprinzip und ihre Historizität," in *Materialien zur aesthetischen Theorie Theodor W. Adornos*, esp. p. 294ff.; see also Bernhard Lypp, "Selbster-

haltung und aesthetische Erfahrung. Zur Geschichtsphilosophie und aesthetischen Theorie Adornos" in the same volume, p. 187ff.; T. Baumeister and J. Kulenkampff, "Geschichtsphilosophie und philosophische Aesthetik. Zu Adornos *Aesthetischer Theorie*, in *Neue Hefte für Philosophie*, vol. 5 (1973), p. 74ff.

11. *Aesthetic Theory*, tr. C. Lenhardt (Routledge and Kegan Paul, 1984), p. 97.

12. *Aesthetic Theory*, p. 191.

13. Adorno, "Der Artist als Statthalter," in *Gesammelte Schriften*, vol. 7 (Frankfurt, 1970), p. 114ff., here p. 124ff.

14. On the relation between Adorno and Lukács, see Dieter Klicke, "Kunst gegen Verdinglichung. Berührungspunkte in Gegensatz von Adorno und Lukács," in *Materialien zur aesethetischen Theorie Theodor W. Adornos*, p. 219ff.

15. Adorno himself speaks of the "truth in the twofold sense" that befalls art (*Aesthetic Theory*, p. 79).

16. See Adorno, "Der Essay als Form," in *Gesammelte Schriften*, vol. 11 (Frankfurt, 1970), p. 9ff.; on this see also my essay "Communication and Reconciliation: Habermas's Critique of Adorno," *Telos* 39 (1979), pp. 45–61.

17. Adorno, *Minima Moralia: Reflections From Damaged Life*, tr. E. F. N. Jephcott (New Left Books, 1974).

18. See T. Baumeister and J. Kulenkampff, "Geschichtsphilosophie und philosophische Aesthetik" and Rüdiger Bubner, "Kann Theorie aesthetisch werden? Zum Hauptmotiv der Philosophie Adornos," both in *Materialien zur aesthetischen Theorie Theodor W. Adornos*.

19. Adorno, "Sociology and Empirical Research," in *The Positivist Dispute in German Sociology*, ed. T. Adorno et al., tr. G. Adey and D. Frisby (Harper, 1976), p. 79.

20. For the limits of such a social theory shaped by the Hegelian mode of thought, see Christel Beier, *Zum Verhältnis von Gesellschaftstheorie und Erkenntnistheorie. Untersuchungen zum Totalitätsbegriff in der kritischen Theorie Adornos* (Frankfurt, 1977), chapter 11.

21. Adorno, "Sociology and Empirical Research," p. 74.

22. Friedrich Pollock, "State Capitalism: Its Possibilities and Limitations," in *The Essential Frankfurt School Reader*, ed. Arato and Gebhardt, pp. 71–94. On the tradition and method of application of this concept in Marxism, see Werner Olle, "Zur Theorie des Staatskapitalismus," in *Probleme des Klassenkampfs* 11/12 (1974), p. 91ff.

23. On Pollock's method of application, see *Studien des Kapitalismus*, ed. H. Dubiel and F. Pollock. On the theoretical context, see H. Dubiel and A. Söllner, "Die Nationalsozialismusforschung des Instituts für Sozialforschung," in *Wirtschaft, Recht und Staat im Nationalsozialismus*, ed. H. Dubiel and A. Söllner (Suhrkamp, 1981), pp. 7–32.

24. [Horkheimer, "The Authoritarian State," in *The Essential Frankfurt School Reader*, pp. 95–117—K.B.] On this, see Giacomo Marramao, "Zum Verhältnis von Politischer Ökonomie und Kritischer Theorie," in *Aesthetik und Kommunikation* 11 (1973), p. 79ff.

25. Adorno, "Reflexionen zur Klassentheorie" in *Gesammelte Schriften*, vol. 8, p. 373ff., esp. p. 380ff. See also Schmucker, *Adorno—Logik des Zerfalls*, p. 51ff.

26. "Late Capitalism or Industrial Society?" (tr. F. van Gelder), in *Modern German Sociology*, ed. V. Meja, D. Misgeld, and N. Stehr (Columbia University Press, 1987), pp. 232–247; here p. 239 [translation modified].

27. Ibid., p. 245.

28. In connection with the third set of alternative interpretations, see Schmucker, *Adorno—Logik des Zerfalls*, p. 63ff.

29. In all his socio-economic writings Adorno begins with the assumption that the propagandistic assertion of the separation between state and economy in liberal capitalism was also actually effective; he thus completely neglects that even in the "classical age" of liberal capitalism a relative degree of economic intervention by the state was an essential factor in capitalist development. For the German example, see especially Joachim Hirsch, *Wissenschaftlich-technischer Fortschritt und politisches System* (Frankfurt, 1971), chapter 1.

30. "Late Capitalism or Industrial Society?," p. 241 [translation modified].

31. *Dialectic of Enlightenment*, pp. 120–167. See also Douglas Kellner, "Kritische Theorie und Kulturindustrie," in *Sozialforschung als Kritik*, ed. W. Bonss and A. Honneth (Suhrkamp, 1982), p. 492ff.

32. Adorno, "Resume über Kulturindustrie," in *Gesammelte Schriften* 10.2 (Frankfurt, 1977), p. 509.

33. See Adorno, "Prolog zum Fernsehen," in *Gesammelte Schriften* 10.2, p. 507ff.

34. Benjamin, "The Work of Art in the Age of Technical Reproduction," in *Illuminations* (Schocken, 1969), pp. 217–251.

35. Adorno, "Television and the Patterns of Mass Culture," in *Mass Culture: The Popular Arts in America*, ed. B. Rosenberg and D. M. White (Free Press, 1957), pp. 474–489.

36. See, for example, "The Psychological Technique of Martin Luther Thomas' Radio Addresses," in *Gesammelte Schriften* 9.1 (Suhrkamp, 1975), p. 7ff.

37. Adorno, "Freizeit," in *Gesammelte Schriften* 10.2, p. 654.

38. Compare Kellner, "Kritische Theorie und Kulturindustrie"; A. Swinglewood, *The Myth of Mass Culture* (London, 1977), chapter 1; David Held, *Introduction to Critical Theory* (London, 1983), chapter 3.

39. "Prolog zum Fernsehen," p. 508.

40. Horkheimer, "Authoritarianism and the Family Today," in *The Family: Its Function and Destiny*, ed. R. N. Anshen (Harper, 1949), pp. 359–374. See also Frankfurt Institute for Social Research, *Aspects of Sociology* (Beacon, 1972), chapter 9.

41. Marcuse, "The Obsolescence of the Freudian Concept of Man" [1963], in *Five Lectures*, tr. J. Shapiro and S. Weber (Beacon, 1970), pp. 44–61; Alexander Mitscherlich, *Society Without the Father* [1963] Harcourt Brace and World, 1969).

42. "Individuum und Organisation," in *Gesammelte Schriften* 8, p. 440ff.

43. T. Adorno, "Anti-Semitism and Fascist Propaganda," in *Anti-Semitism*, ed. [name of editor] (publisher, year); "Freudian Theory and the Pattern of Fascist Propaganda" in *The Frankfurt School Reader*, ed. Arato and Ekhardt, pp. 118–137.

44. See above all T. Adorno, "Die revidierte Psychoanalyse," in *Gesammelte Schriften* 8, p. 20ff.; "Sociology and Psychology," *New Left Review* 46/47 (1966/67), pp. 67–80, 79–97; "Postscriptum," *Gesammelte Schriften* 8, p. 86ff.

45. "Sociology and Psychology," p. 87.

46. Ibid., p. 95. See also p. 93. Compare Adorno, "Society," *Salmagundi* 10/11 (1969/70), pp. 144–153.

47. [This note is absent from the original edition.—A.H.]

48. In *Social Amnesia* (Beacon, 1975) Russell Jacoby has attempted to work out this critique by Adorno (and Marcuse) of the sociological and interactionist reconstruction of psychoanalysis, without however raising the question of the limits and possible errors of this critique. Compare the review essay by Howard Gadlin, "The Return to Freud?," *New German Critique* 7 (1976), p. 122ff. On this whole issue, see also W. Bonss, "Psychoanalyse als Wissenschaft und Kritik. Zur Freudrezeption der Kritischen Theorie," in *Sozialforschung als Kritik*, ed. W. Bonns and A. Honneth (Frankfurt), p. 367ff.

49. Compare Jessica Benjamin, "The End of Internalization: Adorno's Social Psychology," *Telos* 32 (1977), p. 51.

50. "Freudian Theory and the Pattern of Fascist Propaganda," p. 126.

51. Ibid., p. 124.

52. "End of Internalization," p. 55.

53. Ibid., p. 56.

54. Ibid., p. 49.

55. Compare J. Habermas, "Stichworte zur Theorie der Sozialisation" (1968), in *Kultur und Kritik* (Frankfurt, 1973), p. 118ff., esp. p. 181ff.

56. "End of Internalization," p. 44, n. 4.

57. See especially Adorno, "Society," *Salmagundi* 10/11 (1969/1970), pp. 144–153.

58. Hence the title of Adorno's essay referred to in note 42.

Introduction to Part II

1. For a survey of the discussions that have been prompted by Adorno's writings on aesthetics see *Materialen zur ästhetischen Theorie Theodor W. Adornos*, ed. B. Lindner and W. M. Lüdke (Suhrkamp, 1979).

2. An informative survey of Adorno's philosophical writings is T. Baumeister, "Theodor W. Adorno—nach zehn Jahren," *Philosophische Rundschau* 28.1–2, p. 1ff.

3. Adorno's critique of Durkheim ["Einleitung," in E. Durkheim, *Soziologie und Philosophie* (Frankfurt, 1970), p. 7ff.] had lasting effects from this negative perspective.

4. This has already been confirmed by Wolf Lepenies ("Arbeiterkultur. Wissenschaftssoziologische Anmerkungen zur Konjunktur eines Begriffs," *Geschichte und Gesellschaft* 5 (1979), p. 125ff., here p. 134). An interesting exception in this regard is found in a study by Ursula Jaerisch which came out of the Institute for Social Research: *Sind Arbeiter autoritär? Zur Methodenkritik politischer Psychologie* (Frankfurt, 1975). This study relies upon the findings of English research on subcultures.

5. In his project of a social theory of society grounded in a theory of communication Habermas himself makes the claim that he is continuing, with some basic revisions, the original aims of the Frankfurt School; see *The Theory of Communicative Action*, volume 1, chapters 4 and 8. It is even more interesting that Foucault's social theory, which began without any reference to the tradition of critical theory, is increasingly presented as a continuation of Adorno's philosophy of history; see Jochen Hörisch, "Herrscherwort, Geld und geltende Sätze. Adornos Aktualisierung der Frühromantik und ihre Affinität zur poststrukturalistischen Kritik des Subjekts," in *Materialien zur Ästhetischen Theorie*, ed. B. Lindner and W. M. Lüdke, p. 397ff., and J. Bauch, "Reflexionen zur Destruktion der teleologischen Universalgeschichte durch den Strukturalismus und die kritische Theorie," *Archiv für Rechts- und Sozialphilosophie* 65 (1979), p. 81ff.

6. As some of the remarks reveal, the chapter on Foucault was written before his death; I was also unable to take into consideration the second and third volumes of the *History of Sexuality*, which appeared shortly before his death.

Chapter 4

1. See especially Durkheim, *The Elementary Forms of Religious Life*, introduction. On the significance of ethnology for the sociology of Durkheim and the Durkheimian school, see W. Paul Vogt, "Über den Nutzen des Studiums primitiver Gesellschaften. Eine Anmerkung zur Durkheim-Schule 1890–1940," in *Geschichte der Soziologie*, vol. 3, ed. W. Lepenies (Frankfurt, 1981), p. 276ff.

2. *The Order of Things*, p. 378.

3. See Claude Lévi-Strauss, *Structural Anthropology*, especially chapters 2, 3, and 11.

4. Simon Clarke's 1981 critique, *The Foundations of Structuralism*, strikes me as significant. Hans-Heinrich Baumann offers an interesting linguistic critique, "Über französischen Strukturalismus. Zur Rezeption moderner Linguistik in Frankreich und in Deutschland," in *Sprache im technischen Zeitalter* 30 (1969), p. 164ff. Also illuminating is the comparison made by Hermann Lang of Lévi-Strauss's linguistic theory of culture with the approach of Ernest Cassirer in *Die Sprache und das Unbewusste* (Frankfurt, 1973), chapter 4.

5. On Foucault's early work, see Walter Seitters, "Michel Foucault—Von der Subversion des Wissens," in M. Foucault, *Von der Subversion des Wissens* (Munich, 1974), p. 171ff.

6. Paolo Caruso, "Gespräch mit Michel Foucault" [1967], in M. Foucault, *Von der Subversion des Wissens*, p. 13.

7. See especially *Culture, Media, Language: Working Papers in Cultural Studies, 1972–79*, part II, ed. S. Hall, D. Hobson, A. Lowe, and P. Willis (London, 1981).

8. M. Foucault, "Des Denkens des Aussen," in *Von der Subversion des Wissens*, p. 13 ["La pensée du dehors," *Critique* 229 (1966), pp. 523–546].

9. M. Foucault, "Le Langage de l'espace," *Critique* 203 (1964), pp. 378–382. Jean Amery draws attention to the convergence between French structuralism and the literary movement of the "new novel" in chapter 6 of *Unmeisterliche Wanderjahre* (Stuttgart, 1971).

10. "Das Denken von Aussen," p. 57.

11. On the background of structuralist literary interpretation, see H. T. Lehmann, "Das Subjekt als Schrift. Hinweise zur französischen Texttheorie," *Merkur* 374 (1979), p. 665ff., and Reinold Werner, "Einleitung," in Julia Kristeva, *Die Revolution der poetischen Sprache* (Frankfurt, 1978), p. 7ff.

12. *The Order of Things*, chapter 9; "Introduction" to *The Archaeology of Knowledge*, pp. 3–17.

13. Unfortunately I could not take into account Habermas' interpretation of *The Order of Things* in chapter 9 of *The Philosophical Discourse of Modernity*.

14. *The Order of Things*, p. 310.

15. See, for example, Jean Piaget, *Structuralism*, tr. C. Maschler (Harper, 1971), p. 128ff.

16. Piaget, p. 132ff. See, among others, Ian Hacking, "Michel Foucault's Immature Science," *Nous* 13 (1979), p. 39ff., and "The Archaeology of Foucault," in *Foucault: A Critical Reader*, ed. David Couzens Hoy (Blackwell, 1986), pp. 27–40; Richard Rorty, "Beyond Nietzsche and Marx," *London Review of Books* 3 (1981), p. 5ff. On the context of the discussion, see Dirk Koppelberg, "Ende oder Wende der analytischen Philosophie und Wissenschaftstheorie?," *Zeitschrift für allgemeine Wissenschaftstheorie* 12 (1981), p. 364ff.

17. See especially "Marxism and Humanism," in *For Marx*, tr. B. Brewster (Vintage, 1970); *Reading Capital*, tr. B. Brewster (Verso, 1979), p. 158ff.

18. Herbert Schnädelbach's *Geschichtsphilosophie nach Hegel* (Freiburg, 1974) is instructive concerning these differences.

19. Ibid., p. 12.

20. Compare my essay "Geschichte und Interaktionsverhältnisse," in *Theorien des historischen Materialismus*, ed. U. Jaeggi and A. Honneth (Frankfurt, 1977), 405ff.

21. See L. Althusser, "Antwort an John Lewis," in *Was ist revolutionärer Marxismus?*, ed. H. Arenz, J. Bischoff, and U. Jaeggi (Berlin, 1973), p. 35ff.

22. *The Archaeology of Knowledge*, p. 12.

23. Ibid.

24. Compare A. Danto, *Analytical Philosophy of History* (Cambridge, 1965), and H. M. Baumgarten, *Kontinuität und Geschichte* (Frankfurt, 1972).

25. *The Archaeology of Knowledge*, p. 6.

26. Ibid., p. 7; see also pp. 138–139.

27. Of course, the "hermeneutical" basis of archaeological research should not be overlooked. A buried edifice can be reconstructed as a functionally harmonious memorial only to the extent that we can know the intended meaning-context of the individual elements. Foucault underestimates this when he employs the title "archaeology" for an explicitly anti-hermeneutical theoretical program.

28. *The Archaeology of Knowledge*, pp. 6–7.

29. I borrow this concept of "semiological structuralism" from chapter 3 of Vincent Descombes' *Das Selbe und das Andere. Fünfundvierzig Jahre Philosophie in Frankreich 1933–1978* (Frankfurt, 1981). On the context, see also Manfred Frank, *Das Individuelle Allgemeine. Textstrukturierung und -interpretation nach Schleiermacher* (Frankfurt, 1978), p. 48ff., and *Das Sagbare und das Unsagbare* (Frankfurt, 1980); also very helpful is Paul Ricoeur, *Hermeneutik und Strukturalismus* (Munich, 1974), p. 137ff.

30. Of course, with this the viewpoint of the arbitrariness of the sign is radicalized in a manner that goes beyond Saussure; on this, see Rodolphe Gasché, "Das wilde Denken und die Ökonomie der Repräsentation. Zum Verhältnis von Ferdinand de Saussure und Claude Lévi-Strauss," in *Orte des wilden Denkens. Zur Anthropologie von Claude Lévi-Strauss*, ed. Wolf Lepenies and Hans Henning Ritter (Frankfurt, 1970), p. 360ff.

31. M. Frank, *Das Individuelle Allgemeine*, p. 51.

32. See, for example, Kristeva, *Die Revolution der poetischen Sprache*.

33. On Lacan's theory see H. Lang, *Die Sprache und das Unbewusste*; also quite helpful are M. Frank, "Das 'Wahre Subjekt und sein Doppel'. Jacques Lacans Hermeneutik," in *Das Sagbare und das Unsagbare*, p. 114ff., and the volume of *Psyche* (34:10, 1980) dedicated to Lacan.

34. Compare M. Frank, "Eine fundamentalsemiologische Herausforderung der abendländischen Wissenschaft (J. Derrida)," *Philosophische Rundschau* 23 (1976), p. 1ff.; Descombes, *Das Selbe und das Andere*, p. 172ff.

35. This formulation makes intelligible the expression "transcendentalism without a subject," which is often used polemically in the French discussion about structuralism.

36. See Wolfert von Rahden, "Epistemologie und Wissenschaftskritik," in *Konsequenzen kritischer Wissenschaftstheorie*, ed. C. Hubig and W. von Rahden (Berlin, 1978), p. 162ff.

37. An exceptionally informative study on the dependence of *The Archaeology of Knowledge* upon the concept of history worked out in the Annales school is Claudia Honegger's "Michel Foucault und die serielle Geschichte," *Merkur* 407 (1982), p. 500ff.

38. *The Archaeology of Knowledge*, pp. 9–10.

39. Vincent Descombes assigns a somewhat different meaning to the concept of "archaeology" in the framework of Foucault's theory; see *Das Selbe und das Andere*, p. 132. He connects the meaning of archaeology with a research discipline that uncovers the

buried presuppositions of our present. In this sense the "archaeology of knowledge" is a discipline that reconstructs the unacknowledged cognitive presuppositions of our culture. I regard this interpretation as limited since it does not consider that archaeology is primarily a discipline oriented to edifices [*Baudenkmäler*]. If this is taken into account it becomes clear that Foucault attempts to distance methodically his own field of research. The manner in which Foucault attempts to carry this out also makes me skeptical about attempts to explain Walter Benjamin's method for writing the history of modernity with the aid of this concept of "archaeology." For an interesting attempt along these lines see Marc Sagnol, "Walter Benjamin, archeologue de la modernité," *Les Temps Moderne* (1985).

40. *The Archaeology of Knowledge*, p. 16.

41. Roland Barthes, "Die strukturalistische Tätigkeit," *Kursbuch* 5 (1966), p. 190ff.

42. Nancy Fraser uses this concept, which is taken from Husserl's phenomenological method, to characterize the methical attitude of Foucault's later theory of power; see "Foucault on Modern Power: Empirical Insights and Normative Confusions," *Praxis International* 3 (1981), p. 272ff. This concept seems to me to be suited above all for describing the first step in the method of investigation in *The Archaeology of Knowledge*.

43. See, for example, H. M. Baumgarten, *Kontinuität und Geschichte*.

44. *The Archaeology of Knowledge*, p. 24.

45. Ibid., p. 31ff.

46. Ibid., pp. 26–27.

47. Ibid., p. 93.

48. Ibid., p. 89 [English translation modified].

49. Ibid., p. 82.

50. Ibid., pp. 86–87. Also important in this context are Foucault's remarks on the "exteriority" of the statement (p. 125).

51. Ibid., p. 86.

52. For a similar conclusion, reached in different ways, see two earlier interpretations of *The Archaeology of Knowledge*: Gerd Kimmerle, "Die Leere im Denken des verschwendenen Menschen," *Konkursbuch* 5 (1980), p. 111ff.; C. Honegger, "Michel Foucault und die serielle Geschichte."

53. *The Archeology of Knowledge*, pp. 95–96.

54. See Charles Lemert and Garth Gillan, "The New Alternative in Critical Sociology: Foucault's Discursive Analysis," *Cultural Hermeneutics* 4 (1977), p. 309ff.

55. See *Urszenen. Literaturwissenschaft als Diskuranalyse und Diskurskritik*, ed. Friedrich A. Kittler and Horst Turk (Frankfurt, 1977); Harold Woetzel, "Diskursanalyse in Frankreich," *Das Argument* 126 (1980), p. 511ff.

56. *The Archaeology of Knowledge*, p. 107.

57. Ibid., pp. 107–108.

58. On the concept of "exteriority" see ibid., p. 122ff.

59. *The Archaeology of Knowledge*, p. 32.

60. Ibid.

61. Ibid., p. 47.

62. Ibid., p. 33ff.

63. Ibid., pp. 37–38.

64. Ibid., p. 49.

65. Ibid.

66. The concept of discourse in *The Archaeology of Knowledge* has often been interpreted solely from the perspective of a theory of social domination, although this plays almost no role in the text; see, for example, C. Lemert and G. Gillan, "The New Alternative in Critical Sociology: Foucault's Discursive Analysis," and Gerhard Plumpe and Clemens Kammler, "Wissen ist Macht (M. Foucault)," *Philosophische Rundschau* 3/4 (1980), p. 186ff.

67. This is above all a self-criticism of the concept of the *episteme* in *The Order of Things*; see Peter Sloterdijk, "Michel Foucaults strukturale Theorie der Geschichte," *Philosophisches Jahrbuch* 79 (1972), p. 161ff.

68. See p. 424ff. of my essay "Geschichte und Interaktionsverhältnisse" (note 20 above).

69. *The Archaeology of Knowledge*, p. 46.

70. Ibid., pp. 53–54.

71. Ibid., p. 120; but see p. 68ff.

72. Ibid., p. 68 [translation modified].

73. Ibid., p. 216 [translation modified].

74. Ibid., p. 229.

75. Ironically reversing a classical concept within the cultural criticism of life-philosophy ("logocentrism"), Foucault calls European civilization's fear of disorderly discourse "logophobia" (p. 229).

76. See Manfred Frank, "Die Welt als Wunsch und Repräsentation oder Gegen ein anarcho-strukturalistisches Zeitalter" (a critique of G. Deleuze and F. Guattari's *Anti-Oedipus*), in *Fugen. Deutsch-Französisches Jahrbuch für Text-Analytik. 1980* (Olten and Freiburg, 1980), p. 269ff.

Chapter 5

1. On the convergence of the historical investigations from the "first" phase of Foucault's work with Adorno's position, compare Martin Puder's article "Der böse Blick des Michel Foucault," *Neue Rundschau* (1972), p. 315ff.

2. See, for example, Dominique Lecourt, *Marxism and Epistemology: Bachelard, Canguilhem and Foucault*, tr. B. Brewster (Humanities Press, 1975). For a summary of the discussion see P. Sloterdijk, "Michel Foucaults strukturale Theorie der Geschichte."

3. *The Archaeology of Knowledge*, appendix, pp. 215–237. Foucault himself subsequently characterized this lecture as the text of a "period of transition"; see "The History of Sexuality," an interview with Lucetta Finas, in *Power/Knowledge* (Pantheon, 1980), pp. 183–193.

4. On the meaning of this dualism of dispositions in contemporary French social philosophy, see Descombes, *Das Selbe und das Andere*, p. 198ff. See also Alex Callinicos, *Is there a Future for Marxists?* (London and Basingstoke, 1982), chapter 4 ("Power and Desire").

5. This change from a dualistic to a monistic concept of social drive obviously takes the place in Foucault's work that the change from a dualistic to a monistic theory of passion takes in the work of Nietzsche; on the development of Nietzsche's philosophy from this point of view, see Walter Kaufmann, *Nietzsche: Philosopher, Psychologist, Antichrist*, third edition, revised and enlarged (Vintage, 1968). On Foucault's monism of power as borrowed from Nietzsche, see Hinrich Fink-Eitel, "Foucaults Analytik der Macht," in *Die Austreibung des Geistes aus den Geisteswissenschaften*, ed. Friedrich Kittler (Paderborn, 1980), p. 38ff. In what follows, however, I suggest an alternative interpretation.

6. Michel Foucault, "Truth and Power" (interview with Alessandro Fontana and Pasquale Pasquino), reprinted in *Power/Knowledge*, ed. Colin Gordon (Pantheon, 1980), p. 113. In the first part of my argumentation I will more frequently refer to Foucault's conversational utterances, because there he has, provoked in part by questions, made the conceptual presuppositions of his theory of power more explicit than in the historical investigations.

7. "Truth and Power," in *Power/Knowledge*, p. 114ff.

8. See "Die Macht und die Norm," in M. Foucault, *Mikrophysik der Macht* (West Berlin, 1976), p. 114ff. Also see Foucault, "The History of Sexuality: Interview with L. Finas" in *Power/Knowledge*," pp. 183–193.

9. During the course of this I rely on Kaufmann's interpretation of Nietzsche's theory of power (*Nietzsche: Philosopher, Psychologist, Antichrist*). In what follows, though, I reconstruct Foucault's theory of power from a model of action built upon a concept of "struggle" and not from a doctrine of dispositions, as would be suggested by Nietzsche's philosophy. Even though Foucault's text in some places strongly suggests naturalistic or instinct-theoretic characteristics of thought (for instance, in the concept of the "will to knowledge"), for the purposes of a theory of society an action-theoretic interpretation seems to me more meaningful.

10. M. Foucault, *The History of Sexuality*, volume 1, tr. R. Hurley (Vintage, 1980), p. 92.

11. M. Foucault, *Discipline and Punish: The Birth of the Prison*, tr. A. Sheridan (Vintage, 1979), p. 26.

12. *The History of Sexuality*, p. 94.

13. "Die Macht und die Norm," p. 114.

14. "The History of Sexuality: Interview with L. Finas, in *Power/Knowledge*, p. 187. In one place ("Lecture I" in *Power/Knowledge*, pp. 78–92, here p. 90) Foucault claims that the concept of power can be explained solely with the help of the concepts of "struggle," "conflict," and "war."

15. Foucault addresses Hobbes' formula explicitly in "Ein Spiel um die Psychoanalyse. Gesprach mit Angehörigen des Department de Psychanalyse der Universität Paris VIII in Vincennes," in M. Foucault, *Dispositiv der Macht*, p. 118ff., here p. 141.

16. Compare to this the pertinent remarks of Rudolf Burger, "Die luziden Labyrinthe der Bourgeoisie. Marginalien zum Begriff der Macht bei Foucault," in *Kriminalsoziologische Bibliographie* 19/29 (1978), "Foucault und das Gefängnis," p. 60ff., here p. 76.

17. Foucault expresses these basic ideas most clearly in "Ein Spiel um die Psychoanalyse"; see, above all, p. 125ff.

18. "Truth and Power," p. 122. See also "Die Macht und die Norm," p. 115ff.

19. Louis Althusser, "The Ideological State Apparatus," in Althusser, *Lenin and Philosophy*, tr. B. Brewster (Monthly Review Press, 1972).

20. Ideas from Foucault's theory of power obviously also entered into the critique that G. Marramao directed toward the reductive statist theory of power of the Frankfurt School. See G. Marramao, "Die Formveränderung der politischen Konflikts im Spätkapitalismus. Zur Kritik der politiktheoretischen Paradigmas der Frankfurter Schule," in *Sozialforschung als Kritik*, p. 240ff.

21. *Discipline and Punish*, p. 27.

22. In relation to this ethical problematic in Foucault's theory of power, see above all Nancy Fraser, "Foucault on Modern Power: Empirical Insights and Normative Confusions," *Praxis International* 1 (1981), pp. 272–287. See also N. Fraser, "Foucault's Body-Language: A Post-Humanist Political Rhetoric?," *Salmagundi* 61 (1983), pp. 55–70.

23. Foucault, "Die Macht und die Norm," p. 118; *Discipline and Punish*, p. 26.

24. Ibid.

25. See Foucault, "Truth and Power," p. 118; Mark Poster, "Foucault and History," *Social Research* 49 (1982), I, p. 116ff.

26. Talcott Parsons, *The Structure of Social Action* (Free Press, 1968), p. 87ff.

27. Foucault, *The History of Sexuality*, p. 85.

28. Ibid., p. 86.

29. Ibid., p. 136.

30. Foucault, "Die Macht und die Norm," p. 121ff.

31. Ibid., p. 121.

32. See, for example, *Discipline and Punish*, p. 184.

33. See M. Foucault, "Body/Power," in *Power/Knowledge*, p. 55.

34. See Foucault, "Die Macht und die Norm," p. 117.

35. Norbert Elias, *The History of Manners*, volume 1 of *The Civilizing Process*, tr. E. Jephcott (Urizen, 1978); compare Axel Honneth and Hans Joas, *Social Action and Human Nature*, tr. R. Meyer (Cambridge University Press, 1988), p. 119ff.

36. Foucault, *The History of Sexuality*, p. 139.

37. Foucault, *Discipline and Punish*, p. 27.

38. For this view, Johan Galtung's and Pierre Bourdieu's theories of power are good examples.

39. *Discipline and Punish*, pp. 225–226.

40. Ibid., p. 226.

41. Compare Hans-Jörg Stahl, "Von der 'Geschichte des Anderen' zum Monismus der Macht," master's thesis in educational theory, Free University of Berlin, 1981, p. 86ff. With the exception of one short review of *Discipline and Punish* (Ellen K. Reinike-Koberer, "Schwierigkeiten mit Foucault," *Psyche 33* (1979), p. 364ff.), which addressed itself only slightly to problems in scientific theory, I know of no contribution on the part of psychoanalysis that examines Foucault's critique of psychoanalysis in any detail.

42. Compare Hinrich Fink-Eitel, "Foucault's Analytik der Macht."

43. As found in "Die Macht und die Norm," p. 123.

Chapter 6

1. See M. Foucault, "Nietzsche, Genealogy and History," in *Language, Counter-Memory and Practice*, ed. Donald Bouchard (Cornell University Press, 1977), p. 140.

2. Ibid., p. 151.

3. *Discipline and Punish*, p. 305.

4. In what follows I have made use in a few places of some of the formulations used in the chapter on Foucault in A. Honneth and H. Joas, *Social Action and Human Nature*, tr. R. Meyer (Cambridge University Press, 1988), p. 129ff.

5. *Discipline and Punish*, p. 40.

6. Ibid., p. 48.

7. Ibid., pp. 53–54.

8. Ibid., p. 87–88.

9. This type of functionalist analysis is found in the methodology employed by George Rusche and Otto Kirchheimer in *Punishment and Social Structures* [1939] (Russell and Russell, 1968).

10. *Discipline and Punish*, pp. 77 and 86.

11. Ibid., p. 80. Of course, Foucault speaks in many places of an all-encompassing process of the augmentation of social power.

12. However, see the socio-historical objections of Heinz Steinert, "Ist es denn aber auch wahr, Herr F.? *Überwachen und Strafen* unter der Fiktion gelesen, es handle sich dabei um eine sozialgeschichtliche Darstellung," *Kriminalsoziologische Bibliographie* 19/20 (1978), p. 30ff.

13. *Discipline and Punish*, p. 120.

14. Ibid., pp. 138–139.

15. Ibid., p. 141.

16. Alfred Krovoza's *Produktion und Sozialisation* (Frankfurt, 1976) more or less tends toward such a problematic narrowing of the historical perspective.

17. *Discipline and Punish*, p. 170.

18. Ibid., p. 184.

19. Ibid., p. 193 (translation modified).

20. See the impressive examples of the creation of "administrative biographies" by the police in Aaron V. Cicourel's book *The Social Organization of Juvenile Justice* (London, 1976).

21. *Discipline and Punish*, p. 29.

22. E. Durkheim, *The Elementary Forms of Religious Life* (Free Press, 1967), book 3, chapter 8.

23. *Discipline and Punish*, p. 224.

24. Ibid., p. 218.

25. Ibid., pp. 218–219.

26. Ibid., p. 218.

27. See also *The History of Sexuality*, volume 1, p. 106ff.

28. *Discipline and Punish*, p. 232.

29. Ibid., pp. 227–228.

30. See the persuasive objections by A. Giddens, *A Contemporary Critique of Historical Materialism* (University of California Press, 1981), p. 171ff.

31. *Discipline and Punish*, p. 222.

32. *Dialectic of Enlightenment*, p. 246 (German tr.).

Chapter 7

1. J. Habermas, "Knowledge and Human Interests: A General Perspective," appendix to *Knowledge and Human Interests*, tr. J. Shapiro (Beacon, 1971), pp. 301–317.

2. Edmund Husserl, *The Crisis of European Sciences and Transcendental Phenomenology*, tr. D. Carr (Northwestern University Press, 1970), p. 5.

3. This interpretation of Husserl's intention in the *Crisis* is, however, contested; for an essay directed against Habermas's interpretation, see R. Bubner, "What is Critical Theory?," in *Essays in Hermeneutics and Critical Theory*, tr. E. Matthews (Cambridge University Press, 1988), pp. 1–35.

4. Appendix to *Knowledge and Human Interests* (see note 1 above), p. 306.

5. Ibid., p. 307.

6. Ibid.

7. Ibid., p. 308.

8. I refer primarily to the essays on the "positivist dispute" written in the early 1960s. With their aid I attempt to reconstruct the path along the way toward the theory of knowledge up to the position formulated in Habermas' inaugural address.

9. J. Habermas, "Philosophische Anthropologie (Ein Lexikonartikel)," in *Kultur und Kritik*, p. 84ff., here p. 100.

10. Ibid. See also J. Habermas, *Political-Philosophical Profiles* (MIT Press).

11. In this regard, Karl-Otto Apel, who initially shared with Habermas an approach to the philosophy of science from the perspective of an anthropology of knowledge, could also use Heidegger's concept of "care" as a beginning point in his theory of "knowledge-interests" in *Transformation der Philosophie* (Suhrkamp, 1971), vol. 1, p. 22ff. On the status of action as "care" in the epistemology of *Being and Time* see chapter 1 of G. Prauss, *Erkennen und Handeln in Heideggers 'Sein und Zeit'* (Freiburg and Munich, 1977).

12. Habermas, "Philosophische Anthropologie (Ein Lexikonartikel)," p. 76.

13. See *The Positivist Dispute in German Sociology*, ed. T. Adorno (Harper & Row, 1976).

14. Karl Popper, *The Logic of Scientific Discovery* (Harper & Row, 1965), chapter 4. See also Albrecht Wellmer, *Methodologie als Erkenntnistheorie. Zur Wissenschaftslehre Karl R. Poppers* (Frankfurt, 1967).

15. J. Habermas, "Analytical Theory of Science and Dialectics," in *The Positivist Dispute*, pp. 152–153.

16. Ibid., p. 153.

17. Ibid., p. 154.

18. Later Habermas will distinguish more precisely than he does in the context of the "positivist dispute" between questions of object constitution and questions of the determination of truth, between the *a priori* of experience and the criterion of truth.

19. Ibid., p. 155.

20. Ibid., p. 162. See also J. Habermas, "A Positivistically Bisected Rationalism," in *The Positivist Dispute*, p. 198ff., here p. 209.

21. See Joel Whitebook, "The Problem of Nature in Habermas," *Telos* 40 (1979), p. 41ff; Henning Ottmann, 'Cognitive Interests and Self-Reflection," in *Habermas: Critical Debates*, ed. J. Thompson and D. Held (MIT Press, 1982), p. 74ff. See also J. Habermas, "A Reply to My Critics," in Thompson and Held, p. 238ff.

22. Habermas, "A Positivistically Bisected Rationalism," p. 198.

23. Habermas, "Philosophische Anthropologie," p. 102.

24. Ibid.

25. Arnold Gehlen, *Der Mensch*.

26. See J. Habermas, "Between Philosophy and Science: Marxism as Critique," in *Theory and Practice*, tr. J. Viertel (Beacon, 1973); "Literaturbericht zur philosophischen Diskussion um Marx und den Marxismus," p. 387ff.

27. Habermas, "Against a Positivistically Bisected Rationalism," p. 222.

28. Ibid., p. 222.

29. Ibid., p. 221.

30. See the proposed interpretation by W. Bonss, "Empirie und Dechiffrierung von Wirklichkeit. Zur Methodologie bei Adorno," in *Adorno-Konferenz 1983*, ed. L. von Friedeburg and J. Habermas (Frankfurt, 1983), p. 201ff.

31. See H. L. Dreyfus and Paul Rabinow, *Michel Foucault: Beyond Structuralism and Hermeneutics* (Northwestern University Press, 1982), chapters 1 and 4.

32. J. Habermas, "The Hermeneutic Claim to Universality," in *Contemporary Hermeneutics*, ed. Josef Bleicher (RKP, 1980), pp. 181–211.

33. Habermas, "Analytical Theory of Science and Dialectics," p. 160.

34. See the essays referred to in note 26.

35. See Habermas, "Between Philosophy and Science: Marxism as Critique," esp. p. 242ff.

36. On the importance of Merleau-Ponty on Habermas's early interpretation of Marxism, see E. H. Walter, "Die prekäre Vermittlung von Theorie und Praxis in unserer nachrevolutionären Zeit. Anmerkungen zur Geschichtsphilosophie Maurice Merleau-Pontys und Jürgen Habermas," *Archiv für Rechts- und Sozialphilosophie* 50:3, p. 415ff.

37. For a similar model, see K.-O. Apel, "Scientism, Hermeneutics and the Critique of Ideology," in Müller-Vollmer, *Hermeneutics,* pp. 320–345.

38. Habermas, "Analytical Theory of Science and Dialectics," p. 139.

39. Ibid., 139.

40. Ibid., 154.

41. Habermas, "A Positivistically Bisected Rationalism," p. 215.

42. Ibid., p. 219.

43. Appendix to *Knowledge and Human Interests,* p. 313.

44. Ibid., p. 313.

45. Ibid., p. 314.

46. See Habermas, "A Postscript to *Knowledge and Human Interests,*" *Philosophy of Social Science* 3 (1973), p. 176.

Chapter 8

1. On the romanticist aspects of the Marxist concept of labor, see P. Röder, "Von der Frühromantik zum jungen Marx. Rückwärtsgewandte Prophetie eines qualitativen Naturbegriffs," in *Romantische Utopie—Utopische Romantik,* ed. G. Dischner and R. Faber (Hildesheim, 1974), p. 149ff.; Agnes Heller, "Habermas and Marxism," in *Habermas. Critical Debates,* ed. J. B. Thompson and D. Held (London, 1982), p. 21ff. On the problem of such a depleted concept of labor, see Axel Honneth, "Labor and Instrumental Action," *New German Critique* 26 (1982).

2. J. Habermas, "Technology and Science as Ideology," in *Toward a Rational Society,* tr. J. Shapiro (Beacon, 1970), pp. 91–92. Tom McCarthy resolves the confusion that results from this distinction between instrumental action and rational choice: "Habermas considers the distinction important because it permits us to separate the contribution of technical progress to the rationalization of action from the rationalization effected by improvements in decision-making procedures themselves. But it is misleading to present the distinction, as he does here, as one between two *types* of action. Rational decision and the application of technically appropriate means appear rather to be two *moments* of purposive-rational action. In rationally pursuing certain specified ends, the agent must take account of both the available information . . . and the preference rules and decision maxims that he has adopted." (*The Critical Theory of Jürgen Habermas,* p. 24).

3. "Technology and Science as Ideology," p. 92.

4. David Lockwood has compared the role Gramsci played for Marxism to that played by Durkheim for classical sociology: D. Lockwood, "The Weakest Line in the chain? Some Comments on the Marxist Theory of Action," *Research in the Sociology of Work* 1 (1981), p. 435ff.

5. See especially J. Habermas, *On the Logic of the Social Sciences,* tr. S. Nicholsen and J. Stark (MIT Press, 1988), p. 89ff.

6. As the history of sociology indicates, the solution to this problem distinguishes the various trends within the normativistic tradition of social theory. The basic normativistic idea assumes a different theoretical form according to whether the common fact of the normative integration of societies is explained as the result of a universally accepted value system (Parsons), a process of living in a linguistic tradition (hermeneutics), a consensus-producing effect of symbolic power (Bourdieu), or a complicated interplay of consensus-building and power (Habermas, Gramsci).

7. See especially "Technology and Science as Ideology," pp. 81–122, "Labor and Interaction: On Hegel's Jena Writings" [which appears in English translation in *Theory and Practice*], and *Knowledge and Human Interests*, chapters 2, 3, and 12.

8. J. Habermas, *The Structural Transformation of the Public Sphere* [1962], tr. T. Burger (MIT Press, 1989); "Praktische Folgen des wissenschaftlich-technischen Fortschritts," in *Theorie und Praxis*, p. 336ff.; "Dogmatism, Reason and Decision: On Theory and Praxis in our Scientific Civilization," in *Theory and Practice* (Beacon).

9. On the theoretical significance of Habermas' *Structural Transformation of the Public Sphere*, see Jean Cohen, "Why More Political Theory?," *Telos* 40 (1979), pp. 70–94.

10. As is evident, the basic idea of Habermas' communicative ethics is anticipated in this description of the idea of liberal publicity; see especially the discussion of Kant's moral philosophy in section 13 of *The Structural Transformation of the Public Sphere* (pp. 102–117).

11. Ibid., chapters 4 and 7.

12. See also *Texte zur Technokratiediskussion*, ed. C. Koch and D. Senghaas (Frankfurt, 1970).

13. Hans Freyer, "Über das Dominantwerden technischer Kategorien in der Lebenswelt der industriellen Gesellschaft," in *Akademie der Wissenschaften und der Literatur. Abhandlung der geistes- und sozial-wissenschaftlichen Klasse* 7 (Mainz, 1960). It is surprising to see the extent to which the formulations of Habermas' social theory are shaped by contemporary texts of this sort: for more on this, see pp. 263–267 below.

14. See Freyer, ibid., p. 242. In "Technology and Science as Ideology" Habermas speaks of technocratic consciousness as a "common positivistic consciousness," p. 114.

15. See "Technology and Science as Ideology," in *Toward a Rational Society*.

16. Ibid., p. 90.

17. Ibid., p. 93–4.

18. See "Technical Progress and the Social Lifeworld," in *Toward a Rational Society*.

19. Habermas, *On the Logic of the Social Sciences*, p. 173.

20. Ibid., p. 307.

21. Habermas, "Technology and Science as Ideology," p. 93.

22. J. P. Arnason makes a similar argument with the aid of the concept of "goals of production." See "Marx und Habermas," in *Arbeit, Handlung, Normativität. Theorien des Historischen Materialismus 2*, ed. A. Honneth and U. Jaeggi, especially p. 156ff.

23. Cornelius Castoriadis, *Crossroads in the Labyrinth* (MIT Press, 1984); see the chapter on "Technique."

24. Michael Burawoy views the strategies of political domination as an independent dimension of the process of social production ("The Contours of Production Politics," Wissenschaftszentrum Berlin, 1984).

25. Habermas, "Technology and Science as Ideology," p. 115.

26. See J. Habermas, "Historical Materialism and the Development of Normative Structures," in *Communication and the Evolution of Society*, tr. T. McCarthy (Beacon, 1979), pp. 95–129.

27. "Technology and Science as Ideology," p. 96.

28. See above; more generally, see T. McCarthy, *The Critical Theory of Jürgen Habermas*, p. 98ff.

29. "Technology and Science as Ideology," p. 118.

30. Ibid., p. 119.

31. The starting point for a normative concept of ego autonomy, which Habermas had in view in his interpretation of psychoanalysis and later in the outline of a theory of socialization, follows naturally from this; see "Moral Development and Ego Identity," in *Communication and the Evolution of Society*, tr. T. McCarthy (Beacon Press, 1979), pp. 69–94.

32. "Technology and Science as Ideology," p. 96.

33. Ibid., p. 96.

34. Ibid., p. 96.

35. Ibid., p. 98.

36. Ibid., p. 98.

37. See Habermas, "Between Philosophy and Science: Marxism as Critique," in *Theory and Practice*, tr. J. Viertel (Beacon, 1973).

38. "Technology and Science as Ideology," p. 105.

39. Ibid., p. 103.

40. Ibid., p. 106–107.

41. Ibid., p. 113.

42. Ibid., p. 113.

43. Ibid., p. 118–119.

44. On the tension between these two models of history within Marxist theory, to which Karl Korsch had already drawn attention, see C. Castoriadis, *The Imaginary Institution of Society*, tr. K. Blamey (MIT Press, 1987), part I.

45. *Knowledge and Human Interests*, p. 54.

46. Ibid., p. 54.

47. Ibid., p. 55.

48. Bernard Waldenfels has also attempted to understand systematically, on a phenomenological basis, the "struggle," "interruption," and "destruction" of dialogue. See *Das Zwischenreich des Dialogs* (The Hague, 1971), chapter 6.

49. See Habermas, "Labor and Interaction: Remarks on Hegel's Jena 'Philosophy of Mind'," in *Theory and Practice*.

50. *Knowledge and Human Interests*, p. 59.

51. Ibid., p. 58.

52. Ibid., p. 57–58.

53. Ibid., p. 61.

54. If Habermas had abandoned the framework of a philosophy of history, then the struggle for recognition would no longer appear as a reflective process between two classes represented as subjects, but as a conflict between collective actors over the organizational forms of society.

55. See Lucien Goldman, *Dialektische Untersuchungen* (Neuwied and Berlin, 1966); W. W. Mayrl, "Genetic Structuralism and the Analysis of Social Consciousness," *Theory and Society* 5 (1978), p. 19ff.; Karl Mannheim, *Wissenssoziologie* (Neuwied and Berlin, 1964); N. Abercrombie and B. Longhurst, "Interpreting Mannheim," *Theory, Culture and Society* 2 (1983), pp. 5ff. On English sociology of culture, and the work of E. P. Thompson and R. Williams in particular, see John Clarke, *Jugendkulture als Widerstand* (Frankfurt, 1979).

56. With the concept of negotiation, symbolic interactionism attempts to describe those processes of action whereby members of social organizations continuously regulate anew the distribution of tasks and activities and thus are always rearranging the system of organization. For a macro-sociological application of this interesting approach, see Hans Joas, "Arbeitsteilung und Interaktion. Das makrosoziologische Potential des symbolischen Interaktionismus" (manuscript, 1981).

57. See my critical objections in "Moral Consciousness and Class Struggle," *Praxis International* 2 (1982), pp. 12–25. See also David Held, *Introduction to Critical Theory, Horkheimer to Habermas* (University of California Press, 1980), p. 374ff.

Chapter 9

1. See especially Habermas' introduction to *Theory and Practice* (Beacon, 1973).

2. J. Habermas, "A Postscript to *Knowledge and Human Interests*," *Philosophy of Social Science* 3 (1973), pp. 157–189, here p. 182. See also "The Hermeneutic Claim to Universality," in *Contemporary Hermeneutics*, ed. Josef Bleicher (RKP, 1980), pp. 181–211.

3. Ibid., p. 182.

4. That is the guiding thesis of Thomas McCarthy's illuminating exposition, *The Critical Theory of Jürgen Habermas* (MIT Press, 1978).

5. Habermas, "The Hermeneutic Claim to Universality," p. 342. However, the first mention of the idea of a context-free analysis of language-use is found in "Zur Logik der Wissenschaften," in *Zur Logik der Sozialwissenschaften*, p. 265.

6. Compare H. Joas, "Situation-Körperlichkeit-Sozialität. Drei vernachlässigte Dimensionen der soziologischen Handlungstheorie" (manuscript, 1983). Ulf Matthiesen also criticizes the neglect of the corporeal dimension of the social in Habermas' action theory; see *Das Dickicht der Lebenswelt und die Theorie des Kommunikativen Handelns* (Munich, 1983). On the role of the human body within the social sciences, see B. S. Turner, *The Body and Society* (Blackwell, 1984).

7. McCarthy, *The Critical Theory of Jürgen Habermas*, p. 272ff.

8. See J. Habermas, "Vorbereitende Bemerkungen zu einer Theorie der kommunikativen Kompetenz," in *Theorie der Gesellschaft oder Sozialtechnologie. Was leistet die Systemforschung?*, ed. J. Habermas and N. Luhmann (Frankfurt, 1971), p. 101ff.

9. J. Habermas, "Eine Auseinandersetzung mit Niklas Luhmann (1971): Systemtheorie der Gesellschaft oder Kritische Gesellschaftstheorie?," in *Zur Logik der Sozialwissenschaften*, p. 369ff., here p. 398.

10. See especially J. Habermas, "History and Evolution," *Telos* 39 (1979), pp. 5–44.

11. Habermas, *Zur Rekonstruktion des Historischen Materialismus.* For an interesting discussion of Habermas' theory of social evolution, see A. Linkenbach, "Vom Mythos zur Moderne: die Theorie der gesellschaftlichen Entwicklung bei J. Habermas" (dissertation, Frankfurt, 1984).

12. See H. M. Baumgartner, *Kontinuität und Geschichte*, esp. p. 229.

13. Habermas, "Eine Auseinandersetzung mit Niklas Luhmann," p. 484.

14. See Otto Kallschever, "Auf der Suche nach einer politischen Theorie bei Jürgen Habermas," *Aesthetik und Kommunikation* 45/46 (1981), p. 171ff., esp. p. 179.

15. In the following I limit myself to an extremely brief reconstruction of the systematic steps through which Habermas, in *The Theory of Communicative Action*, grounds the approach of a two-tiered theory of society. Thus I necessarily neglect the many highly instructive contributions to the development of action theory and the theory of language, as well as the fascinating interpretations in which he justifies his approach via the history of social theories.

16. Habermas, *Theory of Communicative Action*, I, chapter 1.1.

17. Ibid., p. 76ff.

18. Ibid., p. 275f.

19. Ibid., p. 94f.

20. Ibid., p. 20f. and p. 334.

21. Albrecht Wellmer has undertaken an immanent critique of this approach in a superb interpretation of Adorno's aesthetics: "Truth, Appearance, Reconciliation: Adorno's Aesthetic Redemption of Modernity," *Telos* 62 (1984–85), pp. 89–115.

22. J. Habermas, *The Theory of Communicative Action*, I, p. 101. Habermas admittedly encounters difficulties with his own classification since, on the one hand, he emphasizes the teleological structure of all action and, on the other hand, he describes teleological action as a limiting case of communicative action (see also *The Theory of Communicative Action*, I, pp. 86–88). See also R. Zimmerman, *Utopie, Rationalität, Politik: Zu Kritik, Rekonstruktion und Systematik einer emanzipatorischen Gesellschaftstheorie bei Marx und Habermas*, part II (Alber, 1985).

23. Habermas, *The Theory of Communicative Action*, I, p. 101.

24. See below.

25. *The Theory of Communicative Action*, I, p. 335. The systematic presentation of the concept of the lifeworld begins in *The Theory of Communicative Action*, II, chapter 4.

26. Ibid., p. 70.

27. Ibid., pp. 70–71.

28. *The Theory of Communicative Action*, II, p. 232.

29. Ibid., p. 232.

30. Ibid., p. 232.

31. Ibid., p. 150.

32. Ibid., pp. 153–154.

33. Ibid., p. 156ff.

34. Ibid., p. 180.

35. Ibid., p. 181.

36. Ibid., p. 183.

37. Ibid., p. 171ff.

38. Ibid., p. 171.

39. See *The Theory of Communicative Action*, II, p. 267f.

40. Ibid., p. 307.

41. Ibid., p. 309.

42. I refer here throughout to the interesting review of *The Theory of Communicative Action* by Johannes Berger, "The Linguistification of the Sacred and the De-linguistification of the Economy," *Telos* 57 (1983), pp. 194–205, which was very helpful to me on more than just this point (see especially p. 203). I would also like to mention the essay "The Unhappy Marriage of Hermeneutics and Functionalism," *Praxis Interna-*

tional (1987), in which Hans Joas attempts to develop a theoretical alternative to Habermas.

43. Habermas also grants this, though without permitting it to disturb him; see *The Theory of Communicative Action*, II, p. 310ff.

44. See M. Burawoy, *Manufacturing Consent. Changes in the Labor Process under Monopoly Capitalism* (Chicago, 1979).

45. See J. Habermas, "Remarks on the Concept of Communicative Action," in *Social Action*, ed. G. Seebass and R. Tuomela (Reidel, 1985), pp. 151–178, here p. 153.

46. This terminological fiction results mainly from the fact that, on the one hand, Habermas distinguishes between social action oriented to success and social action oriented to mutual understanding so that two types of symbolically mediated interaction can be defined, while on the other hand he interprets communicative action as a reflexive mechanism for coordinating success-oriented action.

47. See A. Giddens, "Reason Without Revolution: Habermas's Theory of Communicative Reason," in *Habermas and Modernity*, ed. R. Bernstein (MIT Press, 1985).

48. *The Theory of Communicative Action*, II, p. 155.

49. Ibid., p. 196.

50. See Rolf Zimmerman, *Utopie, Rationalität, Politik: Zu Kritik, Rekonstruktion und Systematik einer emanzipatorischen Gesellschaftstheorie bei Marx und Habermas*, part II (Alber, 1985).